HISTORICAL DICTIONARY

The historical dictionaries present essential information on a broad range of subjects, including American and world history, art, business, cities, countries, cultures, customs, film, global conflicts, international relations, literature, music, philosophy, religion, sports, and theater. Written by experts, all contain highly informative introductory essays on the topic and detailed chronologies that, in some cases, cover vast historical time periods but still manage to heavily feature more recent events.

Brief A–Z entries describe the main people, events, politics, social issues, institutions, and policies that make the topic unique, and entries are cross-referenced for ease of browsing. Extensive bibliographies are divided into several general subject areas, providing excellent access points for students, researchers, and anyone wanting to know more. Additionally, maps, photographs, and appendixes of supplemental information aid high school and college students doing term papers or introductory research projects. In short, the historical dictionaries are the perfect starting point for anyone looking to research in these fields.

HISTORICAL DICTIONARIES OF RELIGIONS, PHILOSOPHIES, AND MOVEMENTS

Jon Woronoff, Series Editor

Orthodox Church, by Michael Prokurat, Alexander Golitzin, and Michael D. Peterson, 1996

Civil Rights Movement, by Ralph E. Luker, 1997

North American Environmentalism, by Edward R. Wells and Alan M. Schwartz, 1997

Taoism, by Julian F. Pas in cooperation with Man Kam Leung, 1998

Gay Liberation Movement, by Ronald J. Hunt, 1999

Islamic Fundamentalist Movements in the Arab World, Iran, and Turkey, by Ahmad S. Moussalli, 1999

Cooperative Movement, by Jack Shaffer, 1999

Kierkegaard's Philosophy, by Julia Watkin, 2001

Prophets in Islam and Judaism, by Scott B. Noegel and Brannon M. Wheeler, 2002

Lesbian Liberation Movement: Still the Rage, by JoAnne Myers, 2003

Unitarian Universalism, by Mark W. Harris, 2004

New Age Movements, by Michael York, 2004

Utopianism, by James M. Morris and Andrea L. Kross, 2004

Feminism, Second Edition, by Janet K. Boles and Diane Long Hoeveler, 2004

Jainism, by Kristi L. Wiley, 2004

Methodism, Second Edition, by Charles Yrigoyen Jr. and Susan E. Warrick, 2005

Kant and Kantianism, by Helmut Holzhey and Vilem Mudroch, 2005

Olympic Movement, Third Edition, by Bill Mallon with Ian Buchanan, 2006

Feminist Philosophy, by Catherine Villanueva Gardner, 2006

Logic, by Harry J. Gensler, 2006

Leibniz's Philosophy, by Stuart Brown and Nicholas J. Fox, 2006

Non-Aligned Movement and Third World, by Guy Arnold, 2006

Salvation Army, by Major John G. Merritt, 2006

Epistemology, by Ralph Baergen, 2006

Bahá'í Faith, Second Edition, by Hugh C. Adamson, 2006

Aesthetics, by Dabney Townsend, 2006

Medieval Philosophy and Theology, by Stephen F. Brown and Juan Carlos Flores, 2007

Puritans, by Charles Pastoor and Galen K. Johnson, 2007

Green Movement, Second Edition, by Miranda Schreurs and Elim Papadakis, 2007

Husserl's Philosophy, by John J. Drummond, 2008

Existentialism, by Stephen Michelman, 2008

Zionism, Second Edition, by Rafael Medoff and Chaim I. Waxman, 2008

Coptic Church, by Gawdat Gabra, 2008

Jehovah's Witnesses, by George D. Chryssides, 2008

Hume's Philosophy, by Kenneth R. Merrill, 2008

Shakers, by Stephen J. Paterwic, 2008

Mormonism, Third Edition, by Davis Bitton and Thomas G. Alexander, 2008

Hegelian Philosophy, Second Edition, by John W. Burbidge, 2008

Ethics, by Harry J. Gensler and Earl W. Spurgin, 2008

Bertrand Russell's Philosophy, by Rosalind Carey and John Ongley, 2009

Baptists, Second Edition, by William H. Brackney, 2009

Islam, Second Edition, by Ludwig W. Adamec, 2009

Homosexuality, by Brent L. Pickett, 2009

Buddhism, by Carl Olson, 2009

Holiness Movement, Second Edition, edited by William Kostlevy, 2009

Reformed Churches, Second Edition, by Robert Benedetto and Donald K. McKim, 2010

The Reformation and Counter-Reformation, by Michael Mullett, 2010

Heidegger's Philosophy, Second Edition, by Frank Schalow and Alfred Denker, 2010

Jesus, by Daniel J. Harrington, S.J., 2010

Metaphysics, by Gary Rosenkrantz and Joshua Hoffman, 2011

Shinto, Second Edition, by Stuart D. B. Picken, 2011

The Friends (Quakers), Second Edition, by Margery Post Abbott, Mary Ellen Chijioke, Pink Dandelion, and John William Oliver Jr., 2011

Lutheranism, Second Edition, by Günther Gassmann with Duane H. Larson, and Mark W. Oldenburg, 2011

Hinduism, New Edition, by Jeffery D. Long, 2011

Calvinism, by Stuart D. B. Picken, 2012

Hobbes's Philosophy, by Juhana Lemetti, 2012

Chinese Communist Party, by Lawrence R. Sullivan, 2012

New Religious Movements, Second Edition, by George D. Chryssides, 2012

Catholicism, Second Edition, by William J. Collinge, 2012

Radical Christianity, by William H. Brackney, 2012

Organized Labor, Third Edition, by James C. Docherty and Sjaak van der Velden, 2012

Islamic Fundamentalism, by Mathieu Guidère, 2012

Witchcraft, Second Edition, by Jonathan Durrant and Michael D. Bailey, 2013

Lesbian and Gay Liberation Movements, by JoAnne Myers, 2013

Nietzscheanism, Third Edition, by Carol Diethe, 2014

Human Rights, by Jacques Fomerand, 2014

Welfare State, Third Edition, by Bent Greve, 2014

Wittgenstein's Philosophy, Second Edition, by Duncan Richter, 2014

Civil Rights Movement, Second Edition, by Christopher M. Richardson and Ralph E. Luker, 2014

Sikhism, Third Edition, by Louis E. Fenech and W. H. McLeod, 2014

Marxism, Second Edition, by Elliott Johnson, David Walker, and Daniel Gray, 2014

Slavery and Abolition, Second Edition, by Martin A. Klein, 2014

Historical Dictionary of Environmentalism

Second Edition

Peter Dauvergne

ROWMAN & LITTLEFIELD
Lanham • Boulder • New York • London

Published by Rowman & Littlefield
A wholly owned subsidiary of The Rowman & Littlefield Publishing Group, Inc.
4501 Forbes Boulevard, Suite 200, Lanham, Maryland 20706
www.rowman.com

Unit A, Whitacre Mews, 26-34 Stannary Street, London SE11 4AB

British Library Cataloguing in Publication Information Available

Library of Congress Cataloging-in-Publication Data

Name: Dauvergne, Peter.
Title: Historical dictionary of environmentalism / Peter Dauvergne.
Description: Second edition. | Lanham : Rowman & Littlefield, [2016] | Includes bibliographical references.
Identifiers: LCCN 2016017608 | ISBN 9781442269606 (hardcover : alk. paper)
Subjects: LCSH: Environmentalism—History—Dictionaries.
Classification: LCC GE195 .D358 2016 | DDC 333.7203—dc23 LC record available at https://lccn.loc.gov/2016017608

∞™ The paper used in this publication meets the minimum requirements of American National Standard for Information Sciences Permanence of Paper for Printed Library Materials, ANSI/NISO Z39.48-1992.

Printed in the United States of America

All photos in this book are courtesy of Jennifer Clapp.

Contents

Editor's Foreword

Few topics are more important for all of us than the environment, since we are among the many creatures who live in it and are seriously affected by any problems, let alone major disasters, it encounters. This second edition of *Historical Dictionary of Environmentalism* describes the numerous efforts that are being made to resolve problems and avoid catastrophes. It includes information on environmental pioneers—those who wrote about the topic well before the subject was popular or even had a name—and looks at the most recent information, while tracing the efforts of those who study it and recommending practices that are in humanity's best interests.

Many of the volumes in this particular series deal with controversial topics. One might think that environmentalism would not be among them since we all live on our "spaceship earth" together. Nonetheless, there is controversy over virtually every aspect of it, from causes to solutions to blame, and all too many people assume they have the right views and everyone else is hopelessly wrong. This book is broad enough to examine opinions on all sides of each question while introducing a multitude of issues that are becoming more intractable with time. Some insist that time is running out and we must act immediately, others fear that precipitate action could be dangerous, and yet others think the issue is overblown and that it's best to do nothing. There has recently even been a positive role played by the apparent villains—government and big business.

This updated and expanded edition tackles its topic in several interrelated sections. The list of acronyms is quite long, the chronology traces significant events, and the introduction examines the different and sometimes cooperative efforts of various players—scholars, governments, nongovernmental organizations, and corporations—and what has been achieved so far. But the most important section is once again a substantial dictionary, with specific entries on issues, problems and disasters, conferences, conventions, organizations, and notable individuals, as well as some key countries. There is so much to say about environmentalism that any serious reader will want to refer to some of the more detailed sources listed in the comprehensive bibliography.

The author of this book is Peter Dauvergne, who is a professor of political science at the University of British Columbia, Canada, where he has served as director of the Liu Institute for Global Issues, associate dean in the Faculty of Arts, and senior advisor to the university president. Dr. Dauvergne's research interests include critical global change theory and environmental theory in international relations. These have given him considerable insight into a broad range of issues, both practical and theoretical. He has published extensively, with many books and shorter works. Most of his books deal with global environmental politics and political economy, such as consumption and logging in the Asia-Pacific. This experience has made him an unusually skilled guide to the complex and often controversial field of environmentalism.

Jon Woronoff
Series Editor

Preface

Over the past decade, environmentalism as both a social movement and a belief system has continued to spread and deepen around the world. We see this across governments, civil society, and business. States have signed on to new international environmental agreements, national governments have revised environmental policies and strengthened existing environmental agencies, cities have joined together to participate in international environmental affairs, and towns have implemented new environmental bylaws. New nongovernmental organizations (NGOs) have formed, and long-standing ones (e.g., Greenpeace, Friends of the Earth, and the World Wide Fund for Nature/World Wildlife Fund—WWF) have joined with grassroots movements to continue to push for stronger efforts to protect nature, prevent pollution, and avoid degradation. Meanwhile, just about every one of the world's largest multinational corporations has put forth new visions of their role in advancing sustainably. The first edition of this book has been thoroughly updated and revised (with new entries on countries, events, personalities, issues, and philosophies) to reflect this increase in environmentalism, as well as to respond to a worsening of global environmental problems and the emergence of important new research. The bibliography has been completely revamped to reflect the explosion of research on a wide range of topics, from new citizen mobilizations to new forms of environmental governance to new (and often deteriorating) environmental conditions. Also, significantly, the dictionary entries have been fully brought up to date, with a large number of additional entries to reflect the ongoing rise, and shifting nature, of environmentalism over the past 10 years.

Three trends in environmentalism are especially striking over the last decade. First, the crisis of climate change has risen to the top of the world's agenda. Confidence in the scientific evidence of ongoing warming and greater climatic instability has grown. So has public concern. We can see this growing concern in opinion polls, civil society attendance at climate change negotiations, and an avalanche of scholarly books and media coverage. In 2015 the Canadian government even went as far as renaming its environment department the "Department of Environment and Climate Change." In response to the emerging consensus on the need to act, the world community has called for an increase in global temperatures of no more than two degrees Celsius above preindustrial levels. In recent years this has been the goal of the meetings of the Conference of the Parties for the United Nations Framework Convention for Climate Change, including the 21st convention in Paris in December 2015 to negotiate a new agreement. That meeting, however, agreed to add an aspirational target of no more than 1.5 degrees Celsius. Even in the United States, where skepticism of the science of climate change still runs strong, the political rhetoric has shifted in recent years. At the United Nations Climate Summit in New York City in September 2014, for example, U.S. president Barack Obama called climate change an "urgent and growing . . . threat" that was going to "define the contours of this century more dramatically than any other." The growing crisis of climate change is also shifting the focus of environmentalism—as well as the resources of international, national, and local environmental NGOs—away from long-standing issues of nature conservation and pollution prevention toward advocating more specifically for measures to mitigate and adapt to climate change. Some environmentalists are even starting to express concern that the issue of climate change has come to dominate the environmental movement.

A second striking trend in environmentalism over the past decade has been the shift in the approach of multinational corporations with well-known brands toward a more proactive, assertive stance on environmental matters. Companies such as Walmart, Nike, and McDonald's are now claiming to be sustainability leaders, making grand promises of a future of "100 percent sustainable sourcing," with their home operations and supply chains producing "zero waste," "zero carbon," and "zero deforestation." Sustainability for these corporations is defined as "sustainability of business," not ecological sustainability of the planet. Yet, significantly, the resulting sustainability programs and initiatives, which fall broadly under the older rubric of "corporate social responsibility" (CSR), are going beyond simply protecting corporate reputations, reducing risk, deflecting government regulators, and projecting better images for consumers. Through codes of conduct, standardized management principles, and strategic auditing, these companies are using sustainability programs to gain more control over supply chains as a way of increasing efficiencies and reducing waste. Improvements and gains are incremental, and many environmentalists dispute the overall value once these are seen within the context of rising production and consumption. Still, measured on a per-product-sold basis, there is no question that over the past decade corporations have made real gains in recycling, reducing packaging, and using less energy. At the same time, as part of these "sustainability commitments," corporations have reached out to fund and partner with many mainstream NGOs, such as Coca-Cola partnering with the WWF.

This extension of "corporate sustainability" connects to a third striking trend in environmentalism over the past decade: the growing embrace of business and markets as a "solution" for global environmental problems, including the crisis of climate change. Partly, this trend arises out of a growing frustration with the inability of states to make headway through formal treaties. But it also reflects a growing belief within and outside governments in the efficiency (and to a lesser extent effectiveness) of market solutions. In this context more NGOs, especially those with large budgets and staff, are reaching out to partner with business to co-brand fund-raising campaigns, establish and extend certification organizations, and co-market eco-products. To be clear, as this book highlights time and again, radical environmentalism remains strong. We see this, for example, with the Occupy Movement of 2011. And we see this with ongoing protests by activists to oppose oil drilling in the Arctic, deforestation in the tropics, and hazardous waste dumps in poor neighborhoods. Yet, as we'll also see in the second edition of this book, the growing embrace of markets and business over the past decade is bolstering more middle-of-the-road environmental groups and worldviews, moderating environmentalism as a whole as more of the mainstream embraces a less confrontational politics in relation to consumer capitalism.

This book forms part of a comprehensive series of books covering social movements and belief systems under the adept editorship of Jon Woronoff. To facilitate the rapid and efficient location of information and to make this book as useful a reference tool as possible, extensive cross-references have been provided in the dictionary section. Within individual entries, terms that have their own entries are in **boldface type** the first time they appear. Related terms that do not appear in the text are indicated in the *See also*. *See* refers to other entries that deal with the topic.

Acknowledgments

I would like to thank the Social Sciences and Humanities Research Council of Canada and the Canada Research Chairs Program for their funding, which supported a team of graduate students who for several years methodically collected research for the first edition of this book. Special thanks to Kaija Belfry for coordinating this project and to the team of adept researchers under her guidance: Nicolas Dragojlovic, Josh Gordon, Talusier Arbour La-Salle, Jane Lister, Vanessa Meadu, Nicolas Sternsdorff, and Colin Trehearne. I am also indebted to Kate Neville for fact-checking and assistance with dictionary entries (especially the country entries), to Sharon Goad for editorial support and assistance with the bibliography, and to Jennifer Clapp for her photographs and photograph descriptions. My thanks as well to Jon Woronoff for his helpful advice and support on both editions of this book.

Acronyms and Abbreviations

AA	AccountAbility
ABN	L'Autorité du Bassin du Niger (Niger Basin Authority)
ACF	Australian Conservation Foundation
ADEME	Agence de l'Environnement et de la Maîtrise de l'Energie (Environment and Energy Efficiency Agency) (France)
AEPS	Arctic Environmental Protection Strategy
AIA	advance informed agreement
ARPA	Programa Áreas Protegidas da Amazônia (Amazon Protected Areas Programme)
ASEAN	Association of Southeast Asian Nations
ASEM	Asia-Europe Meeting
AZAP	Arid Zone Afforestation Project (Nigeria)
BAPA	Bangladesh Poribesh Andolon (Bangladesh Environment Movement)
BCSD	Business Council for Sustainable Development
BEN	Bangladesh Environment Network
BIO	Biotechnology Industry Organization
BPA	bisphenol A
CASBEE	Comprehensive Assessment System for Building Environmental Efficiency (Japan)
CBD	Convention on Biological Diversity
CCAMLR	Convention on the Conservation of Antarctic Marine Living Resources
CCP	Cities for Climate Protection
CDM	Clean Development Mechanism
CELA	Canadian Environmental Law Association
CEN	Coalition of Environmental NGOs (Bangladesh)
CERES	Coalition for Environmentally Responsible Economies
CFCs	chlorofluorocarbons

CFN	Commission du Fleuve Niger (Niger River Commission)
CI	Conservation International
CIEL	Center for International Environmental Law
CITES	Convention on International Trade in Endangered Species of Wild Fauna and Flora
CLRTAP	Convention on Long-Range Transboundary Air Pollution
COAG	Council of Australian Governments
COFEMA	Consejo Federal de Medio Ambiente (Federal Council of the Environment) (Argentina)
CONAMA	Comisión Nacional del Medio Ambiente (National Commission for the Environment) (Chile)
COP	Conference of the Parties
COPUOS	Committee on the Peaceful Uses of Outer Space (in the United Nations)
COSEWIC	Committee on the Status of Endangered Wildlife in Canada
CRT	cathode ray tube
CSA	Canadian Standards Association
CSE	Centre for Science and Environment (India)
CSR	corporate social responsibility
DDT	dichlorodiphenyltrichloroethane
Defra	Department for Environment, Food and Rural Affairs (Great Britain)
DPRK	Democratic People's Republic of Korea (North Korea)
ECO	Environmental Challenge Organisation (Singapore)
EDF	Environmental Defense Fund (United States)
EEZ	exclusive economic zone
EIA	Environmental Investigation Agency
EKC	environmental Kuznets curve
ELF	Earth Liberation Front
EMAS	Eco-Management and Audit Scheme
EMS	Environmental Management System (of the ISO)
ENB	*Earth Negotiations Bulletin*
EPA	Environmental Protection Agency

EPFIs	Equator Principles Financial Institutions
EPR	extended producer/product responsibility
ETC	Erosion, Technology and Concentration (Action Group on)
EU	European Union
FAO	Food and Agriculture Organization
FBI	Federal Bureau of Investigation (United States)
FERN	Forests and the European Union Resource Network
FLO	Fairtrade Labelling Organizations International
FOEI	Friends of the Earth International
FSC	Forest Stewardship Council
FUNAM	Fundación para la Defensa del Ambiente (Environment Defense Foundation) (Argentina)
FUNBIO	Fundo Brasileiro para a Biodiversidade (Brazilian Biodiversity Fund)
GDP	gross domestic product
GEF	Global Environment Facility
GEN	Global Ecolabelling Network
GM	genetically modified
GMO	genetically modified organism
GNP	gross national product
GRAIN	Genetic Action Resources International
GRI	Global Reporting Initiative
GROZA	Zelenaya Alternativa (Green Alternative) (Russia)
GW	gigawatts
HCB	hexachlorobenzene
HCFCs	hydrochlorofluorocarbons
HELCOM	Helsinki Commission (Finland)
HFCs	hydrofluorocarbons
HIV/AIDS	human immunodeficiency virus/acquired immunodeficiency syndrome
IBAMA	Instituto Brasileiro do Meio Ambiente e dos Recursos Naturais Renováveis (Brazilian Institute of Environment and Renewable Natural Resources)

IBDF	Instituto Brasileiro de Desenvolvimento Florestal (Brazilian Institute of Forestry Development)
IBF	International Biofuels Forum
ICC	Inuit Circumpolar Conference
ICED	International Center for Environment and Development
ICLEI	Local Governments for Sustainability
ICMM	International Council on Mining and Metals
IFAW	International Fund for Animal Welfare
IIED	International Institute for Environment and Development
IISD	International Institute for Sustainable Development
IMF	International Monetary Fund
IMO	International Maritime Organization
INBio	Instituto Nacional de Biodiversidad (National Biodiversity Institute) (Costa Rica)
INCR	Investor Network on Climate Risk
INRIC	International Network of Resource Information Centers
IPAM	Instituto de Pesquisa Ambiental da Amazônia (Institute for Environmental Research in Brazil)
IPCC	Intergovernmental Panel on Climate Change
ISA	Instituto Socioambiental (an institute in Brazil to promote social and environmental rights)
ISEE	International Society for Ecological Economics
ISEW	Index of Sustainable Economic Welfare
ISO	International Organization for Standardization
IUCN	International Union for Conservation of Nature
IWC	International Whaling Commission
LEED	Leadership in Energy and Environmental Design
LVEMP	Lake Victoria Environmental Management Project (Africa)
MEWR	Ministry of the Environment and Water Resources (Singapore)
MINAE	Ministerio de Ambiente y Energía (Ministry of the Environment and Energy) (Costa Rica)
MNC	multinational corporation
MoE	Ministry of Environment (South Korea)

MoEF	Ministry of Environment and Forests (Bangladesh)
MoEFCC	Ministry of Environment and Forests (India)
MOSOP	Movement for the Survival of the Ogoni People (Nigeria)
MSC	Marine Stewardship Council
MV SZOPK	Slovensky Zvaz Ochrancov Prirodky a Krajiny (Slovak Association of Protectors of Nature and Landscape)
MW	megawatts
NASA	National Aeronautics and Space Administration
NCEP	National Committee on Environmental Planning (India)
NEPA	National Environmental Policy Act (United States)
NEWS!	Network of European Worldshops
NFZT	Nuclear Free Zone Treaty (South Pacific)
NIMBY	not in my backyard
NGO	nongovernmental organization
NRDC	Natural Resources Defense Council
ODA	Official Development Assistance
OECD	Organisation for Economic Co-operation and Development
OPEC	Organization of the Petroleum Exporting Countries
PBDE	polybrominated diphenyl ethers
PCB	polychlorinated biphenyl
PCSD	Philippine Council for Sustainable Development
PEFC	Programme for the Endorsement of Forest Certification
PIROP	Pacific Islands Regional Ocean Policy
POPs	persistent organic pollutants
PRA	participatory rural appraisal
PVC	polyvinyl chloride
RAN	Rainforest Action Network
RCMS	Responsible Care Management System
REDD	Reduced Emissions through Avoided Deforestation and Degradation
RENOVE	Rede Nacional de Organizações da Sociedade Civil para as Energias Renováveis (a network of NGOs to promote renewable energy in Brazil)

RFF	Resources for the Future
RSPO	Roundtable on Sustainable Palm Oil
RTS	Reclaim the Streets
SARA	Species at Risk Act (Canada)
SCAR	Scientific Committee on Antarctic Research
SEC	Singapore Environment Council
SEDUE	Secretaría de Desarrollo Urbano y Ecología (Secretariat of Urban Development and Ecology) (Mexico)
SEMA	Secretaria Especial do Meio Ambiente (secretariat for the environment under the jurisdiction of the Minister of the Interior in Brazil)
SEPA	State Environmental Protection Administration (China)
SFI	Sustainable Forestry Initiative
SGLS	Singapore Green Labelling Scheme
SINAC	Sistema Nacional de Áreas de Conservación de Costa Rica (National Conservation Areas System of Costa Rica)
SNUC	Sistema Nacional de Unidades de Conservação (National System of Conservation Units in Brazil)
SPREP	South Pacific Regional Environment Programme
TACIS	Technical Assistance to the Commonwealth of Independent States (a program of the European Commission)
TAMAR	Tartarugas Marinhas (Sea Turtles, a Brazilian NGO)
TIS	Svaz Pro Ochranu Přírody a Krajiny (Yew Tree, the Union for the Protection of Nature and Landscape) (Czechoslovakia)
TRAFFIC	Trade Records Analysis of Fauna and Flora in Commerce
TWN	Third World Network
UN	United Nations
UNCCD	United Nations Convention to Combat Desertification
UNCED	United Nations Conference on Environment and Development
UNCLOS	United Nations Convention on the Law of the Sea
UNCSD	United Nations Commission on Sustainable Development
UNDP	United Nations Development Programme
UNEP	United Nations Environment Programme

UNESCO	United Nations Educational, Scientific and Cultural Organization
UNFCCC	United Nations Framework Convention on Climate Change
UNFPA	United Nations Fund for Population Activities
UNOOSA	United Nations Office for Outer Space Affairs
U.S.	United States
USAID	United States Agency for International Development
USSR	Union of Soviet Socialist Republics
UTG	United Tasmania Group (Australia)
WALHI	Wahana Lingkungan Hidup Indonesia (Indonesian Forum for Environment)
WBCSD	World Business Council for Sustainable Development
WFTO	World Fair Trade Organization
WMO	World Meteorological Organization
WRI	World Resources Institute
WWF	World Wide Fund for Nature/World Wildlife Fund

Chronology

1601 Russia: One of the worst famines in Russia's history begins, lasting until 1603 and killing up to one-third of the population.

1626 United States: Plymouth Colony passes an ordinance for cutting and selling timber.

1642 China: Near the end of the Ming dynasty (1368–1644), General Gao Mingheng breaches dikes to fight a peasant uprising, one of the first recorded uses of water as a military tool.

1666 Japan: Tokugawa Shogunate takes control of logging and promotes tree planting to reduce soil erosion and flooding.

1669 France: Forest Code is established to regulate wood production for the navy.

1681 Mauritius: Last Mauritius dodo (*Raphus cucullatus*) dies. **United States:** Proprietor of Pennsylvania, William Penn, decrees that one acre (0.4 hectares) of old-growth forest must remain for every five cleared.

1710 United States: Massachusetts protects waterfowl in coastal regions.

1722 Easter Island: Dutch explorer Jacob Roggeveen visits on Easter Sunday, surprised to find an ecological wasteland littered with majestic stone monuments.

1730 India: More than 300 Bishnois in what is now the state of Rajasthan are killed trying to prevent logging.

1798 Great Britain: Thomas Malthus's *An Essay on the Principle of Population* is published.

1804 International: World population reaches one billion.

1829 France: Statute to protect fish is enacted (still in effect).

1845 Prussia (present-day Germany): Regulations for industrial air pollution are introduced.

1859 South Africa: Cape Colony government passes Forest Protection Act.

1861 Mexico: Forest Service and forest ranger corps are established.

1862 France/Vietnam: First of a series of French ordinances to create forest reserves in Cochinchina (Vietnam) is enacted.

1864 India: Forest Service is founded. **United States:** George Perkins Marsh's *Man and Nature* is published, a foundational study of scientific conservation.

1865 Great Britain: First private group for environmental protection forms the Open Spaces Society. William Stanley Jevons publishes *The Coal Question*, demonstrating how the efficiency gains from steam engines did not lead to a decline in coal production but rather to an increase (becoming known as the Jevons paradox or rebound effect of efficiency gains). **India:** First Indian Forest Act is passed. **Java (controlled by the Netherlands):** Forest legislation is passed.

1866 Germany: Ernst Haeckel coins the term *ecology*.

1869 Egypt: Suez Canal opens, creating the first saltwater passage between the Mediterranean Sea and Red Sea; species previously blocked by hypersaline lakes begin to move between the seas, with the Mediterranean especially invaded by Red Sea species.

1871 United States: *American Sportsman* becomes the first publication to weave together the topics of conservation, hunting, fishing, and natural history.

1872 United States: Yellowstone National Park becomes the world's first national park (March). Nebraska sets aside 10 April as a holiday to plant trees (which in 1885 becomes a legal holiday, with the date now 22 April).

1873 Australia: Forest Tree Act passes in South Australia.

1879 Australia: First national park is established: Royal National Park in New South Wales.

1885 Canada: Banff National Park is established.

1892 United States: John Muir cofounds the Sierra Club.

1894 New Zealand: Tongariro National Park is established.

1895 United States: Wildlife Conservation Society is founded with headquarters at the Bronx Zoo in New York City.

1897 Thailand: Royal Forest Department is set up to manage revenue from teak forests.

1899 Thailand: All forests in Thailand are declared government property.

1900 International: First "international" conference on the environment is held in London in order to protect African wildlife. Parties adopt the Convention for the Preservation of Animals, Birds and Fish in Africa (May).

1905 Great Britain: In a London newspaper, Dr. Henry Antoine Des Voeux describes the London fog as "smog" (combining "smoke" and "fog"), popularizing the term. **United States:** National Audubon Society is established from local Audubon clubs set up in the late 1800s.

1906 Mexico/United States: Mexico and the United States sign the Convention on the Equitable Distribution of the Waters of the Rio Grande (for irrigation purposes), one of the first international environmental agreements (May).

1908 United States: President Theodore Roosevelt hosts a conference on conservation that leads to the formation of 38 state conservation commissions.

1914 United States: Once the most common bird in eastern North America, the last passenger pigeon dies in a Cincinnati zoo.

1916 International: Convention for the Protection of Migratory Birds concludes (August).

1921 United States: Thomas Midgley Jr. discovers that adding tetraethyl lead to gasoline can reduce engine knock, the beginning of the leaded gasoline industry.

1926 South Africa: National Parks Act is enacted.

1927 International: World population reaches two billion. **France:** French scientist and explorer Louis Lavauden coins the term *desertification*.

1928 United States: Thomas Midgley Jr. discovers chlorofluorocarbons (CFCs), later sold under the trademark Freon to cool refrigerators.

1933 International: Convention Relative to the Preservation of Fauna and Flora in Their Natural State opens for signature (November).

1934 Argentina: A national parks system is established.

1935 United States: Wilderness Society is founded.

1939 Switzerland: Paul Hermann Müller (1899–1965) discovers the "high efficiency" of dichlorodiphenyltrichloroethane (DDT) as an insecticide (for which he receives a Nobel Prize in 1948).

1946 International: International Convention for the Regulation of Whaling opens for signature (December). **Bikini Atoll:** Atomic bomb is tested in July, the first of over 20 in Micronesia over the next 12 years; nuclear fallout leaves behind a devastating toll, convincing many to oppose nuclear tests on ecological grounds.

1948 International: International Union for Conservation of Nature (IUCN) is founded. **Great Britain:** Six hundred die in London from fog laced with particulate matter and sulfuric acid. **India:** Mohandas Karamchand (Mahatma) Gandhi (1869–1948) is assassinated.

1949 United States: Aldo Leopold's *A Sand County Almanac* is published, which would shape the environmental movement into the 1950s and 1960s.

1950 Bangladesh: Government begins to manage fish resources under the Protection and Conservation of Fish Act.

1951 International: International Plant Protection Convention opens for signature (December). **Czechoslovakia:** Communist Party forcibly disbands all "decorative" clubs, including organizations concerned with landscape preservation that—as part of the nascent preservationist movement prior to World War I—had approximately 50,000 members in 378 clubs. **Iran:** Government nationalizes oil, straining relations with Great Britain and the United States. **United States:** Nature Conservancy is founded, although roots go back to 1915.

1952 Great Britain: "Killer fog" contributes to 4,000–7,000 deaths in London (December). **United States:** Resources for the Future is founded, the first think tank in the United States to focus solely on energy, environmental issues, and natural resources.

1954 International: International Convention on Pollution of the Sea by Oil opens for signature (May). **United States:** Bell Laboratories develops a silicon photovoltaic cell able to convert enough sunlight to power electrical equipment.

1955 Israel: Wildlife Protection Law is enacted.

1956 China: The first nature reserve is established. **Great Britain:** Clean Air Act is passed. **Japan:** Minamata disease, a neurological condition, is officially "discovered" in villagers living upstream from Minamata Bay (linked in 1959 to methyl mercury from the Chisso industrial plant).

1958 International: Convention on the Continental Shelf, the Convention on the Territorial Sea and Contiguous Zone, and the Geneva Convention on Fishing and Conservation of the Living Resources of the High Seas open for signature (April). **Czechoslovakia:** Yew Tree, the Union for the Protection of Nature and Landscape (TIS)—the first conservation group—is formed; it is not completely independent, however, as it works within the state apparatus and, thus, supports the Soviet regime.

1959 International: Main international organization for space law, the United Nations and its Committee on the Peaceful Uses of Outer Space (COPUOS), becomes a permanent body of the General Assembly. Antarctic Treaty opens for signature (December). **Vietnam:** Vietnam War (1959–1975) begins, causing widespread environmental damage over the next decade and a half as the United States sprays herbicides, such as the dioxin-containing Agent Orange, to defoliate forests.

1960 International: World population reaches three billion. Paris Convention on Third Party Liability in the Field of Nuclear Energy opens for signature (July).

1961 International: World Wildlife Fund is founded (today known simply as the WWF). **South Korea:** Government enacts a new Forest Law to promote reforestation, the country's first environmental law.

1962 United States: Rachel Carson's *Silent Spring* is published, which for many marks the start of the modern environmental movement.

1963 International: Berne Convention on the International Commission for the Protection of the Rhine against Pollution opens for signature (April). Vienna Convention on Civil Liability in the Field of Nuclear Energy opens for signature (May). **Israel:** Government passes first law for national parks. **Soviet Union:** *Oktiabr* publishes the most famous of the essays related to Lake Baikal, "Luminous Eye of Siberia," by Vladimir Chivilikhin.

1964 International: Convention for the International Council for the Exploration of the Sea opens for signature (September).

1966 International: International Convention for the Conservation of Atlantic Tunas opens for signature (May). **South Korea:** Protests in Pusan against air pollution from an oil-fired power station spur emerging environmental citizen activism. **United States:** Scientists concerned about the effects of dichlorodiphenyltrichloroethane (DDT) establish the Environmental Defense Fund (which incorporates the following year). Kenneth Boulding publishes "The Economics of the Coming Spaceship Earth."

1967 Great Britain: *Torrey Canyon* sinks off the coast of England, spilling over 30 million gallons of crude oil.

1968 International: African Convention on the Conservation of Nature and Natural Resources opens for signature (September). **United States:** Paul Ehrlich publishes *The Population Bomb*. Garrett Hardin publishes in the journal *Science* what would become one of the most cited articles of all time, "The Tragedy of the Commons."

1969 International: United Nations establishes the Fund for Population Activities (UNFPA). **Canada:** Don't Make a Wave Committee forms in Vancouver, the beginning of what later becomes Greenpeace. **Czechoslovakia:** Yew Tree, the Union for the Protection of Nature and Landscape (TIS)—the first conservation group—splits in two, giving rise to the Slovak Union of Nature Conservationists (with the original organization continuing in some areas). **United States:** David Brower founds Friends of the Earth after resigning as executive director of the Sierra Club.

1970 International: United Nations General Assembly adopts the Declaration of Principles Governing the Seabed and the Ocean Floor, and the Subsoil Thereof, beyond the Limits of National Jurisdiction (December). **Germany:** Paul Crutzen of the Max Planck Institute for Chemistry in Mainz raises the possibility that nitrogen oxides from fertilizers and supersonic aircraft could be damaging the ozone layer. **Japan:** The Diet holds a special session that passes 14 new laws to regulate pollution. **United States:** First Earth Day held on 22 April. Group of law students and attorneys founds the Natural Resources Defense Council to influence environmental laws. Environmental Protection Agency (EPA) is established.

1971 International: Ramsar Convention on Wetlands of International Importance Especially as Waterfowl Habitat opens for signature (February). International Institute for Environment and Development is founded with a base in London. **Brazil:** Economist José Lutzemberger founds Gaucho Association for the Protection of the Natural Environment. **Canada:** Department of Environment is established. Group of activists founds Greenpeace in Vancouver. **France:** Environment Ministry is established. **Great Britain:** World Wide Opportunities on Organic Farms begins, eventually evolving into a worldwide network of national organizations to link travelers wanting to volunteer (in exchange for food and accommodation) on organic farms.

1972 International: United Nations Conference on the Human Environment is held in Stockholm (June). Convention on the Prevention of Pollution by Dumping of Wastes and Other Matter (London Convention) opens for signature (November). Club of Rome authors publish *The Limits to Growth*. United Nations Environment Programme is established with its headquarters in Nairobi, Kenya. United Nations establishes World Environment Day to be held every year on 5 June. **Australia:** United Tasmania Group (UTG) forms, which some environmental historians consider the world's first green party. **Singapore:** A Ministry of the Environment is created. **United States:** Pesticide dichlorodiphenyltrichloroethane (DDT) is banned.

1973 International: Convention on International Trade in Endangered Species of Wild Fauna and Flora opens for signature (March). International Convention for the Prevention of Pollution from Ships opens for signature (November). **Bangladesh:** Wild Life (Preservation) Order is enacted. **Great Britain:** E. F. Schumacher publishes *Small Is Beautiful*. Under the name PEOPLE, Europe's first green party is founded (renamed the Ecology Party in 1975 and the Green Party in 1985). **India:** Chipko Movement emerges when villagers in the Himalayan Mountains start hugging trees to stop logging. **Israel:** Environmental Protection Service is established. **Norway:** Arne Naess publishes "The Shallow and the Deep, Long-Range Ecology Movements" in *Inquiry*, coining the phrase *deep ecology*. **United States:** Endangered Species Act is enacted.

1974 International: World population reaches four billion. **Finland:** Helsinki Convention (Convention on the Protection of the Marine Environment of the Baltic Sea Area) is adopted (replaced in 1992 by a new Helsinki Convention). **France:** Françoise d'Eaubonne coins the term *eco-feminism*, merging environmentalism and feminism into a new intellectual movement. René Dumont contests the French presidential elections with an environmental platform. **Germany:** Federal Environmental Agency is established. **Mexico:** Symposium on development and environment is held at Cocoyoc, hosted by the United Nations Environment Programme and the United Nations Conference on Trade and Development (October). The Cocoyoc Declaration represents one of the earliest uses of the phrase *sustainable development*. **United States:** Lester Brown founds the Worldwatch Institute (based in Washington, D.C.). Mario J. Molina and F. Sherwood Rowland publish an article hypothesizing that chlorofluorocarbons (CFCs) might be destroying the ozone layer.

1975 International: Convention on Registration of Objects Launched into Outer Space opens for signature (January). **Australia:** Peter Singer publishes *Animal Liberation*, a highly influential book within the animal rights movement. **Bikini Atoll:** People of Bikini file first of many lawsuits against the United States for the environmental and health consequences of nuclear testing in the region. **New Zealand:** Plan to clear-cut 340,000 hectares of forest in South Island is abandoned after widespread public opposition.

1976 International: Convention on International Trade in Endangered Species of Wild Fauna and Flora (CITES) lists Asian elephants as a species threatened with extinction, thus banning commercial trade internationally. **Australia:** Tasmania Wilderness Society is founded, changing its name in 1984 to the Wilderness Society. **France:** Conservation Act creates a legal foundation for protecting the natural environment, although implementation proves difficult. **Nigeria:** Government begins the Arid Zone Afforestation Project.

1977 International: United Nations Conference on Desertification is held in Nairobi, Kenya (August–September). **Argentina:** Wildlife Foundation established to protect biodiversity. **Bangladesh:** Department of Environment is established. **Canada:** Paul Watson founds the Earthforce Society in Vancouver (which is incorporated in the United States as the Sea Shepherd Conservation Society in 1981). **Germany:** First eco-labeling scheme is launched: the "Blue Angel" program. **Kenya:** Wangari Maathai founds the Green Belt Movement. **South Korea:** Government passes an Environmental Preservation Act, the first attempt to develop comprehensive environmental legislation. **United States:** Herman Daly publishes one of his most influential books, *Steady-State Economics*.

1978 Argentina: Local office of Greenpeace opens. **Malaysia:** Sahabat Alam Malaysia (Friends of the Earth Malaysia) is established. **United States:** Government evacuates the first homeowners from Love Canal in Niagara Falls, New York, following a grassroots campaign to expose poisons leaking into yards and basements. **West Germany:** Environmentalists in local elections present candidates under a "Green List" (*Grüne Liste Umweltschutz*), the first use of the term *green* to describe a political party.

1979 International: Geneva Convention on Long-Range Transboundary Air Pollution opens for signature (November). Convention on the Conservation of Migratory Species of Wild Animals opens for signature (June). Greenpeace International is officially founded to connect a half dozen loosely affiliated groups. **China:** Government puts in place its one-child policy. Government enacts its first major environmental legislation, the Environmental Protection Law for Trial Implementation. **Great Britain:** James Lovelock publishes *Gaia: A New Look at Life on Earth*, popularizing his Gaia hypothesis. **Taiwan:** Environmental Protection Bureau forms out of the Department of Environmental Health. **United States:** Three Mile Island nuclear facility experiences a core meltdown of one of two reactors. The name "Earth First!" appears to describe a new radical environmental group willing to take direct action to "protect" the environment. **West Germany:** Green Party is founded.

1980 International: Convention on the Conservation of Antarctic Marine Living Resources opens for signature (May). **Brazil:** The nongovernmental organization Projeto TAMAR (Projeto Tartarugas Marinhas, or Sea Turtles Project) is founded to protect sea turtles and promote marine conservation. **India:** Prime Minister Indira Gandhi orders a 15-year ban on logging in the Himalayan forests, a victory for the Chipko Movement. **Indonesia:** Indonesian Forum for Environment (Wahana Lingkungan Hidup Indonesia, WAL-HI) is established as a network of nongovernmental and community-based organizations. **United States:** First eco-feminist conference takes place in Amherst, Massachusetts.

1981 Ireland: The Ecology Party is established. **South Africa:** National Conservation Strategy is implemented. **Sweden:** Green Party, Miljöpartiet de Gröna, is founded. **United States:** Julian Simon publishes *The Ultimate Resource*, challenging the intellectual foundation of environmentalism. Donella and Dennis Meadows found the International Network of Resource Information Centers (INRIC) to advance systems-oriented analysis and activism. New administration of Ronald Reagan cuts the budget of the Environmental Protection Agency.

1982 International: United Nations General Assembly adopts a World Charter for Nature (October). United Nations Convention on the Law of the Sea opens for signature (December). International Whaling Commission declares a moratorium on commercial whaling. **Argentina:** Environmentalists found the Fundación para la Defensa del Ambiente (FUNAM, or Environment Defense Foundation). **India:** Vandana Shiva establishes the Research Foundation for Science, Technology and Ecology. **Mexico:** The government establishes a Secretariat of Urban Development and Ecology (SEDUE). **Soviet Union:** Two feeder rivers, Amu Darya and Syr Darya, stop emptying into the Aral Sea. **United States:** World Resources Institute is founded to produce independent and scientific policy research and analysis on environmental issues. Amory Lovins founds the Rocky Mountain Institute as an entrepreneurial nonprofit organization to advance environmental efficiencies.

1983 International: United Nations General Assembly forms the World Commission on Environment and Development, which meets for the first time the following year. **Canada:** Green Party is established. **European Community:** Following a global environmental campaign, a two-year ban is imposed on the import of whitecoat harp seals, leading to a collapse in prices and markets that in effect ends Canada's commercial seal hunt. **West Germany:** German Green Party becomes the first new party to enter the German Parliament in 60 years. **India:** Appiko Movement, following in the tradition of the Chipko Movement, begins a nonviolent struggle to save trees by hugging them. **Iran:** Government restricts traffic in the city center to combat air pollution. **United States:** Seven million tires burn in Virginia.

1984 International: Environmental Investigation Agency, with offices in London and Washington, D.C., is founded to investigate "crimes" against the environment. **Chile:** President Augusto Pinochet establishes a National Commission for Ecology to draft a national environmental framework (although it never completes its task). **Europe:** Green parties capture 12 seats in the European Parliament. **France:** The political party Les Verts (the Greens) is formed. **India:** Toxic gas leak kills thousands in Bhopal (December). **Malaysia:** Third World Network, an international network of nongovernmental organizations across developing countries, is founded with an international secretariat in Penang. Swiss activist Bruno Manser moves to Sarawak where he lives with the Penan people and helps to organize local resistance to logging. **Spain:** Confederation of the Greens is founded. **United States:** Green Party is founded.

1985 International: International Tropical Timber Agreement opens for signature (April). Vienna Convention for the Protection of the Ozone Layer opens for signature (March). Randall Hayes establishes the Rainforest Action Network (with offices in San Francisco and Tokyo) to protect rain forests and the rights of indigenous peoples living in these forests. **Brazil:** Chico Mendes founds the National Council of Rubber Tappers. **Canada:** The Canadian Chemical Producers' Association launch Responsible Care, an environmental management system for chemicals. **New Zealand:** French agents sink the Greenpeace ship *Rainbow Warrior*.

1986 International: Convention for the Protection of the Natural Resources and Environment of the South Pacific Region opens for signature (November). **Brazil:** The nongovernmental organization Pro-Natura is founded to promote better environmental management. **Soviet Union:** Nuclear disaster occurs at Chernobyl, Ukraine. **Switzerland:** National Swiss Green Party (Grüne Partei der Schweiz) forms.

1987 International: Montreal Protocol on Substances That Deplete the Ozone Layer opens for signature (September). World Commission on Environment and Development releases *Our Common Future* containing the now widely accepted definition of sustainable development. World population reaches five billion. **Bolivia:** Conservation International brokers an exchange of US$650,000 in debt relief for an agreement with the government to conserve 1.5 million hectares of tropical forests, the world's first debt-for-nature swap. **Czechoslovakia:** Environmental group MV SZOPK (Slovensky Zvaz Ochrancov Prirodky a Krajiny, or Slovak Association of Protectors of Nature and Landscape) releases a damning report titled *Bratislava Nahlas* (Bratislava Aloud)—the government responds harshly, bringing the editor of the report up on criminal charges. **United States:** Conservation International, a nongovernmental organization working to conserve worldwide biodiversity, is founded.

1988 International: First genetically modified plants are grown. The World Meteorological Organization and the United Nations Environment Programme establish the Intergovernmental Panel on Climate Change (IPCC). **Brazil:** Chico Mendes, leader of Brazil's rubber tappers, is murdered. **Phi-**

lippines: The Philippines becomes the first country in Asia to participate in a WWF debt-for-nature swap. **Sweden:** Green Party, Miljöpartiet de Gröna, becomes the first new political party in 70 years to win a seat in the Swedish Parliament.

1989 International: Basel Convention on the Control of Transboundary Movements of Hazardous Wastes and Their Disposal opens for signature (March). Wellington Convention for the Prohibition of Fishing with Long Driftnets in the South Pacific opens for signature (November). Convention on International Trade in Endangered Species of Wild Fauna and Flora prohibits the international trade in ivory. International Society for Ecological Economics is founded. **Canada:** Kalle Lasn and Bill Schmalz found Adbusters Media Foundation as an anticorporate and anticonsumption movement. **Europe:** Green parties win 32 seats in the European Parliament, the most to date. **Philippines:** Government bans timber exports following floods, although illegal logging and deforestation continue. **Thailand:** Government bans commercial logging in natural forests. **United States:** Oil tanker *Exxon Valdez* spills over 40 million liters of crude oil into Prince William Sound off the coast of Alaska.

1990 International: An international association of local governments called the International Council of Local Environmental Initiatives is established (now called ICLEI: Local Governments for Sustainability). **Argentina:** Federal government creates the Consejo Federal de Medio Ambiente (COFEMA, or Federal Council of the Environment) to manage and coordinate environmental protection. **Canada:** International Institute for Sustainable Development is established in Winnipeg to promote sustainable development worldwide. **Malaysia:** Bruno Manser, now a well-known environmental activist fighting for the rights of the Penan people of Borneo, leaves Sarawak to launch an international campaign to raise awareness of the plight of the Penan people and the Bornean rain forests. **United States:** Clean Air Act Amendments establish a sulfur dioxide cap-and-trade program. Goldman Environmental Prize is established to honor grassroots environmentalists in Africa, Asia, Europe, islands and island nations, North America, and South and Central America.

1991 International: Bamako Convention on the Ban of Import into Africa and the Control of Transboundary Movement and Management of Hazardous Wastes within Africa opens for signature (January). Protocol on Environmental Protection to the Antarctic Treaty opens for signature (October). Global Environment Facility is piloted to provide environmental project grants to developing countries. United Nations General Assembly passes a moratorium on high-seas drift-net fishing. Swiss industrialist Stephan Schmidheiny founds the Business Council for Sustainable Development (BCSD) to participate in the 1992 United Nations Conference on Environment and Development. **Great Britain:** Protest group Reclaim the Streets emerges in London as part of a direct-action movement against automobiles. **Russia/Soviet Union:** End of the Soviet Union contributes to an economic crisis in the Russian Federation, further straining environmental conditions. **Sweden:** Government imposes a carbon tax on oil, coal, and natural gas to promote renewable energy. **United States:** David Foreman, cofounder of Earth First!, publishes *Confessions of an Eco-Warrior*. Greens/Green Party USA forms, emerging from a group called the Green Committees of Correspondence.

1992 International: Framework Convention on Climate Change opens for signature (May). Convention on Biological Diversity opens for signature (June). United Nations Conference on Environment and Development (also known as the Earth Summit and Rio Summit) held in Rio de Janeiro (June). Newly independent countries bordering the Aral Sea sign the first of a series of agreements to manage the Aral basin. **Bangladesh:** Environmental Lawyers Association is founded. **Germany:** Petra Kelly, a founder of the West German Green Party, is murdered. **Great Britain:** Earth Liberation Front (ELF) emerges as a "leaderless" global resistance to capitalism and environmental destruction. **Singapore:** Ministry of the Environment establishes a Green Labelling Scheme.

1993 International: With funding from the WWF, the Forest Stewardship Council is established to support certification of sustainable forest practices. **China:** Plans to construct the world's largest hydroelectric dam, the Three Gorges Dam on the Yangtze River, move ahead, despite opposition from many human rights activists and environmentalists. **European Union:** Eco-management and audit scheme, or EMAS, is introduced as a voluntary program to audit an organization's environmental impacts.

1994 International: Convention on Nuclear Safety opens for signature (June). United Nations Convention to Combat Desertification in Countries Experiencing Serious Drought and/or Desertification, Particularly in Africa, opens for signature (October). Mostafa Kamal Tolba, former head of the United Nations Environment Programme, founds the nonprofit International Center for Environment and Development (ICED) to finance environmental projects in developing countries. **Chile:** A general environmental framework is enacted. **China:** Government begins to implement the China Action Plan for Biodiversity Conservation. Construction begins on the Three Gorges Dam. First formal environmental nongovernmental organization is established (Friends of Nature, initially called the Academy for Green Culture). **Germany:** Constitution of the Federal Republic of Germany is amended to include environmental protection. **Great Britain:** Reclaim the Streets emerges to protest the M11 highway through Claremont Road, London, becoming one of the main organizations in the anti-road/anti-car movement. **United States:** American Forest and Paper Association establishes the Sustainable Forestry Initiative as a voluntary certification standard to promote sustainable management and responsible purchasing practices.

1995 International: Straddling Stocks Convention opens for signature (December). Kenya, Uganda, and Tanzania establish the Lake Victoria Environmental Management Project to manage the lake basin. **Brazil:** Nongovernmental Brazilian Biodiversity Fund is established. **Costa Rica:** Government creates a Ministry of the Environment and Energy and passes an overarching environmental law. **European Union:** Environmental auditing scheme EMAS opens for participation. **Great Britain:** Shell's plan to decommission and sink a facility for storing and loading oil in the North Sea (the *Brent Spar*) causes a global controversy. **Nigeria:** Military regime hangs Ken Saro-Wiwa with eight others after trumped-up charges follow protests against Shell's environmental impact in Ogoni Territory. **Southeast Asia:** Cambodia, Lao PDR, Thailand, and Vietnam establish the Mekong River Commission to manage river development (April).

1996 International: Comprehensive Nuclear Test Ban Treaty opens for signature (although still not in force) (September). **Arctic:** Arctic Council is formed to coordinate nonmilitary matters, support environmental strategies, and promote sustainable development. **Australia:** Australian Greens formed. **China:** "Green Lights" program is set up to promote energy-efficient lighting. **Cuba:** Havana passes bylaws so the city only produces organic food. **Great Britain:** Institute for Social and Ethical AccountAbility is founded (now called AccountAbility) to support socially accountable business practices. **South Africa:** Government puts in place a new constitution that includes the right to water in its bill of rights.

1997 International: Convention on the Law of the Non-navigational Uses of International Watercourses opens for signature (May). Convention on Supplementary Compensation for Nuclear Damage opens for signature (September). Kyoto Protocol to the United Nations Framework Convention on Climate Change opens for signature (December). Marine Stewardship Council, a nonprofit international organization dedicated to the sustainable use of marine fisheries, is founded. Global Reporting Initiative is launched as a joint project between the Coalition for Environmentally Responsible Economies (CERES) and the United Nations Environment Programme to strengthen corporate reporting on sustainability. **China:** Energy Conservation Law is passed. **Cuba:** National Environmental Strategy is put in place. **Indonesia:** Forest fires sweep across the islands of Sumatra and Borneo. Asian financial crisis adds to the country's (and Southeast Asia's) environmental woes. **Japan:** The hybrid Toyota Prius is launched. **Mexico:** Ecologist Green Party wins a seat in the national Senate.

1998 International: Convention on Access to Information, Public Participation in Decision Making, and Access to Justice in Environmental Matters opens for signature (June). Protocol on Heavy Metals opens for signature (June). Protocol on Persistent Organic Pollutants opens for signature (June). Rotterdam Convention on the Prior Informed Consent Procedure for Certain Hazardous Chemicals and Pesticides in International Trade opens for signature (September). **Africa:** Federation of Green Parties is established. **North Korea:** Government enacts the National Biodiversity Strategy and Action Plan to protect biodiversity.

1999 International: World population reaches six billion. An umbrella organization for national forest certification schemes, the Programme for the Endorsement of Forest Certification (PEFC), is launched to promote sustainable forest management. **Great Britain:** For the first time the Green Party wins a seat in the European Parliament. **India:** National Green Party registers as a political party. **South Africa:** The Green Party of South Africa forms. **Switzerland/Malaysia:** Swiss environmentalist Bruno Manser paraglides onto the front lawn of the chief minister of Sarawak to protest logging. **United States:** After living for 738 days in a giant California Redwood tree, Julia Butterfly Hill comes down after the company Pacific Lumber agrees to preserve the tree. Antiglobalization protestors disrupt meetings of the World Trade Organization and International Monetary Fund in Seattle, drawing global publicity to the anger among activists over the economic inequalities and environmental injustices of the global trading system.

2000 International: Cartagena Protocol on Biosafety to the Convention on Biological Diversity opens for signature (January). United Nations launches the Global Compact (July). United Nations hosts the Millennium Summit, which produces eight Millennium Development Goals, including achieving environmental sustainability. In 2000 Paul Crutzen and ecologist Eugene F. Stoermer (1934–2012) argue for renaming the Holocene Epoch (which dates from the end of the last major Ice Age some 12,000 years ago) the "Anthropocene" to reflect the geologic impact of *Homo sapiens*. **Brazil:** Brazilian Network of Civil Organizations for Renewable Energy is founded to promote renewable energy. **Great Britain:** Hundreds of guerrilla gardeners plant flowers and vegetables in London's Parliament Square on May Day (1 May).

2001 International: Stockholm Convention on Persistent Organic Pollutants opens for signature (May). Global Greens established. **Denmark:** Bjørn Lomborg publishes an English translation of his book *The Skeptical Environmentalist*, which would go on to become a best seller, with some seeing it as "proof" that environmental activists were exaggerating environmental problems with false statistics. **United States:** New administration of George W. Bush withdraws from the Kyoto Protocol, a decision most analysts see as effectively ending the protocol's chances of ever entering into force. Green Party of the United States (not to be confused with the Greens/Green Party USA) is created out of the Association of State Green Parties (1996–2001). September 11 terrorist attacks on the World Trade Center and Pentagon profoundly alter global politics.

2002 Africa: World Summit on Sustainable Development held in Johannesburg, South Africa. South Africa, Mozambique, and Zimbabwe establish the Great Limpopo Transfrontier Park—linking South Africa's Kruger National Park, Mozambique's Limpopo National Park, and Zimbabwe's Gonarezhou National Park—creating the largest park in Africa and one of the largest cross-border conservation areas in the world. **Antarctica:** Larsen B ice shelf, 200 meters thick with a surface area of over 3,000 square kilometers, breaks apart, a result, most scientists agree, of warmer temperatures from climate change. **Brazil:** Government establishes the Amazon Protected Areas Programme to protect millions of hectares of forests (with the goal of protecting 50 million hectares in the Amazon by 2012). Tumucumaque National Park is created as the world's most extensive tropical forest park. **Pakistan:** Green Party is established. **Vietnam:** Government creates a Ministry of Natural Resources and develops a National Strategy for Environmental Protection.

2003 International: Equator Principles, a voluntary initiative by leading financial institutions with support from the World Bank, is launched. It establishes principles to raise the standard of social and environmental risk assessment in major project financing. **Canada:** Species at Risk Act (SARA) is enacted. **China:** Government establishes Cleaner Production Promotion Law and the Environment Impact Assessment Law. Filling begins for the huge reservoir for the Three Gorges Dam. **Japan:** Japan hosts the Third World Water Forum in Kyoto. **Philippines:** To address worsening air pollution, the government sets hydrocarbon emission standards for motorcycles and motorized tricycles and requires emissions testing to register motor vehicles. **Sweden:** Government introduces Tradable Green Certificates to promote renewable electricity production.

2004 International: Parties to the Convention on International Trade in Endangered Species of Wild Fauna and Flora (CITES) agree to act against the unregulated trade in African ivory. Tsunami devastates many coastal and island communities in the Asia-Pacific region. The Roundtable on Sustainable Palm Oil is founded to certify responsibly and sustainably produced palm oil from tropical forested regions. **Arctic:** Arctic Council publishes the Arctic Climate Impact Assessment, predicting devastating consequences of climate change for life in the Arctic. **Bangladesh:** Green Party founded. **Europe:** European Green Party forms. **Kenya:** Wangari Maathai wins the Nobel Peace Prize for the Green Belt Movement, providing recognition of the growing global consensus about the importance of environmental stability for world peace. **Latvia:** Founder of the Latvian Green Party, Indulis Emsis, becomes the world's first "green" prime minister. **South Korea:** Political party Korea Greens is launched.

2005 International: Initiated by the United States, the Asia-Pacific Partnership on Clean Development and Climate is launched as an alternative approach to the Kyoto Protocol for addressing climate change (besides the United States, the group includes Australia, China, India, Japan, and South Korea). Year ends as the warmest in over a century. **Arctic:** Ayles ice shelf off the northern coast of Ellesmere Island (800 kilometers south of the North Pole) breaks off and floats to sea. **Bangladesh:** Government establishes the Sundarban Tiger Project to protect wild tigers. **Bolivia:** Noel Kempff Climate Action Project becomes the world's first project to use a third party to certify "avoided deforestation." **Europe:** An Emissions Trading Scheme for greenhouse gases becomes operational (covering almost half the European Union's emissions of carbon dioxide). **France:** Parliament ratifies an environmental charter, making the French Constitution the first to include the precautionary principle. **Russia:** Government ratifies the Kyoto Protocol, allowing the protocol to enter into force without the United States (the rules required at least 55 countries contributing at least 55 percent of 1990 greenhouse gas emissions). **Spain:** The government allows commercial genetically modified (GM) corn imports, making it the only country in the European Union to allow imports of GM crops.

2006 International: United Nations declares it the "International Year of Deserts and Desertification." **Canada:** Green Party wins 4.5 percent of the popular vote in the federal election. **China:** Scientists, searching the Yangtze River, are unable to find any Yangtze dolphins and declare the species "likely extinct," making it the first extinction of a large vertebrate in more than 50 years, for many in China and abroad a shocking end to one of the world's oldest animals (scientists estimate the species was more than 20 million years old). **Sub-Saharan Africa:** Region completes a phaseout of leaded gasoline, making it the first developing region to do so.

2007 International: Brazil, China, the European Commission, India, South Africa, and the United States launch the International Biofuels Forum (IBF) to advance biofuels markets. **Australia:** Just hours after being sworn in as prime minister, Kevin Rudd of the Labour Party ratifies the Kyoto Protocol (3 December) and creates a new Department of Climate Change. **Costa Rica:** The government announces plans to become the first carbon-neutral country (aiming for 2021). **Israel:** An explosion at the Makhteshim Agan chemical plant in Ramat Hovav releases hazardous waste into the surrounding area. **Russia:** National park is created to protect the Siberian tiger. **United States:** Al Gore, along with the Intergovernmental Panel on Climate Change, wins the Nobel Peace Prize. His film, *An Inconvenient Truth*, wins two Academy Awards, including best documentary film.

2008 International: Oil prices go over US$100 a barrel, spurring efforts to increase energy efficiencies and dampening interest in gas-guzzling automobiles. Global food crisis develops, and United Nations secretary general Ban Ki-moon establishes a Task Force on the Global Food Security Crisis. **Canada:** Stores pull products with bisphenol A (such as some plastic water bottles) after Health Canada becomes the world's first government agency to issue an alert about its dangers. **China:** Ministry of Environmental Protection replaces the State Environmental Protection Administration. Lead-up to the 2008 Olympics in Beijing draws global attention to China's urban environmental record. Work on the Three Gorges Dam continues, with the aim of finishing in 2009. **Poland:** Country hosts a global conference on climate change with the aim of moving international negotiations forward. **United States:** With its habitat disappearing as sea ice melts, the polar bear is listed as a threatened species under the Endangered Species Act.

2009 International: The 15th Conference of the Parties (COP 15) to the UN Framework Convention on Climate Change (UNFCCC) meets in Copenhagen, Denmark; observers roundly declare the Copenhagen Summit a failure. **Australia:** The state of Queensland declares a state of emergency after a massive oil spill in the Coral Sea. **Great Britain:** Protestors descend on the G20 Summit to demand more action to address climate change. **Kenya:** Worst drought in over a decade; ranchers illegally enter parks and nature reserves in search of water. **Peru:** Police shoot indigenous and environmental protestors obstructing a road near Bagua city, killing scores of people. **United States:** Federal government establishes the Pacific Remote Islands Marine National Monument, a massive noncontiguous marine protected area (extended in 2014).

2010 International: States sign the Nagoya Protocol to the Convention on Biological Diversity specifying "access to genetic resources and the fair and equitable sharing of benefits arising from their utilization." The number of vehicles goes over one billion. **Canada:** The federal government's health agency lists the synthetic petrochemical bisphenol A, or BPA, a common ingredient in plastic, as a toxic substance. **France:** Les Verts (the Green party) merged with Europe Écologie (formed in 2009 and gaining quick electoral successes) to form Europe Écologie—Les Verts (Europe Ecology—The Greens). **Haiti:** An earthquake shatters the country, killing more than

200,000 people; cholera breaks out. **Hungary:** A wave of noxious red sludge spills from an aluminum factory and flows into the Danube River. **Iceland:** A volcanic eruption spews ash and disrupts air travel across Europe for a week. **Indonesia:** Norway offers the government US$1 billion (over multiple years) to support forest conservation and reduce global carbon emissions by avoiding deforestation. **Pakistan:** Severe flooding disrupts the lives and food supplies of 20 million people. **United States:** Millions of barrels of oil spill into the Gulf of Mexico after an explosion at BP's *Deepwater Horizon* oil rig.

2011 International: The world population reaches seven billion. **Canada:** Elizabeth May becomes the first member of the Green Party to be elected to the federal parliament (then the first to be reelected in 2015). The federal government announces it is withdrawing from the Kyoto Protocol. **Germany:** Following countrywide protests after a meltdown at Japan's Fukushima Daiichi nuclear power facility, German chancellor Angela Merkel announces the phaseout of Germany's nuclear power capacity by 2022. **Japan:** Tsunami kills more than 15,000 people; waves strike the Fukushima Daiichi nuclear power facility, triggering a meltdown and the worst radiation release since Chernobyl in 1986. **Kenya:** Wangari Maathai, founder of the Green Belt Movement (1977) and winner of the Nobel Peace Prize (2004), passes away. **United States:** Following a call by the anticonsumerist magazine and advocacy group Adbusters to "Occupy Wall Street," antiglobalization and anticorporate activists converge in New York City to protest inequality and injustice, launching the Occupy Movement. Taren Stinebrickner-Kauffman founds the advocacy group SumOfUs to use social media to campaign for more responsible and sustainable business practices.

2012 International: United Nations holds the Conference on Sustainable Development in Rio de Janeiro to move along the goals of the UN Conference on Environment and Development held in Rio in 1992; worldwide, environmentalists express frustration at the outcomes of what is popularly known as Rio+20. **Australia:** The government passes a new law to ban the import of illegal timber. **Brazil:** Hosting Rio+20 puts Brazil's environmental record under a global spotlight, especially deforestation of the Amazon, one of the world's richest sources of biodiversity. **France:** National government establishes the Natural Park of the Coral Sea to protect marine life around its territory of New Caledonia. **United States:** Flooding from hurricane Sandy devastates parts of New York and New Jersey, raising public concern for climate change.

2013 International: The concentration of carbon dioxide in the atmosphere reaches 400 parts per million, raising alarms among climate change scientists, as this would seem to be the highest levels for millions of years. States sign the Minamata Convention, an international agreement to control mercury (named to honor the history of Minamata, Japan, where in the 1950s and 1960s hundreds of people died of mercury poisoning from local seafood). **China:** Reducing air pollution rises up the government's agenda as cities experience severe smog. **Indonesia:** Raging fires across the outer islands of Indonesia cause air pollution in some areas of Malaysia and Singapore to reach record levels; as is true every year, oil palm estates set many of these fires as a way of clearing and fertilizing land. **Russia:** To protest oil drilling in the Arctic, Greenpeace protestors scale a Gazprom oil platform in the Pechora Sea; security forces arrest the 30-person crew of the Greenpeace ship *Arctic Sunrise*, sparking worldwide outrage until the release of the "Arctic 30" at the end of the year.

2014 International: In a historic agreement, the United States and China agree on joint action to cut greenhouse gas emissions. New York City hosts the United Nations Climate Summit; here, dozens of governments, corporations, environmental groups, and indigenous organizations sign the New York Forest Declaration, pledging to strive for the end of deforestation by 2030. Dozens of well-known multinational corporations, including Cargill, General Mills, Johnson & Johnson, Kellogg's, L'Oréal, Mars, and Procter & Gamble pledge "zero deforestation," joining others such as Nestlé. The Nagoya Protocol to the Convention on Biological Diversity goes into force. **China:** Government announces it will step up its "war on pollution." **Nicaragua:** Government moves forward with the Grand Canal, both deeper and larger than the Panama Canal; ecologists express concerns over the consequences for protected areas and Lake Nicaragua. **United States:** California is hit by drought; water restrictions put in place as crops suffer. The state of California announces a ban on plastic bags (to go into effect in 2015/2016), the first U.S. state to do so.

2015 International: The 21st Conference of the Parties (COP) of the United Nations Framework Convention on Climate Change is held in Paris, France (December), and succeeds in negotiating a new international climate change agreement (called the Paris Agreement, it extends the climate change framework and replaces the Kyoto Protocol commitments ending in 2020). Year ends as the warmest ever recorded. **Australia:** The federal government announces it had met its 2020 greenhouse gas emission reduction targets early; critics respond with derision. **Bangladesh:** Prime Minister Sheikh Hasina receives a UN "Champion of the Earth" award for her climate change policies. **Bolivia:** New legislation welcomes oil and gas exploration within the country's 22 protected areas, upsetting conservation groups worldwide. **Canada:** The federal government of Canada renames its environment department the "Department of Environment and Climate Change." **Chile:** As air pollution reaches exceptionally dangerous levels, for the first time since 1999 the city of Santiago declares an emergency, closing factories and canceling events. **China:** The government revises its 1979 one-child policy to allow for two children as of 2016. **France:** Government restricts planned protests at the Paris climate change negotiations following deadly terrorist attacks in November. **Great Britain:** The government establishes Pitcairn Marine Reserve, the world's largest contiguous marine reserve, linking the islands around Pitcairn Island in the middle of the Pacific Ocean. **South Africa:** The UN awards the Black Mamba Anti-Poaching Unit, a small group of unarmed and mostly female rangers, for its successful efforts to reduce poaching and illegal bush hunting in a nature reserve within the Greater Kruger National Park. **United States:** The state of California announces a delay in implementing the ban on plastic bags after challengers collected enough signatures to require a referendum. President Barack Obama rejects the fourth phase of the Keystone XL Pipeline System, which would have greatly expanded the capacity of the Canadian province of Alberta to transport oil to U.S. refineries (and thus reach new export markets).

Introduction

The history of environmentalism is woven into the history of global ecological change. Before the 1960s, the word *environment*, in the relatively rare instances when it appeared in print, referred primarily to the home or work environment, not to nature, ecosystems, or the earth. Efforts to balance human societies with nature's capacity to adapt certainly has a much longer history than the more modern meaning of the word *environment*, extending back to when nomadic hunters and gatherers were allowing animals and plants to regenerate, settled indigenous communities were developing cultural practices of living *within* nature, and ancient Greek and Roman philosophers were reflecting on the consequences of different political and social orders for the natural world. By as early as the 17th century, various scholars and state officials were already calling for greater efforts to preserve, conserve, and manage natural systems. By the 19th and early 20th centuries, as consumption of natural resources began to rise alongside industrial production and growing populations, more and more governments, including some colonizers, began to implement "scientific" management of resources (such as sustained yield management for timber) to try to ensure more efficient use of natural resources and lessen unnecessary degradation and unwanted consequences (such as soil erosion and flooding). Some governments, writers, and ordinary citizens began to worry, too, about the quality of air and unsanitary conditions in industrializing cities. Many began to advocate for measures to preserve the "countryside" and "nature" by, for example, establishing national parks to preserve scenic beauty or species for viewing (e.g., birds) or hunting (e.g., bears) in natural settings.

Still, the word *environment* only began to take on its more modern political, social, ecological, and global meaning during the 1960s and early 1970s as public demands for cleaner and safer living conditions became more vocal, as newly formed nongovernmental groups began to lobby governments and campaign to influence consumers and corporations, and as global-scale problems began to move up national and international political agendas. Today, the concept of "the environment" is highly political, with definitions varying across and within societies. Some see the word *environment* as shorthand for *natural ecosystem*—for rain forests, oceans, deserts, and wetlands, as well as the atmosphere, climate, and ozone layer. For them, protecting the global environment is about protecting the earth itself *from* growing numbers of people. For others, the word *environment* includes, or is more about, the living spaces for humans: the air in towns and cities, the garbage in streets,

1

the rats and disease in dirty cities, the sewage in canals and oceans, and the industrial poisons in wells and lakes. Thus, "managing" the environment is more about making the spaces where people reside cleaner, safer, and more pleasant; preserving "natural" beauty for hikers and birdwatchers; and ensuring efficient economic growth and sufficient resources for future generations.

The understanding of environmental*ism* is even more contested. Most would agree the "ism" connotes a movement advocating for change to reduce the impact of humans on the environment (with its multiple definitions). But who are the legitimate environmental*ists*? Most would agree that ideas like "sustainable development" and the "precautionary principle"—as well as knowledge of the causes and consequences of escalating problems (deforestation, desertification, biodiversity loss, ozone depletion, climate change)— infuse environmentalism with beliefs and values, shaping arguments and prescriptions. And most, too, would agree that an environmentalist, by definition, believes that environmental problems are real and that some action is necessary (or at least potentially beneficial).

But what action? Here, little consensus exists among environmentalists on the best path forward. Some stress the need for better science and technologies, more trade, and more investment to reduce poverty and ensure more efficient production and distribution of environmental resources. Others emphasize the need for stronger international laws and state regulations. Still others stress the need to reform the globalizing capitalist world order to eliminate South-North inequalities, foreign debts, and exploitative multinational corporations. And still others see the only way for lasting change to occur is to shift global consciousness to alter lifestyles, reduce human populations, and decrease consumption.

To capture this diversity within environmentalism, this dictionary takes a global tack with a focus on ideas, events, institutions, initiatives, and green movements since the 1960s. It strives to avoid a common error made by many histories of environmentalism, which tend to exaggerate the input of the wealthy countries of Europe and North America and understate the influence of Africa, Asia, South and Central America, and the polar regions. It aims as well for a more comprehensive analysis than most histories of the modern environmental movement, understanding environmentalism as emerging not only from grassroots and formal nongovernmental associations, but also from corporate, governmental, and intergovernmental organizations and initiatives. This assumes that the ideas and energy infusing environmentalism with political purpose arise from hundreds of thousands of sources, from corporate boardrooms to bureaucratic policies to international negotiations to activists. Thus, environmentalists are not only indigenous people blocking a logging road, Greenpeace activists protesting a seal hunt, or green candidates contesting an election; an equal or larger number of environmentalists are working within the Japanese bureaucracy to implement environmental policies, within the World Bank to assess the environmental impacts of loans, within Walmart to green its purchasing practices, or within intergovernmental forums to negotiate international environmental agreements.

Understanding environmentalism in this way reveals that, unlike in the 1960s, as a movement it is no longer on the political fringes but is now a driving global force reforming state policies, international law, business practices, and community life everywhere. To chart the contours of this powerful movement, and to provide necessary background for the dictionary entries, this introduction divides environmentalism into four categories that, although overlapping slightly, are in significant ways distinctive: scholarly environmentalism, governmental environmentalism, nongovernmental environmentalism, and corporate environmentalism.

SCHOLARLY ENVIRONMENTALISM

Environmentalism, more so than other social and political movements, can suddenly shift and reorient in unexpected directions following groundbreaking scientific research or the development of new ways of understanding from the social sciences and humanities. Other new ideas have taken root following a best-selling book or popular essay. One of the most influential essays in the intellectual history of environmentalism goes back to 1798 when Thomas Malthus published the first edition of *An Essay on the Principle of Population*, which predicted that a worldwide famine would one day ensue because population, left unchecked, rises exponentially while food production can only increase arithmetically. One of the most influential books was Rachel Carson's *Silent Spring* (1962), which many people believe ushered in modern environmentalism by raising American (and over time global) consciousness with regard to the environmental dangers of chemicals such as dichlorodiphenyltrichloroethane (DDT). But many other books and essays have shaped environmentalism, too.

Before Carson, books such as Aldo Leopold's *A Sand County Almanac* (1949) were influencing the emerging environmental movement in the United States. Numerous best-selling books and popular articles would also follow Carson's *Silent Spring*, with many of the authors inspired by a belief that environmentalists must reach a global audience to bring about necessary reforms. One particularly influential book from the late 1960s was Paul Ehrlich's *The Population Bomb* (1968), with its metaphor of the earth bombed by an exploding human population, leaving it no longer able to feed the starving survivors. One of the most cited academic articles of all time came out in the same year: Garrett Hardin's article "The Tragedy of the

Commons," which sees the history of access to and the collapse of the English commons as analogous to access to and the collapse of shared environments in modern times. The idea of a global environment began to emerge around this time as well, reinforced as astronauts took stunning pictures of a fragile and borderless earth from space, an image that soon became a symbol of global environmentalism (and common on book covers). This image also reinforced a growing sense in both the First and Third Worlds of mutual vulnerability of increasingly entwined economies and ecosystems.

Three especially influential books in the 1970s were *The Limits to Growth* (1972) by Donella Meadows, Dennis Meadows, Jørgen Randers, and William Behrens III; *Small Is Beautiful* (1973) by E. F. Schumacher; and *Steady-State Economics* (1977) by Herman Daly. *The Limits to Growth*, using groundbreaking computer simulations to argue that economies would one day crash into the earth's finite resources, convinced many people to question the value of unrestrained economic growth. *Small Is Beautiful* took these critiques further and proposed reforming the global economy to decentralize and democratize decision making and ensure appropriate technology scaled for a quality community life. *Steady-State Economics* added further to a growing vision among some environmentalists about how to manage economic life sustainably and became a foundational text for the emerging field of ecological economics.

Some influential books were also written by politicians, such as Petra Kelly's *Fighting for Hope* (1984) (she was one of the founders of the West German Green Party). Other influential books and articles came out of governmental forums. The World Commission on Environment and Development, set up by the United Nations in 1983 to develop ideas for bringing together the goals of development with the values of environmentalism, published a report in 1987 called *Our Common Future* that included a definition of sustainable development that to this day continues to guide most governments and many nongovernmental organizations (NGOs): "development that meets the needs of the present without compromising the ability of future generations to meet their own needs."

Although rarer, corporate leaders have also authored influential books, such as *Changing Course* (1992) by Swiss industrialist Stephan Schmidheiny, who founded the Business Council for Sustainable Development (BCSD) in 1991. More common is for books to receive a significant boost in publicity as business leaders praise them. One example is economist Julian Simon's *The Ultimate Resource* (1981). Another is journalist Gregg Easterbrook's best seller, *A Moment on the Earth* (1995). An even more dramatic example is the best-selling translation of Danish political scientist's Bjørn Lomborg's *The Skeptical Environmentalist* (2001), a Cambridge University Press book with more than 3,000 footnotes. Best-selling books critical of environmentalism, however, remain much less common than ones about the global environmental "crisis" or ones calling for global reforms to "save" the planet from humanity. The list of influential books in this category is long: four examples are Herman Daly's *Beyond Growth* (1996), Jared Diamond's *Collapse* (2005), Bill McKibben's *Deep Economy* (2007), and Naomi Klein's *This Changes Everything* (2014). A few environmental movies, too, have been highly influential in shaping public debates and global consciousness; one of the best known is Al Gore's documentary film *An Inconvenient Truth* (2006), which won two Academy Awards and was one of the reasons Gore won the 2007 Nobel Peace Prize.

GOVERNMENTAL ENVIRONMENTALISM

Collective efforts to control nature started in earnest 8,000 to 15,000 years ago as nomadic hunters and gatherers began turning to settled agriculture. Large civilizations emerged as inventions like the animal-drawn plow, the wheel, numbers, and writing began to change political and social life. Often, these same civilizations began to clear forests, degrade land, and pollute local waters. Environmental collapse even toppled a few great civilizations, such as Mesopotamia (a land between the Tigris and Euphrates Rivers, part of contemporary Iraq), where a badly designed irrigation system slowly poisoned the land with salt. Until some 200–300 years ago, however, environmental problems were primarily local; only with the industrial revolution did human activities start to cause noticeable regional and global environmental damage.

One reason for the increasing global damage was the rise in the production and burning of fossil fuels (such as coal). Another was the growing global population, which jumped from one billion people in the early 1800s to over two billion by the end of the 1920s. A third reason was the rising consumption of natural resources from places far from producers and consumers (with colonial administrations often facilitating this "trade"). The evidence of severe damage was already clear by the late 19th and early 20th centuries. On some days, smog in cities such as London and New York became thick enough to kill. Once abundant species, such as the Plains bison of North America, were brought to near extinction; a few, such as the passenger pigeon, even went extinct (in 1914). By then, some governments were starting to respond by passing new national and regional policies to promote conservation of wildlife and better resource management. Canada and the United States, for example, signed the Migratory Birds Treaty in 1918.

State environmentalism began to take off after the late 1960s, however, as more and more people (especially in wealthy countries) began to demand better living conditions and as "global" environmental problems began to emerge. By the beginning of the 1970s, various governments were establishing environmental departments and agencies. The United States, for example, created the Environmental Protection Agency (EPA) in 1970. The following year, Canada set up its Department of the Environment, and France established its Environment Ministry. A year later, Singapore established a Ministry of the Environment. By this time many governments were also putting together negotiating teams to participate in international environmental negotiations. One outcome was the United Nations Conference on the Human Environment, held in June 1972 in Stockholm, Sweden.

The Stockholm conference was the first international United Nations conference for state officials on the environment and a sign of the growing importance of environmentalism for governments worldwide. The only heads of state to attend were Swedish prime minister Olof Palme and Indian prime minister Indira Gandhi; still, the turnout was impressive, with about 1,200 delegates from over a hundred countries attending (although, disappointingly for the organizers, Russia and the communist bloc countries boycotted the conference to protest the exclusion of East Germany). The conference revealed, however, some fundamental differences in how governmental environmentalism was emerging in developed and developing countries. Delegates from wealthier states tended to stress issues such as industrial pollution, nature conservation, and population growth. Delegates from poorer states tended to stress the need for development, arguing that rich conservationists should not deny the world's poor the benefits of economic growth. Sharp differences emerged as well over who was responsible for solving (and thus financing the solutions to) global environmental problems. Many delegates from the Third World saw global capitalism as a cause of poverty and a core reason for the pressures on natural environments, especially with global economic institutions such as the World Bank and the International Monetary Fund pressuring developing countries to export natural resources on declining terms of trade. These delegates coined the phrase *the pollution of poverty* to express the idea that the greatest global environmental threat was in fact poverty and that the only solution for poverty was international economic reforms.

In the end, the official conference documents—the nonbinding Declaration on the Human Environment (with 26 principles), the Action Plan for the Human Environment (with 109 recommendations), and the Resolution on Institutional and Financial Arrangements—did not stress these calls to reform the global economy. The conference did, however, raise the profile of global environmental issues within states, and it revealed the complexity and diversity of worldviews about the causes and consequences of global environmental change. It also led to the creation of the United Nations Environment Programme (UNEP), officially launched in 1973 with its headquarters in Nairobi, Kenya, and with Canada's Maurice Strong as its first executive director. It was not designed as a strong institution—more a coordinating program than a specialized agency with a significant budget. Both the First and Third Worlds supported this. The First World did not want to fund a large institution; the Third World did not want an institution able to interfere with development goals.

After the Stockholm Conference, rising oil prices in 1973–1974 rocked the global economy—inflation soared, economic growth slowed, and foreign debt increased in many Third World countries, particularly in Latin America and Africa. Such turbulence deflated some of the more ambitious environmental plans after Stockholm, especially in countries with heavy debts and weak economies. Still, governmental environmentalism continued to strengthen. In 1973 the United States passed the Endangered Species Act, and Bangladesh enacted the Wild Life (Preservation) Order. In 1974 West Germany set up its federal Environment Agency, and Mexico hosted a symposium on development and environment in Cocoyoc, formulating some of the earliest conceptions of sustainable development. Just after Stockholm, states also signed some noteworthy international environmental treaties, including the Convention on the Prevention of Marine Pollution by Dumping of Wastes and Other Matter (the London Convention of 1972, which entered into force in 1975) and the Convention on International Trade in Endangered Species of Wild Fauna and Flora (CITES, 1973, which entered into force in 1975).

In the second half of the 1970s and the first half of the 1980s, conservative governments more hostile to environmentalism came to power in the United States and Great Britain, and many developing economies fell further into debt. Nevertheless, governmental environmentalism was continuing to strengthen, partly because of advances in scientific understanding (such as the dangers of chlorofluorocarbons [CFCs] for the ozone layer and the link to skin cancer); partly because of disasters such as the 1979 U.S. nuclear accident at Three Mile Island and the 1984 Union Carbide chemical leak in Bhopal, India; and partly because of increasing pressure from grassroots and nongovernmental environmentalism (and thus, in democracies, pressure from voters). More and more states established environmental agencies, including increasingly in the developing world (for example, Bangladesh established its Department of Environment in 1977, and Taiwan created its Environmental Protection Bureau in 1979). States also continued to sign and ratify international environmental agreements, such as the 1979 Convention on the Conservation of Migratory Species of Wild Animals (which entered into force in 1983), the 1979 Convention on Long-Range Transboundary Air Pollution (which entered into force in 1983), and the 1980 Convention on the Conservation of Antarctic Marine Living Resources (which entered into force in 1982).

Global environmental issues began to move up the list of government priorities in the second half of the 1980s. States continued to negotiate and sign international environmental treaties, including the 1985 Vienna Convention for the Protection of the Ozone Layer, the 1987 Montreal Protocol on Substances That Deplete the Ozone Layer, and the 1989 Basel Convention on the Control of Transboundary Movements of Hazardous Wastes and Their Disposal. By the end of the 1980s, the debate was centering on the concept of sustainable development, drawing on the definition from the 1987 report by the World Commission on Environment and Development, *Our Common Future*.

This report, commonly called the Brundtland Report after its chair Gro Harlem Brundtland, was an ingenious compromise between those wanting more development and those wanting more environmental protection. It did not assume any necessary limits to growth, and it saw industrialization and natural resource production, under correct management, as suitable, even essential, for some countries. The report saw poverty as a core cause of unsustainable development. Thus, the only way forward was to stimulate—not slow—economic growth, although not the unchecked growth of the 1960s and 1970s, but growth arising from sustainable development. It called for developed countries to transfer more environmental technologies and economic assistance to the Third World. It also recommended better education and food security as well as more controls on population growth.

The growing consensus around the Brundtland concept of sustainable development culminated in a 1989 United Nations General Assembly resolution to hold the first summit of world leaders on the global environment, what became the 1992 United Nations Conference on Environment and Development (UNCED), held in Rio de Janeiro, Brazil. Popularly called the Rio or Earth Summit, this was the largest conference ever held by the United Nations, with 117 heads of state participating and 178 national delegations. The official conference also included thousands of NGO representatives; thousands more also attended a parallel NGO forum. Most state delegates endorsed the Brundtland definition of sustainable development, although many from developing countries also called for far more economic assistance and technology transfers from the First World to balance the additional costs of green growth.

The Rio Summit reinforced the view among state leaders that more economic growth was necessary for a healthy global environment. It produced several important consensus documents: the Rio Declaration on Environment and Development (a set of 27 principles on the rights and responsibilities of states for environment and development) and Agenda 21 (a 300-page action program to promote sustainable development). It also produced the Non-Legally Binding Authoritative Statement of Principles for a Global Consensus on the Management, Conservation and Sustainable Development of All

Types of Forests, and it opened two conventions for signature: the United Nations Framework Convention on Climate Change and the Convention on Biological Diversity.

The decade after the Rio Summit saw environmental issues again slide down the list of state priorities as threats of terrorism, chemical and biological warfare, and a financial crisis in Asia took center stage. State negotiators nevertheless kept signing and ratifying environmental treaties. The Convention on Biological Diversity entered into force in 1993. The United Nations Convention on the Law of the Sea, first opened for signature in 1982, entered into force in 1994. The United Nations Convention to Combat Desertification in Countries Experiencing Serious Drought and/or Desertification, Particularly in Africa, was opened for signature in 1994 (and entered into force in 1996). The Kyoto Protocol to the United Nations Framework Convention on Climate Change was opened for signature in 1998. And the Stockholm Convention on Persistent Organic Pollutants (POPs) was opened for signature in 2001. State negotiators also continued to review the progress of Agenda 21 and the implementation of sustainable development, including a 1997 special session of the United Nations General Assembly (commonly called the Earth Summit+5) that paved the way for the 2002 World Summit on Sustainable Development in Johannesburg, South Africa.

The Johannesburg Summit, also called Rio+10, was designed to evaluate the progress toward sustainable development, establish mechanisms to implement the Rio goal, and develop a global strategy to reach the United Nations' Millennium Development Goals. Global environmental change was no longer at the top of the global agenda (the terrorist attack on the World Trade Center and Pentagon on 11 September 2001 profoundly changed foreign policy priorities worldwide). Still, the Johannesburg Summit was a landmark event reaffirming the importance of governmental environmentalism; although fewer heads of state attended (about 100) than in the case of the Rio Summit, overall the conference was even larger than Rio, with more than 10,000 delegates from more than 180 countries, at least 8,000 civil society representatives, and about 4,000 members of the press. The official documents from the Johannesburg Summit were similar to the Rio Summit in terms of their broad support for sustainable development. The two most significant ones were the Johannesburg Declaration on Sustainable Development, a list of nonbinding challenges and commitments, and the Johannesburg Plan of Implementation. Like the Rio Summit, the Johannesburg Summit added yet another layer to environmentalism. It further raised the profile of environmental issues among world leaders and within state bureaucracies, it cemented sustainable development as the core organizing concept for governmental environmentalism, and it brought many nongovernmental organizations and community groups into partnerships with business and governments to implement policies to promote sustainable development.

NONGOVERNMENTAL ENVIRONMENTALISM

Among ordinary citizens, concern over deteriorating local and global environmental conditions began to increase in the late 1960s and early 1970s. Symbolic of this was the first Earth Day in April 1970, which saw some 20 million people rally at one of the largest organized demonstrations ever held in the United States. At the same time, more and more environmental activists were creating national and transnational organizations to lobby governments and corporations and to rally public support. The World Wildlife Fund (later renamed the World Wide Fund for Nature except in the United States and Canada), which started in 1961 with fund-raising headquarters in Switzerland, was evolving into an international network of national offices. By the early 1970s, it had already established a US$10 million trust fund to cover administrative expenses. Greenpeace was also beginning to take shape after a group of activists set sail in 1971 from Vancouver for Amchitka, an island off Alaska, to "bear witness" to U.S. nuclear testing. The same year four groups—from England, France, Sweden, and the United States—founded Friends of the Earth International to coordinate environmental campaigns.

Over the next decade, networks of environmental activism began to deepen. Greenpeace, for example, evolved into a multinational enterprise as more than 20 groups in North America, Europe, Australia, and New Zealand adopted the name Greenpeace. In 1979 the Canadian Greenpeace Foundation, facing financial and organizational difficulties, agreed to create a new international organization called Greenpeace International (with its headquarters in Amsterdam). By the 1980s this new structure was allowing Greenpeace to coordinate campaigns and fund-raising in ways not unlike the advertising and sales strategies of a multinational corporation. Some Greenpeace activists stole a page from advertisers, using daring stunts to reach front pages and prime time, repeating messages and images to embed new meanings and emotions into the public psyche. There were many successes. For example, whales became "majestic" and seals "cuddly," and whaling and sealing were recast in the minds of many people as senseless slaughters.

Friends of the Earth International (FOEI) was continuing to grow and evolve over this time as well. In the second half of the 1970s, the number of national offices in the federation increased (primarily in developed countries). Such expansion began to necessitate more organizational capacity. The federation decided to set up a small international secretariat in 1981 (rotating from country to country) to assist with coordinating and running the increasingly large annual meetings. Two years later the number of groups in the federation reached 25, and the members decided to elect an executive committee to oversee the issues dealt with at the annual meetings. Two years after this, the European members decided to create the first regional coordinating office in Brussels. The number of national offices in the federation was continuing to grow, with more joining through the 1980s from Africa, Asia, and Latin America. The first member from Eastern Europe—Poland's Polski Klub Ekologiczny—joined in 1985. A year later the number of members was at 31, and for the first time a national office in the developing world hosted the annual meeting (Sahabat Alam Malaysia, or Friends of the Earth Malaysia). The mandate was expanding, with more national offices from developing countries, and by the mid-1980s, FOEI was campaigning to protect tropical rain forests and indigenous forest dwellers.

The increase in the number of World Wildlife Fund/World Wide Fund for Nature (WWF) projects and campaigns is yet another typical example of the growth of many nongovernmental environmental organizations from the mid-1970s to the mid-1980s. In 1973 the WWF launched Project Tiger (with the Indian government) to try to save India's endangered tigers. Its first worldwide tropical rain forest campaign—covering Africa, Latin America, and Southeast Asia—began two years later. In 1976 the WWF launched an ambitious marine campaign—called The Seas Must Live—to establish sanctuaries for dolphins, seals, turtles, and whales. The WWF was focusing more as well on monitoring and strengthening controls on trade in animals and plants (including ivory and rhino horn). It cooperated with the International Union for Conservation of Nature (IUCN) to create a new organization in 1976 called TRAFFIC (Trade Records Analysis of Fauna and Flora in Commerce). The end of the decade saw the WWF raise over US$1 million in a campaign to "Save the Rhino" from poachers.

By then the WWF was a truly international institution with a mandate well beyond its original focus on endangered species and habitat loss—one that many within the organization now felt required more cooperation with governments to integrate conservation into development strategies. The WWF was also emerging as an actor in more formal international structures—for example, cooperating with the IUCN and the UNEP to launch in 1980 a World Conservation Strategy endorsed by the United Nations. Meanwhile, its number of regular supporters was continuing to grow—sitting at about one million by the early 1980s.

Since the 1980s the capacity of environmental activists to influence governments, public attitudes, and corporations has continued to expand. Today, thousands of groups—big and small—form networks advocating for change. These can include celebrity consumer advocates like Ralph Nader. They can include innovative NGOs like Adbusters that practice "culture jamming," running spoof ads and counter-ads to encourage people to *not* consume. They can include grassroots movements like the Green Belt Movement in Kenya, which under the leadership of Wangari Maathai (winner of the 2004 Nobel Peace Prize) has been able to plant more than 50 million trees across Africa. And they can include local groups of just a couple of people working to protect a patch of land in a village. A few environmental groups, however—ones like Greenpeace, Friends of the Earth, and the WWF—now sit as big multinational players in this thicket of diverse environmental voices. Greenpeace International now has millions of contributors and offices in dozens of countries. Friends of the Earth also has millions of members and supporters, with over 70 national groups and over 5,000 local ones. And the WWF now has close to five million regular supporters, operating in over 80 countries and funding more than 2,000 conservation projects.

Over the last decade more of these activists have been cooperating with governments to achieve "mutual" goals. For groups like the WWF, this strategy has resulted in many successful projects. In recent years, for example, the WWF has been able to assist with establishing millions of hectares of protected forests. This includes, for example, in 2006 convincing Brunei Darussalam, Indonesia, and Malaysia to commit to the WWF's Heart of Borneo initiative to protect the biological diversity of 220,000 square kilometers of forests on the island of Borneo. The WWF has also been cooperating with governments to strengthen environmentalism in local communities as well—such as working with the Malagasy government on an environmental syllabus for primary schools, training locals as wildlife scouts in Zambia, and training gold miners in Suriname. It is collaborating as well with scientists to conduct research, on occasion making original discoveries, such as when a team of WWF divers found a new coral reef off the coast of Thailand in 2006.

The WWF is also partnering with many companies. "The WWF sees a future in which the private sector makes a positive contribution to the well-being of the planet," explains a website pamphlet called *The Nature of Business*. "To achieve this, WWF engages in challenging and innovative partnerships with business to drive change." A few examples show the diversity and range of activities. WWF-Sweden has worked with the food company Tetra Pak to establish policies for responsible wood purchases and to mitigate climate change. WWF-India has worked with the Austrian crystal firm Swarovski to establish a wetlands visitor center in India's Keoladeo National Park. WWF-U.S. has worked with Coca-Cola to promote water conservation. And WWF-Denmark has worked with the pharmaceutical firm Novo Nordisk on a policy to reduce the firm's carbon dioxide emissions. The WWF has also partnered with many firms on policies to reduce greenhouse gases—including multinationals such as IBM, Johnson & Johnson, Nike, and Polaroid.

NGOs such as the WWF have been especially eager to develop partnerships for eco-labeling programs. Two of the most influential programs are the Forest Stewardship Council (FSC) and the Marine Stewardship Council (MSC). Today, the FSC, founded in 1993 primarily using WWF funds, is the world's most recognizable logo for sustainable forest management, with retailers like Home Depot relying on FSC-certified wood to market sustainable timber. The MSC, founded in 1996 by the WWF and the Unilever food conglomerate, is now the most recognizable international eco-labeling program for sustainable seafood, gaining worldwide publicity in 2006 when Walmart—the world's biggest retailer—pledged to only buy wild seafood from fisheries meeting MSC standards. The partnering of some NGOs with governments and firms does not mean activists are no longer challenging from the periphery of power. If anything, there are more activists than ever before, in part because the Internet allows for a cheap and easy global presence. Still, as the preface to this book emphasizes, the trend in recent years has been toward more partnerships and a more commercial focus to all environmentalism.

CORPORATE ENVIRONMENTALISM

Corporations in a few sectors, such as forestry, have long histories of working toward "environmental" objectives such as sustainable yields. The purpose, however, was primarily about improving efficiency, reducing waste, and managing long-term risks to profits, not conservation or environmental protection. As governmental and nongovernmental environmentalism was strengthening and spreading during the 1960s and 1970s, most corporations in most sectors tried to block, stall, or counteract environmental regulations and criticisms. Tactics varied across cultures and economic settings, but the core objective—to stop environmentalism from cutting into profits—was the same. In countries like the United States, business executives financed political parties, deployed industry scientists to create uncertainty, lobbied politicians, and sued government departments such as the Environmental Protection Agency. In countries like the Philippines and Indonesia, multinational and local corporations funded military operations, bribed enforcement officers, and gave millions of dollars to politicians and their families.

The corporate approach to the challenges of environmentalism started to change in the 1980s. This occurred partly because government regulations and civil society pressures were forcing corporations in many countries to alter their practices. And it occurred partly because more and more firms began to see opportunities to gain competitive advantages and increase efficiencies by engaging with, rather than opposing, environmentalism. One example is Responsible Care, which began in 1985 as a voluntary commitment by the chemical industry to improve the health, safety, and environmental performance of chemical operations. By the end of the 1980s, multinational corporations were working toward developing a more constructive role in international environmental negotiations. The willingness of DuPont (the chemical company) to develop substitutes for CFCs, for example, was instrumental in moving along the international agreement to phase out ozone-depleting substances. By 1991, Swiss industrialist Stephan Schmidheiny had founded the Business Council for Sustainable Development to participate more effectively in the upcoming 1992 United Nations Conference on Environment and Development, as well as to facilitate business efforts to achieve sustainable development and develop a green image.

Since this conference, just about every multinational corporation (MNC) has now created an environment section and put in place internal guidelines to advance sustainable development. Programs similar to Responsible Care are now common, and their reach is extending. Responsible Care, for example, is now operating around the world, with uptake accelerating after the International Council of Chemical Associations passed a Responsible Care Global Charter in 2005 to encourage adoption of national Responsible Care programs. Together, "corporate environmentalists" advocate a business approach to environmentalism, including policies such as eco-efficiency (a business strategy to maximize resource efficiencies and minimize ecological impacts to produce more with less), market liberalization, industry self-regulation, corporate codes of conduct, and voluntary eco-labeling and certification schemes. They participate in international meetings and "partnerships" with governments, communities, and NGOs (especially with more moderate groups such as the WWF). They have also become increasingly active in developing international environmental policy, such as the Kyoto Protocol, advocating for flexible, voluntary, trade- and market-based instruments.

A common business label for this approach to environmentalism is corporate social responsibility, or what is now commonly called CSR. Often corporate brochures describe this as meeting a "triple bottom line": economic, social, and environmental. Such an approach requires companies to be diligent producers, sometimes even going "beyond compliance" with existing environmental regulations (especially in poorer countries with relatively low standards). The phrase *corporate social responsibility* first began to spread in the 1970s and 1980s in response to calls from nongovernmental groups and some states for stricter national and international regulations (including an initiative to develop a United Nations code of conduçt) for multinational corporations. In the 1990s, CSR began to take hold as a standard policy for MNCs, and today just about every MNC uses the phrase to frame its approach toward, and input into, national and international environmental policy.

Supporters of corporate environmentalism see these contributions as a practical and effective way to advance sustainable development. For some it is a way for MNCs to raise environmental standards in developing countries, such as the policy of the Swedish firm Electrolux to require suppliers and contractors in developing countries to follow its code of conduct. For other supporters, it is a way to expand niche eco-markets into profitable global ones. Corporate environmentalism is, they argue, currently encouraging many markets to grow, such as for wind and solar power, organic foods, fair trade coffee, and sustainable timber. For them the case of fair trade coffee is indicative. For decades this was a tiny market prodded along by the energy of international activists and farmers in the developing world, but today it is expanding quickly as big coffee chains like Starbucks purchase more fair trade coffee as part of their sustainability policies under the rubric of corporate social responsibility. Another revealing trend for supporters of corporate environmentalism is the growth of forest certification schemes, which now cover hundreds of millions of hectares of forest.

Not everyone is enthusiastic about the growing strength of corporate environmentalism, and many remain highly skeptical of the increasingly assertive claims of "sustainability leadership" over the past decade by companies such as Walmart, Coca-Cola, and Nestlé. Critics see many of these claims as disingenuous public relations—what some call *greenwash*—to conceal business as usual: that is, more profits from more production and more consumption, all of which requires more natural resources and generates more waste. As the preface discusses, some critics, too, are increasingly worried that corporate environmentalism is undermining the radicalism of grassroots, nongovernmental, and Third World environmentalism as more and more groups and community leaders join corporate partnerships in an effort to achieve concrete changes without disrupting the economic growth arising from corporate investment and trade.

THE FUTURE OF ENVIRONMENTALISM

Environmentalism, then, involves hundreds of international environmental groups, thousands of national groups, and tens of thousands of local ones. It also includes hundreds of international agreements, hundreds of national environmental agencies, and countless environmental sections in other organizations—from ones in MNCs to ones in regional and international organizations. Environmental concepts such as sustainability, sustainable development, the precautionary principle, corporate social responsibility, and eco-labeling percolate from all of these sources. Every year new ideas, refinements, policies, institutions, markets, and problems continue to enter into environmental debates and discourses—so many from so many different sources that one dictionary could not possibly capture all of it. Thus, this book strategically skips across issues, concepts, time, organizations, and cultures, not with any pretense of producing a definitive dictionary, but rather with the aim of producing an inclusive, wide-ranging, and global history of environmentalism.

ACCOUNTABILITY (AA). Founded in 1996 as the Institute for Social and Ethical AccountAbility, AccountAbility, or AA, promotes socially accountable business practices, including increasing the credibility of **sustainability** reports. Its members include private firms, civil society organizations, and research bodies. AA first published its AA1000 framework in 1999 as a principles-based standard applicable to any sector of any size in any region. It is designed to help organizations strengthen accountability and social responsibility by improving social and ethical accounting, auditing, and reporting. By engaging stakeholders in consultative processes, AA aims to increase transparency and improve organizational performance. In 2016 hundreds of organizations were using or referring to the AA1000 series of standards as part of strategies to advance **corporate social responsibility**.

ACID RAIN. Scottish chemist Robert Angus Smith coined the term *acid rain* in the mid-1800s after speculating that emissions from local **coal**-burning factories were making rainfall in the English city of Manchester unusually acidic. The main pollutants producing acid rain are sulfur dioxide and nitrogen oxides, which are released into the atmosphere as by-products of industrial processes and transportation, especially from burning fossil fuels. Smokestacks can contribute to acid rain by spewing pollutants above the inversion layer, which reduces local **pollution** but can cause pollution to travel as much as 1,000 kilometers on higher winds. Acid rain creates many problems, including acidification of lakes, harming aquatic life, damaging terrestrial plants and forests, harming human health, and damaging buildings and monuments.

Controlling acid rain requires transboundary cooperation. Acid deposition is particularly bad in Asia, partly because **China** relies heavily on burning coal for energy. Efforts to promote transboundary cooperation on acid rain and air pollution include the 1979 **Convention on Long-Range Transboundary Air Pollution (CLRTAP)** protocol to reduce sulfur emissions or transboundary fluxes by at least 30 percent (Sulphur Emissions Reduction Protocol). *See also* EMISSIONS TRADING; KOREA, SOUTH; SWEDEN.

ADAPTATION. Adapting to **climate change** is increasingly seen as a political and societal necessity as the average surface temperature is on track to rise by the end of this century by at least 1.5 degrees Celsius above preindustrial levels. More likely, many climate scientists are now saying, is a rise of 2–4 degrees Celsius, which would bring about mass extinctions, wild storms, severe droughts, and rising sea levels. Given this possibility, advocates of adaptation call for governments and communities to start the process of adapting to these consequences immediately: build dykes and dams, prepare to abandon low-lying valleys and island states, put in place more resilient food systems, and develop disaster protocols. Critics of adaptation worry that these efforts are deflecting demands for mitigation and accommodating the status quo, as the poor are being told to adapt to climate change so lifestyles of opulence can continue.

ADAPTIVE MANAGEMENT. Adaptive management takes a holistic and systems approach to managing resources in complex ecosystems, emphasizing ongoing experimentation and continual learning. Since its development in the early 1970s, it has been defined in various ways across different jurisdictions and ecosystems. Generally, its practices resemble scientific methods, although some key differences exist. Adaptive management integrates uncertainty: specifically, it assumes that ecosystems evolve with multiple equilibriums. Its methods of experimentation also differ. In particular, it is done at a management scale (thousands of hectares) without strict controls rather than within a controlled experiment of, say, a few square meters. Adaptive management assumes that ecological and economic systems are integrated and coevolve. This requires decision makers to remain open and flexible—to receive, understand, and respond to positive or negative signals in the physical and social environment and to change management responses accordingly.

Adaptive management is most commonly employed as a way to oversee ecosystems such as fisheries, forests, and wildlife. The concept was refined and developed by **C. S. Holling** and Carl J. Walters at the University of British Columbia (**Canada**) in the 1970s; further advances were made during Holling's time as director of the International Institute for Applied Systems Analysis in Vienna, Austria, from 1981 to 1984.

ADBUSTERS. Adbusters Media Foundation is a nonprofit activist network cofounded in Vancouver, **Canada**, in 1989 by Kalle Lasn (a documentary filmmaker) and Bill Schmalz (a wilderness filmmaker and photographer). Adbusters sees itself as an anticorporate social movement, using a method of social change it calls "culture jamming," defined by best-selling Canadian author **Naomi Klein** in her book *No Logo* as "the practice of parodying advertisements and hijacking billboards in order to drastically alter their messages" (280).

The network's primary means of communication is its *Adbusters* magazine, which, after starting in 1989 with 5,000 copies, has grown into a magazine with a circulation that at times has exceeded 100,000 digital and print copies. The magazine publishes six times a year and has subscribers from scores of countries, although most live in the **United States**. The foundation also operates a website (www.adbusters.org), offering services to support environmental campaigns in making "uncommercials" and "subvertisements." In recent years, Adbusters has pulled off some high-profile campaigns, including buying space on CNN to advertise TV Turnoff Week and Buy Nothing Day and purchasing a full-page advertisement in the *New York Times* for its Unbrand America campaign. Adbusters' most influential moment came in 2011 when, under the Twitter hashtag #OccupyWallStreet, it called on activists everywhere to descend on New York City on September 17 (Lasn's mother's birthday) to "occupy" Wall Street to protest inequality and the destruction of the planet. This call launched Occupy Wall Street and the **Occupy Movement**, although Adbusters did not attempt to lead or direct the subsequent global uprising.

AFFORESTATION. *See* REFORESTATION.

AFRICA. *See* KENYA; NIGERIA; SOUTH AFRICA; SUB-SAHARAN AFRICA; UNITED NATIONS CONVENTION TO COMBAT DESERTIFICATION IN COUNTRIES EXPERIENCING SERIOUS DROUGHT AND/OR DESERTIFICATION, PARTICULARLY IN AFRICA.

AGENDA 21. Agenda 21, a document arising from the 1992 **United Nations Conference on Environment and Development**, is a nonbinding plan to achieve **sustainable development** for the 21st century. The result of years of preparatory meetings, it reflected the emerging consensus among state negotiators that global environmental **sustainability** would require cooperation and partnerships across developed and developing countries. The specifics of how to share the financing of sustainable development—by far the most contentious topic at the 1992 conference—were never resolved, although Agenda 21 does call for more Official Development Assistance (ODA).

ALTERNATIVE ENERGY. *See* RENEWABLE ENERGY.

AMAZON. The Amazon basin covers roughly seven million square kilometers—nearly 5 percent of the world's land surface—and contains four to five million square kilometers of tropical rain forest. Close to two-thirds of the Amazon is in **Brazil**; the rest is in **Bolivia**, Colombia, Ecuador, French Guiana, Guyana, Peru, Suriname, and Venezuela. It is a rich source of **biodiversity**, by some estimates containing, for example, around 30 percent of all plant species. Approximately 20 million people reside in the Amazon basin, including over 200,000 indigenous people. Since the 1980s, a global environmental movement has been campaigning to protect the Amazon—in particular the old-growth forests of the Brazilian Amazon. **Chico Mendes**, a Brazilian rubber tapper, was one of the best-known activists until his assassination in 1988. This diverse movement has managed to advance research and spotlight many injustices and environmental disasters; however, in terms of slowing **deforestation**, it has been less effective. The Brazilian Amazon, for example, lost over 17 million hectares of forest in the 1990s alone—an area the size of Uruguay. The total deforested area had reached nearly 60 million hectares by the beginning of the 21st century. Since the mid-2000s deforestation has declined in the Brazilian Amazon, although ranchers continue to convert forests into pasture to supply the export market for beef, and, to a lesser extent, farmers continue to burn logged forests to grow crops such as soybeans (burning is a cheap and quick way to clear land and fertilize soil). *See also* GOLDMAN ENVIRONMENTAL PRIZE; ILLEGAL LOGGING.

ANIMAL LIBERATION FRONT (ALF). Emerging in the 1970s, the Animal Liberation Front is a radical, direct-action movement to prevent the inhumane treatment of animals, which for ALF includes laboratory testing, industrial meat production, fur farming, and zoos. The organization is leaderless and underground, with members "joining" by taking action to stop animal abuse. ALF claims that it is "nonviolent": every possible precaution is taken to avoid injuring anyone when it "liberates" animals and fights against "speciesism," a prejudice the movement places alongside racism and sexism. ALF describes the owning of animals as akin to slavery; only vegans or vegetarians can act on its behalf. At times ALF cooperates with the **Earth Liberation Front (ELF)**, which emerged in the 1990s to fight more explicitly for the liberation of the earth (including its animals), and members cross over. The U.S. government has declared both ALF and ELF to be domestic **"ecoterrorists"** since the early 2000s, severely constraining the activities of both ALF and ELF in the **United States**. *See also* SINGER, PETER (1946–).

ANIMAL RIGHTS. *See* ANIMAL LIBERATION FRONT (ALF); SINGER, PETER (1946–).

ANTARCTICA. The Antarctic accounts for 10 percent of the earth's total land surface, roughly equal in size to Europe and the **United States** combined. The southern circumpolar seas also comprise nearly 10 percent of the world's oceans. The Antarctic continent is home to more than 800 species of plant life (approximately 350 are lichens), eight types of seals, 12 cetacean species, and about 45 different species of birds. It is the only continent without trees; only two flowering plants have been discovered. Antarctica's ice sheet contains 70–75 percent of the world's freshwater reserves and 90 percent of the earth's ice. On average, the ice sheet is about 2,000 meters thick; if all of this ice were to melt, global sea levels would rise by 60 meters or so.

Extreme weather conditions mean the ecosystems in Antarctica are especially fragile and vulnerable to any disturbance. The lowest temperature ever recorded on earth was near the South Pole on 21 July 1983 at the Soviet Vostok station (-89.2 Celsius, or -128.6 Fahrenheit). Antarctica is also one of the world's driest places, receiving less precipitation than the Sahara Desert.

Antarctica, except for the indirect effects of **greenhouse gases** and **ozone depletion**, suffers from little atmospheric **pollution**. Trawlers have exploited some **fishing** grounds, and several species are close to commercial collapse. **Whaling** also put some species at risk prior to the moratorium on commercial whale hunting by the International Whaling Commission (IWC) in the mid-1980s.

The Southern Ocean and boundless ice were too rough for early explorers, and until the 19th century, most states ignored Antarctica (considered *terra nullius*, or belonging to nobody). **Great Britain** was the first country to claim sovereignty over Antarctica in 1908. **New Zealand**, **Australia**, Norway, **France**, **Argentina**, and **Chile** would later claim sovereignty over various parts (some overlap, notably the claims by Great Britain, Argentina, and Chile). The Antarctic treaty was signed in 1959, and it came into force in 1961. The treaty forbade new sovereignty claims while neither recognizing nor delegitimizing existing ones. The treaty only allows nonmilitary research (and bans nuclear weapons testing). Initially, it did not include environmental protection clauses. However, in 1964 the Antarctic Treaty Consultative Parties passed the Agreed Measures for the Conservation of the Antarctic Fauna and Flora. Since then the parties to the treaty have negotiated other conventions as well, including the Conservation of Antarctic Seals (1972) and the **Convention on the Conservation of Antarctic Marine Living Resources** (1980). In 1991, the parties agreed to halt all **oil** and mineral exploration and exploitation for another 50 years, an amendment called the Environmental Protocol to the Antarctic Treaty, or the Madrid Protocol (which came into force in 1998). *See also* ARCTIC; SEALING.

ANTHROPOCENE. The Holocene Epoch, beginning roughly 12,000 years ago as the last major Ice Age came to a close, is the standard name for the latest geologic epoch of the Quaternary Period, which began 2.6 million years ago. In 2000, Paul Crutzen, along with ecologist Eugene F. Stoermer (1934–2012), argued in the *Global Change* newsletter of the International Geosphere-Biosphere Programme that the ecological consequences of *Homo sapiens* had been so far reaching and damaging since the late 1700s as to constitute a new geologic epoch, which they called the "Anthropocene." Stoermer had been referring to the current epoch as the Anthropocene since the 1980s. The backing of Crutzen, however, gave the idea international publicity; five years earlier, Crutzen, along with Mario J. Molina and F. Sherwood Rowland, had won a Nobel Prize in Chemistry for theorizing the long-term consequences of **chlorofluorocarbons (CFCs)** for **ozone depletion**.

Well before the year 2000, many ecologists had talked broadly of the geologic "age of *Homo sapiens*." Since Crutzen and Stoermer's article, however, the term *Anthropocene* has been appearing with increasing frequency in both academic and popular writing. In 2009 a working group of a subcommission of the International Commission on Stratigraphy of the International Union of Geological Sciences began evaluating the merits of officially recognizing the Anthropocene. Besides the beginning of industrialization in the late 1700s, other starting dates have been proposed, including the beginning of agriculture 10,000 years ago, the early 1600s as **ecological imperialism** took off, and the mid-1900s with the beginning of the atomic age. The working group is scheduled to report in 2016.

APPIKO MOVEMENT. *See* INDIA.

ARAL SEA. The Aral Sea, in Central Asia, was once the world's fourth-largest lake. In just three decades, as governments and industry diverted its inflows for agriculture and hydroelectricity, its surface area shrank by half and its level fell by 15 meters, leaving this saline lake almost as salty as an ocean by the early 1990s. **Desertification** in the region increased, and soil quality deteriorated. The remaining water became increasingly polluted from sewage waste and the rising use of pesticides and herbicides to maintain agricultural output, leaving it unsafe for human consumption. Local fish could not adapt, and commercial **fishing** ended.

Authorities in the former Soviet Union declared the region an ecological catastrophe at the tail end of the communist regime. After the breakup of the Soviet Union in the early 1990s, degradation of the Aral Sea turned into an international problem involving the new nations of Kazakhstan, Kyrgyzstan, Tajikistan, Turkmenistan, and Uzbekistan. In February 1992, the new states signed the first of a series of agreements to manage the Aral basin. The **Global Environment Facility**, together with the World Bank, ran a project between 1998 and 2003 to improve water management, collect data, raise awareness, and restore wetlands in the region. Some progress is occurring in terms of improving environmental management; nevertheless, the Aral Sea is continuing to contract.

ARBOR DAY. *See* MARSH, GEORGE PERKINS (1801–1882).

ARCTIC. The Arctic is located around the North Pole. Countries with sovereignty over areas of the Arctic are **Canada**, Greenland (territory of Denmark), **Russia**, the **United States**, Iceland, Norway, **Sweden**, and **Finland**. Little international effort was made to conserve the Arctic environment before the 1970s, with a 1973 agreement to preserve polar bears as one of the first attempts. The first form of air **pollution** in the Arctic was called "Arctic haze" and was seen by airplane pilots in the mid-1950s; it was also seen by indigenous people. Not until the 1980s did scientists confirm that the cause of the haze was aerosol particles traveling over the Arctic from industrial Europe and Russia.

Notably, for most of the Cold War, states did not account for environmental impacts. In contrast to **Antarctica**, where the Scientific Committee on Antarctic Research (SCAR) was set up to coordinate efforts, nothing equivalent was put in place for the Arctic. There was the Arctic Ocean Sciences Board and the Comité Arctique International (International Arctic Committee), but the former Soviet Union did not participate and the organizations did not have the means to coordinate large-scale research. In October 1987, however, with the Arctic now containing ships, weapons, nuclear fuel, and radioactive waste, Mikhail Gorbachev did call for environmental cooperation.

In the late 1980s a number of treaties were negotiated to better manage the Arctic environment. In August 1990, the scientific organizations of the eight Arctic states agreed to form the International Arctic Science Committee as an international **nongovernmental organization**. In 1991, the environmental ministers of the eight Arctic nations issued the Rovaniemi Declaration, which outlined an Arctic Environmental Protection Strategy (AEPS). They identified six critical problems: **persistent organic pollutants (POPs)**, radionuclides, heavy metals, **oil**, acidification, and noise. In 1996 the Arctic Council was formed to coordinate nonmilitary matters and the AEPS among Arctic states, as well as to promote **sustainable development** and interest in the Arctic. In November 2004, the Arctic Council published the Arctic Climate Impact Assessment, which raised alarm bells over the severe impact of **climate change** on the Arctic. While the Arctic Council is an intergovernmental organization, indigenous groups, such as the Inuit Circumpolar Conference (ICC), have permanent participant status. The ICC, formed in 1977, has been critical of the AEPS for focusing too much on conservation and not enough on how to ensure livelihoods in Arctic communities. *See also* STOCKHOLM CONVENTION ON PERSISTENT ORGANIC POLLUTANTS.

ARGENTINA. Argentina's landscape is diverse. It contains the fifth-largest desert in the world (the Patagonian desert), the Andes Mountains, subtropical rain forests, and scrubland, as well as substantial agriculture (e.g., soy, wheat, vegetable oils, and beef). It is also a major exporter of **oil** and **natural gas**; **mining** for gold, zinc, silver, magnesium, and copper is also increasingly important.

The 1970s and 1980s saw the founding of several influential environmental **nongovernmental organizations**. The Wildlife Foundation was set up in 1977 to protect **biodiversity**; a branch of **Greenpeace** opened in 1978. The Fundación para la Defensa del Ambiente (FUNAM, or the Environment Defense Foundation) was set up in 1982; an influential founding member was Raúl Montenegro, an Argentinean biologist, environmentalist, and activist who won the Right Livelihood Award in 2004 (often described as the Alternative Nobel Prize, it is awarded for work on ecology and poverty alleviation). The Federación Amigos de la Tierra Argentina was founded in 1984 (joining **Friends of the Earth** International in 1985). The group Environment and Natural Resources was created in 1985 (with a specialty in legal services). City Foundation was established in 1995 to promote civic participation.

In 1990 the government established the Consejo Federal de Medio Ambiente, or Federal Council of the Environment (COFEMA), a federal agency tasked with environmental protection, including helping to coordinate provincial-level efforts. In 2002 the government passed a general law on the environment. Argentina also has a long history of **national parks**, creating a national parks system in 1934, a process that began in 1903 with donation of land in the Andes that later became part of a larger protected area. Today, there are 33 national parks; the country also has 14 **United Nations Educational, Scientific and Cultural Organization (UNESCO)** World Biosphere Reserves and nine World Heritage Sites.

AUSTRALIA. Environmental management in Australia involves several levels of government. The peak coordinating body is the Council of Australian Governments (COAG), an intergovernmental forum including the prime minister, state premiers, territory chief ministers, and the president of the Australian Local Government Association.

Two major environmental **nongovernmental organizations** in the country are the Australian Conservation Foundation (ACF), established in 1966, and the **Wilderness Society**, established in 1976 under the name Tasmania Wilderness Society. Some environmental historians consider the United Tasmania Group (UTG), which arose in 1972 as part of a campaign to save Lake Pedder in Tasmania from plans to develop hydroelectricity, as the world's first **green party** (it was at least one of the world's first green political organizations to compete in elections). The green movement would strengthen and develop out of various forest campaigns across Australia in the 1980s. In 1992, the Australian Greens, a confederation of eight state and territory Greens, was formally established as a national party.

Invasive species have been a particularly grave threat to Australia's **biodiversity**. Australia was active in negotiating the **Convention on Biological Diversity**, signing and ratifying the agreement in 1992. It established the National Environment Protection Council Act in 1994, a National Reserve System Programme in 1996 under the National Strategy for the Conservation of Australia's Biodiversity, the National Environment Protection Measures (Implementation) Act in 1998, and the Environment Protection and Biodiversity Conservation Act—its main environmental legislation—in 1999.

Australia is the world's driest inhabited continent, and water has been a long-standing environmental issue. Numerous regional and basin-specific water agreements have been created, including the 1965 Western Australia (South-West Region Water Supplies) Agreement Act, the 1968 and 1980 Western Australia Agreement (Ord River Irrigation) Acts, the Dartmouth Reservoir Agreement Act, and the 1993 Murray-Darling Basin Act. Joint efforts of national, state, and territorial governments to create a more comprehensive framework for water management led to the adoption of the National Action Plan for Salinity and Water Quality in 2000 and the National Water Initiative in 2004, the creation of the National Water Commission in 2004, and the passing of the 2007 Water Act.

Although Australia's **Cities for Climate Protection** program has been supporting local action to reduce **greenhouse gases** since 1997, Australia—like the **United States**—was notably absent from the **Kyoto Protocol** until 2007. The transition in 2007 from John Howard's conservative government to the Labor Party, under Kevin Rudd, brought with it Australia's ratification of the Kyoto Protocol and the creation of its Department of Climate Change (disbanded in 2010). Going into the December 2015 Conference of the Parties (COP) of the **United Nations Framework Convention on Climate Change** in Paris, the federal government under Prime Minister Malcolm Turnbull announced that it had now met its 2020 reduction target for greenhouse gases. Many climate specialists were not impressed, however, arguing that Australia's target was too low, and further that the government's calculations of so-called progress were designed to conceal that Australia's overall effort was still lagging behind many advanced economies.

AUTOMOBILES. A mere handful of wealthy citizens in wealthy countries owned automobiles at the beginning of the 20th century. Today, there are more than a billion cars and commercial vehicles emitting significant amounts of **greenhouse gases**. Globally, automobiles account for about one-fifth of carbon dioxide emissions related to energy and cause many premature deaths—over 1.2 million people die every year in traffic collisions—with especially high death rates in the Third World.

Still, the number of motor vehicles keeps rising as automakers roll out over 85 million a year, with the fast-growing economies of **China** and **Brazil** leading new registrations; if trends continue, the total number of vehicles will reach three billion by the middle of this century. Some jurisdictions—such as London and **Singapore**—do attempt to reduce traffic congestion with financial incentives and penalties, and a rare few, such as Toronto Island in **Canada**, ban automobiles. However, in the vast majority of places, environmental campaigns to ban or restrict automobiles have failed. There is also no effort to negotiate an international environmental agreement for automobiles. Instead, governments and **nongovernmental organizations** tend to rely on technological advances (such as catalytic converters, fuel injection, and seat belts), education campaigns, and international trade to improve the safety and environmental efficiency of automobiles. *See also* CRITICAL MASS; HYBRID AUTOMOBILES; LEADED GASOLINE; RECLAIM THE STREETS (RTS); TIRES.

B

BANGLADESH. The first environmental legislation in Bangladesh was put in place during British colonial rule, including public parks, agricultural regulations, and sanitation laws in the early 20th century. After partition and prior to independence from Pakistan in 1971, Bangladesh's forests were administered under the Provincial Forest Department and the Bangladesh Forest Industries Development Corporation (the Bangladesh Forest Research Institute was also created in the mid-1950s). During this time, fisheries resource management began with the 1950 Protection and Conservation of Fish Act. Forests were transferred to the jurisdiction of the Ministry of Agriculture in 1971. Post-independence also saw the government establish further measures such as the 1973 Bangladesh Wild Life (Preservation) Order and the 1983 Marine Fisheries Ordinance.

The Department of Environment was formed in 1977 and was replaced by the Ministry of Environment and Forests (MoEF) in 1989. Further development of environmental planning occurred during the early 1990s, with the MoEF creating the National Environment Management Action Plan in 1992, the Forestry Master Plan in 1993, and the Bangladesh Environment Conservation Act in 1995. The Forest Department is involved in conservation efforts and in 2005 started the Sundarban Tiger Project to protect wild tigers.

Advocates work from within the country and abroad to promote environmental action. The Bangladesh Environmental Lawyers Association was created in 1992 to advocate for environmental legislation, while in 1998 nonresident Bangladeshis formed the Bangladesh Environment Network (BEN) to facilitate environmental communication. BEN helped to initiate the International Conference on Bangladesh Environment in 2000, which sparked the formation of the nongovernmental environmental network Bangladesh Poribesh Andolon (BAPA). The Coalition of Environmental NGOs (CEN) performs a similar role as an umbrella group for a network of **nongovernmental organizations**.

One of the more serious environmental and public health issues confronting Bangladesh is arsenic in drinking water, especially in shallow wells (called tube wells), which is exposing millions of people to arsenic levels in water above what the World Health Organization considers safe. Recurring and intensifying droughts are causing suffering among some of the world's poorest communities. Meanwhile, rising sea levels and flooding are increasingly grave threats in low-lying regions of Bangladesh. In 2015 the United Nations presented Sheikh Hasina, the prime minister of Bangladesh, with a UN "Champion of the Earth" award to commend her government's responses to climate change.

BASEL CONVENTION ON THE CONTROL OF TRANSBOUNDARY MOVEMENTS OF HAZARDOUS WASTES AND THEIR DISPOSAL. The Basel Convention was concluded in Basel, Switzerland, in 1989 and entered into force in 1992. This international treaty is designed to protect the environment and human health from the creation, movement, and disposal of **hazardous wastes**. By 2016, there were 183 parties to the agreement, including all countries in the Organisation for Economic Co-operation and Development (OECD) except for the **United States**, which has signed but not ratified the agreement.

The agreement is an example of the influence of several emerging principles of global environmentalism. To some extent it integrates the principles of "duty of care" and "polluter pays": that waste producers have a duty, as well as the legal and financial responsibility, to dispose of their waste safely. The agreement reflects a belief in the "proximity principle": that the disposal of waste should be as close as possible to the source of origin, taking into account the availability of environmentally sound disposal sites.

The Basel Convention also reflects some values of the **environmental justice** movement. In particular, it aims to prevent wealthier states from transferring hazardous wastes to poorer ones (an increasingly common practice in the 1980s). Many environmental groups—and some states—seeing such practices as morally wrong and unsustainable called for a total ban on transboundary movements of hazardous wastes. In the end the Basel Convention did not ban such movements outright, instead setting limits and regulating transport. However, to address some of the ethical concerns around trading waste, it did establish a principle of ensuring "prior informed consent" from those at risk. A 1995 amendment to the convention, called the Basel Ban Amendment, goes further and prohibits to a far greater extent the export of hazardous waste from developed to developing countries. It is, however, not yet in force in international law, although many signatories do abide by it. *See also* MINAMATA CONVENTION ON MERCURY; POLLUTER PAYS PRINCIPLE.

BHOPAL GAS LEAK. A toxic gas leak in December 1984 at a pesticide plant in the city of Bhopal, **India**, is often called the world's worst industrial disaster. The plant was run by Union Carbide India, a subsidiary of the U.S. parent company, Union Carbide Company (now owned by Dow Chemical Company). After investigating, Union Carbide claimed the cause of the "accident" was employee sabotage. Activists discounted this "story," instead seeing the "disaster" as evidence of the grave dangers for workers and ecologies of producing chemicals without adequate safety measures or staff training, where multinational corporations set up shop in the world's poorest regions to exploit low standards and cut costs. Estimates of casualties vary, generally from 2,000 to 20,000 people dead (with higher estimates including cases of related illnesses, such as cancer) and 50,000 to 70,000 poisoned and/or left with disabilities (such as scarred lungs, blindness, and loss of speech and memory). The nongovernmental Bhopal Medical Appeal estimates that half a million people were exposed to the gas methyl isocyanate and at least 100,000 still suffer from the consequences today.

Union Carbide, in a 1989 out-of-court settlement, agreed to pay US$470 million to the Bhopal victims. The company has also taken other small measures to assist with cleanup and compensation. Human rights and environmental groups, however, widely see these efforts and monies as utterly inadequate.

BIKINI ATOLL. The history of Bikini Atoll after World War II brought the dangers of nuclear testing to the attention of the environmental movement. Bikini is one of 29 atolls and five islands comprising the Marshall Islands in Micronesia. The **United States** chose to locate its nuclear testing program at Bikini because it was away from regular air and sea routes. In March 1946, the United States began to relocate the 167 inhabitants of Bikini "temporarily" to Rongerik Atoll, 125 miles away. In July 1946, the United States detonated the fourth atomic bomb ever (after Los Alamos, Hiroshima, and Nagasaki) in the Bikini Atoll. Over the next 12 years, as the people of Bikini suffered terrible hardships, the United States tested over 20 atomic and hydrogen bombs in this region. The United States allowed a small number of people to return to Bikini in the late 1960s. As the long-term environmental effects of radiation became clearer, however, the United States again relocated the locals in 1978.

The people of Bikini filed the first of many lawsuits against the U.S. government in 1975. Since then, a series of successful suits created a relocation and resettlement fund as well as a trust fund. Seeking further reparations, the people of Bikini launched another lawsuit in 2006. The United States completed its cleanup of the region in 1980. Even today many scientists do not consider it safe for permanent settlement, however, and most of the Bikini people continue to live on the Marshall Islands, although a tourist industry for diving and **fishing** does exist now on Bikini Atoll.

BIODIVERSITY. Scientists have now described just under two million species of animals, plants, fungi, protists, and bacteria. The total number of species is likely somewhere between 8 and 9 million, although some put the number far higher.

Processes such as **deforestation, desertification**, and **climate change** are contributing to the deaths of 10 to 500 species every day. Much of this loss of biological diversity, or biodiversity (a word coined by Harvard biologist **Edward O. Wilson** in his 1988 edited book *Biodiversity*), involves microscopic organisms deep in oceans and forests. Still, even animal and plant species are going extinct—over 1,000 since the beginning of the 17th century—at rates 50 to 100 times higher than natural ones (assuming average life spans of 5 to 10 million years for a species).

At the global level, the **Convention on Biological Diversity (CBD)** functions as an umbrella agreement to protect biodiversity. Many other multilateral agreements are also now in place to protect biodiversity, including, for example, the **Convention on International Trade in Endangered Species of Wild Fauna and Flora (CITES)** and the **Convention on Wetlands of International Importance Especially as Waterfowl Habitat**. *See also* ANTARCTICA; AUSTRALIA; COSTA RICA; NATURE CONSERVANCY; THE PHILIPPINES.

BIOFUELS. The definitions and categories of biofuels are not always consistent but generally include biomass, biogas, bioethanol, and biodiesel. Primary biofuels rely on unprocessed organic material, such as the direct combustion of wood; secondary biofuels tend to be agrofuels (derived from agricultural products) and are processed. First-generation biofuels, mainly biodiesel and bioethanol, are made directly from food crops by fermenting plant-derived sugars to produce ethanol. In contrast, second-generation fuels are predominantly made from the residual nonfood parts of crops, such as the stems and leaves, or from things like wood chips or the leftover skins from fruit pressing. Second-generation biofuels are not yet commercially viable on a large scale.

Many advocates of biofuels see them as an environmentally friendly alternative to fossil fuels as an energy source, particularly for transportation. Unlike fossil fuels, which produce large amounts of **greenhouse gases** from underground stores, in theory biofuels are carbon neutral because any carbon released while using them as fuel is carbon the plants or trees absorbed during growth. Any reduction in net emissions, however, also depends in part on the environmental impact of the production cycle.

Worldwide, the use of biofuels for transportation is still relatively low, but many are predicting a steady increase in consumption going forward. **Brazil** and the **United States** are currently global leaders in biofuel production, and some countries, including within the European Union, have contemplated mandatory inclusion of biofuels in their energy policies and **climate change** strategies. In recent years, however, a growing number of environmental groups have turned against biofuels, calling for moratoriums as evidence mounts of serious ecological and social costs. Many analysts still argue that biofuels can diversify energy sources while enhancing rural economic development. Yet, critics respond, producing enough to meet the demand from global automobile and industrial markets has the potential to cause a global food shortage for the world's poor as prices for crops like corn rise. Critics worry, too, that biofuel markets will create even more incentives for developing countries to turn forests and farms into industrial plantations. At a minimum, many environmentalists are now calling for life-cycle analysis of the costs and benefits to account for impacts on water, energy, **biodiversity**, land degradation, climate change, and social and economic development. *See also* OIL; PEAK OIL.

BIOPIRACY. *See* SHIVA, VANDANA (1952–).

BIOTECHNOLOGY. The term *biotechnology* fuses the words *biology* and *technology* to describe the use of living organisms and biological systems to create or modify products or technological processes (such as genetically modifying agricultural crops). Biotechnology is growing in importance as a force of global change; the term also now appears in international agreements, such as the **United Nations Convention on Biological Diversity**. For advocates, biotechnology can produce many benefits: everything from improving food yields to preventing the spread of diseases. For opponents, it is one of the most dangerous of all technologies, as altering life forms brings with it the potential for unpredictable and uncontrollable spillover effects across food chains, ecosystems, and human health. *See also* GENETICALLY MODIFIED ORGANISMS (GMOs).

BISHNOIS OF RAJASTHAN. The Bishnois of the Indian state of Rajasthan are renowned worldwide for their commitment to environmentalism and nature. A community of Hinduism, their history goes back to the followers of Jambaji or Jambeshwar Bhagavan (1451–1537). Jambaji asked his followers to adopt 29 principles: two principal tenets forbid the cutting down of trees and the killing of animals. He also called for compassion for all living things, nonviolence, truth, vegetarianism, and no use of intoxicants. Bishnois derive their name from this list of principles, with *bis*[*h*] meaning "twenty" and *no/ noi/nou* meaning "nine": thus, followers are sometimes called "twenty-nin-ers." In one often-recounted story, over 300 Bishnois were killed in 1730 while attempting to stop the felling of trees around their village. Some see the Bishnois ethic, including the idea of hugging trees to protect them, as a significant predecessor of, and influence on, modern environmental move-ments such as the **Chipko Movement**. *See also* INDIA.

BISPHENOL A (BPA). Bisphenol A, or BPA, is a synthetic petrochemical and a core ingredient in polycarbonate **plastic**. It is one of the latest in a long list of chemicals—from **dichlorodiphenyltrichloroethane (DDT)** to **chlorofluorocarbons (CFCs)** to perfluorinated chemicals (PFCs)—that en-vironmentalists have campaigned to ban for health and ecological reasons. Volumes of BPA have been rising since the 1950s (with major producers including Bayer, Dow Chemical, GE Plastics, and Sunoco). Today, it is one of the most common chemicals, present in hard, clear plastic water and baby bottles; microwavable plastics; dental sealants; compact disks; sports hel-mets; and canned foods.

Trace amounts of BPA, which can mimic the female hormone estrogen, are migrating into the environment and into people. Scientists at Stanford University, trying to figure out what was interfering with their tests on the estrogen properties of yeast in the early 1990s, were the first to discover that BPA was leaching into water from plastic polycarbonate flasks. Since then the chemical industry continues to assert that it is safe, but hundreds of experiments over the last decade have found possible links to cancer, low sperm counts, and the early onset of puberty. The first class-action lawsuit to draw on this research was against five manufacturers of baby bottles, filed in Los Angeles in March 2007. In 2008, Health **Canada** became the first government agency to alert the public that it was getting ready to list BPA as a toxic substance; stores across the country immediately pulled products containing BPA from the shelves. In 2010, Health Canada listed BPA as a toxic substance. Concern in other jurisdictions, however, has been less pro-nounced. In the **United States**, for example, following a review of the latest scientific studies, the Food and Drug Administration concluded in 2014 that exposure to low levels is safe.

BLUE ANGEL PROGRAM. *See* ECO-LABELING.

BOLIVIA. Despite substantial natural resources, Bolivia is one of the poorest countries in South America and is part of the Heavily Indebted Poor Countries debt relief initiative of the World Bank and International Monetary Fund. To build the economy, the government, especially under the leadership of President Gonzalo Sánchez de Lozada from 1993 to 1997, adopted a contentious strategy of partial privatization of state enterprises. In 2000, large protests and riots erupted over a public-private partnership between the city of Cochabamba and a subsidiary of Bechtel Corporation for water provision in the city. Violent police responses, resulting in the deaths of several protestors, led to international headlines of "water wars," and the Bolivian government withdrew the contract. Protests in 2003 and 2005 over the privatization of **natural gas** resources also led to violent strikes and roadblocks, contributing to the resignation of Sánchez de Lozada in 2003 and his successor, Carlos Mesa, in 2005. In 2006, Evo Morales was elected president, with a platform including the "renationalization of gas"; the leader of the Movement for Socialism (MAS) party, he is now in his third presidential term, which began in 2014.

Bolivia has participated in some innovative environmental programs. It was the site of the world's first debt-for-nature swap. In 1987, **Conservation International** brokered an exchange of US$650,000 in debt relief for an agreement by the Bolivian government to protect 1.5 million hectares of tropical lowlands. In 2005, the Noel Kempff Climate Action Project—started in 1997 by the **Nature Conservancy**, the Fundación Amigos de la Naturaleza (Friends of Nature Foundation, a **nongovernmental organization** started in 1988), the Bolivian government, and three energy companies—became the world's first project to use third-party international standards to certify "avoided **deforestation**."

Bolivia has 22 protected areas, including the Madidi National Park, one of the most biodiverse spots on earth. Although Bolivia has always allowed some commercial and livelihood activities in its protected areas, President Morales has positioned himself internationally and domestically as a defender of "Mother Earth." In 2015, however, the government passed a new law explicitly allowing oil and gas exploration within its protected areas—a decision that upset conservation groups at home and abroad.

BOULDING, KENNETH E. (1910–1993). Born in Liverpool, England, Kenneth Boulding was a professor at the University of Michigan (1949–1967) and at the University of Colorado at Boulder (until he retired). Influential in the field of **ecological economics**, he is credited in particular with developing the interdisciplinary field of systems theory for the study of nature, science, and society. He was also a founding thinker in evolutionary economics, which brings together the study of economics and biological evolution. His 1966 essay "The Economics of the Coming Spaceship Earth" also helped to popularize the metaphor of **"spaceship earth,"** although the idea was in usage by then (including, for example, in a 1963 book titled *Operating Manual for Spaceship Earth*).

BOVÉ, JOSÉ (1953–). A sheep farmer and trade unionist, Joseph (José) Bové has gained international fame as an "alter-globalization" activist, advocating for social justice alternatives to globalization and opposing industrial agriculture and **genetically modified organisms (GMOs).** Born in Talence, France, he won over 1 percent of the vote in the first round of the 2007 French presidential elections, running on a leftist platform promoting international integration that placed human rights, social justice, environmental protection, and democracy above economic interests.

Bové's participation in environmental and social movements ranges from official political action to more radical civil disobedience and activism. He helped found the agricultural union Confédération Paysanne (Peasant Confederation) in 1987 to promote organic farming and oppose industrial agriculture. In the late 1980s and early 1990s, Bové led protests against agricultural land-use regulations and held hunger strikes to demand more government support for farmers. He served time in prison in 1976 for destroying military documents as part of a protest against a plan to displace sheep farms with an expanded military camp (the plan was eventually canceled). He again served prison time in 2002 for damaging a McDonald's franchise to protest the chain's use of hormone-treated beef, as well as in 2003 and 2005 for destroying genetically modified crops.

Bové has participated in **Greenpeace** protests, including on the *Rainbow Warrior* to oppose nuclear weapons testing, and attended the antiglobalization protests at the World Trade Organization meeting in Seattle in 1999. He has also been active in La Via Campesina (International Peasant Movement), which started in 1993 to promote small and medium-sized agriculture; a fair economy; gender parity; social justice; and sustainable food, land, and resource use. Since 2009 Bové has served as a member of the European Parliament, elected as part of a coalition of French political parties called Europe Écologie.

BRAZIL. Since the 1960s the Brazilian government—with many setbacks along the way—has been expanding its capacity to manage the environment. In 1962 it created a Fisheries Ministry; in 1965, it put in place a new forestry code, followed in 1967 by the Instituto Brasileiro de Desenvolvimento Florestal (IBDF, or Brazilian Institute of Forestry Development). Efforts continued as well into the 1970s and 1980s. For example, in 1973 the government set up a special secretariat for the environment under the jurisdiction of the minister of the interior (Secretaria Especial do Meio Ambiente, or SEMA).

In 1985 the government created a Ministry of Urban Development and the Environment (Ministério do Desenvolvimento Urbano e Meio Ambiente). In 1998 the National Congress approved the Environmental Crimes Act, restructuring the previous legislation dealing with environmental crimes and damage.

Many environmental **nongovernmental organizations (NGOs)** have also been established in Brazil over the last few decades. For example, in 1980, Projeto TAMAR (Tartarugas Marinhas, or Sea Turtles) was created, an NGO for sea turtle and marine protection and conservation. In 1986 Pro-Natura was founded, an NGO more broadly addressing **sustainable development** in Brazil before becoming international after the 1992 Rio Earth Summit. (That year a **green party** [the Partido Verde] also formed.) In 1988, **Conservation International** set up a project in Brazil; a Brazilian chapter was officially launched two years later. In anticipation of the Earth Summit, a group of NGOs also created the Brazilian NGO and Social Movements Forum, an umbrella organization for a network of environmental activists.

Other NGOs also continued to form. For example, in 1994 the Institute for Social and Environmental Studies in Southern Bahia formed to promote conservation of the Atlantic Coastal Forest. In the same year, the Instituto Socioambiental (ISA) was created to promote social and environmental rights. The following year the Instituto de Pesquisa Ambiental da Amazônia (IPAM, or Amazon Institute for Environmental Research), an organization to protect the **Amazon**, was set up. In 2000 the Rede Nacional de Organizações da Sociedade Civil para as Energias Renováveis (RENOVE, or Brazilian Network of Civil Organizations for Renewable Energy) was also established as a network of NGOs striving to promote **renewable energy** in Brazil's sustainable development plans.

In the 1970s the government began to invest in **biofuels**, in 1975 establishing Proálcool, a national ethanol program. Today, Brazil is a global leader in biofuels. For example, in 2007 Brazil—in partnership with **China**, the European Commission, **India**, **South Africa**, and the **United States**—launched the International Biofuels Forum (IBF) to support biofuels markets.

Over the last 30 years, **deforestation** in the Brazilian Amazon—one of the world's richest sources of **biodiversity**—has attracted intense global criticism. The 1988 murder of **Chico Mendes**, a well-known activist and rubber tapper, also brought worldwide condemnation. For decades this criticism did little to slow deforestation rates, with Brazil for many years losing more forest than any other country—frequently around three million hectares (seven million acres) a year, well ahead of **Indonesia** at about two million hectares (five million acres). A major cause of deforestation in the Amazon region is cattle ranching to supply the beef export industry (ranchers often burn down logged forests as a cheap way to clear land for pastures).

The government did establish the Programa Áreas Protegidas da Amazônia (ARPA, or Amazon Protected Areas Programme) in 2002, which by 2006 had set aside 18 million hectares of protected areas. Its goal is to protect 50 million hectares in the Amazon—thus expanding and maintaining the Sistema Nacional de Unidades de Conservação (SNUC, or National System of Conservation Units). It is run by Brazil's national environmental protection agency, the Instituto Brasileiro do Meio Ambiente e dos Recursos Naturais Renováveis (IBAMA, or the Brazilian Institute of Environment and Renewable Natural Resources), supported by the **Global Environment Facility**, the World Bank, the **World Wide Fund for Nature/World Wildlife Fund (WWF)**, Fundo Brasileiro para a Biodiversidade (FUNBIO, or the Brazilian Biodiversity Fund, a nonprofit and nongovernmental association founded in 1995), the German government's Cooperation Bank, the German Cooperation Agency, and civil society organizations.

In May 2008, Marina Osmarina Silva Souza resigned as minister of the environment, a post she had held since 2003. Silva, an environmental activist who worked with Chico Mendes in the Association of Rubber Tree Tappers in the 1980s, was reportedly frustrated by internal squabbling within and between government departments over how to best pursue sustainable development. This squabbling may have partly been a result of the decision in 2007 by President Lula da Silva to divide IBAMA into two agencies, leading to a strike by IBAMA, which saw this move as a way to circumvent rigorous **environmental impact assessments** of hydroelectric projects. Silva was replaced by Carlos Minc, who helped to found the Green Party of Brazil.

Since then Silva has run two times for president of Brazil, in 2010 as head of the Green Party and in 2014 as head of the Socialist Party. She is widely regarded for her efforts to curb deforestation during her time as minister of the environment, although since 2014 she has alienated some of her fellow environmentalists by backing hydroelectric dams in the Amazon and offshore oil drilling. After she resigned as minister of the environment, however, the Brazilian government continued to crack down on illegal logging, ranching, and land clearing in the Brazilian Amazon. According to Brazilian government data, the rate of deforestation in the decade after 2005 has been far lower (75 percent lower in some years) than it was in the decade before 2005.

BREAKTHROUGH INSTITUTE. Ted Nordhaus and Michael Shellenberger founded the Breakthrough Institute in 2003 to promote a new environmentalism of hope and pragmatism. The institute advances the philosophy of **"eco-modernism,"** which sees technology as the means for delinking economic growth from ecological destruction. The Breakthrough Institute shot to prominence after Nordhaus and Shellenberger published the controversial text, *The Death of Environmentalism* in 2004. *See also* ECO-BUSINESS; ECO-EFFICIENCY.

BRENT SPAR. The plan by the **oil** company Shell UK to decommission and sink the *Brent Spar*, a facility for storing and loading oil in the North Sea off the coast of Scotland, created a storm of controversy in 1995 as **Greenpeace** took its case against the sinking to the global media. Activists and journalists occupied the *Spar*, video recorders in hand, protesting the lack of disclosure and the risk of toxic contamination. Greenpeace worried, too, that sinking the *Brent Spar* would set a precedent for other deep-sea dumping of oil facilities. Drivers boycotted Shell service stations throughout Europe; a few activists even vandalized Shell property. Throughout, Shell UK continued to maintain that its research showed that deep-sea disposal was a sound environmental option. Greenpeace countered with evidence that the *Brent Spar* contained far more oil and toxic waste than Shell was revealing. After investigating, independent researchers concluded that at least some of Greenpeace's data were inaccurate, overestimating the environmental risk.

Nevertheless, confronting a global outcry and a critical popular press, Shell decided to rescind its decision and agreed to reevaluate its options. Greenpeace, meanwhile, retracted its estimate of the amount of oil left on the *Brent Spar*, stating that its initial calculations involved an inadvertent error. Shell then initiated a two-year process of stakeholder consultation, eventually deciding in 1998 to reuse the *Spar* as a ferry quay in Norway. This outcome was part of a more general shift in the direction of global environmentalism during this period, as many other corporations and nongovernmental groups also began to shift strategies away from confrontation and toward more practical dialogue with stakeholders.

BROWER, DAVID (1912–2000). David Brower was executive director of the **Sierra Club** from 1952 until 1969, when he left to found **Friends of the Earth**. He founded or helped to launch numerous other environmental bodies and conferences as well, including the Earth Island Institute, the League of Conservation Voters, and the Brower Fund.

Brower and others proposed the creation of the United Nations World Heritage Site to protect **biodiversity**, ecosystems, and the geological importance of key places. In 2000 he resigned from the board of the Sierra Club because he felt the organization was not treating overpopulation and immigration as serious environmental problems.

BRUNDTLAND, GRO HARLEM (1939–). Brundtland was one of the world's most influential leaders behind the strengthening of global environmental institutions in the 1980s and 1990s. Born in Norway, she began her career as a medical doctor before entering politics as a member of the Norwegian Labour Party. Brundtland became minister of the environment in 1974; then, seven years later, at the age of 41, she was elected as the youngest, and first female, prime minister of Norway. Over the next decade and a half, Brundtland won three elections, serving as prime minister for a total of about 10 years. Her most significant impact on the evolution of global environmentalism came when she served as chair of the 1983–1987 **World Commission on Environment and Development**, the group responsible for consolidating a definition of the concept of **sustainable development** as well as developing a consensus for holding the 1992 **United Nations Conference on Environment and Development**. The commission's report, formally called *Our Common Future*, is frequently referred to as the Brundtland Report. From 1998 to 2003 Brundtland also served as director general of the World Health Organization, moving the organization in many innovative directions, including more focus on the links between environmental change and health. As of 2016, she was serving as deputy chair of The Elders, a group of "independent" former world leaders initiated by Nelson Mandela in 2007 to provide advice and guidance on international affairs, aiming to promote "peace and human rights."

BUBONIC PLAGUE. The bubonic plague is one of three plague forms, along with septicemic and pneumonic. It is thought to be responsible for three pandemics: the plague of Justinian (approximately 541 AD to 760 AD) in the Mediterranean basin and perhaps as far as England and Northern Europe; the Black Death (approximately 1347–1352) in medieval Europe, which killed a third to half of the European population; and the plague of Asia (approximately 1898–1948), killing millions in **China**, Southeast Asia, Hong Kong, and **India**. Some in the environmental movement worry that a new disease will soon strike humans once again, sweeping across a globalized world of industrial farms with even greater intensity and speed than the bubonic plagues of the past (one example is the bird flu).

BUTTERFLY HILL, JULIA (1974–). In the late 1990s, Julia Butterfly Hill gained worldwide publicity after living for 738 days in a giant California redwood tree (which she called Luna) to stop loggers from cutting it down. Initially, she did this on her own, although groups such as **Earth First!** later supported her. In 1999 the company Pacific Lumber agreed to preserve Luna;

in exchange, Hill agreed to vacate the tree. Today, her courage, spirit, and commitment to save California's redwood forest continue to inspire other environmental activists and tree-sitting campaigns.

C

CANADA. In 1971 the Canadian government established a department called Environment Canada to manage and regulate environmental matters, although the departments of Natural Resources Canada and Fisheries and Oceans Canada play key roles, too. Canada has also passed new and stronger environmental regulations over the last five decades, including the Canada Water Act in 1970, the Canada Forestry Act in 1989, and the Canadian Environmental Protection Act—a central piece of environmental legislation—in 1999. In 1994, the government created the Canadian Environmental Assessment Agency to promote **sustainability** and public participation in development projects.

Other important environmental initiatives include establishing its Committee on the Status of Endangered Wildlife in Canada (COSEWIC) in 1977, which acts as an advisory board to the Species at Risk Act (SARA), enacted in 2003. **National parks** were first managed through the Dominion Parks Branch, created in 1911. This later became the National Parks Branch, the Canadian Parks Service, Parks Canada, and then the Parks Canada Agency. The Canada National Parks Act, passed in 1930, was amended in 2000. Environment Canada created the Environmental Choice Program in 1988 as an **eco-labeling** program using the EcoLogo certification. The program also helped to found the Global Ecolabelling Network in 1994.

Canada has put in place many regulations around fisheries, although its record includes some spectacular failures, such as the collapse of the Atlantic cod industry in the early 1990s. This breakdown led to a two-year moratorium on cod **fishing**, followed by an extension of the moratorium and additional fisheries restrictions in 1994, limited reopenings in 1999, subsequent reclosures in 2003, and limited fishing since then. By 2012, signs were appearing of a possible resurgence of the Atlantic cod off the coast of the Canadian province of Newfoundland, with tests looking especially promising in 2015.

Canada and Canadians have been active in advancing environmentalism in the international sphere. **Maurice Strong** has been one of the most influential individuals. He was secretary general of the 1972 **United Nations Con-**

ference on the Human Environment, the first executive director of the United Nations Environment Programme, and the secretary general of the 1992 Earth Summit. Canada hosted meetings to negotiate the reduction of ozone-depleting substances and signed the Montreal Protocol in 1987. Canada ratified the Kyoto Protocol in 2002 and hosted the 2005 United Nations Framework Convention on Climate Change Conference (UNFCCC COP11/Kyoto Protocol MOP1) in Montreal. Sheila Watt-Cloutier, an Inuit environmental activist and spokesperson, is another Canadian with considerable influence over the course of global environmentalism. She became the international chair of the Inuit Circumpolar Conference in 2002 and has been especially active on the Stockholm Convention on Persistent Organic Pollutants and on climate change. Under the leadership of the Conservative prime minister Stephen Harper (2006–2015), however, Canada's reputation as an international environmental leader went down considerably, with other states and nongovernmental organizations (NGOs) widely critical of such decisions as the one in 2006 to back out of Kyoto commitments and replace them with a "made in Canada" plan. Taking office in November 2015, the Liberal government of Prime Minister Justin Trudeau vowed to reclaim Canada's position as an international environmental leader, including on climate change, renaming Environment Canada "Environment and Climate Change Canada."

Canada has a vibrant history of environmental activism. Vancouver was the birthplace of Greenpeace in the early 1970s, leading to the founding of Greenpeace International in 1979. The Canadian Environmental Law Association (CELA) was founded in 1970 to advocate for environmental law reforms and enforcement; in 1984 the Canadian Environmental Defence Fund, later known as Environmental Defence, was created to provide support (legal, scientific, and organizational) to citizens and grassroots groups. In 1963, environmentalists in British Columbia aligned themselves with the Sierra Club of the United States; eventually, in 1989, a Canadian national office was established in Ottawa (which was legally incorporated in 1992).

The Canadian Environmental Network was established in 1977 to support NGO participation in consultations with government. In 1990, the David Suzuki Foundation was created. The Green Party of Canada was established in 1983, running 60 candidates in the federal election in 1984. It won 6.7 percent of the popular vote in the 2008 election, leaving it as the largest party in Canada without a seat in the federal Parliament. Elizabeth May, a former executive director of the Sierra Club of Canada, became the Green Party leader in 2006, winning the Green Party's first seat in Canada's House of Commons in 2011 and again in 2015.

CANADIAN STANDARDS ASSOCIATION, CSA Z809. An example of the global trend toward environmental certification, CSA Z809 (together with CSA Z808) provides a framework for voluntary forestry management design, implementation, and registration in **Canada**. Published by the Canadian Standards Association (a not-for-profit private-sector organization), approved by the Standards Council of Canada, and developed by consensus among various stakeholders (although unanimity was not required), these criteria were originally published in 1996 and then updated in 2003. Participants included industry, individual owners, governments, academics, scientists, technical experts, aboriginal peoples, trade unions, consumer groups, conservationists, and environmental and social organizations. Certification requires an initial (and later periodic) third-party independent audit performed by an auditor certified by the Standards Council of Canada. Among sustainable forestry certification schemes, CSA Z809 has one of the highest requirements for public participation. *See also* ECO-CERTIFICATION; PROGRAMME FOR THE ENDORSEMENT OF FOREST CERTIFICATION (PEFC); SUSTAINABLE FOREST MANAGEMENT.

CAP-AND-TRADE. *See* EMISSIONS TRADING.

CARBON TAX. A carbon tax is a tax on carbon dioxide emissions. It can take many forms; a common one is a direct levy on carbon-based fuels; another, less common, is a tax based on the total carbon dioxide emissions of a corporation. Supporters see "green taxes" as a straightforward and effective way to change consumer and corporate behavior by internalizing the costs of **pollution** into production and prices. Advocates also see these as a way to finance government and societal efforts to comply with national regulations and international agreements (such as the emission targets under the **Kyoto Protocol**). Critics worry that carbon taxes cause inflation, with unequal effects and unclear consequences. Some argue that carbon taxes are little more than government revenue grabs on the back of environmentalism. *See also* EMISSIONS TRADING.

CARRYING CAPACITY. The idea of carrying capacity is at the core of many debates in environmentalism, although definitions differ across disciplines. In ecology, a common focus is on the number of individuals of a given species that an ecosystem can support over the long term without damaging the ecosystem. This assumes that resources (water, land, food) limit population growth. That is, when a species exceeds the available resources, the population will die back to a natural sustainable level. Defining carrying capacity in this way makes its application to humans a bit tricky, as factors such as technology, morality, or consumption patterns can alter its utility. Malthusians and ecological economists do tend to use the concept in this way, especially to analyze the limits of the earth's capacity to support life. Among Malthusians and neo-Malthusians, a common example of humans exceeding carrying capacity is **Easter Island**. However, for humans, many environmentalists also use the idea of carrying capacity to focus more on how much consumption and waste is safe and possible within ecosystems (which may include built systems, such as for water and sewage). *See also* ECOLOGICAL ECONOMICS; MALTHUS, THOMAS ROBERT (1766–1834).

CARSON, RACHEL (1907–1964). Born in Pennsylvania, Carson graduated in 1932 with a master's in zoology from Johns Hopkins University in Maryland. She joined the U.S. Bureau of Fisheries (now the Fish and Wildlife Service) as a scriptwriter for science radio shows, eventually rising to become chief editor of publications in 1949. In 1951, Carson published *The Sea around Us*, winner of the U.S. National Book Award for nonfiction. In 1952 she left the Fish and Wildlife Service to write full time. Many consider the public outcry following her 1962 book, *Silent Spring*, the beginning of modern environmentalism. In that text, Carson elegantly asks, "Can anyone believe it is possible to lay down such a barrage of poisons on the surface of the earth without making it unfit for all life?" The book's critique of the deadly effects of **dichlorodiphenyltrichloroethane (DDT)** influenced **United States** president John F. Kennedy to ask his Scientific Advisory Committee to investigate, leading to a 1963 report highly critical of the impact of pesticides on human health and the environment. Carson was diagnosed with breast cancer in 1960 but continued to work on *Silent Spring* even after the cancer spread to her lymph nodes and bones. She succumbed to cancer less than two years after the publication of *Silent Spring*.

CARTAGENA PROTOCOL ON BIOSAFETY. *See* CONVENTION ON BIOLOGICAL DIVERSITY.

CENTER FOR INTERNATIONAL ENVIRONMENTAL LAW (CIEL). The Center for International Environmental Law is a nonprofit organization set up in 1989. It aims to use international law and institutions to protect ecosystems, safeguard human health, and promote justice and **sustainability**. It works as well to incorporate the principles of ecology and justice into international law. Its offices are located in Washington, D.C., and in Geneva, Switzerland, although the center covers issues in dozens of countries. CIEL is an example of the increasing importance of **nongovernmental organizations** that focus on strengthening the legal powers and influence of global environmentalism.

CFCs. *See* CHLOROFLUOROCARBONS (CFCs).

CHERNOBYL NUCLEAR MELTDOWN. On 26 April 1986, a reactor core exploded at the Chernobyl nuclear power plant in the Ukraine (then part of the Soviet Union), with fires and further explosions continuing into early May. By then, this had become the world's worst nuclear power accident, releasing at least six times more radioactivity than the 1979 accident at **Three Mile Island** (in the **United States**). A radioactive cloud floated over a large part of Europe and what was then the Soviet Union. Authorities evacuated over 100,000 people around the power plant during the meltdown; over 200,000 more were relocated in subsequent years. This accident, along with many years of media stories about the long-term environmental and health consequences at the Chernobyl site and in surrounding regions, gave further impetus to a growing movement against nuclear power in the 1980s and 1990s. The movement gained further strength after the meltdown of **Japan**'s Fukushima Daiichi nuclear power facility in 2011, the worst accident since Chernobyl. Today, tens of thousands of people still suffer from illnesses linked to radiation exposure from Chernobyl, and millions of people continue to live in contaminated areas that authorities now consider safe.

CHILE. Stretching along the Pacific Coast of the lower part of South America, Chile is home to the world's driest desert, the Atacama Desert, located in northern Chile. The central and southern regions contain vast temperate forests and agricultural lands, while the southern tip in Patagonia has ice fields. Chile also claims a section of **Antarctica**. Chile's economy depends on natural resources, with 80–90 percent of its exports coming from mineral (especially copper), agricultural, forestry, and fishery products.

Responding to political pressure, President Augusto Pinochet created the National Commission for Ecology in 1984, with the mission to draft a national environmental framework. It never accomplished this task, however. In 1994, Chile enacted into law a general environmental framework, which aimed to prevent further environmental degradation by making environmental assessment reports mandatory for new investments. Alongside, the government created the Comisión Nacional del Medio Ambiente (CONAMA, or National Commission for the Environment), the environmental agency in charge of enforcing the new law. CONAMA, however, has not had enough funding or staff to enforce the new regulatory framework consistently or fully. A grassroots environmental movement also exists in Chile, but a general lack of civic participation after the end of the Pinochet dictatorship in 1990 has left it with inconsistent influence over public policy.

Major environmental issues for Chile include **deforestation**, **mining**, and **fishing**. In the case of fishing, for example, most estimates put the annual catch well over the maximum **sustainable yield**. The industry has tended to go through repeated boom-and-bust cycles, turning to new species after each bust. Chile is also developing into a leading producer of farmed fish, with salmon aquaculture in the southern part of the country now a booming business. Some ecologists are critical of the large amounts of waste and the large amounts of antibiotics involved in the industry; others, though, see this as a way to alleviate commercial pressure on natural fish populations. In 2015 Chile was the world's second-biggest producer of farmed salmon, behind only Norway. Antibiotic use in Chile's farmed salmon industry has gone up even more following a bacterial outbreak in 2013, however, and in response some retailers have been scaling back purchase orders in recent years, such as Costco in 2015.

Some cities in Chile also suffer from extreme air **pollution**. On bad days in Santiago, for example, pollution can far exceed levels that the **United States** Environmental Protection Agency or the World Health Organization deem "unhealthy." In 2015 as air pollution reached increasingly dangerous levels, Santiago declared a state of emergency, temporarily closing factories and urging residents to stay inside. This was the first time since 1999 that the government had resorted to emergency measures to try to lessen air pollution.

CHINA, PEOPLE'S REPUBLIC OF. Rapid economic growth over the last few decades is contributing to many environmental problems in China, including water **pollution**, scarcity, and flooding; natural disasters (droughts, floods, and landslides); **desertification**; **deforestation**; **hazardous waste**; **biodiversity** loss; air pollution; and **acid rain**. The government has passed many environmental laws, but often economic priorities prevail or enforcement is poor. The close ties between environmental management and economics in China is evident even in its international activities; for example, the Ministry of Finance is the focal point for the **Global Environment Facility** in China and works closely with the Ministry of Environmental Protection. In some cases, however, enforcement is much stronger than in other developing countries. For example, China, through its one-child policy, has been strictly controlling population growth since 1979, although in 2015 the government revised this policy to a two-child policy as of 2016.

The government established the Environmental Protection Leadership Group in 1973. Later, this became the State Environmental Protection Administration (SEPA), which in 2008 was replaced by the Ministry of Environmental Protection. The first major environmental legislation was the Environmental Protection Law for Trial Implementation, created in 1979; a formal law for environmental protection was established 10 years later. The government created the Law on Protection of the Ocean Environment in 1982 (with amendments in 1999), the State Environmental Protection Committee and the Water Pollution Prevention and Control Law in 1984, the Air Pollution Prevention and Control Law in 1987, and the Water and Soil Conservation Law in 1991. The China Environmental Culture Promotion Association was created by SEPA in 1992, and the Environmental Resources Committee was created in 1993.

China created its first nature reserve in 1956; by the end of 2014, over 2,700 reserves were in place, covering around 15 percent of China's total land area. In 1992, China joined the Ramsar Convention on Wetlands and today has over 250 natural wetland reserves. China also started the National Plan for Wetland Protection Actions in 2000 and approved the National Program for Wetland Protection Engineering in 2003. The **United Nations Educational, Scientific and Cultural Organization (UNESCO)** currently designates 31 reserves in China as World Biosphere Reserves, including the Hanma Biosphere Reserve in Inner Mongolia added in 2015.

In 1994, the government implemented the China Action Plan for Biodiversity Conservation. It is also party to the **Convention on Biological Diversity** and has set up wildlife breeding centers and protection projects for species such as the red ibis and the giant panda. In 2003, China also established a National Expert Commission on the Protection of Biological Species Resources. Still, many species remain under severe threat; for example, in 2006, the **International Union for Conservation of Nature (IUCN)** declared the Yangtze River dolphin critically endangered, a species now considered to be functionally extinct. China also participates in regional environmental management. In 1996, China became a dialogue partner of the Association of Southeast Asian Nations (ASEAN), and in 2007 it added "environment" to the priority areas of cooperation. China also became a dialogue partner of the Mekong River Commission in 1996 and now provides information to assist with flood control in downstream states.

China's approach to resource management, especially water, has included large-scale engineering projects. In 1994, construction began on the **Three Gorges Dam** on the Yangtze River with the plan to develop the world's largest hydroelectric power source. Early planning stages involved advising from the **United States,** but the United States withdrew in 1993 following an increasingly vocal international outcry over environmental impacts and violations of human rights. The dam opened in 2008 and was completed in 2012.

Over the past two decades, the government has been adopting a new focus on environmental issues, with a "green strategy" that includes developing a "revolving economy," clean production methods, green consumption, new energy resources, and increasing resource-use efficiency. It started the Green Lights program in 1996 to promote energy-efficient lighting and passed the

Energy Conservation Law in 1997. It is working to reduce the costs of pollution from production and promoting more ecological processes for industry. It is developing "eco-areas" to promote regional **sustainable development** and to integrate economic growth, social progress, and environmental management. The implementation of a program for prevention and control of water pollution was started in 2001. In 2003, new environmental legislation included the Cleaner Production Promotion Law and the Environmental Impact Assessment Law. That year also saw the Regulations on Conversion of Farmlands to Forest (to promote **reforestation**) enter into force; it was also the first year the government required annual reporting on pollution control in key watersheds. In 2004, SEPA concluded 12 international environmental protocols and multilateral environmental negotiations, including the ratification of the **Stockholm Convention**. The government has since launched the EPA-China Environmental Law Initiative to encourage dialogue with the United States on environmental regulations. The government has also been investing and promoting solar and wind energy as a way of advancing energy security, and by 2015 China was a world leader in the development of solar and wind power technology.

China's first formal environmental **nongovernmental organization**, Friends of Nature (initially Academy for Green Culture), was founded in 1994. Thousands of environmental NGOs have been set up since then. The lead-up to the 2008 Olympics in Beijing brought further focus on environmental issues, especially air quality in Beijing, as well as intense scrutiny from international environmental and human rights groups.

CHIPKO MOVEMENT. The Chipko Movement emerged in 1973 when a small number of female villagers in the Himalayan Mountains of **India**, following a Gandhian philosophy of nonviolent resistance, began to hug trees in an effort to save them from loggers and thus protect the culture and survival of the village. In 1980, with the movement now extending (without any formal organization or ties between groups) to other Himalayan villages (and including some men), Indian prime minister Indira Gandhi ordered a 15-year ban on logging in the Himalayan forests. Since then, this grassroots movement has spontaneously spread across India, inspiring villagers who hope to prevent the loss of traditional land and forest rights without resorting to violence.

CHLOROFLUOROCARBONS (CFCs). Searching in 1928 for a safer way to cool refrigerators, **Thomas Midgley Jr.** took just three days to discover chlorofluorocarbons (CFCs): a stable, odorless, nontoxic, and nonflammable compound, later sold by DuPont and General Motors under the trademark Freon. The new compound seemed totally safe—so safe, as Midgley demonstrated at the 1930 American Chemical Society meeting, that it was possible to breathe it in and blow out a candle. Soon, companies everywhere were using similar compounds in the class of CFCs, not only to cool refrigerators, freezers, and air conditioners, but also to make foams and insulations as well as to propel aerosols and fire extinguishers. It would take over four decades before Mario J. Molina and F. Sherwood Rowland (in a 1974 article in the journal *Nature*) put forth the startling theory that CFCs, with millions of tons now in use, might be leaking from consumer products and drifting into the stratosphere, then splitting apart and triggering a chain reaction that was destroying the ozone layer. This theory, which won Molina and Rowland the 1995 Nobel Prize in Chemistry, changed global environmental relations, leading eventually to a series of international agreements to phase out the production and consumption of CFCs (most notably, the 1987 **Montreal Protocol on Substances That Deplete the Ozone Layer**). *See also* OZONE DEPLETION.

CITIES FOR CLIMATE PROTECTION. A campaign by **ICLEI: Local Governments for Sustainability**, Cities for Climate Protection (CCP) supports cities that adopt policies and implement changes to decrease local emissions of **greenhouse gases** and improve air quality; it also assists with efforts to advance urban **sustainability**. First initiated in 1993, by 2016 over 1,200 local governments were participating in CCP, from **Australia** and **Japan** to **Mexico** and the **United States**. The ICLEI reports on the actions of local governments through forums such as **United Nations** conferences on **climate change**. Goals include, for example, working toward becoming carbon-neutral communities; concrete measures include, for example, developing more sustainable street lighting.

CLIMATE CHANGE. Of all the global environmental problems, climate change is arguably the most far reaching, as well as the most difficult to solve. It is sometimes called global warming since the stimulus for climate change is rising average temperatures on the earth's surface, but this is a less precise term because shifting ocean currents and weather patterns mean some areas may become colder. Over the 20th century the average surface temperature of the earth increased by roughly 0.6 degrees Celsius, making it the warmest century of the last millennium. The vast majority of scientists now agree this is occurring because the atmosphere is trapping more heat, a process analogous to rolling up a car window on a hot day. The main reason this is happening is the increase in **greenhouse gases**—in particular, carbon dioxide, methane, and nitrous oxide—from human activities. Just about every aspect of modern life seems to add greenhouse gases, including manufacturing, cattle, **automobiles**, and energy (such as burning **coal**, **oil**, and **natural**

gas). Other environmental problems, such as forest fires and **deforestation**, are also leaving the atmosphere with higher concentrations of carbon dioxide.

A primary scientific source for understanding climate change is the Intergovernmental Panel on Climate Change (IPCC), established in 1988 by the World Meteorological Organization (WMO) and the **United Nations Environment Programme (UNEP)**. So far, it has published five comprehensive assessment reports (1990, 1995, 2001, 2007, and 2014), contributing to a growing consensus that climate change is real, with the potential for great harm.

These reports show that the problem of rising temperatures appears to be worsening. The 2000s was the warmest decade since instrumental measuring began in 1861, while 2015 was the warmest year. The IPCC expects the 21st century to get even warmer, with average surface temperatures rising by as much as 4–6 degrees Celsius above preindustrial levels. Many models now predict that this century will see the fastest rate of change in the last 10,000 years or so. A rise of 3–5 degrees Celsius would, most scientists now agree, profoundly alter wind, rain, and snow patterns. The international community has set a target of a temperature increase of no more than two degrees Celsius (with an aspirational target of no more than 1.5 degrees Celsius), including negotiators at the 21st Conference of the Parties (COP) of the United Nations Framework Convention on Climate Change held in Paris, France, in December 2015. One possible consequence is an increase in the magnitude and frequency of severe weather—such as hurricanes, tornados, hailstorms, and droughts. Another possible consequence is a rise in sea levels, which could displace millions of people living in low-lying coastal areas in places such as **Bangladesh** or submerge low-lying countries such as the Marshall Islands and the Maldives. Such changes would impact nearly every ecological issue, including melting ice caps in the **Arctic**, deforestation, **desertification**, **biodiversity**, and the extinction of **endangered species**.

Developing countries tend to see the First World as primarily responsible for climate change, as developed countries accounted for the majority of greenhouse gas emissions during the 20th century. Political leaders in the First World, however, commonly emphasize the need for a global effort to tackle climate change, especially with greenhouse gas emissions from countries such as **China** now edging toward levels found in the rest of the world. Still, governmental positions regarding climate change do not split cleanly along North–South lines. The European Union and **Japan**, for example, have supported an international treaty to address climate change, while the **United States** and **Australia** (until 2007) have been far more skeptical of the value of such a treaty, at times even questioning the science of climate change. Meanwhile, in the developing world, the states in the Organization of Petroleum Exporting Countries (OPEC) have generally opposed efforts to reduce oil consumption, while the 44 countries and observers in the Alliance of Small Island States support such efforts in the hopes of slowing the rise in sea levels.

The **United Nations Framework Convention on Climate Change** is the main international agreement to slow greenhouse gas emissions. Over the past few decades, large numbers of environmental groups have been participating in negotiations to strengthen and extend this framework convention, with record levels of interest in the 21st COP in Paris in 2015. There are, however, many environmental groups that see international agreements as inherently weak and insufficient and instead call for sweeping changes to the global economy, as **Naomi Klein** called for in her 2014 book *This Changes Everything*. Some worry that the process of climate change will soon reach a "**tipping point**," spiraling into a catastrophic ecological collapse. Others, such as environmental skeptic **Bjørn Lomborg** in his 2007 book *Cool It*, argue that such scenarios exaggerate the probable consequences of warmer average temperatures. *See also* ADAPTATION; ANTARCTICA; ANTHROPOCENE; COALITION FOR ENVIRONMENTALLY RESPONSIBLE ECONOMIES (CERES); OCEAN ACIDIFICATION; SUSTAINABILITY.

COAL. Coal, along with **oil** and **natural gas**, is one of the world's three main fossil fuels. It is primarily used to generate electricity at large utilities or for energy-intensive industries like cement manufacturing. Worldwide, it is the largest source of fuel for electricity generation. It is the world's second-largest source of primary energy needs, behind oil. Over 100 countries mine coal. The largest known reserves are in the **United States**, **Russia**, and **China**. Other major producers include **India**, **Indonesia**, **Australia**, and **South Africa**. Australia and Indonesia are the world's largest coal exporters. China is by far the largest producer and consumer as coal-fired power stations fuel rapid economic growth.

Environmentalists have long challenged the cost-benefit calculations of relying on coal to generate electricity. It is the "dirtiest" of the fossil fuels, polluting the air with particulates, spewing sulfur (a cause of **acid rain**), and emitting carbon dioxide into the atmosphere (a cause of **climate change**). Open-pit coal **mining** also scars local landscapes. Many governments have implemented measures to mitigate the environmental effects of coal use, such as the U.S. Clean Air Act Amendments of 1990 that created a sulfur dioxide cap-and-trade program. Firms have also put in place clean coal technologies—sometimes because of legislation, sometimes voluntarily—to reduce, for example, the emissions of sulfur, nitrogen oxides, and mercury. Nevertheless, coal-fired power plants remain one of the world's major sources of **pollution**, and in 2015 the International Energy Agency was still predicting that coal consumption would continue to keep rising for many years to come by more than 2 percent per year. *See also* REBOUND EFFECT.

COALITION FOR ENVIRONMENTALLY RESPONSIBLE ECONOMIES (CERES). Founded in 1989, CERES promotes environmental and social responsibility among corporations and within capital markets from its office in Boston, Massachusetts. One of its most significant accomplishments was the founding in 1997 of the **Global Reporting Initiative (GRI)**, a joint initiative with the **United Nations Environment Programme** to develop global guidelines for reporting on the economic, social, and environmental performance of corporations, governments, and **nongovernmental organizations**. In 2002, the GRI became an independent international body; now based in Amsterdam, it is used by thousands of companies as an international standard for reporting environmental, economic, and social performance.

Another major accomplishment is the Investor Network on Climate Risk (INCR), which CERES launched in 2003 at the first Institutional Investor Summit on Climate Risk at the **United Nations**. INCR began with 10 investors managing US$600 billion in assets; today it includes more than 100 investors (such as asset managers, pension funds, and foundations) with over US$10 trillion in assets. INCR promotes improved disclosure and better practices in managing the business risks and opportunities arising from **climate change**. *See also* CORPORATE SOCIAL RESPONSIBILITY (CSR).

COCOYOC DECLARATION. *See* SUSTAINABLE DEVELOPMENT.

COFFEE. Coffee is one of the world's top-ten legal export crops by value. For many centuries, growing coffee involved intercropping, with farmers planting trees for shade, soil balance, and homes for birds (which eat insects that harm coffee plants). Today, many plantations grow coffee directly under the sun, producing as much as six times more coffee per hectare than more traditional methods but requiring intensive use of fertilizers and pesticides that can pollute waterways and degrade soils. Movements to promote **sustainability** and **fair trade** in the coffee sector became popular in the 1990s (although in Europe the first attempts to promote fair trade were appearing as far back as the 1950s) and have gained momentum since 2000. The core idea of **fair trade coffee** is for consumers to pay a premium to guarantee a minimum price for farmers even in periods of low world market prices (and thus promote social stability and sustainable production). Today, many certified fair trade farms also produce organic, or shade, coffee, and although these still comprise a small percentage of global output, sales are slowly increasing. *See also* ECO-CERTIFICATION.

CONSERVATION INTERNATIONAL (CI). Founded in 1987 and based in the **United States**, the nonprofit organization Conservation International (CI) works to conserve natural ecosystems and global **biodiversity**. To achieve this goal, CI relies on a mix of science, economics, policy, and community participation. The focus is on biodiversity hot spots, or wilderness and marine regions with high biodiversity. As of 2016, CI was employing more than 1,000 people and operating in more than 30 countries, mostly developing ones. CI also funds more than 2,000 conservation partners and claims it has helped set up more than 1,200 conservation areas around the world. *See also* BOLIVIA; MARINE PROTECTED AREAS (MPAs).

CONVENTION ON BIOLOGICAL DIVERSITY. The Convention on Biological Diversity was opened for signature at the **United Nations Conference on Environment and Development (UNCED)** in 1992 and entered into force the following year. Most of the world has joined this international treaty—with 196 parties to the agreement at the beginning of 2016. The primary objective is to conserve biological diversity (**biodiversity**) and promote sustainable use of biological resources. The task is formidable. So far scientists have been able to identify around two million species of plants, animals, insects, and microorganisms. A common scientific estimate of the total number of species is in the range of eight to nine million, but some have put the number as low as two million and some as high as 100 million. Preserving biodiversity includes protecting this diversity of species as well as the genetic differences within each species. It includes, too, protecting the variety of ecosystems occurring in, for example, forests, deserts, mountains, wetlands, lakes, rivers, oceans, and agricultural landscapes. Two binding provisions of the convention (Articles 6 and 20) include measures to conserve biodiversity through sustainable use, research and training, public education, impact assessments, technology transfers, and financing.

In 2000, the Conference of Parties to the Convention on Biological Diversity adopted a supplementary agreement called the Cartagena Protocol on Biosafety (named after Cartagena, Colombia). It aims to protect biological diversity from the possible threat posed by living organisms modified through **biotechnology**. It draws on a **precautionary approach** as defined in the Rio Declaration from the 1992 UNCED to establish an advance informed agreement (AIA) procedure to ensure that governments receive sufficient information to make informed decisions before agreeing to import modified organisms. It also created a Biosafety Clearing-House to exchange information on living modified organisms and help countries implement the Cartagena Protocol. There were 170 parties as of December 2015.

The Convention on Biological Diversity and the Cartagena Protocol on Biosafety both facilitate international dialogues on preserving the biodiversity of the earth as a whole, the value of which is now a foundational principle of global environmentalism.

CONVENTION ON INTERNATIONAL TRADE IN ENDANGERED SPECIES OF WILD FAUNA AND FLORA (CITES). The text for the Convention on International Trade in Endangered Species of Wild Fauna and Flora—more commonly called CITES—was agreed upon in 1973. This international treaty entered into force in 1975 and as of 2015 had 181 parties (signatories that have ratified the convention). CITES is designed to safeguard wild plants and animals that are, or may be, threatened with extinction as a result of international trade. It provides a framework for parties to adopt appropriate domestic legislation and enforcement procedures. In this way, to varying degrees, it protects tens of thousands of species of animals and plants, from live specimens to dried herbs.

Appendixes I and II are especially important. Appendix I of CITES lists species threatened with extinction. The rules prohibit international trade in these species for commercial purposes. Trade for noncommercial purposes requires permission from both the exporting and importing countries. Examples on this list include apes, giant pandas, cheetahs, leopards, tigers, elephants, and rhinoceroses, as well as some mussels, orchids, and cacti. Appendix II includes species that are not immediately under threat of extinction but may become so unless trade is controlled, as well as some species similar in appearance to the ones in appendix I (to make it harder for smugglers and illegal loggers to deceive authorities by claiming that appendix I species are similar-looking appendix II species). Trade in appendix II species only requires an export permit, which authorities can issue as long as the trade will not harm the survival of the species.

For the evolution of global environmentalism, CITES has set important precedents for the need—at least in circumstances where ecologies or species are nearing collapse—to restrict or even ban international trade. *See also* BIODIVERSITY; ENDANGERED SPECIES; IVORY TRADE.

CONVENTION ON LONG-RANGE TRANSBOUNDARY AIR POLLUTION (CLRTAP). The Convention on Long-Range Transboundary Air Pollution, or CLRTAP, was responding in part to a growing scientific consensus on the acidification of Scandinavian lakes from sulfur emissions in continental Europe, thus confirming the need for international cooperation to address the ability of air pollutants to damage environments thousands of kilometers away. Signed in 1979 in Geneva, Switzerland, CLRTAP entered into force in 1983. Eight protocols have subsequently been added to address monitoring and evaluation of air pollutant transmission; sulfur emissions; nitrogen oxides; volatile organic compounds; **persistent organic pollutants**; heavy metals (especially cadmium, lead, and mercury); and acidification, eutrophication, and ground-level ozone. As of the beginning of 2016, 51 countries were party to CLRTAP. A related agreement is the 2000 **Stockholm Convention on Persistent Organic Pollutants**. *See also* ACID RAIN; MINAMATA CONVENTION ON MERCURY.

CONVENTION ON THE CONSERVATION OF ANTARCTIC MARINE LIVING RESOURCES (CCAMLR). The Antarctic Treaty System is a series of agreements, including the 1980 Convention on the Conservation of Antarctic Marine Living Resources (CCAMLR), created to regulate relations among states in the Antarctic. The Antarctic Treaty, signed in 1959 and in force from 1961, is designed to promote scientific research and maintain peaceful relations among states in **Antarctica**. It thus puts territorial claims in abeyance and forbids military activity, except to support scientific research, and prohibits nuclear tests and the disposal of nuclear waste. In addition to the CCAMLR, the Antarctic Treaty System also includes the Protocol on Environmental Protection (1991) and the Convention on the Conservation of Antarctic Seals (1972).

The CCAMLR, which entered into force in 1982, was negotiated primarily to improve the management of krill catches and other marine life in the Southern Ocean. The convention adopts a **precautionary approach** to reduce risks due to high uncertainty in the understanding of conservation in Antarctica. The Secretariat of the Commission for the Convention on the Conservation of Antarctic Marine Living Resources is located in **Australia**. The commission monitors compliance with the convention. Significant challenges, however, confront this mandate, including the sheer size and harsh conditions of the Southern Ocean, which make it very difficult, for example, to monitor and control illegal **fishing**.

CONVENTION ON THE PREVENTION OF MARINE POLLUTION BY DUMPING OF WASTES AND OTHER MATTER. The Convention on the Prevention of Marine Pollution by Dumping of Wastes and Other Matter—commonly called the London Convention—was signed in 1972 in London and entered into force in 1975. It was amended in 1978, 1980, 1989, 1993, 1996 (with a protocol designed to replace the 1972 convention), and 2006 with an amendment to the protocol. The International Maritime Organization (IMO) administers the provisions of the convention and protocol. There were 87 parties to the convention in 2015.

The London Convention codifies a general prohibition against deliberate dumping of wastes and "other matter" (other than standard operational discharges) by vessels and aircraft at sea. Different substances face different restrictions, depending on factors like persistence, degradability, tendency to bioaccumulate, and toxicity. It also allows some exceptions for safety and emergencies. The 1972 London Convention bans the dumping of substances listed in Annex I (the black list): mostly toxic chemicals and some synthetics. Meanwhile, dumping substances listed in Annex II (the gray list) requires a "special permit." The 1996 protocol (known as the "London Protocol"), which entered into force in 2006, is more restrictive than the 1972 convention. It restructured the 1972 convention to create a "reverse list," so parties are not allowed to dump any waste or other matter not listed in Annex I (rather than ones listed). It also links more effectively to other international environmental agreements, such as the **Basel Convention on the Control of Transboundary Movements of Hazardous Wastes and Their Disposal**. Significantly, it invokes the **precautionary approach**, requiring shipowners to take appropriate measures if harm from dumping wastes is deemed likely, even if there is no conclusive scientific proof of a direct causal link between the discharge of wastes and harm to the marine environment. It further invokes the **polluter pays principle**, meaning in principle that the polluter should pay for the cost of **pollution** (as well as avoid merely transferring this cost to another location). Currently, both the convention and the protocol will be in force in parallel for some time, with the protocol gradually becoming the primary international legal instrument as more and more parties ratify it (45 parties as of 2015). *See also* HAZARDOUS WASTE.

CONVENTION ON WETLANDS OF INTERNATIONAL IMPORTANCE ESPECIALLY AS WATERFOWL HABITAT. The Convention on Wetlands was signed in Ramsar, **Iran**, in 1971 and entered into force in 1975. This international treaty, known as the Ramsar Convention on Wetlands, had 169 state parties as of 2015. It defines wetlands broadly, including natural marshes, lakes, rivers, mangroves, and **coral reefs** as well as fishponds, rice paddies, reservoirs, and salt pans. The primary purpose is to conserve and protect wetlands, including flora and fauna (especially waterfowl) relying on wetlands. It does so by encouraging governments to follow a principle of "wise use," establish nature reserves, fund research, train personnel, and cooperate across jurisdictions. Wise use of wetlands is defined as "their sustainable utilization for the benefit of humankind in a way compatible with the maintenance of the natural properties of the ecosystem." The convention also created the List of Wetlands of International Importance (each party must contribute at least one listing). Today, there are over 2,200 entries on the list, covering around 210 million hectares. Each year, on 2

February, the date of the adoption of the convention, the Ramsar Secretariat also helps to celebrate World Wetlands Day. *See also* BIODIVERSITY; CHINA, PEOPLE'S REPUBLIC OF.

CORAL REEFS. A mix of living coral and skeletal material, coral reefs are found in shallow, mostly clear tropical waters. About 100 countries have them; one of the best known is **Australia**'s Great Barrier Reef. Significant sources of animal and plant **biodiversity**, these fragile ecosystems support over one-quarter of all known marine life and are often called the rain forests of the sea; as a result, various governments and environmental groups (e.g., **Conservation International**) are working to save them. Still, many (e.g., those on **Indonesia**'s coastline) remain under grave threat from recreational divers (who can disturb and damage them), destructive **fishing** techniques (such as using explosives or cyanide), **pollution** (such as **oil** and pesticides), and **climate change** (which, for example, is warming waters and can cause coral to expel algae and turn white—called bleaching). Some scientists are now projecting that if trends continue, most of the world's remaining coral reefs will die or fundamentally change over the next few decades. *See also* CONVENTION ON WETLANDS OF INTERNATIONAL IMPORTANCE ESPECIALLY AS WATERFOWL HABITAT; MARINE PROTECTED AREAS (MPAs); OCEAN ACIDIFICATION.

CORPORATE SOCIAL RESPONSIBILITY (CSR). Corporate social responsibility, or CSR, is a business approach which assumes not only that companies have a duty to protect social and environmental values but that it generally makes good business sense to do so. It is not the same as charity work; rather, it presumes that everyday business activities should reflect these values. Many firms explain this in terms of meeting a "triple bottom line," with economic, social, and environmental accounting. Such accounting requires firms to be conscientious producers, at times voluntarily going "beyond compliance" with existing laws (especially in developing countries with low standards).

The phrase *corporate social responsibility* began to spread in the 1970s and 1980s in response to calls for stronger national and international regulations (such as a **United Nations** code of conduct) on multinational corporations. Corporations began to stress the need for voluntary regulatory measures, or **industry self-regulation**. In the 1990s CSR solidified as standard policy for multinational corporations with the strengthening of global environmentalism and pressure from a growing antiglobalization campaign. Over the past decade it has gained even more momentum as most of the world's largest multinational manufacturers and retailers—Nike, Nestlé, Procter & Gamble, Walmart, Coca-Cola, and McDonald's, among many others—have turned increasingly to CSR initiatives as a way of increasing efficiencies, reducing waste, enhancing quality controls, and controlling diffuse supply chains. Today just about every large multinational corporation declares a CSR policy for shareholders and the public. Advocates of CSR see this as a practical and effective way to shift the globalization of capitalism toward more **sustainable development**. Critics attack CSR as disingenuous public relations to conceal business as usual—as little more than what some call **greenwash**. *See also* ACCOUNTABILITY (AA); COALITION FOR ENVIRONMENTALLY RESPONSIBLE ECONOMIES (CERES); ECO-BUSINESS; ECO-CERTIFICATION; ECO-EFFICIENCY; EQUATOR PRINCIPLES; GLOBAL COMPACT; MARKET LIBERALISM; WORLD BUSINESS COUNCIL FOR SUSTAINABLE DEVELOPMENT (WBCSD).

COSTANZA, ROBERT (1950–). Robert Costanza is cofounder and past president of the **International Society for Ecological Economics (ISEE)** and was chief editor of the society's journal *Ecological Economics* from its first issue in 1989 until 2002. In 1997 Costanza put the value of the world's ecosystem services at about US$33 trillion a year, an often-cited estimate for many years afterward. Until 2002, he was the director of the University of Maryland Institute for Ecological Economics, then director of the Gund Institute for Ecological Economics at the University of Vermont (2002–2010), then a professor at Portland State University from 2010 to 2012. One of the world's most cited ecological economists, he is currently a professor at the Australian National University's Crawford School of Public Policy in Canberra, **Australia**. *See also* DALY, HERMAN (1938–); GEORGESCU-ROEGEN, NICHOLAS (1906–1994).

COSTA RICA. With the world's highest species density and 5 percent of the world's **biodiversity**, Costa Rica has set aside around a quarter of its lands and forests for environmental protection. Since the mid-1990s the government has been compensating landowners for **reforestation** and forest conservation (as part of its payments for environmental services initiatives). The Sistema Nacional de Áreas de Conservación de Costa Rica (SINAC, or National Conservation Areas System) includes many biological reserves, forest reserves, **national parks**, protected zones, and wildlife refuges. The government also coordinates tree planting.

Over the last few decades, energy, resource, and environmental issues have fallen under the purview of several government agencies, with the Ministry of Energy and Mines created in 1980; the Ministry of Industry, Energy, and Mines in 1982; the Ministry of Natural Resources, Energy, and Mines in 1988; and most recently the Ministry of the Environment and Energy (MINAE). Along with MINAE, the government established an overarching environmental law, national and regional environmental councils, and a national technical secretary for the environment.

Ecotourism comprises a significant part of Costa Rica's economy. Renewable sources generate over 90 percent of Costa Rica's energy, and in 2007 the government announced plans to become the first carbon-neutral country (by 2021). It has also incorporated environmental concerns into its trade relations, including the 2001 Canada–Costa Rica Agreement on Environmental Cooperation (a side agreement to the Canada–Costa Rica Free Trade Agreement).

Costa Rica has many civil society and environmental advocacy organizations. These include the Centro Científico Tropical (Tropical Science Center), created in 1962 to focus on biodiversity research and protection, and the Instituto Nacional de Biodiversidad (INBio, or National Biodiversity Institute), established in 1989 to research and manage biodiversity. International environmental NGOs, such as the **World Wide Fund for Nature/World Wildlife Fund (WWF)** and **Conservation International**, have also long worked in Costa Rica. *See also* RENEWABLE ENERGY.

CRITICAL MASS. Emerging in San Francisco in the early 1990s, Critical Mass is a decentralized, leaderless, and memberless global cycling movement. It has little organizational structure other than arranging for a time (often the last Friday of every month) and place for bicyclists to gather for a ride through a city, often, although not always, following a spontaneous route (these occur around the world with little coordination and with different degrees of planning). Noncompetitive and festive events, these rides aim to raise awareness by bringing together enough cyclists to create a "critical mass" able to disrupt traffic and draw attention to the dangers of riding bicycles in cities designed for **automobiles** (and the corresponding need for more environmentally friendly transportation). In some cases, these rides occur on other celebratory environmental days, such as **Earth Day** (22 April). On occasion, Critical Mass events involve altercations between cyclists blocking traffic and annoyed drivers; the resulting publicity, as some cycling organizations lament, does little to advance the interests of those wanting to cycle safely in cities.

CUBA. The decline of the former Soviet Union in the late 1980s contributed to a fall in **oil** supplies in Cuba, along with decreased aid (including agricultural products, fertilizers, pesticides, and animal feed) from its former communist supporter. This caused economic and production troubles in Cuba, but it also spurred along some positive environmental changes. The government, for example, promoted urban agriculture after the decline of food markets in the early 1990s, and local governments allowed the use of state-owned vacant land in Havana for community gardens. Basic Units for Cooperative Production, created in 1993 to restructure state-run farms, were used for organizing some of the urban agricultural activities. In 1996, Havana passed bylaws that only **organic food** could be produced in the city.

Domestic oil exploration, initiated after the fall of the Soviet Union, is ongoing. In 2006, test drilling took place in the North Cuba Basin. Cuba also has large reserves of nickel and is a producer of cobalt, a nickel **mining** byproduct.

The 1990s also came with an increase in nongovernmental activity, including the establishment of the organizations ProNaturaleza (Sociedad Cubana para la Protección del Medio Ambiente, or Cuban Society for the Protection of the Environment) and the Fundación de la Naturaleza y el Hombre (Foundation of Nature and Humanity). The Cuban government incorporated the Rio Earth Summit resolutions into its constitution in 1992 and created a National Environmental Strategy in 1997. The transition in leadership from Fidel to Raúl Castro beginning in 2008, however, put Cuba's environmental future on a new trajectory. Improving diplomatic relations with the United States since 2015 will bring many challenges, such as an increase in high-end tourism, but this could also bring many opportunities, such as infrastructure investment and conservation funding.

D

DALY, HERMAN (1938–). Herman Daly, an emeritus professor at the University of Maryland, is one of the best-known ecological economists. A former senior economist at the World Bank, his critiques of the environmental effects of trade have been especially influential. One of his most influential books was *Steady-State Economics* (1977). *See also* COSTANZA, ROBERT (1950–); ECOLOGICAL ECONOMICS.

DAMS. *See* GOLDMAN ENVIRONMENTAL PRIZE; HYDROELECTRICITY; NARMADA DAM; THREE GORGES DAM.

DDT. *See* DICHLORODIPHENYLTRICHLOROETHANE (DDT).

DEEP ECOLOGY. The term *deep ecology* was coined by Arne Naess (1912–2009) in a 1973 article titled "The Shallow and the Deep, Long-Range Ecology Movement: A Summary" in a journal Naess founded called *Inquiry*. Naess, arguably the most influential Norwegian philosopher of the 20th century, was a professor at the University of Oslo. After publishing this article he became a leading intellectual figure in what some now call the deep ecology movement. One of the aims of deep ecology is to critique materialism, consumerism, and capitalism. It strives as well to integrate religious and philosophical traditions into ecological reasoning and ethics. Followers move beyond a simple focus on solving particular environmental problems by going "deeper," taking a holistic and relational approach, seeing, for example, humans as one part of nature. Such an approach requires a questioning of the purpose of life and fundamental values.

In contrast, shallow ecology sees humans as separate from nature, producing superficial analysis by assuming that nature is comprised of separate, discrete "things." This shallow approach also accepts a world order with unjust and unsustainable outcomes—one that prioritizes economic growth and draws down natural resources to feed excessive consumption. Unlike deep ecology, a shallow ecology approach proposes solutions like **recycling** and more efficient production rather than fundamental changes to basic principles and practices.

For followers of the deep ecology movement, the destruction of nature becomes equal to the destruction of humanity. Here, humans should not exploit nature except to satisfy essential needs, striving instead for a sustainable existence. Supporters assume, too, that all life has the same inherent value. A radical wing of deep ecology calls for a revolution—over the years a few have even advocated violence—to reestablish the harmony between people and nature lost in modern times. For Naess, however, deep ecology is a moral philosophy of reimagining the place of humans in the global environment, one best achieved through eco-centric values, Gandhian nonviolence, cultural diversity, and simple living. Critics see the ideas of philosophers like Naess as naive or reckless and the "solutions" of more radical followers of a deep ecology philosophy as dangerous or even misanthropic. *See also* ANIMAL LIBERATION FRONT (ALF); EARTH LIBERATION FRONT (ELF); ECOTERRORISM.

DEEPWATER HORIZON **OIL SPILL.** *See* UNITED STATES.

DEFORESTATION. Defined in basic terms as the permanent loss of forest cover, deforestation is one of the greatest stresses on the global environment. By some estimates, more than half of the earth's original forests are now gone, most of them disappearing during the 20th century. Every year the area of forests continues to decrease by millions of hectares, with the biggest losses in Asia, Africa, and South America. The loss of forests as a sink for carbon (trees store and absorb carbon dioxide) contributes to **climate change**. Logging, decaying wood, and forest fires also release carbon, adding further to **greenhouse gases**.

Worldwide, deforestation now accounts for around 15 percent of annual anthropogenic emissions of carbon dioxide. Deforestation is also a significant cause of soil erosion, flooding, and **biodiversity** loss, especially in the tropics. In developed countries with temperate forests, **reforestation** and stricter environmental management over the last half century have slowed some of the environmental damage; here, the total forest area is now growing, although generally not with complex forests, but with tree plantations. The overall rate of tropical deforestation remains high, with rates in countries like **Indonesia** and **Brazil** particularly so, although in recent years rates have been rising in West Africa and the Mekong region of Southeast Asia. In these places the process of deforestation often begins with destructive logging. Loggers open the canopy, leaving forests drier; littered with debris; and more accessible to developers, plantation owners, ranchers, and swidden (sometimes called slash-and-burn) farmers. Burning is the cheapest way to clear these degraded forests; out-of-control fires, such as the **Indonesian forest fires of 1997–1998**, are a common result, with fires once again raging across Indonesia's outer islands in 2015.

For centuries the debate over how, and to what extent, to preserve forests has been at the heart of environmentalism. Still, unlike most environmental issues, no international agreement exists for forestry. Efforts to develop one failed at the 1992 **United Nations Conference on Environment and Development**. Since then a series of international meetings have been held to discuss the possibility of negotiating such an agreement, but so far no formal negotiations have begun. Countless numbers of environmental **nongovernmental organizations**—like **Greenpeace**, the **World Wide Fund for Nature/World Wildlife Fund (WWF)**, and the **Rainforest Action Network**—are currently campaigning to save forests. Many do not support the idea of negotiating an international treaty, worrying that producers would dominate the process and seeing too much diversity of causes and solutions to deforestation for a treaty to work effectively. Some of these groups instead call for local bans on logging, timber exports, and clearing land for ranches and plantations. Others, such as the **Forest Stewardship Council**, are working with timber companies and governments to establish programs to certify that internationally traded products from forests are managed in a sustainable way. *See also* BISHNOIS OF RAJASTHAN; CHIPKO MOVEMENT; EASTER ISLAND; ECO-FORESTRY; ENVIRONMENTAL KUZNETS CURVE (EKC); GREEN BELT MOVEMENT; ILLEGAL LOGGING; MARSH, GEORGE PERKINS (1801–1882); THE PHILIPPINES; THAILAND.

DESERTIFICATION. Desertification, defined as a process, involves incremental decreases in the productive capacity of arid, semiarid, and dry subhumid ecosystems. Defined as a result, desertification is the creation of desertlike conditions following degradation of nondesert land. Causes vary, but two of the most significant and common are climatic changes and human activity. Overexploitation and inappropriate land use in dry ecosystems are two primary ways humans cause desertification. More specifically, grazing livestock, logging, collecting firewood, and tilling and irrigating land for agriculture can damage or destroy the flora that keeps soil in place.

French scientist and explorer Louis Lavauden coined the term *desertification* in 1927; André Aubreville popularized it in 1949. The drought in western Africa from 1968 to 1973, which killed 200,000 people and millions of animals, launched desertification onto the international agenda. In 1974, the **United Nations** General Assembly called for an international conference on desertification. The first UN Conference on Desertification was held in Nairobi, **Kenya**, in 1977. The 1992 **United Nations Conference on Environ-**

ment and Development put forth a new integrated approach to combat desertification, which led to the 1994 **United Nations Convention to Combat Desertification** (which came into force in 1996). As of 2016, there were 196 parties to this convention. The year 2006 was the International Year of Deserts and Desertification, and the UN designates 17 June as the World Day to Combat Desertification. *See also* NIGERIA; SUB-SAHARAN AFRICA.

DICHLORODIPHENYLTRICHLOROETHANE (DDT). Dichlorodiphenyltrichloroethane, more commonly known as DDT, is a synthetic pesticide effective against mosquitoes that spread malaria and lice that transfer typhus. The chemist Paul Hermann Müller (1899–1965) of Switzerland was awarded the 1948 Nobel Prize in Physiology or Medicine for saving millions of lives by discovering in 1939 the "high efficiency" of DDT as an insecticide. Since then scientists have learned that DDT can build up in animals (including humans), becoming toxic and causing cancer. **Rachel Carson**'s best-selling 1962 book, *Silent Spring*, was one of the first to alert the public to the deadly effects of pesticides such as DDT, leaving many in the **United States** seeing the acronym as little more than an industrial poison. The United States banned DDT in 1972.

Today, many countries ban or significantly restrict its use. The **Stockholm Convention on Persistent Organic Pollutants**, which went into force in 2004, has also put in place an international treaty to begin to control the production, use, and trade of DDT. This convention still allows DDT to control malaria, however, a disease that continues to kill millions of people every year. *See also* ENVIRONMENTAL DEFENSE FUND (EDF); PERSISTENT ORGANIC POLLUTANTS (POPs); PLASTIC; SYNTHETIC CHEMICALS.

DRIFT NETS. In the 1980s, drift nets on the high seas were spanning tens of kilometers. Generally, trawlers would set these near the ocean's surface to drift with the wind and currents, indiscriminately catching everything, including noncommercial species, commercial species below the minimum size for markets, as well as dolphins, sharks, and turtles. Also, pieces of the nets were routinely lost, further killing and harming sea life. By the end of the 1980s, a worldwide environmental campaign to ban these nets was gaining strength, especially in the tuna industry (responsible for drowning at least 100,000 dolphins a year). Facing a consumer backlash, by the beginning of the 1990s, many of the world's largest tuna-canning companies—such as StarKist, Chicken of the Sea, and Bumble Bee Foods—stopped buying tuna caught in drift nets and began to market "dolphin-safe" tuna. In 1991, the

General Assembly of the **United Nations** passed a moratorium on the use of large-scale drift nets on the high seas (effective from 1992). Illegal drift-net **fishing** still occurs, but drift nets now kill far fewer dolphins each year.

E

EARTH DAY. Gaylord Nelson, **United States** Democratic senator from Wisconsin, was the first to call publicly for an Earth Day. The first Earth Day was held on 22 April 1970 and was modeled after the nonviolent Vietnam War protests. Across the United States, around 20 million people rallied as part of an "environmental teach-in," one of the largest organized public demonstrations in American history and a defining moment in American environmentalism. Earth Day was an outgrowth of increasing environmental concern in the United States in the 1960s, in part as best-selling books like **Rachel Carson**'s *Silent Spring* and **Paul Ehrlich**'s *The Population Bomb* raised public awareness. In the wake of the 1970 Earth Day, the U.S. government created the United States Environmental Protection Agency and took steps to pass and strengthen environmental legislation. In 1990, Earth Day became a global event. Promoters of Earth Day estimate that each year, including in 2015, over half a billion people celebrate Earth Day across just about every country.

Earth Day is sometimes confused with an international celebration to mark the spring equinox in the Northern Hemisphere (around 21 March) and reconfirm the need to care for the global environment; it is also called Earth Day and was also first held in 1970. On occasion, Earth Day is also confused with **World Environment Day**.

EARTH FIRST!. A radical environmental movement, Earth First! is comprised of small groups that take direct action to protect natural environments. Pioneered in 1979–1980 by American environmental activists David Foreman, Mike Roselle, Howie Wolke, Ron Kezar, and Bart Koehler, it promotes the values of biocentrism through grassroots education, litigation, and civil disobedience. Early acts by Earth First! in the **United States** included what the group called ecotage, acts of environmental sabotage such as tree spiking (driving nails into trees to make it dangerous to cut into them). In 1989, the U.S. government charged five members, including Foreman, with planning to destroy an electrical transmission tower in Arizona. All, except Foreman who was not directly involved, received jail time in federal prison. Foreman was placed on probation for five years for distributing copies of his book *Ecodefense: A Field Guide to Monkeywrenching*.

By 1990, many of the founders of the U.S. group had quit the organization, some of whom founded the less radical environmental group, the Wildlands Project, and some of whom joined to form the **Earth Liberation Front**. Today, besides in the United States, Earth First! also has chapters in **Great Britain**, **Canada**, **Australia**, the **Philippines**, and the Czech Republic, among others. Participants share a common goal of taking direct action to defend remaining natural areas from humans. Many Earth First! activists have been influenced by the writings of Edward Abbey (*The Monkey Wrench Gang*), the **deep ecology** philosophy, and anarchist political philosophy. *See also* ANIMAL LIBERATION FRONT (ALF); ECOTERRORISM.

EARTH LIBERATION FRONT (ELF). Founded in **Great Britain** in 1992, the Earth Liberation Front (ELF) is a "leaderless" resistance to capitalism and environmental destruction comprising secret cells of individuals willing to resort to sabotage, but with precautions to avoid harming people or animals (such as burning down vacant housing developments or closed car dealerships), a practice some call ecotage. Today, ELF is a small global movement whose members (who call themselves "elves") on occasion cooperate with the **Animal Liberation Front (ALF)**. Its capacity to function and expand has been severely constrained after the **United States** Federal Bureau of Investigation (FBI) classified the ELF in 2001 as a domestic terrorism threat and its members as **ecoterrorists**. *See also* ECOTERRORISM.

EARTH NEGOTIATIONS BULLETIN (ENB). See INTERNATIONAL INSTITUTE FOR SUSTAINABLE DEVELOPMENT (IISD).

EARTH SUMMIT. *See* UNITED NATIONS CONFERENCE ON ENVIRONMENT AND DEVELOPMENT (UNCED).

EASTER ISLAND. Among those who see humanity on a path toward ecological collapse, the history of Easter Island is a common metaphor for the planet's future. Located in the southeastern Pacific (around 2,300 miles/ 3,700 kilometers from **Chile**), its name in English derives from the first recorded visit by Dutch explorer Jacob Roggeveen on Easter Sunday in 1722. As Jared Diamond describes vividly in his best-selling 2005 book *Collapse*, Roggeveen was amazed to find hundreds of giant stone statues (called *moai*), with many erected on massive stone platforms (called *ahu*). Yet, at the same time, the small island was in environmental ruins, without a single tree over 10 feet tall; by then, the Polynesian population had crashed from a peak of between 1,400 and 1,600, with the remaining people struggling to survive. For centuries, large trees were cut down to drag and lift the massive stones to build ever-bigger monuments to the gods, causing **deforestation** and contributing to the loss of wild food, a decline in seaworthy canoes for **fishing**, a decrease in wood for cooking and heat, high rates of soil erosion, and a fall in crop yields. Starvation became widespread; military factions overthrew the chiefs and priests; civil wars erupted; and, to survive, people began to hide in caves and possibly even turned to cannibalism.

Critics of the use of Easter Island as a metaphor for today's escalating global crisis argue that its extreme isolation means it is a unique historical case, unlike modern societies able to trade and bring in new natural resources, people, and technologies. Some scholars have also claimed that Diamond and other environmental scholars have exaggerated the collapse of life on Easter Island. *See also* NAURU.

EASTERN GARBAGE PATCH. Hundreds of kilometers north of Hawaii, the Eastern Garbage Patch (also called the Great Pacific Garbage Patch) is a "dead" zone of the vast Pacific Ocean now filled with floating **plastic** pellets from the breakdown of everything from grocery bags to cigarette lighters to foam cups. Covering an area that some estimate could be around the size of the state of Texas in the **United States** (although estimates vary considerably), it is located within the North Pacific Gyre, a 26-million-square-kilometer clockwise vortex of calm winds and slow-moving water. The Garbage Patch, the nonprofit Agalita Marine Research Foundation estimates, now contains more than five kilograms of plastic per square kilometer, an amount six times the concentration of zooplankton in this region. Usually no deeper than 10 meters below the surface, much of this plastic waste has broken down into tiny pellets that can resemble food to jellyfish and lantern fish (a major source of food for dolphins, sharks, tuna, and whales). Many environmentalists stress the ecological and health consequences of so much plastic entering the world's food chains; many also see this as a metaphor for the consequences of throwaway capitalism and the shadow effects of consumption.

ECO-BUSINESS. Peter Dauvergne and Jane Lister coined the term *eco-business* to describe the **sustainability** policies of multinational brand corporations since the mid-2000s. In the 2013 MIT Press book *Eco-Business*, they show how corporations with global brands have been increasingly implementing initiatives framed as sustainability—such as codes of conduct, certification standards, supplier audits, recycling and waste management policies, smart packaging programs, and environmental reporting—as business tools to compete for sales, profits, and customers, as well as to increase control over global supply chains. Eco-business helps these companies to improve reputations, secure higher-quality inputs, and better manage risks as the scarcity of natural resources rises. It also reduces waste and energy use per product sold and pushes suppliers to cut prices.

Eco-business has proven especially valuable since the global financial crisis of 2008 as a way for multinational manufacturers (e.g., Coca-Cola, Nike, Nestlé, Procter & Gamble), big-box retailers (e.g., Walmart, Home Depot, Costco), and food chains (e.g., McDonald's) to lower costs, keep down consumer prices, and expand operations. These firms claim that such gains demonstrate environmental leadership and **corporate social responsibility**. They further claim to be making progress toward a suite of far-reaching "aspirational" goals: 100 percent **renewable energy**, 100 percent sustainable sourcing, zero waste, zero **deforestation**, and carbon neutrality, among others. Eco-business has innate limits, however, on how far it can advance global sustainability. As Dauvergne and Lister document, eco-business is fundamentally geared toward increasing corporate sales and profits and expanding production and consumption, doing far more to advance the interests of business than the sustainability of the earth's ecosystems. *See also* ECO-CERTIFICATION; ECO-EFFICIENCY; ENVIRONMENTAL DEFENSE FUND (EDF); GLOBAL COMPACT; WORLD BUSINESS COUNCIL FOR SUSTAINABLE DEVELOPMENT (WBCSD); WORLD WIDE FUND FOR NATURE/WORLD WILDLIFE FUND (WWF).

ECO-CERTIFICATION. Eco-certification assesses business processes and/or products to evaluate whether they conform to a particular environmental standard. It is a voluntary mechanism relying on the market to promote **corporate social responsibility**, accountability, and **sustainable development**. Conformance can be determined in three ways: an internal audit (self-certification), an industry association audit, or an independent verifier (third-party certification). Typically, eco-certified organizations or products receive an **eco-label** to inform consumers, although not all eco-certification programs have an eco-label (e.g., **International Organization for Standardization [ISO]** 14001). The first eco-label certification program was **Germany**'s Blue Angel program created in 1977. Other product certifications now include Green Seal (**United States**), Eco Mark (**Japan**), Eco-label (European Union), NF Environnement (**France**), Nordic Swan (Scandinavia), and the Environmental Choice/EcoLogo Program (**Canada**).

Beyond ISO 14001 and the European Union's **Eco-Management and Audit Scheme (EMAS),** an increasing number of eco-certification programs now serve multinational businesses. These include the international **Forest Stewardship Council (FSC), Marine Stewardship Council (MSC),** and **Roundtable on Sustainable Palm Oil (RSPO)** programs, as well as numerous **organic food** and **coffee** certification programs. Eco-certification standards tend to fall into two categories: systems standards and performance standards. A systems standard (e.g., ISO 14001) specifies the elements of a required management system, whereas a performance standard specifies outcome goals and objectives (e.g., FSC). Sometimes, as more eco-certification schemes enter the marketplace, these begin to compete for legitimacy, as in the case of sustainable forestry standards with the FSC and the **Programme for the Endorsement of Forest Certification (PEFC)**. The Global Ecolabelling Network (GEN) was founded in 1994 to facilitate the harmonization of eco-certification labeling programs.

ECO-EFFICIENCY. Industry coined the term *eco-efficiency* in the period leading up to the 1992 **United Nations Conference on Environment and Development**. It describes a business strategy where companies maximize resource efficiencies and minimize ecological impacts to produce more competitively priced goods and services (generating more with less). The idea is to create both economic and environmental benefits by integrating environmental values into business practices. Economic benefits can include fewer risks, lower costs for environmental cleanups, and larger market shares by improving performance and corporate images (and thus brand value). Environmental benefits can arise as more efficient firms use less energy and natural resources and produce less waste per unit of output. Proponents of eco-efficiency, such as **ecological modernization** theorists, see this as a way to reframe environmental stewardship so it becomes a standard corporate tool to try to gain a competitive advantage. Here, environmental management becomes a business opportunity rather than a cost; thus, going "beyond compliance" with environmental regulations becomes part of normal corporate operating procedures (often under a more general rubric of pursuing **corporate social responsibility**).

Proponents of eco-efficiency see this as one of the most significant business strategies for achieving **sustainable development**. Businesses that adopt an eco-efficient approach will eventually drive other firms into bankruptcy, leaving behind a global network of corporations able to produce more products with less resource inputs, and willing to set ambitious long-term environmental goals, such as zero-emission production. Critics charge that eco-efficiency is merely a repackaging for consumers of long-standing business efforts to maximize profits and minimize financial costs and therefore overstates the environmental benefits (in addition to justifying weak government regulations). *See also* ECO-BUSINESS; ECO-MODERNISM; MARKET LIBERALISM.

ECO-FEMINISM. Eco-feminist thought began to develop in the 1970s, emerging alongside and as part of protests for peace, labor rights, and animal liberation, as well as environmental and women's movements. In 1974, Françoise d'Eaubonne coined the term *eco-feminism*, or what some call *ecological feminism* (uniting environmentalism and feminism). It is an intellectual movement connecting the patriarchal oppression of women (often including other groups, too) with human domination and exploitation of the natural world.

Eco-feminists stress the interconnections between all forms of oppression: for example, racism, heterosexism, and ageism. Many see misogyny as rooted in the opposition and separation of nature and culture. Many also see women as central to ecological thought because women are "closer" to nature, be it by natural/innate connections (sometimes labeled as *radical eco-feminism*) or by cultural/historical developments (sometimes labeled as *materialist/constructivist eco-feminism*). For these thinkers ecological change affects women more than men; thus, with more at stake, women are often central to efforts to stop environmental degradation (at least compared to other movements). Examples include **Love Canal**, the **Chipko Movement**, and the **Green Belt Movement**. Prominent thinkers in this tradition include Carol J. Adams, Irene Diamond, Greta Claire Gaard, Carolyn Merchant, Maria Mies, Starhawk, and **Vandana Shiva**. *See also* ENVIRONMENTAL JUSTICE.

ECO-FORESTRY. This term stands for ecologically based or eco-centric forestry. Its origins go back over a hundred years; early notions, for example, are found in debates between **John Muir**, the founder of the **Sierra Club**, and **Gifford Pinchot**, head of the **United States** Forest Service from 1905 to 1910. The primary aim of eco-forestry is to harvest—and then care for—natural forests in ways that allow self-regulating and self-renewing processes to maintain **biodiversity** and ecological integrity (such as for soils and watersheds). Today, in contrast to maximizing output and profits through industrial forestry, eco-forestry avoids practices such as clear-cutting, plantations, and pesticides and instead aims to harvest forests selectively, more along the lines of a 19th-century family homestead. *See also* SUSTAINABLE FOREST MANAGEMENT; SUSTAINABLE YIELD.

ECO-LABELING. Eco-labeling uses a label or logo to inform consumers that a product has met certain environmental standards. Generally it is voluntary and certified by third parties (usually either a government or a **nongovernmental organization**). The first eco-labeling scheme was in **Germany** in 1977, called the Blue Angel program. Schemes in **Canada, Japan**, and the **United States** followed in the late 1980s, and the idea spread in the

1990s. Today, large numbers of national governments employ labeling schemes. The **International Organization for Standardization** has also created eco-labeling standards.

Many environmentalists support eco-labeling, but only when the criteria are clear and the outcomes improve environmental performance; otherwise, they worry that it can become a sophisticated form of **greenwashing**. Some economists also argue that eco-labels can distort trade, with only marginal benefits for protecting environmental values. In particular, because they are most common in developed countries, eco-labels can function as a barrier to trade, with disproportionate costs for export-oriented economies in the developing world. In response, to promote principles of equivalency and mutual recognition for eco-labeling, some within the environmental movement are working to harmonize procedures to measure and assess environmental impacts across jurisdictions.

ECOLOGICAL ECONOMICS. An interdisciplinary field of inquiry integrating ecology and economics, ecological economics combines economic theory with ideas from thermodynamics, systems theory, and ecology. It assumes that economies function within physical environments (rather than outside, as is common in other economic approaches). Thus, an economy is not an isolated, self-sustaining system but relies on—and is limited by—flows of energy, materials, and ecosystem services.

Many ecological economists build on these assumptions to argue that a rising global population with rising per capita consumption is increasingly putting the earth above its biological **carrying capacity**. **Nicholas Georgescu-Roegen**'s pioneering research on the concept of *entropy* influenced this field; so have the writings of **Kenneth Boulding** and **Herman Daly**. The books of **E. F. Schumacher**, especially the best seller *Small Is Beautiful* (1973), also shaped this field. Another important leader in this field is **Robert Costanza**, who cofounded the **International Society for Ecological Economics (ISEE)** in 1989, which publishes the peer-reviewed academic journal *Ecological Economics* (first volume, February 1989).

Supporters see this field as one on the cutting edge of critical economic inquiry into understanding the root causes of environmental degradation and the growing global crisis. Critics, including many in the field of inquiry commonly called environmental economics, argue that ecological economists tend to underestimate the power of ingenuity and technology to substitute for resource scarcity and natural capital (which explains why everything from food to energy has managed to keep up with exponential population growth). *See also* ECOLOGICAL FOOTPRINT.

ECOLOGICAL FOOTPRINT. William Rees and Mathis Wackernagel developed the concept of an *ecological footprint* to measure the environmental impact of human lifestyles. It calculates the average amount of productive land and water necessary to sustain current levels of consumption and waste. The measure concentrates on the impacts of food, water, housing, transportation, and consumer goods and services. An individual's footprint is the total area in global hectares (one hectare of average biological productivity) required to support his or her lifestyle. The data set in 2010 put the average footprint at 2.7 global hectares per person. Sharp differences, however, exist across the globe. Across Africa it was about 1.5 hectares per person. In contrast, it was 4.7 in **Great Britain** and 7.2 in the **United States**. Today, according to these calculations, the global ecological footprint is at least 2.5 times higher than in the early 1960s and at least 1.5 times over the planet's regenerative capacity. The concept of ecological footprint is now common in educational programs, environmental campaigns, and the Western media. Critics argue that it is more of a political tool to raise environmental consciousness than an accurate scientific measure, as it underestimates the potential of new technologies and the value of international trade and financing.

ECOLOGICAL IMPERIALISM. The historian Alfred W. Crosby (1931–), emeritus professor at the University of Texas at Austin, developed and popularized the concept of "ecological imperialism" to describe the biological consequences of European conquest and colonization of the "New World" from 900 to 1900. In his 1986 book, *Ecological Imperialism*, he highlighted three biological sources of sweeping ecological change—European diseases, animals, and plants. The diseases that devastated indigenous populations included smallpox, influenza, dysentery, measles, whooping cough, diphtheria, tuberculosis, and sexually transmitted diseases. Introduced animals, insects, and amphibians that altered ecosystems included honeybees, cows, horses, pigs, dogs, rabbits, sheep, and rats. Introduced crops and plants that changed landscapes included dandelions, wheat, barley, rye, grazing grasses, and grapevines. So great were the consequences of ecological imperialism—in some places killing 80–95 percent of the indigenous population—that some scholars argue that the beginning of the **Anthropocene** epoch is best dated in the early 1600s. *See also* ENVIRONMENTAL JUSTICE.

ECOLOGICAL MODERNIZATION. Ecological modernization theory is a strand of environmental thought drawing primarily on the environmental and economic histories of Western Europe after World War II. German political scientist Martin Jänicke coined the term *ecological modernization* in the late 1970s, although many see German sociologist Joseph Huber as the founder of the "theory" with his writings in the 1980s. Many other social scientists (at first from Western Europe, then later from many other developed countries) added further to the empirical and conceptual foundations of this theory. The gist is straightforward: putting in place stricter environmental regulations does not need to impede economic or social development and with appropriate policies can even increase the competitiveness of industry.

Ecological modernization theory assumes that a restructuring of global capitalism, along with the institutions of modernity, can relieve ecological pressures (rather than cause environmental crises) and allow sustainable economic growth. States can do this in particular by transforming the ecological impact of production and consumption. This requires that governments guide markets and promote innovative technologies to increase efficiency, use less energy, deplete fewer resources, and recycle waste, thus producing greener economic growth. Governments need as well to create incentives for firms to go beyond compliance—that is, go beyond the legal environmental rules in various jurisdictions. Here, states need to develop a policy framework so that firms see protecting the environment not as a cost but as a business opportunity to improve competitiveness.

Some critics accuse proponents of ecological modernization of being Eurocentric—of describing the institutional practices of countries like the Netherlands, **Germany**, and **Great Britain** rather than developing a real theory exportable to poor countries. Other critics stress that the theory underestimates the power of structural inequalities in the current world order. Still others contend that the theory only captures a slice of the process of global change, highlighting progress in wealthy states while overlooking the escalating global environmental crisis. *See also* DEEP ECOLOGY; ECO-EFFICIENCY; ENVIRONMENTAL KUZNETS CURVE (EKC); *THE LIMITS TO GROWTH*; SIMON, JULIAN (1932–1998).

ECO-MANAGEMENT AND AUDIT SCHEME (EMAS). The European Union's Eco-Management and Audit Scheme—commonly called EMAS—is a voluntary program for regular site audits of an organization's impacts on the environment by independent, accredited experts. It was introduced in 1993 and opened for participation in 1995. It aims to enhance the credibility of organizations that go beyond minimum legal compliance and strive to improve environmental performance on a continual basis. Registered organizations can use the EMAS logo to demonstrate a commitment to environmental goals. The scheme initially targeted the industrial sector but now includes the service sector. It goes beyond the requirements of the **International Organization for Standardization**, as participating organizations must not only implement an environmental management system complying with ISO 14001 but also publish a performance statement verified by an external assessor. *See also* ECO-CERTIFICATION; ECO-LABELING.

ECO-MODERNISM. The primary proponent of eco-modernism is the **Breakthrough Institute**, a **nongovernmental organization** founded by Ted Nordhaus and Michael Shellenberger in 2003. Eco-modernists call for an environmentalism of hope, not fear and worry. Exuding optimism, they challenge those who call for **limits to growth** to curb overexploitation of the planet, as well as those who call for constraints on population growth, such as **Paul Ehrlich** and other "Malthusians." They call instead for "eco-pragmatism," arguing that technology and ingenuity can allow for more economic growth without harming the natural world. More efficient and intensive use of land can produce more food, including meat. Reengineering of suboptimal production can produce more consumer products with less resources. Eco-modernists envision far more people living in eco-friendly megacities. *See also* ECO-EFFICIENCY; MALTHUS, THOMAS ROBERT (1766–1834); MARKET LIBERALISM; MEADOWS, DONELLA (1941–2001).

ECOSYSTEM MANAGEMENT. Ecosystem management has multiple definitions. At a general level, it is a systems approach to resource management that integrates ecological, economic, and social goals into land-use decisions and practices. Many definitions stress that the aim is to sustain ecological integrity (not just species) while still meeting economic needs and societal values. This assumes that each generation should manage renewable natural resources so that succeeding generations will have comparable resources: in this way it is a means for achieving **sustainable development**. Key themes to achieve this include balancing human and ecological needs, managing systems rather than components, defining management areas ecologically rather than politically, assessing longer time horizons, and employing an **adaptive management** approach. The origins are complex and involve multiple inputs; one source in the **United States** was the discussions among ecologists and conservationists in the 1920s and 1930s about the need for nature reserves of sufficient size to conserve wildlife species and **biodiversity**. The Central and Eastern European origins of the concept emerged more through the discipline of landscape ecology after World War II.

ECOTAGE. *See* EARTH FIRST!; EARTH LIBERATION FRONT (ELF).

ECOTERRORISM. The **United States** Federal Bureau of Investigation (FBI) defines *ecoterrorism* within its domestic terrorism unit as the criminal use or threatened use of violence by a subnational group in the name of an environmental cause. The FBI estimates that ecoterrorists caused hundreds of millions of dollars of property damage over the last decade. Some environmentalists contest this definition of *ecoterrorism*, seeing it as government-speak to scare the public into thinking of radical environmentalism as terrorism. Some of these radical environmentalists, such as former **Greenpeace** member **Paul Watson** (now leader of the Sea Shepherd Conservation Society and, as of 2015, refusing to comply with Interpol extradition notices to face charges in Costa Rica and Japan), turn the definition of *ecoterrorism* inside out, defining it as acts by governments and corporations that terrorize species and the earth. *See also* ANIMAL LIBERATION FRONT (ALF); EARTH LIBERATION FRONT (ELF).

ECOTOURISM. Definitions vary, but generally ecotourism aims to limit the footprint of tourists on local ecosystems and communities. Sometimes called responsible tourism, it assumes that with controls, tourism can infuse local economies with valuable income (including foreign currency in poorer countries), which can then finance **sustainable development** and ease pressures on governments to export industrial agriculture crops and natural resources to maintain basic services and service foreign debts. In practice, the concept does not always take on these meanings, however, as creative marketers use it to draw tourists into remote and exotic places to experience nature (with, in effect, ecotourism becoming little more than a way to promote adventure tourism to tropical rain forests, glaciers, or **coral reefs**). Established in 1990, the nonprofit International Ecotourism Society advances general "principles of ecotourism" and promotes specific ecotourist destinations in every region of the world. *See also* COSTA RICA; MARINE PROTECTED AREAS (MPAs); WWOOF.

ECO-WARRIOR. The term *eco-warrior* generally refers to someone who is willing to protect the environment with radical acts like eco-sabotage or tree spiking. The Canadian environmentalist **Robert "Bob" Hunter**, a cofounder of **Greenpeace**, is often credited with coining the term. American environmentalist David Foreman, cofounder of the radical environmental organization **Earth First!**, popularized the term with his 1991 book *Confessions of an Eco-Warrior*. Today, the term is often diluted to refer to activists campaigning with tactics ranging from rallies to filing legal appeals. *See also* SWAMPY (DANIEL HOOPER) (1974–).

EHRLICH, PAUL R. (1932–). A professor in the Department of Biological Sciences at Stanford University in California, Paul Ehrlich is best known for his analyses of the impact of population growth on the health of the global environment. His most famous book, *The Population Bomb*, was published in 1968, selling millions of copies. Following in the tradition of **Thomas Malthus**, Ehrlich foresaw a collapse of the global environment under the pressures of exponential population growth on a planet with finite resources. For humans, such a collapse would mean widespread famine, social instability, and a dieback of the population. To avoid this future, Ehrlich advocated strict controls on population growth, such as **China**'s one-child policy. Environmentalists such as Ehrlich are sometimes called neo-Malthusians, a line of reasoning more popular in the late 1960s and 1970s than today, in part because many of the predictions of doom have failed to happen.

EMISSIONS TRADING. Two types of market-based instruments for environmental policy include taxing **pollution** and trading pollution permits (which includes emissions trading). Many in the environmental movement now see emissions trading (with a cap on the amount of pollution) as a practical—and potentially effective—way to handle complex environmental problems such as **climate change**. Advocates see the trading or buying of pollution credits, such as for carbon, as more flexible and cost effective than government regulations, with greater capacity to account for significant differences in abatement costs across many sources and jurisdictions.

The concept of emissions trading goes back to the late 1960s (including, for example, in the work of **Herman Daly**). Since then, the number of specific schemes has been growing steadily. The **United States** introduced credit-based emissions trading schemes in the 1970s and 1980s as part of its air-quality policy. A 1990 amendment to the U.S. Clean Air Act established a cap-and-trade system (in effect since 1995) for sulfur dioxide emissions, a major cause of **acid rain**. The **Kyoto Protocol to the United Nations Framework Convention on Climate Change** established an "emissions trading mechanism." The European Union (EU) also has an Emissions Trading Scheme for **greenhouse gases** that became operational in 2005 (covering sources accounting for nearly half of the EU's overall emissions of carbon dioxide). In 2008 the government of British Columbia became the first in **Canada** to introduce cap-and-trade legislation for large emitters, with the goal of reducing the province's greenhouse gas emissions by one-third by 2020. Negotiators at the 21st Conference of the Parties (COP) of the **United Nations Framework Convention on Climate Change** held in Paris, **France**, in 2015 considered emissions trading one of the most valuable policy mechanisms for meeting emission reduction commitments. *See also* CARBON TAX.

ENDANGERED SPECIES. A species is "endangered" when its population is so low it could soon become extinct over all (or at least most) of its natural range. Biologists sometimes distinguish between three levels of threat: local extinction, where a species no longer lives in its original habitat but exists elsewhere (sometimes referred to as "extirpated"); ecological extinction, where so few are left that the species can no longer carry out its natural role (e.g., as predator or food) in its ecosystems (sometimes called "functional extinction"); and biological extinction, where the species no longer exists. Related, a "threatened" species is one that is still abundant, but declining numbers suggest it might become endangered in the near future unless something is done.

The current rate of extinction due to man-made causes for animal and plant species is 50 to 100 times higher than it is for natural causes. **Climate change** is one of the greatest threats to species: an increase of just 0.8 to 2.0 degrees Celsius (1.4 to 3.6 degrees Fahrenheit), for example, could "commit" a quarter of plant and animal species to extinction by 2050 (although scientific uncertainty is very high with such predictions, and estimates vary widely). Other causes of rising numbers of endangered species include **deforestation**, poaching, alien species, **pollution**, land clearance, soil erosion, and trade in endangered species, to name just a few.

The international community, to control trade in endangered species, negotiated the 1973 **Convention on International Trade in Endangered Species of Wild Fauna and Flora (CITES)**, which, as of 2015, had 181 parties. At the 1992 **United Nations Conference on Environment and Development**, over 150 countries also signed the **Convention on Biological Diversity** to protect **biodiversity**, including endangered species (an agreement which, at the beginning of 2016, had 196 parties). **Nongovernmental organizations**, such as the **International Union for Conservation of Nature (IUCN)** and the **World Wide Fund for Nature/World Wildlife Fund (WWF)**, have also played an important role in efforts to protect endangered species. *See also* ADAPTATION; ENVIRONMENTAL INVESTIGATION AGENCY (EIA); ILLEGAL LOGGING; IVORY TRADE; NATURE CONSERVANCY; OCEAN ACIDIFICATION.

ENVIRONMENTAL CITIZENSHIP. No single definition of *environmental citizenship* exists, but the basic idea is to bring the environmental rights and responsibilities of individuals into citizenship. Such approaches identify the role of attitudinal change in bridging the self-interest and environmentally responsible actions of consumers. Promoting environmental citizenship has been gaining in popularity among governments and environmentalists as a way to engage civil society and promote **sustainability**. It is also a way to highlight that relying on taxes and financial incentives is not the only means to motivate changes in individual environmental behavior.

ENVIRONMENTAL DEFENSE FUND (EDF). Part of a wave of **nongovernmental organizations** formed in North America and Europe in the 1960s and early 1970s, the Environmental Defense Fund was founded in the **United States** in 1966 (and incorporated in 1967) by scientists concerned about the effects of **dichlorodiphenyltrichloroethane (DDT)** on wildlife on

Long Island, New York. In 2000 it changed its name to Environmental Defense but later switched back to its original name. Headquartered in New York City, in 2015 the Environmental Defense Fund had around a million members and offices across the United States (as well as offices in **China**, **Mexico**, and **Great Britain**). It runs a variety of campaigns, including ones over the years on **climate change**, species **preservation**, human health, and oceans and marine life. Its primary strategy for change relies on collecting strong scientific evidence to work with businesses and communities on market-based solutions for environmental protection and, if necessary, to take its case through the U.S. courts. Some critics feel that the Environmental Defense Fund has caved to business interests by advocating market-based compromises and partnering with businesses such as Walmart and McDonald's; supporters, however, see it as one of the most practical and effective "scientific" advocacy organizations working for cleaner and safer environments in the United States. *See also* CORPORATE SOCIAL RESPONSIBILITY (CSR); ECO-BUSINESS; MARKET LIBERALISM.

ENVIRONMENTAL ECONOMICS. *See* ECOLOGICAL ECONOMICS.

ENVIRONMENTAL IMPACT ASSESSMENTS. This is a management technique to predict and assess the environmental consequences of a proposed project. Proponents see this as an essential tool to mitigate the environmental damage of development as well as to block destructive activities. Most environmentalists see environmental impact assessments as necessary, although most agree they are an imperfect tool, prone to underestimating long-term spillovers on ecosystems. Critics argue that without systematic government and societal input and controls, there is a high degree of uncertainty in many of the estimates and scenarios, and corporations can manipulate them to get a green light for business as usual.

ENVIRONMENTAL INVESTIGATION AGENCY (EIA). Founded in 1984, the Environmental Investigation Agency (EIA) is a **nongovernmental organization** with offices in London and Washington, D.C. Its mission is to investigate international "crimes" against the environment. Its investigators go undercover to document illegal activities through film, photographs, and scientific evidence. Campaigns include exposing trade in **endangered species**, poaching, **illegal logging**, and illegal trade in ozone-depleting substances. More specifically, the EIA has gone undercover in **Indonesia** to document illegal logging, in Sri Lanka and the Maldives to trace illegal trade in marine turtle shells, and in **Japan** to expose the killing of porpoises.

ENVIRONMENTAL JUSTICE. The concept of *environmental justice* brings together movements for social justice and environmentalism. Some analysts see it as arising out of the **United States** in the 1980s, although it is in many ways a result of countless struggles worldwide for environmental rights. The environmental justice movement highlights socioeconomic and political processes creating—or reinforcing—the unequal distribution of environmental harms, such as situating dirty factories in poor and marginalized neighborhoods or exporting **hazardous waste** from developed countries to developing ones. Causes of environmental crises, according to environmental justice theorists, lie not only in the global economy but also in factors such as systemic racism, gender discrimination, and a neocolonialist global system. One solution to enhance environmental justice is to end (or at least confront) environmental racism, a term that more specifically refers to how racism can cause discriminatory environmentalism, where environmental laws, industrial locations, cleanup or phaseout efforts, representation on environmental agencies, and environmental priorities favor one group (usually a majority) at the expense of another (usually a minority). *See also* ECO-FEMINISM; ECOLOGICAL IMPERIALISM.

ENVIRONMENTAL KUZNETS CURVE (EKC). The environmental Kuznets curve (EKC)—in the shape of an inverted U—graphs the relationship between rising per capita incomes (x-axis) and rising **pollution** (y-axis) during the process of industrialization, a relationship similar to the one between per capita income and income inequality, first proposed by 1971 Nobel Prize winner Simon Kuznets. The EKC shows that pollution (such as **smog**, mercury, and lead) rises in the early stages of development as governments pursue economic growth but then begins to decline once per capita income reaches high enough levels.

This inverted U occurs for several reasons. It happens because citizens demand better living conditions. It occurs because corporations and governments now have the financial and institutional capacity to respond effectively. And it happens because growing economies naturally shift from heavy industry to service and information industries. The EKC generally relies on data for industrial pollution rather than depletion of natural resources, although a few studies have found a correlation between lower rates of **deforestation** and higher incomes in Asia, Latin America, and Africa. **Japan**'s history of industrial pollution in the 1960s and 1970s—going from one of the world's most polluted countries with few environmental controls to one of the cleanest with relatively strong environmental measures—matches the EKC especially well.

Many environmentalists see valuable lessons to be learned from the EKC. For advocates, it shows the need for economic growth and higher per capita incomes to advance environmentalism. Many advocates further contend that it is possible to "tunnel" through the middle of the inverted U in countries with low per capita incomes, raising per capita incomes with less environmental damage. This can be done through eco-markets, free trade, new technologies, appropriate policies, and international organizations. Critics counter that the EKC is a fallacy, more ideology than reality, allowing states to justify pollution during the early stages of industrialization. It fails as a theory for issues like municipal waste, **biodiversity** loss, and carbon dioxide emissions. It ignores, too, that a decline of particular pollutants in one country may occur because dirty industries move overseas, improving local conditions in wealthy states but causing global conditions to deteriorate. *See also* ECO-MODERNISM.

ENVIRONMENTAL RACISM. *See* ENVIRONMENTAL JUSTICE.

ENVIRONMENTAL SECURITY. The concept of environmental security only began to draw widespread interest after the end of the Cold War in the 1990s (building on a few earlier essays). Security theorists had long recognized the significance of the conflict environment (whether at sea or on land, on hills or on mountains). But after the Cold War, some analysts began to advocate broadening the security discourse to include nontraditional security threats, ranging from earthquakes to resource scarcity to environmental degradation.

Definitions of environmental security have proven contentious, and official statements, policy, and international agreements have provided disparate understandings. Three main understandings tend to reappear: a **deep ecology** emphasis on global ecological security; a human security emphasis on social justice; and a national security emphasis on the propensity, or not, of resource scarcity and environmental degradation to cause violent conflict. *See also* FINLAND.

EQUATOR PRINCIPLES. The Equator Principles, a voluntary initiative launched in 2003 by leading financial institutions with support from the World Bank, establish benchmarks to raise the standard of social and environmental risk assessment in project financing. Revised principles became effective from 2014. These principles include appropriate consultation with affected stakeholders and management of impacts on wildlife and indigenous peoples. Institutions that adopt these principles, known as Equator Principles Financial Institutions (EPFIs), must put in place internal policies and processes consistent with the principles, agreeing that "negative impacts on project-affected ecosystems and communities should be avoided where possible, and if these impacts are unavoidable, they should be reduced, mitigated and/or compensated for appropriately." At the beginning of 2016, 81 financial institutions had adopted the principles as part of a broader commitment to **corporate social responsibility**. EPFIs from the **United States** include the Bank of America, Citigroup, JPMorgan, and Wells Fargo. Ones from **Great Britain** include Barclays, HSBC, and Lloyds Banking Group. Ones from **Japan** include Mizuho Corporate Bank and the Bank of Tokyo-Mitsubishi UFJ. Ones from **Canada** include the Royal Bank of Canada and the Bank of Montreal. The National Bank of Abu Dhabi joined in 2015. Supporters see the Equator Principles as a practical and effective way to advance the goals of corporate social responsibility. Critics see them as yet another example of the increasing amount of **greenwash** coming out of the corporate world.

EUROPE ECOLOGY—THE GREENS. See FRANCE.

E-WASTE. *See* HAZARDOUS WASTE.

EXTENDED PRODUCER/PRODUCT RESPONSIBILITY (EPR). Extended producer/product responsibility, or EPR, is a policy instrument where governments place responsibility for postconsumer waste on producers. EPR principles were formalized in the early 1990s with the help of the Organisation for Economic Co-operation and Development (OECD). It is a market-based approach to **sustainable development**, internalizing the costs of waste into the production process and thus creating incentives for producers to shift to more environmentally friendly designs and manufacturing processes. Design changes can reduce material inputs and increase reusability and recyclability. EPR uses a life-cycle analysis of the environmental impacts of a product, from inception and production (upstream) to use and disposal (downstream). The idea is to shift the traditional balance of responsibilities relating to waste management from municipalities and taxpayers to manufacturers and consumers. In this sense it is an extension of the **polluter pays principle**. EPR can include rules to require manufacturers to take back used goods, economic instruments (deposit/refund schemes), and performance standards.

One of the most successful examples of an EPR policy is the German Green Dot System (Duales Systeme Deutschland), which has significantly decreased packaging waste in **Germany**. In contrast, in North America, EPR still tends to focus on end-of-life management (i.e., industry funding for municipal **recycling** programs) or on reducing toxins in products. Some industries have developed voluntary **product stewardship** systems to avoid regulation, although environmentalists are often critical of the lack of targets, transparency, and accountability, and various studies suggest that industry-led EPR programs are only effective when supported by government regulation.

Some producers express concerns about the potential negative impacts of EPR policies on trade and competition. Other issues include the risk of free riding, orphan products (i.e., when the producer goes out of business), and existing/preexisting products. Nevertheless, EPR appeals to environmentalists with both conservative and liberal political leanings. On the one hand, it removes waste management from the general tax base and uses market mechanisms to achieve change. On the other hand, it places responsibility on producers and consumers—that is, on the polluters.

EXXON VALDEZ OIL SPILL. On 24 March 1989, the *Exxon Valdez* **oil** tanker grounded on Bligh Reef in Prince William Sound, Alaska. At the time the resulting oil spill was the largest in the history of the **United States** and one of the world's worst environmental accidents at sea, polluting the sound and over 550 kilometers of the Alaskan shoreline with 11 million gallons (41 million liters) of unrefined crude oil. The spill killed tens of thousands of migratory birds as well as countless marine organisms. The year after the disaster, the U.S. Congress passed the Oil Pollution Act.

Exxon ended up spending billions of dollars on the cleanup and settling lawsuits. Today, those lobbying for stricter environmental rules to govern international transportation continue to point to the *Exxon Valdez* as an example of the ecological and financial dangers of shipping oil. Those advocating for far stricter controls on oil production more generally also now point to the 2010 oil spill in the Gulf of Mexico (following an explosion at BP's *Deepwater Horizon* oil rig) as further evidence of the ongoing danger for marine life and human health.

F

FAIR TRADE. This approach to trading aims to establish more equal transactions between buyers and suppliers to support community development through access to international trade. It often relies on direct trade with producers to guarantee a minimum price and thus ensure more stable incomes and fairer prices, even when world market prices are falling. It can also involve other support for producers, such as social premiums to support better labor conditions, low-interest credit in times of hardship, and up-to-date market information.

The idea of trading fairly has a long history in bartering between neighbors and among communities. The modern-day fair trade movement first began to take shape during the 1960s around the import of Third World handicrafts into Europe. It soon spread to agricultural products—first **fair trade coffee** and tea, then sugar, bananas, nuts, dried fruits, and wine, among many others. The movement did not take off as a major economic force, however, until fair trade labels and certification programs took hold after the 1990s.

Two key fair trade organizations are the Fairtrade Labelling Organizations International (Fairtrade International, or FLO) and the World Fair Trade Organization (WFTO). Proponents of fair trade see it as a realistic and effective way for consumption in the First World to promote development in the Third World. Critics see it as little more than a token, doing more to relieve the guilt of the wealthy "cappuccino class" than to promote better environmental and social conditions in developing countries.

FAIR TRADE COFFEE. Fair trade in **coffee** began in the 1960s as part of the fair trade movement in Europe. It spread into North America in the 1980s as small-scale roasters started importing directly from cooperatives at above-market prices. It remained a niche market until the late 1990s, when certification programs began to expand the potential for fair trade coffee to reach mainstream markets.

The world's largest coffee chain, Starbucks, started serving fair trade coffee in 2000 as part of its policy of **corporate social responsibility**. Its purchases grew quickly, from just under 650,000 pounds in 2001 to hundreds of millions of pounds of fair trade certified coffee today. Supporters of fair trade stress how quickly sales are now rising for products like coffee, although, as many critics point out, these still comprise a small percentage of total consumption of natural resources from the Third World.

FAJARDO MENDO, PABLO. *See* GOLDMAN ENVIRONMENTAL PRIZE.

FARMED MEAT. Records suggest that per capita meat consumption in most traditional agricultural societies was rarely above 5–10 kilograms a year. Today, consumption of farmed meat is one of the greatest strains on the global environment. Global per capita meat consumption more than doubled from 1950 to 2010. And, as per capita consumption continues to increase, the number of pigs (over 1 billion), cattle (over 1.4 billion), sheep and goats (over 1.8 billion), and chickens (over 20 billion) continues to rise, a trend that will continue for some time. Most countries are still well behind leaders like the **United States,** with each person on average now consuming over 125 kilograms a year and rising.

Industrial meat farms emit significant **greenhouse gases** (belching and flatulent livestock, for example, account for a significant portion of global methane emissions, especially ones fattened on artificial feed containing things like corn, soy, and antibiotics). Since the 1960s, various **nongovernmental organizations** have campaigned to raise awareness about the environmental consequences and inhumane conditions of meat farms. But, compared to campaigns for whales or seals or elephants, these have gained little traction among states, corporations, and the general public. *See also* INTERNATIONAL CONVENTION FOR THE REGULATION OF WHALING; SEALING.

FIJI. *See* MELANESIA.

FINLAND. Although Finland's economy has many energy-intensive industries, it also has substantial coniferous taiga forests, many lakes, and little arable land, and thus the government has kept a strong focus on the environment. In 2004, it initiated a national strategy to adapt to **climate change**. This strategy also included **environmental security**, with particular attention to climate change threats, as part of its comprehensive security and defense strategy. The Ministry of the Environment oversees environmental issues in conjunction with the Ministry of Agriculture and Forestry and state-run regional environment centers. The Ministry of the Environment also runs a research wing, the Finnish Environment Institute. Meanwhile, Metsähallitus, a state-owned enterprise, is responsible for Finland's **national parks** and most of its nature reserves. During Finland's presidency of the European Union in 2006, its environmental focus was on air quality, **biodiversity**, climate change, marine life, and waste management.

Finland is part of the Helsinki Commission (HELCOM), the governing organization of the Helsinki Convention (Convention on the Protection of the Marine Environment of the Baltic Sea Area) of 1974. It is also a member of the Arctic Council, created in 1996 by Finland, **Canada**, Denmark, **Iceland**, Norway, **Russia**, **Sweden**, and the **United States** to promote cooperation on **Arctic** issues, including the environment.

The government has also established the Finnish Forest Certification Council and System as a branch of the **Programme for the Endorsement of Forest Certification (PEFC)** schemes. The Finnish Association for Nature Conservation (the largest environmental **nongovernmental organization** in Finland), the Finnish Nature League, and **World Wide Fund for Nature (WWF)**–Finland are all members of the **Forest Stewardship Council**. The Green League, Finland's main **green party**, registered as a political party in 1987, although previously various green-oriented candidates had run in elections without establishing a formal party (though some had cooperated as a list of candidates). At the beginning of 2016, the Green League held 15 seats in the Finnish Parliament.

FISHING. Large marine fishing states include **China**, Peru, the **United States**, **Japan**, **Chile**, **Indonesia**, and **Russia**, which in some recent years have accounted for as much as half of the global catch. Worldwide, the vast majority of the fish catch occurs within the 200-mile exclusive economic zones under national jurisdiction. Countries with "distant-water" fishing fleets such as Russia, Japan, **Spain**, Poland, **South Korea**, and **Taiwan** are responsible for the majority of the catch in international waters.

The 1982 UN Agreement for the Implementation of the Provisions of the **United Nations Convention on the Law of the Sea** relating to the Conservation and Management of Straddling Fish Stocks and Highly Migratory Fish Stocks sets out principles and international standards for the conservation and management of straddling and migratory fish stocks. In 1995, the **United Nations** adopted an international agreement on straddling and highly migratory fish stocks to implement these principles and international standards, which entered into force in 2001.

Estimates of remaining fish stocks vary widely and are hard to verify. Nevertheless, many marine biologists now agree that overfishing, **pollution**, and **climate change** mean many commercial species are in crisis, with stocks crashing. Over the last half century, for example, the stocks of large predatory fish—including cod, flounder, marlin, swordfish, and tuna—have fallen by at least 90 percent. The once seemingly infinite northern cod crashed in the early 1990s, although there were some signs of a population resurgence in 2015. Still, even as stocks fall, and even with international agreements on fish stocks now in place, the global marine catch remains far above the 1950 total of 16 million tons annually and currently sits at above 90 million tons, an amount most environmentalists see as many times above a sustainable catch.

FOOD NOT BOMBS. Comprising dispersed, small, independent, consensus-oriented groups of volunteers, the Food Not Bombs movement aims to promote social justice, more equitable and less wasteful consumption, and **sustainability** by serving free vegan and vegetarian food to the hungry and poor. Volunteers do this in part as a protest against war, capitalism, and poverty, and in part to reduce waste with a practical approach to alleviating hunger, especially among the homeless (whenever possible, the free food comes from surplus stock from bakeries, fruit and vegetable markets, and grocery stores that would otherwise be thrown away). The movement started in Cambridge, Massachusetts, in the early 1980s, spread to San Francisco in the late 1980s, and then went worldwide, with hundreds of loosely tied and fluidly organized chapters. Many of these "environmental" groups overlap with movements against globalization and war and for animal rights and vegetarianism. *See also* NONGOVERNMENTAL ORGANIZATIONS (NGOs).

FOREMAN, DAVID (1947–). *See* EARTH FIRST!; ECO-WARRIOR.

FORESTS. *See* AMAZON; DEFORESTATION; FOREST STEWARD-SHIP COUNCIL (FSC); ILLEGAL LOGGING; ROUNDTABLE ON SUS-TAINABLE PALM OIL (RSPO).

FOREST STEWARDSHIP COUNCIL (FSC). The Forest Stewardship Council, or FSC, is a nonprofit international organization founded in 1993, with funding primarily from the **World Wide Fund for Nature/World Wildlife Fund (WWF)**. It was originally based in Oaxaca, **Mexico**, but later moved to Bonn, **Germany**. Its mandate is to improve forest management by more effectively taking into account long-term economic, social, and environmental impacts. Its members include forest industries, indigenous peoples, certification bodies, community groups, and environmental organizations. Today, the FSC has hundreds of members from scores of countries, with its decision-making bodies providing equal representation for developed and developing countries.

The FSC is supporting the development of local, national, and regional environmental standards for forest management. Its primary function, however, is to accredit and monitor organizations which certify that products are from "a well-managed forest"—defined as one that meets the FSC's Principles and Criteria of Forest Stewardship. FSC representatives also monitor certified forests to ensure compliance. According to the FSC, its logo on a wood product is designed to provide a "credible guarantee" to the consumer that they are buying timber products from a sustainable source. Its label is gaining increasing market strength, and large retailers such as Office Depot and Home Depot are now selling significant quantities of FSC-certified paper and wood.

The FSC is an example of a growing trend among environmentalists since the early 1990s that has gained increasing momentum over the past decade: to change corporate behavior by influencing consumer demand with voluntary eco-labels. *See also* DEFORESTATION; ECO-CERTIFICATION; ECO-LABELING; MARKET LIBERALISM; SUSTAINABLE FOREST MANAGEMENT.

FOSSIL FUELS. *See* COAL; NATURAL GAS; OIL; PEAK OIL.

FRACKING. *See* NATURAL GAS.

FRANCE. France has a long history of national environmental legislation. An 1810 decree created the category of "licensed sites," requiring permission for highly polluting and hazardous operations. A 1917 act created the Licensed Sites Inspectorate. In 1930, the National Heritage Act allowed for the **preservation** of architectural and natural sites on aesthetic, historic, or scientific grounds, but it was not very effective with respect to environmental protection. Early attempts to establish nature parks included Fontainebleau in 1861 (near Paris), but all of today's nine **national parks** were created since 1963.

The Environment Ministry was established in 1971. The 1976 Nature Conservation Act provides a legal basis for protection of the natural environment, although it is rather general, and implementation has been difficult. Specific measures include **environmental impact assessments** and the authorization of public-interest environmental litigation by state-recognized environmental groups, as well as the creation of nature reserves. France has many specific environmental laws: one example is the 1975 Waste Act. European legislation also supplements France's environmental legislation, including the 1979 European Birds Directive, the 1992 Habitats Directive, and the 1993 Landscapes Act, which supports the preservation of the aesthetic quality of urban and rural areas.

Moreover, France has a long history of regulating fresh water for everything from fisheries to agriculture. Regulation of fisheries goes back to an 1829 statute on fish protection under the *code rural*—still used in court actions today. The 1964 and 1992 Water Acts, and over 20 pieces of European legislation, also form a legal basis for water management. The 1964 Water Act, for example, created the "river basin" as the key unit with respect to water protection. Municipalities (of which there are over 36,000) also hold key management and implementation responsibilities in this area and are strongly represented on basin committees, as are state and industrial interests. These committees set charges for matters such as water consumption and **pollution** (in line with the environmental taxation framework).

Environmental taxation in France relies in part on the **polluter pays principle**. The key agency is the Agence de l'Environnement et de la Maîtrise de l'Energie (ADEME), or the Environment and Energy Efficiency Agency, which was established in 1990. This agency receives public funding and taxes charged on practices such as landfill waste disposal, use of **oil**, industrial air pollution, and noise from airports. Tax revenue is partly returned to industry to subsidize environmental measures.

French environmentalism was primarily about conservation until the 1950s. The radicalism of the 1960s was a turning point, with environmentalism beginning to reflect a broader critique of consumer society. The "Vanoise affair" was the first major mobilization of this new environmentalism (arising over a proposal to build a ski resort in Vanoise National Park in 1969). The movement generated more than 500,000 protest letters and managed to stop the project. Another key issue mobilizing environmentalism at this time was **nuclear power**. The antinuclear movement began in the early 1970s, prompted by the 1974 Mesmer Plan, which aimed to provide 70 percent of France's electricity through nuclear power by 1985. Clashes at a demonstration in Malville in 1977 led to a split in the antinuclear movement between environmentalists and the extreme left (Trotskyites and Maoists) over the use of political violence. A major victory for the antinuclear movement was the cancellation of the Plogoff nuclear plant project in 1981.

The first environmental candidate stood in the 1973 legislative elections. In 1974, presidential candidate René Dumont, running on an environmental platform, gained 1.3 percent of the first-round vote. From the beginning there were tensions within the environmental movement between those who wanted to build centralized parties and structures (the organizers) and those who wanted to engage in more direct action (radicals). A split also developed between those wanting to develop an independent and exclusively environmental party without a close affiliation with either the Left or the Right and those wanting to form a common oppositional social movement.

These two strands eventually united to create Les Verts (The Greens) in 1984. In 1986, Antoine Waechter won the leadership and succeeded in pushing through a policy of full independence from other parties (both right and left). In 1989, Les Verts elected a record number of candidates in the municipal and European elections. Political support for the party, however, was undercut by other environmental politicians such as Brice Lalonde, who became state secretary for the environment in François Mitterrand's Socialist government in 1988. Politically oriented environmentalists agreed to run a single campaign in 1993; despite running high in the polls, however, the party did not manage to elect a member of Parliament.

In 1995, Dominique Voynet ran for president of Les Verts and launched a new strategy of alliance with the Socialist Party. In 1997, the Left won the legislative elections, including eight seats (for the first time) in the National Assembly for Les Verts. Voynet was appointed minister of environment and town and county planning in the Socialist government. As part of government, Les Verts succeeded in stopping the Super-Phoenix and Le Carnet nuclear plants (which they had failed to block earlier) and took on an important role in the Kyoto Conference on **climate change**. Les Verts was set back in the 2007 French presidential election, however, when Voynet achieved less than 1.6 percent of support in the first round, the party's worst result.

In 2010, Les Verts merged with Europe Écologie (founded in 2009) to form Europe Écologie–Les Verts, or Europe Ecology—the Greens. The party has fared especially well in regional council elections (holding more than 260 seats in 2015) but has also elected many members to the French National Assembly (with 17 in 2015), the French Senate (with 12 in 2015), and the European Parliament (with 6 in 2015). In recent years France has also taken on a leadership role in climate change negotiations, with Paris hosting the December 2015 Conference of the Parties (COP) of the **United Nations Framework Convention on Climate Change**, the most important global climate negotiation and agreement to date. *See also* BOVÉ, JOSÉ (1953–).

FREON. *See* CHLOROFLUOROCARBONS (CFCs).

FRIENDS OF THE EARTH. In 1969, **David Brower** founded the environmental **nongovernmental organization** Friends of the Earth after resigning as executive director of the **Sierra Club**. With its headquarters in San Francisco and advocacy staff in Washington, D.C., the organization quickly became influential in the **United States**, during the 1970s leading campaigns against the construction of supersonic transport and for restoration of the Florida Everglades.

In 1972, most of the Washington advocacy staff resigned after disagreements arose over the organization's structure and Brower's style of leadership. They founded the Environmental Policy Center and shortly afterward the Environmental Policy Institute (the two groups formally merged in 1977). Opposed by Brower and the activist wing, in 1985 the board of

Friends of the Earth decided to restructure and move its headquarters to Washington, D.C. Bower resigned and moved fully to the Earth Island Institute based in San Francisco (which he had founded in 1982).

In 1989, Friends of the Earth merged with the Oceanic Society and the Environmental Policy Institute, effectively reuniting with the group from the 1972 split. They resolved to pursue global environmental issues. Despite this turmoil, membership in Friends of the Earth went from 7,000 in 1970–1971 to 35,000 in 2002–2003. In 2005, Friends of the Earth expanded again with a merger with the Bluewater Network. The U.S. branch of Friends of the Earth was also instrumental in fostering Friends of the Earth International, now the world's largest network of grassroots organizations, with 75 national organizations, over 5,000 local groups, and about 2 million supporters worldwide.

G

GAIA HYPOTHESIS. James Lovelock developed the Gaia hypothesis in the 1970s, with his 1979 book *Gaia: A New Look at Life on Earth* helping to popularize it. Since then, Lovelock and many others (notably, microbiologist Lynn Margulis, 1938–2011) have further refined and tested the hypothesis, with some now calling it a theory with predictive power. Today, the idea of Gaia (named after the Greek earth goddess) continues to challenge many of the assumptions underlying environmental policies and institutions. It understands the earth as a living, self-regulating, and adaptive superorganism. No single organism makes life on earth possible, and no organism, not even humans, can disturb the earth without severe consequences, as Gaia adapts to sustain the whole system.

Many scientists reject the Gaia hypothesis as more fantasy than empirical reality. Many environmentalists also refer to Gaia more as a metaphor than a theory or hypothesis. They talk about the earth as alive to stress the vulnerability and interdependence of life on the planet. They also do so to stress the need for a more holistic and spiritual understanding of the "global environment." In many cultures this more general idea, however, predates Lovelock by at least several centuries. In the late 18th century, for example, the Scottish naturalist James Hutton (1726–1797)—a founding figure of modern geology—was writing that the earth was a "living world."

GANDHI, MOHANDAS KARAMCHAND (MAHATMA) (1869–1948). Born in **India**, Mahatma Gandhi completed a law degree in England in 1891 before moving to **South Africa** in 1893. He led a nonviolent campaign in South Africa against discrimination toward Indians before returning to India in 1914, where he was a leader in the struggle for Indian independence from the British. He is best known for his method of nonviolent resistance called satyagraha, or "devotion to truth," which has inspired human rights, civil society, and environmental movements worldwide. A vegetarian, Gandhi was a proponent of simple living in harmony with local conditions, and both his life and writings have inspired many strands of environmental thought. He was assassinated by a Hindu extremist.

GENETICALLY MODIFIED ORGANISMS (GMOs). The first genetically modified (GM) plants were grown experimentally in the late 1980s.
Already by 2003, one-third of all corn and three-quarters of soybeans were
GM crops in the **United States**. Today the vast majority of crops in both the
United States and **Canada** are genetically modified. **Argentina** and **China**
also have extensive GM plantations. GM crops are particularly controversial
in Europe, and **Japan** also bans several GM crops as well as long-grain rice
imports from the United States (which contain genetically modified organisms).

Supporters stress the value of engineering crops such as corn and cotton to
reduce the need for pesticides and herbicides as well as to increase yields to
feed the burgeoning global population (at 7.4 billion in 2016 and on track for
10 billion around the year 2050). Critics worry about the long-term consequences of altering nature without a full understanding of how this will affect
ecosystems with complex feedbacks (such as pesticide-producing GM crops
possibly leading to a new generation of superpests). Some in the environmental movement also question the morality of putting patents on life forms,
and some worry that GMOs will push even more farmers into producing cash
crops for export in the developing world. In 2002, several African nations
refused to take food aid (corn) from the United States because of a lack of
guarantees that it was GMO free. *See also* BOVÉ, JOSÉ (1953–); FRANCE;
SHIVA, VANDANA (1952–); SPAIN; THAILAND.

GEORGESCU-ROEGEN, NICHOLAS (1906–1994). A Romanian economist, Nicholas Georgescu-Roegen was a founding thinker in the field of
ecological economics and thermoeconomics (which applies the principles of
thermodynamics to the study of economics). His 1971 book *The Entropy
Law and the Economic Process* has been especially influential. *See also*
COSTANZA, ROBERT (1950–); DALY, HERMAN (1938–).

GEOTHERMAL ENERGY. Geothermal energy relies on the earth's natural heat to produce power. Humans have always known about this source of
energy, from hissing steam vents, erupting geysers, boiling mud pots, and
bubbling hot springs. The first attempt to generate electricity from geothermal steam was made in Italy in 1904. Today, it is possible to drill thousands
of meters into the earth to release high-pressure steam able to drive large
turbine generators.

Normally, economically extractible heat (four kilometers or less) concentrates where hot or molten rocks are at relatively shallow depths. One example of an area with intense thermal activity is the "ring of fire" around the
Pacific Ocean.

The world's largest producer of geothermal electricity is the **United States**, in 2015 followed by the **Philippines, Indonesia, Mexico, New Zealand**, and Italy. Geothermal energy also plays a significant role in Iceland, where around a third of energy production is geothermal power. Overall, however, geothermal power generates less than 1 percent of the world's energy.

The environmental movement has tended to support efforts to tap geothermal power, as the ecological consequences are much less than alternatives like **coal**, **natural gas**, and **oil**. Typically, a geothermal plant releases only 1–3 percent of the carbon dioxide emissions of a fossil fuel plant. Nevertheless, some concerns do exist, such as the impact of power plants on land stability and surrounding ecosystems.

GERMANY. Germany has a long tradition of environmental legislation. One of the first was an 1845 statute regulating industrial processes likely to cause air **pollution** in Prussia. The foundation of the current era was put in place following reforms by Willy Brandt's center-left coalition in 1969. This produced the 1970 Immediate Program for Environmental Action. Most crucially, a 1972 amendment to the Basic Law (the constitutional document) increased the competency of the federal state (called the Bund) over environmental policy. It gave concurrent legislative power in waste management, air pollution control, noise abatement, protection from radiation, and criminal law relating to environmental protection matters. It gave the Länder (the federal units) competence only after the Bund became involved.

The federal Environmental Agency was founded in 1974; still, with the government facing an **oil** crisis and economic recession, environmental policy was not a top political priority from 1974 to 1978. From 1979 to 1989, a grassroots environmental movement began to strengthen. The German Green Party was founded in 1979–1980 and was first elected to the Bundestag in 1983. In 1986, the Environmental Agency was subsumed under a more powerful Federal Ministry for the Environment, Nature Conservation and Nuclear Safety. In the first half of the 1990s, however, environmentalism again slid down the list of national priorities as debates over the financing of German reunification took center stage.

For the past few decades Germany's environmental policy has rested on three key principles: the **precautionary principle**, the **polluter pays principle**, and the cooperation principle. Of lesser importance are the common burden principle and the international cooperation principle. Although environmental policy is largely federal, the Länder are still highly influential. The Länder are represented in the Bundesrat and can vote on most federal legislation. They retain some competency over environmental policy when the Bund does not become involved. And the Bund depends on the Länder for implementation of most environmental laws (municipalities are also key to implementation). The result is cooperative federalism and joint decision making in developing environmental policy.

Typically, policies favor command-and-control approaches rather than market instruments to internalize environmental costs. The style of German environmental policy is legalistic, with detailed setting of standards. Usually, statutes take the form of "framework legislation," with specific standards set by regulators in the federal bureaucracy and published as ordinances. That said, there is generally significant consultation with stakeholders.

Germany has long had a strong antinuclear sentiment within its environmental movement (which itself has been an influential political force since the 1970s). Still, in 2010, roughly one-fifth of Germany's energy production came from nuclear power plants, although the government was slowly scaling back on nuclear power (with plans for a full phaseout by 2036). Antinuclear protests in Germany following the meltdown of **Japan**'s Fukushima Daiichi nuclear power facility in 2011, however, sped along the process; shortly afterward German chancellor Angela Merkel announced that all nuclear power plants would be closed by 2022 as Germany accelerated plans to expand its **renewable energy** capacity.

Under a plan known as Energiewende, or the Energy Transition toward renewable sources (e.g., solar, bioenergy, and wind) and away from nuclear energy, in 2014 Germany became the first major economy to sustain economic growth while reducing overall energy consumption, a model of growth praised by the World Bank and many climate specialists. *See also* GREEN PARTY; KELLY, PETRA (1947–1992).

GLASS. Glass is made from natural resources such as silica sand, soda ash, and limestone. In theory, it is possible to recycle it indefinitely, as its production does not create significant waste. Some countries in Europe are now **recycling** over 85 percent—and in many countries recycling rates are climbing. Most glass containers, for example, now contain up to 35 percent postconsumer glass. This uses less energy than quarrying and reduces landfill waste (it takes one million years for glass to break down naturally).

But, as some environmentalists stress, recycling glass can involve "downcycling," where each instance of recycling diminishes the quality as broken glass contaminates the process (poorer-quality glass often becomes filler for construction sites or roads). The solution is to sort glass by color, but this requires a committed public and first-rate collection programs. Some glass is also more difficult to recycle, such as cathode ray tubes (CRTs) in old televisions and computer monitors, which contain multiple layers of chemically treated glass. One solution to such complex recycling is for governments to impose **extended producer responsibility** for disposal.

GLOBAL COMPACT. The **United Nations** launched the Global Compact in 2000 to encourage corporations to pursue responsible citizenship by aligning operations with 10 "universally accepted principles" for human rights, labor, the environment, and anticorruption. Today, it includes thousands of participants, including over 8,000 businesses across scores of countries. Participation is purely voluntary, and there is no capacity to monitor or enforce compliance. Once a year, however, the UN expects each member to submit a case study of how they are implementing the principles. Members are also supposed to commit to these principles in their mission statements, newsletters, and annual reports.

Advocates of the Global Compact see it as a way to encourage **corporate social responsibility** and global citizenship. Critics contend that it is yet another feel-good measure that helps corporations to **greenwash** business as usual. *See also* PRECAUTIONARY APPROACH/PRINCIPLE; RESPONSIBLE CARE.

GLOBAL ENVIRONMENT FACILITY (GEF). The Global Environment Facility, or GEF, is an international organization involving three implementing agencies: the World Bank, the United Nations Development Programme, and the **United Nations Environment Programme**. It disburses grants and provides technical assistance to cover the additional costs for developing countries of projects with a global environmental goal, such as reducing **climate change**, ozone loss, **persistent organic pollutants**, or **biodiversity** loss. Beginning as a pilot program in 1991, GEF is now one of the world's biggest sources of financing for global environmental projects in the Third World, distributing about US$14.5 billion in grants and more than US$75 billion in cofinancing from other sources as of 2015.

Some **nongovernmental organizations** have been highly critical of GEF's policy of focusing funds on covering the incremental cost of the global reach of projects; others have been unhappy with the significant influence of the World Bank over policy and approaches. Reforms to the governance of GEF, however, have helped to mute criticism and integrate civil society groups into its decision-making structure and projects. *See also* CHINA, PEOPLE'S REPUBLIC OF; VIETNAM.

GLOBAL REPORTING INITIATIVE (GRI). Created in 1997, the Global Reporting Initiative (GRI) is a joint venture between the **Coalition for Environmentally Responsible Economies (CERES)** and the **United Nations Environment Programme**. It brings together over 100 organizations, including corporations, **nongovernmental organizations**, consultant organizations, and universities. The objective is to strengthen the comparability and credibility of **sustainability** reporting by encouraging companies to report on social and environmental performance with the same degree of rigor (including preparing for audits) as with financial performance.

To support this, the GRI has developed specific reporting guidelines for the industry sector. In the early 2000s, several hundred companies relied on the guidelines to issue reports; today, thousands of firms use some form of triple-bottom-line accounting (economic, social, and environmental) in line with the guidelines. Such companies include 3M, AT&T, General Motors, Ford, Shell, DuPont, McDonald's, Dow Chemical, Nike, Canon, Electrolux, Ericsson, and France Telecom. This initiative is one of an increasing number in a global movement to promote corporate social and environmental responsibility. *See also* CORPORATE SOCIAL RESPONSIBILITY (CSR); ECO-BUSINESS.

GLOBAL WARMING. *See* CLIMATE CHANGE.

GM CROPS. *See* GENETICALLY MODIFIED ORGANISMS (GMOs).

GOLDMAN ENVIRONMENTAL PRIZE. Founded in 1990 by Richard and Rhoda Goldman, the Goldman Environmental Prize is now the world's largest prize to honor grassroots environmentalists in Africa, Asia, Europe, islands and island nations, North America, and South and Central America. Six prizes worth US$175,000 each are awarded annually. Past recipients include **Wangari Maathai** of **Kenya** (1991), **Ken Saro-Wiwa** of **Nigeria** (1995), Marina Silva of **Brazil** (1996), and Alexander Nikitin of **Russia** (1997).

The 2008 winners were Pablo Fajardo Mendo and Luis Yanza of Ecuador, Marina Rikhvanova of Russia, Ignace Schops of Belgium, Feliciano dos Santos of Mozambique, Jesús León Santos of **Mexico**, and Rosa Hilda Ramos of Puerto Rico. Fajardo and Yanza won for leading a community-based class-action lawsuit (possibly the world's largest ever) against the company Texaco for dumping millions of gallons of crude **oil** and billions of gallons of wastewater into the Ecuadorian **Amazon** from 1964 until the end of 1990. Rikhvanova won for leading an environmental movement to protect Lake Baikal in **Siberia**—the oldest and deepest lake in the world, which the **United Nations Educational, Scientific and Cultural Organization (UNESCO)** declared a World Heritage Site in 1996—from construction of an oil pipeline and a uranium enrichment facility. Schops won for his work bringing together industry, governments, **nongovernmental organizations**, and local communities to raise the funds and build a consensus to establish the first and only **national park** in Belgium—the Hoge Kempen National Park, which opened in 2006—a process the **International Union for Con-**

servation of Nature (IUCN) hopes to use to create more national parks worldwide. Santos won for his use of traditional music, through his band Massukos, to raise environmental awareness and promote innovative solutions to managing water and sanitation in Mozambique (such as using composting toilets able to turn human waste into valuable fertilizer). León won for leading a democratic movement of farmers in the Mixteca region of Oaxaca, Mexico, to adapt traditional Mixteca indigenous practices to restore ecosystems (planting, for example, more than one million native trees and building irrigation systems to prevent soil erosion). Ramos won for leading an environmental movement to hold industry responsible for polluting the low-income neighborhood of Cataño (within greater San Juan, Puerto Rico), then lobbying the United States Environmental Protection Agency to use the millions of dollars of **pollution** fines to protect the Las Cucharillas Marsh beside Cataño.

The 2015 winners of the Goldman Prize were Marilyn Baptiste (for campaigning against **mining** in **Canada**), Berta Cáceres (for opposing a megadam in Honduras), Phyllis Omido (for exposing chemical poisoning from a smelter plant in Kenya), Jean Wiener (for advocating for a **marine protected area** in Haiti), Howard Wood (for advocating for a marine protected area in Scotland), and Myint Zaw (for opposing a megadam in Myanmar).

GORE, AL (1948–). Born in Washington, D.C., Albert Arnold "Al" Gore Jr. was the 45th vice president of the **United States**, serving President Bill Clinton from 1993 to 2001. After losing the 2000 presidential election to George W. Bush, Gore returned to his earlier work of raising awareness about global environmental problems. In 2007, Gore was awarded the Nobel Peace Prize for his efforts to publicize and solve the problem of **climate change** (he won along with the Intergovernmental Panel on Climate Change). The documentary film *An Inconvenient Truth* (which won two Academy Awards), the accompanying book (which became a best seller), and a worldwide speaking tour were core to his strategy of raising global consciousness about climate change. In 2013 he published *The Future: Six Drivers of Global Change*.

GREAT BRITAIN. Great Britain's **green party** (the first in Europe) was founded in 1973 under the name PEOPLE, becoming the Ecology Party in 1975 and the Green Party in 1985. In the 1990s, it split into the Green Party of England and Wales, the Scottish Green Party, and the Green Party in Northern Ireland. As of 2015, the Green Party of England and Wales had three members in the European Parliament, one in the House of Lords, and one in the House of Commons.

The Department for Environment, Food and Rural Affairs, known as Defra, is the primary government department responsible for environmental management. The Environment Act was passed in 1995, which established the Environment Agency for England and Wales and the Scottish Environment Protection Agency. A strategy for **sustainable development** for the United Kingdom was launched in 2005. Great Britain is also party to numerous international environmental treaties, including the **Kyoto Protocol**, which it ratified in 2002, reducing emissions largely in line with its commitments.

Great Britain has a long history of environmentalism. Early conservation efforts included a network of nature reserves initiated in 1912 through the Society for the Promotion of Nature Reserves. This organization became the Society for the Promotion of Nature Conservation in 1976, the Royal Society for Nature Conservation in 1981, and the Royal Society of Wildlife Trusts in 2004. The oldest conservation organization, the Open Spaces Society, was founded in 1865. Many others have formed since then. A few examples include the **World Wide Fund for Nature (WWF)**–UK in 1961 (the first national organization in the WWF network), WaterAid in 1981 (an international **nongovernmental organization** focused on water and sanitation), and **Reclaim the Streets** in 1991. Two significant environmental issues in Great Britain are **genetically modified organisms** and pesticides, with strong consumer support for strict regulations on both. In 1997, the Genetic Engineering Network was established. In 2002, coordination of the Pesticide Action Network Europe was transferred to London from **Germany**. *See also* ANTARCTICA; EARTH LIBERATION FRONT (ELF); GUERRILLA GARDENING; WWOOF.

GREAT PACIFIC GARBAGE PATCH. *See* EASTERN GARBAGE PATCH.

GREEN ARCHITECTURE. Green architecture is also called sustainable architecture or green building. Broadly, it aims to use fewer natural resources and energy and build into, rather than on top of, nature. Thus, architects need to see structures as part of an ecosystem rather than as isolated units. Such ideas have a long history but did not begin to gain ground until the 1970s, partly as the **oil** crisis in the early 1970s spurred interest in improving energy efficiency. Publications, such as the journal *Architectural Design*, began to track and promote green designs, such as using traditional or recycled materials and designing ecologically sound buildings. Today, green architects work to improve the efficiency of heating, water circulation, ventilation, and power. Other aspects include sustainable use of resources, long-term planning to allow buildings to adapt to new uses, and green densification. One example of a certification program to promote sustainable architecture is LEED (Leadership in Energy and Environmental Design). *See also* TAIWAN.

GREEN BELT MOVEMENT. Wangari Maathai (1940–2011) founded this women's civil society organization in 1977 to reverse **deforestation** in **Kenya**, which was causing soil erosion and water shortages as well as creating a shortage of wood, a primary source of energy for 90 percent of rural villagers and low-income city residents. The movement relies mostly on women to plant tree seedlings in both rural and urban green belts. It depends on donations to purchase seedlings and compensate workers (who receive a small amount of money for each tree that survives).

So far the Green Belt Movement has planted more than 50 million trees across Africa. This tree planting also provides opportunities for the movement to advocate for good governance, environmental stewardship, peaceful democratic change, and the protection of human rights. "The planting of trees is the planting of ideas," explains Maathai. "By starting with the simple act of planting a tree, we give hope to ourselves and to future generations."

Kenya's Green Belt Movement has inspired similar movements in at least a dozen other countries. Maathai won the 2004 Nobel Peace Prize, an honor enthusiastically applauded by those who believe grassroots environmentalism is an effective way to promote world peace. *See also* ECO-FEMINISM; NONGOVERNMENTAL ORGANIZATIONS (NGOs); REFORESTATION.

GREENHOUSE GASES. Greenhouse gases in the atmosphere, such as carbon dioxide, methane, and nitrous oxides, keep the earth warm by trapping heat. These gases are necessary to sustain life. However, more is not better, as the trapped heat can cause a warming of the planet's surface. Using a vivid metaphor, some compare the process to rolling up a car window on a hot day. Greenhouse gases occur both naturally and as a result of human activity. The amounts of human-induced greenhouse gases have been rising steadily over the last three decades. For example, the global output of carbon dioxide in 2015 was more than 60 percent higher than 1990 levels. Over the last decade, the emphasis of much of global environmentalism has been on shifting toward addressing ways to slow or halt the amount of greenhouse gases drifting into the atmosphere. The most significant international agreement to address the main greenhouse gas—carbon dioxide—is the **Kyoto Protocol to the United Nations Framework Convention on Climate Change**. *See also* AUTOMOBILES; BIOFUELS; CARBON TAX; CITIES

FOR CLIMATE PROTECTION; CLIMATE CHANGE; COAL; DE-FORESTATION; EMISSIONS TRADING; FARMED MEAT; INDONE-SIA; NATURAL GAS; PEAK OIL; SIBERIAN PERMAFROST.

GREEN PARTY. Using the word *green* to describe a political party dates to 1978 when a group of environmentalists listed their candidates under a "Green List" in German local elections. Many analysts, however, see the United Tasmania Group in **Australia** (1972) as the world's first green party and the PEOPLE/Ecology Party in **Great Britain** (1973) as the first green party of Europe (even though initially these parties did not use the word *green* for the name of the party). Definitions and emphases vary across countries and time, but generally green parties tend to support a platform around environmental **sustainability**, social justice, participatory/grassroots democracy, nonviolence, opposition to nuclear technology, and local communities and economies.

The German Green Party was officially formed in 1979–1980; in 1983, with a list of members that included **Petra Kelly**, it became the first new party to enter the German Parliament in 60 years. Over the next decade the German Greens slowly consolidated (with some setbacks, such as the 1990 elections) and by the 1990s were represented in most provincial parliaments. Green parties have also emerged in many other countries and have entered parliament in countries such as Belgium, **Canada**, Italy, **New Zealand**, and **Sweden**. Compared to these places, however, the political victories and influence over public policy of the German Greens put them in a different category. In contrast, the Green Party of the **United States** has had little political success or influence, which is sometimes attributed to the presence of energetic apolitical environmental organizations, the two-party system, the political culture, and lack of a system of proportional representation, as in **Germany**. *See also* BRAZIL; CANADA; FINLAND; FRANCE; RUSSIA; SPAIN.

GREENPEACE. The first recorded use of the name "Greenpeace" was in the *Vancouver Sun* on 15 February 1970, describing plans of the Don't Make a Wave Committee to sail the vessel *Greenpeace* to Amchitka, Alaska, to stop a nuclear weapons test by the **United States**. Before long, it was one of the best-known environmental activist groups, generating worldwide publicity for its campaigns to halt nuclear testing, **whaling**, and **sealing** off the east coast of **Canada**. Groups with the same name began to spring up around the world, and Greenpeace International was officially founded in 1979 from a half dozen loosely connected groups.

Today, Greenpeace has around three million supporters and campaigns in scores of countries. Greenpeace does not accept corporate, government, or political party funds, and fund-raising continues to rely on individual donations. It engages in nonviolent civil disobedience and confrontation, research, treaty negotiation participation, market pressure, clean alternative development, public education, and engagement with legislatures. Four main goals have defined Greenpeace in recent years: protect **biodiversity**; prevent land, air, and water **pollution**; end nuclear threats; and promote peace, disarmament, and nonviolence. Current campaigns include halting **climate change**, protesting oil drilling in the **Arctic**, protecting old-growth forests, ending tropical **deforestation**, stopping the whale hunt, encouraging sustainable trade, and eliminating toxic chemicals. *See also BRENT SPAR*; ECOTERRORISM; GREENWASH; HUNTER, ROBERT "BOB" (1941–2005); NONGOVERNMENTAL ORGANIZATIONS (NGOs); *RAINBOW WARRIOR*.

GREEN REVOLUTION. The phrase *Green Revolution*—reportedly coined by William Gaud (a former director of the **United States** Agency for International Development) in a 1968 speech—describes the changes after World War II to increase agricultural output with high-yield seeds, fertilizers, pesticides, irrigation, and advanced machinery. The result was a substantial increase in the output of crops such as wheat, maize, and rice in developing countries such as **Mexico, India**, and the **Philippines**. Supporters see this as evidence of the power of human ingenuity and technological innovation to overcome food shortages even when populations are growing quickly. For some, too, it confirms the tendency of environmentalism to exaggerate problems, such as the principle, first put forth by **Thomas Malthus** in a 1798 essay, that mass starvation must one day ensue because population, left unchecked, will increase exponentially while food production can only increase arithmetically.

Critics of the Green Revolution counter by pointing to the impact of irrigation systems on declining freshwater supplies; **pollution** from fertilizers and pesticides; high rates of tropical **deforestation**; the growth of industrial estates in the tropics for soy, **palm oil**, and beef; and the loss of **biodiversity** due to the planting of millions of hectares of monocultures. Some environmentalists, too, stress how the shift to industrial agriculture tends to favor plantation owners and multinational corporations while turning subsistence farmers into low-paid laborers with a less nutritional diet and less satisfying work.

GREEN TAXES. *See* CARBON TAX.

GREENWASH. The term *greenwash*, which combines the words *green* and *whitewash*, refers to the efforts of corporations to portray more responsible environmental images when in fact practices remain business as usual. Corporate efforts to improve environmental images took off in the late 1980s and early 1990s with the rise in environmental awareness among governments and consumers. More and more firms began to adopt voluntary green codes of conduct, to pursue more environmentally benign production methods (**eco-efficiency**), and to stress environmental concern in their advertising and public relations. The term *greenwash* gained currency shortly before the 1992 **United Nations Conference on Environment and Development** when **Greenpeace** published *The Greenpeace Book of Greenwash*.

Today, **nongovernmental organization** activists critical of corporate "green talk" are most likely to use this term as a pejorative way of suggesting that firms are trying to fool consumers and "hijack" environmentalism for the pursuit of profits or competitive advantage. The nongovernmental organization CorpWatch, for example, presents "Greenwash Awards" to offending companies. *See also* CORPORATE SOCIAL RESPONSIBILITY (CSR); ECO-BUSINESS; WORLD BUSINESS COUNCIL FOR SUSTAINABLE DEVELOPMENT (WBCSD).

GUERRILLA GARDENING. Guerrilla gardening is a diffuse movement where people illegally plant seeds or seedlings in urban spaces, such as on vacant lots, back alleys, traffic medians, and commercial land. The majority of guerrilla gardeners are in Europe, especially in **Great Britain**. Many portray guerilla gardening as a revolution or a war, taking action in secret and at night, using language such as "troop digs" and "peace talks." The movement, however, calls for nonviolent direct action for inner-city renewal rather than violent uprisings; some members are also now working openly with locals. Most guerrilla gardeners are pursuing both symbolic and practical goals. They target industrialization, commercialization of nature, capitalist food production, unequal land ownership, and the disappearance of public green spaces. They see it as a way to preserve **biodiversity**, engage in hands-on change, and reconnect to nature through personal stewardship of public space. An example of a major event was May Day (1 May) 2000, when the grassroots group **Reclaim the Streets** organized hundreds of guerrilla gardeners to dig up London's Parliament Square and plant flowers and vegetables.

The phrase *guerrilla gardening* goes back to the 1970s, although the movement only gained significant numbers of followers in the last two decades. In many places the practice has a long history, however, with people without land planting food for sustenance on another person's property. Today, guerrilla farming for sustenance still continues in many developing countries.

HAECKEL, ERNST (1834–1919). Holding doctorates in medicine and zoology, the German Ernst Haeckel coined the terms *Darwinism* and *ecology* (along with many other terms). Haeckel was highly influential in his time, his works in support of Darwinism outselling Darwin's original *On the Origin of Species*. He also helped to establish the field of oceanography, consulting on the first noncommercial exploration of the deep sea, the *Challenger* expedition of 1873–1876. Later, Haeckel's scientific reputation would suffer when he admitted falsifying data, but his reputation in the art world remained strong as a result of his work of naturalist illustration, *Art Forms in Nature*. One of his many quotes, "politics is applied biology," would also become notorious in Nazi propaganda.

HARDIN, GARRETT JAMES (1915–2003). Hardin wrote "The **Tragedy of the Commons**" (*Science*, 1968), one of the most cited academic articles of all time. Born in Dallas, Texas, he obtained his Ph.D. in microbiology from Stanford University in 1941. He was professor of human ecology at the University of California, Santa Barbara, until retiring in 1978. He remained active in academic life, however, for another two decades, publishing 27 books and over 350 articles during his career.

A central figure in the field of human ecology, Hardin focused much of his research on human overpopulation and degradation of ecosystems. His publications included the controversial "Living on a Lifeboat" (in *BioScience* in 1974), which uses the metaphor of a lifeboat to argue that for humanity to survive it is the ethical duty of the people in stable and wealthy countries to let the poor of the world fend for themselves; otherwise everyone will drown because of insufficient space (**carrying capacity**) in the lifeboats (wealthy states).

Hardin's views were contentious throughout his long career. In 1997, he wrote an open letter to the American Civil Liberties Union arguing that, because of the ecological cost to society, having children should not be an individual right (even though he had four children). He was also a member of the Hemlock Society for the right to assisted suicide. His spouse, Jane, suffered from Lou Gehrig's disease, and shortly after their 62nd wedding anniversary, they committed suicide together.

HAZARDOUS WASTE. Hazardous waste includes toxic chemicals, infectious waste, and radioactive material. Characteristics include ignitability, corrosivity, reactivity, and toxicity. Developed countries are the biggest producers of hazardous waste. As a global issue, managing hazardous waste took on greater urgency in the 1980s as First World states began exporting increasing amounts to the Third World. Large numbers of **nongovernmental organizations**, including ones such as **Greenpeace**, as well as many states began to call for a ban (or at least clear restrictions) on trade in hazardous waste. An international treaty—called the **Basel Convention**—was negotiated in 1989 and entered into force in 1992 to better control the movement and disposal of hazardous waste across borders. Partly as a result, by the mid-1990s the export of toxic waste to the Third World was declining.

At the beginning of 2016 there were 183 parties to the Basel Convention. Still, trade in hazardous waste remains extensive, with some problems still growing, such as electronic waste, or e-waste. In recent years the amount of e-waste has been increasing at a rate of 3–5 percent per year, almost three times faster than municipal waste (less than one-fifth of e-waste is recycled safely). In many places, e-waste is now equal to roughly the amount of **plastic** packaging waste, as millions of tons pile up as consumers upgrade cell phones, computers, and other electrical goods. Much of the e-waste from North America is being exported to Asia. *See also* NUCLEAR POWER/ ENERGY.

HOLLING, C. S. "BUZZ" (1930–). Crawford Stanley "Buzz" Holling received his Ph.D. from the University of British Columbia in 1957, where he would also research and teach for many years. Currently, he is Emeritus Eminent Scholar and Professor in Ecological Sciences at the University of Florida after a career that saw him contribute to modern predator-prey theory, **panarchy** theory, and the resilience of nonlinear ecological systems. Holling also initiated the Resilience Alliance, a semiformal global group designed to share environmental knowledge and maintain links between theory, empirical reality, and policy institutions. He was the founding editor in chief (until 2001) of the online open-access journal *Conservation Ecology*, now called *Ecology and Society*.

HUNTER, ROBERT "BOB" (1941–2005). Born in **Canada**, journalist Bob Hunter was a founding member of **Greenpeace**, serving as president of the Greenpeace Foundation from 1973 to 1977. *Time* magazine chose him as one of the top-ten "eco-heroes" of the 20th century. A writer with a flair for original prose, Hunter is widely credited with coining the terms *eco-warrior*, *mindbombs*, and *rainbow warriors*.

HYBRID AUTOMOBILES. In 1881, Gustave Trouvé of **France** built a three-wheel electric automobile able to travel at about 12 kilometers per hour. In 1899, an electric vehicle set the world speed record. By 1900, the market for **automobiles** was almost equally divided between steam, electricity, and gasoline; however, 1900 to 1912 became the golden age of electric vehicles, which were quieter and easier to start than automobiles with a hand crank. The first mass production of a hybrid car, combining electric and gasoline propulsion systems, was the "Woods Gasoline-Electric" in 1916.

By the early 1920s, however, electric vehicles virtually disappeared as automobiles powered by a gasoline engine began to take over markets. Interest in electric cars reappeared in the 1960s as air **pollution** worsened in many industrialized cities. General Motors, for example, built an experimental hybrid car in 1969.

Mass production of hybrids, however, did not begin until 1997 with the launch of the Toyota Prius. Ten years later, all of the major automakers were investing in hybrids, with these vehicles now comprising a small but slowly growing share of the global market. Many environmentalists support hybrid and electric automobiles as a small step toward more **sustainable development**, although few would see them as a long-term solution for addressing the global environmental impact of the more than one billion automobiles and commercial vehicles now on the world's roads. *See also* RENEWABLE ENERGY.

HYDROELECTRICITY. *See* RENEWABLE ENERGY.

I

ICLEI: LOCAL GOVERNMENTS FOR SUSTAINABILITY. ICLEI is an international association of local governments (as well as national and regional local government associations) committed to **sustainable development**. Its membership includes more than 1,000 cities, towns, and counties across more than 80 countries. A World Secretariat oversees the ICLEI (located in Bonn, Germany).

The idea to create an international network to coordinate local responses to global environmental management came from a 1989 meeting of 35 local governments from **Canada** and the **United States** to discuss **ozone depletion**. With support from the International Union of Local Authorities and the **United Nations Environment Programme**, ICLEI was founded as the International Council of Local Environmental Initiatives in 1990. The name was changed in 2003 to ICLEI: Local Governments for Sustainability to better reflect current environmental problems. At the same time, the organization shifted its mandate, mission, and charter to focus on **sustainability**. One of its important campaigns is **Cities for Climate Protection**. ICLEI also promotes city **biodiversity**, low-carbon transportation and waste management, water conservation, **renewable energy** systems, green buildings, and the tracking and accounting of greenhouse gases.

ILLEGAL LOGGING. Examples of illegal activities in the forest industry range from timber smuggling, to logging protected species, to logging in nature reserves. Regions with widespread illegal logging include the **Amazon** basin, Central Africa, Southeast Asia, and **Russia**. Estimates of the extent of illegal logging are difficult to confirm; still, in some cases, as in **Indonesia**, most analysts agree that at times it has comprised well over half of total timber production.

Poor villagers are often blamed for illegal logging, but just as often, national or multinational forest companies either pay locals a wage or agree in advance to buy the lumber. Also, in some cases these same firms are bribing government and military officers. Illegal logging can generate income for *some* local people; however, this involves many costs, including lost income from forest products, lost job opportunities, less government revenue, threats to physical security, loss of access to forest resources, forest degradation, corruption, and lack of respect for laws.

The **United Nations Convention on International Trade in Endangered Species of Wild Fauna and Flora** is one of the international legal instruments intended to prevent illegal trade in timber. Another important international legal instrument is the **Convention on Biological Diversity**. Also important is the International Tropical Timber Organization (established in 1986). Voluntary certification under the **Forest Stewardship Council** is yet another mechanism to try to rid the global market of illegal lumber.

The collective goal of these institutions and agreements is to ensure that all of the tropical timber in international trade is from sustainably managed forests; however, critics argue that these global efforts are failing to meet this aim. Some critics go further and see this international system as encasing a vast network of illegal loggers, many working openly, in legitimacy. *See also* DEFORESTATION.

INDEX OF SUSTAINABLE ECONOMIC WELFARE (ISEW). Ecological economists **Herman Daly** and John Cobb created this index for the **United States** in 1989. It builds on Manfred Max-Neef's "threshold hypothesis"—that costs exceed benefits when macroeconomic systems expand beyond a certain threshold. Since then, researchers have applied the Index of Sustainable Economic Welfare (ISEW) to many other countries. It is designed to provide a more comprehensive indicator of economic welfare than standard national accounting systems, such as gross national product (GNP) and gross domestic product (GDP). Although the formula varies slightly, generally it is computed as follows: ISEW = personal consumption weighted by income inequality + domestic labor + nondefense-related public expenditure − defense-related private expenditure − the difference between expenditure on consumer durables and service flow from consumer durables − costs of environmental degradation − depreciation of natural resources + capital adjustments.

Advocates also see ISEW as a way to demonstrate that continued growth is unsustainable. Other related measures include the Genuine Progress Indicator, the Sustainable Net Benefit Index, Gross National Happiness, the Happy Planet Index, and the widely used Human Development Index of the United Nations Development Programme.

INDIA. Mohandas Gandhi was an influential thinker and activist in the emergence of the modern environmental movement in India. In his first book, *Hind Swaraj* (Indian Home Rule), published in 1909, Gandhi rejected industrialization as the way forward for India. This reflected his "back-to-the-land" ethos, offering an alternative: minimizing consumption, reusing materials, and relying on agricultural villages. His legacy inspired many local environmental movements in India, including the Narmada Bachao Andolan (Save the Narmada Movement), led by Medha Patkar with the aim of stopping construction of the Sardar Sarovar Dam, one of the dams in the **Narmada Dam** project; the **Chipko Movement**, begun in 1973 when villagers in a Himalayan village began hugging local hornbeam trees to halt logging; and the Appiko Movement, begun in 1983 in the tradition of the Chipko Movement, with villagers in southern India struggling to save their forests (*appiko* is the local term for hugging).

India has a long history of grassroots and community environmentalism and activism. More formal environmental organizations are also now common. A few examples include the Indian Environmental Society, a **nongovernmental organization** founded in 1972 with a focus on education, policy, and environmental and resource management (together with the Ministry of Environment and Forests); the Indian Environmental Society set up the National Green Corps in 2001 to promote environmental awareness among children; TERI, the Energy and Resources Institute set up in 1974 to advance research and development; the Centre for Science and Environment (CSE), which Anil Agarwal (1947–2002) founded in 1980 to promote knowledge-based activism; and Navdanya, started in 1991 by **Vandana Shiva** to counter corporate control of agricultural and genetic resources (especially by the multinational company Monsanto).

The Indian government's five-year economic plans have increasingly taken environmental concerns into consideration. The Fourth Plan (1969–1970 to 1973–1974) was the first with an **environmental impact assessment**; the Sixth Plan (1980–1985) included an entire chapter on environment and development. This did not, however, prevent India from experiencing one of the world's worst environmental disasters, the 1984 **Bhopal gas leak**, where toxic gas at a pesticide plant run by Union Carbide India (a subsidiary of Union Carbide in the **United States**) killed thousands of people. The Twelfth Plan (2012–2017) continues to integrate environmental planning and management, although sustaining a high rate of economic growth remains a top priority.

Today, the Ministry of Environment, Forest and Climate Change (MoEFCC) is the key bureaucratic actor, having succeeded the National Committee on Environmental Planning (NCEP), which was set up in the 1970s. Important environmental legislation includes the Forest Conservation Act of 1980 (amended by Act 89 of 1988); the Water (Prevention and Control of Pollution) Act of 1974 (amended in 1988); the Air (Prevention and

Control of Pollution) Act of 1981, subsequently amended in 1987; the Environment (Protection) Act of 1986 (amended in 1991); and the National Green Tribunal Act of 2010.

INDONESIA. An archipelago of some 17,000 islands, Indonesia, with the world's largest system of **coral reefs** and sweeping rain forests, is home to 15–20 percent of the world's plant and animal species. The economy depends in large part on natural resources, especially agriculture, forestry, **mining, oil**, and **natural gas**. In recent years it has also been expanding its production of **biofuels**, from both bioethanol (e.g., sugar and cassava) and biodiesel (e.g., crude palm oil). The country has vast hydroelectric potential, but this is largely undeveloped.

Deforestation and air quality are two of its biggest environmental problems. Indonesia is one of the world's largest emitters of **greenhouse gases** (ranking fifth in 2014), in part because of massive and regular forest fires, high rates of deforestation, and rising consumption of fossil fuels. The government has put in place some regulatory programs to combat **pollution**, including the Blue Sky Program, an air-quality program established in 1992. However, in 2002, then president Megawati Sukarnoputri transferred environmental responsibilities to the Office of the State Minister for the Environment and disbanded the Environmental Impact Control Agency, but he did not establish legal enforcement powers and thus weakened regulatory institutions.

Moreover, the currency and economic crash from the 1997–1998 Asian financial crisis was a significant setback for environmentalism, as the government put aside regulations on industry to promote economic recovery, as natural resource and agricultural exports soared to earn foreign exchange, and as enforcement of environmental laws slipped as officers looked for ways to earn a decent living. During the financial crisis, Indonesia was also battling extensive forest fires and severe droughts.

The fall of President Suharto's dictatorship in 1998 did little to improve environmental management. In the case of forestry, Suharto's legacy of unsustainable logging, distribution of timber concessions to reward allies and appease opponents, and dismal enforcement and widespread corruption left the sector in ruins. Deforestation rates remain very high today (averaging 1–2 million hectares a year from 2009 to 2016), with **illegal logging** and timber smuggling rampant as villagers demand a share of the profits and as logging companies exploit broken monitoring and enforcement systems. Some progress has been made to improve forest management, including new laws (that at least on paper are better). Various regional efforts have also been put in place to improve forest management, such as the World Bank's East Asia and Pacific Forest Law Enforcement and Governance Initiative, started in 2001 at the East Asia Ministerial Conference in Bali, and the 2002 ASEAN Agreement on Transboundary Haze Pollution (in force from 2003).

Indonesia also participates in many international environmental initiatives. It ratified the **Kyoto Protocol** in 2004 (signed in 1998) and hosted the 2007 **United Nations Framework Convention on Climate Change** Conference (UNFCCC COP13) in Bali. Initially focused on supporting Clean Development Mechanism (CDM) projects under the Kyoto Protocol, Indonesia shifted to supporting projects to promote Reduced Emissions through Avoided Deforestation and Degradation (REDD) + Conservation (REDD+). These are also supported by **Australia** through its Global Initiative on Forests and Climate and its Kalimantan Forests and Climate Partnership. Indonesia is also part of a planned World Bank pilot project for a Forest Carbon Partnership Facility.

Indonesia's nongovernmental sector has been growing and strengthening since the fall of President Suharto. Founded in 1980, the Indonesian Forum for Environment (WALHI, or the Wahana Lingkungan Hidup Indonesia) did function during Suharto's reign, as a network of **nongovernmental organizations** and community-based associations and also as a member of **Friends of the Earth** International. The fall of Suharto, however, has allowed WALHI more scope to criticize government policies and influence civil society. WALHI joined Friends of the Earth International in 1989 and today comprises over 475 member organizations across Indonesia. *See also* INDONESIAN FOREST FIRES, 1997–1998.

INDONESIAN FOREST FIRES, 1997–1998. Fires on the outer islands of **Indonesia** during 1997–1998 burned as much as 10 million hectares of forests and peat moss, covering Indonesia, Malaysia, and **Singapore** in a smoky haze. Environmentally, this was one of the worst fires in recent history. Over that time, the fires accounted for over one-fifth of the world's carbon dioxide emissions. They did irreparable damage to **biodiversity** and ecological integrity in the region and caused health problems for millions of people. As well, these fires revealed to a global audience the dangers of destructive logging and land clearing in tropical countries. Firms intentionally lit many of the fires to clear land for palm oil plantations (using fires is cheap and fertilizes the soil). Much of the forestland that burned was previously logged and degraded, leaving it dry, littered with debris, and susceptible to so-called controlled fires getting out of control. *See also* DEFORESTATION.

INDUSTRY SELF-REGULATION. Industry self-regulation is an alternative to direct governmental command-and-control regulation. It can involve government on a continuum from voluntary self-regulation to mandatory self-regulation. Two basic strategies tend to shape corporate strategies to self-regulate: the first emphasizes internal regulation, auditing, and control; the second emphasizes obligations arising from a set of corporate values, sometimes called a corporate code of conduct, developed after consulting with stakeholders. Critics argue that self-regulation allows industry to appear to be regulating environmental matters without taking any meaningful action. Moreover, some critics add, it allows some firms a free ride while allowing others too much influence over regulations. Supporters see this as a highly efficient and effective way to bring corporations into environmentalism. An example of industry self-regulation is **Responsible Care** in the chemical industry. *See also* CORPORATE SOCIAL RESPONSIBILITY (CSR); ECO-BUSINESS.

INTERGOVERNMENTAL PANEL ON CLIMATE CHANGE (IPCC). *See* CLIMATE CHANGE.

INTERNATIONAL CENTER FOR ENVIRONMENT AND DEVELOPMENT (ICED). *See* TOLBA, MOSTAFA KAMAL (1922–).

INTERNATIONAL CONVENTION FOR THE REGULATION OF WHALING. Signed in 1946, the Whaling Convention, based on the principles of an earlier agreement in 1937, was set up to manage the **whaling** industry through conservation of stocks. Fifteen countries signed the 1946 convention; as of 2016, there were more than 90 parties to the convention (since its inception, various parties at various times have withdrawn from the convention, such as **Canada** in 1982 and the **Philippines** in 1988, and some parties, such as Norway and **Sweden**, have withdrawn and rejoined).

The convention also set up the International Whaling Commission (IWC), membership of which requires formal acceptance of the 1946 convention. The convention requires the IWC to base decisions on scientific advice. The Schedule to the Convention governs how parties to the convention can conduct whaling. It specifies allowable catches, seasons, and limits (regulating whales by species, size, breeding status, and age) and also establishes sanctuaries and boundaries. The schedule requires, among other things, parties to the convention to report whale catches. *See also* ANTARCTICA.

INTERNATIONAL INSTITUTE FOR ENVIRONMENT AND DEVELOPMENT (IIED). Founded in 1971, the International Institute for Environment and Development, or IIED, is an international policy research institute and **nongovernmental organization** based in London. Its work focuses on sustainable and equitable global development. Earthscan Publishing was originally under its auspices, and it published the *World Resources Report*. It was also an originator of the Participatory Rural Appraisal (PRA) method of development. Starting in 1973, IIED was led by **Barbara Ward**; during her tenure (until her death in 1981), the organization grew rapidly. After her death, IIED turned its smaller office in the **United States** into the **World Resources Institute**, which took over publication of the *World Resources Report*. Today, the organization remains active in promoting **sustainable development**, striving in particular to support vulnerable groups in the development process.

INTERNATIONAL INSTITUTE FOR SUSTAINABLE DEVELOPMENT (IISD). Established in 1990, the International Institute for Sustainable Development, or IISD, is a nonprofit international policy research organization based in Winnipeg, **Canada**, to support **sustainable development** globally. It arose out of Canada's response to the 1987 **World Commission on Environment and Development**. It is funded by the Canadian International Development Agency, the International Development Research Centre, Environment Canada, and the government of Manitoba. It also receives funding from international sources (including **United Nations** agencies) as well as governmental project funding. Today, it focuses in particular on supporting transparent and effective international negotiations. It publishes the *Earth Negotiations Bulletin* (*ENB*), which provides independent reporting on international environmental negotiations (partly relying on Ph.D. candidates, thus supporting new and more-informed research on international environmental law and politics).

INTERNATIONAL ORGANIZATION FOR STANDARDIZATION (ISO) 14000, 14001, AND 26000. The International Organization for Standardization (ISO), with a central secretariat in Geneva, is the world's largest developer of international standards. These include technical ones for manufacturing as well as ones for environmental management. The ISO is a **nongovernmental organization** without legal power to enforce the implementation of standards. Instead, it develops standards through consensus and voluntary participation among member countries (numbering 162 in 2015). Today, it is one of the biggest global voluntary initiatives involving industry, with the **World Trade Organization** officially recognizing ISO standards and labels.

ISO 14000 is a series of voluntary environmental standards. These include ones for auditing, performance, and labeling and, most significantly, the ISO 14001 Environmental Management System (EMS) Standard. This standard is the only one to allow for certification from an external authority. To be eligible, a community or organization must comply with the local environmental laws where they operate. Also, they must implement practices and procedures for a system of environmental management: one with a policy to minimize harm, prevent **pollution**, and continually improve environmental performance.

The ISO has also established ISO 26000 as a voluntary "guidance standard" for social responsibility. It was published in 2010 and is designed to be consistent with the ISO 14001 Environmental Management System Standard. Unlike ISO 14001, the ISO 26000 does not include requirements or certification.

INTERNATIONAL SOCIETY FOR ECOLOGICAL ECONOMICS (ISEE). Founded in 1989, the International Society for Ecological Economics (ISEE) is a nonprofit, **nongovernmental organization** dedicated to advancing the understanding of the field of **ecological economics**. It assists members and societies by publishing a journal and books as well as holding meetings and coordinating common interests. The first president was **Robert Costanza**; Sabine O'Hara of the University of the District of Columbia (**United States**) was the president in 2016–2017.

INTERNATIONAL UNION FOR CONSERVATION OF NATURE (IUCN). Established through the **United Nations Educational, Scientific and Cultural Organization (UNESCO)** in 1948 as the International Union for the Protection of Nature, the organization was renamed the International Union for Conservation of Nature and Natural Resources in 1956. It was referred to as the World Conservation Union from 1990 to 2008 but now goes by the name International Union for Conservation of Nature (IUCN). In response to early criticism of its First World image, the International Union for Conservation of Nature began to conceive conservation in relation to the needs of the developing world, articulating in 1980 a World Conservation Strategy that put it at the forefront of the **sustainable development** movement.

Today, it is the world's largest and oldest conservation network. Headquartered in Gland, Switzerland, IUCN has more than 1,000 staff in scores of offices worldwide. Its members include over 1,000 governmental and **nongovernmental organizations** (including corporations and communities) and more than 10,000 volunteer experts. Its mission is to promote conservation, **biodiversity**, and sustainable resource use through scientific research, education, field projects, political dialogue, and practical solutions for improving development and environmental management. IUCN focuses specifically on promoting **ecosystem management**, environmental education, environmental and socioeconomic policy, environmental law, protected and conservation areas, and species survival. To date, it has assisted over 75 countries to implement national strategies for conservation and biodiversity. *See also* SOUTH AFRICA; WORLD WIDE FUND FOR NATURE/WORLD WILDLIFE FUND (WWF).

INTERNATIONAL WHALING COMMISSION (IWC). *See* WHALING.

INVESTOR NETWORK ON CLIMATE RISK (INCR). *See* COALITION FOR ENVIRONMENTALLY RESPONSIBLE ECONOMIES (CERES).

IRAN. Politics and natural resources are closely linked in Iran, which still has large undeveloped reserves of **oil** and **natural gas**. In 1951, Iran nationalized oil, a decision that strained relations with **Great Britain** and the **United States** and may have contributed to the coup in 1953. The 1980–1988 Iran-Iraq War, following the Islamic/Iranian revolution of 1978, was in part a struggle over control of the oil fields.

The Department of Environment, initially created as the Iranian Wildlife Association in 1956, oversees environmental legislation in Iran. Passed in 1972, the Environment Protection and Enhancement Act was amended in 1992. With support from the United Nations Development Programme, Iran also developed the Strategic Environmental Assessment and Environmental Impact Assessment programs. The Iranian government also manages a significant conservation program, and, as of 2015, the government had designated more than 115 areas as "protected," including 23 **national parks**.

Recent governments have worked to reduce urban air **pollution**, especially in the capital, Tehran. As a first step, in 1983 traffic was restricted in the city center. Subsequent actions have included dedicated bus lanes, converting vehicles to compressed natural gas and liquefied petroleum gas, and conducting a 1995–1997 study for an Integrated Master Plan for Air Pollution Control (funded by **Japan**).

In 1998, the Department of the Environment created the Participation Bureau to provide legal and logistical assistance to **nongovernmental organizations (NGOs)**. Over 460 environmental NGOs, according to the bureau, were created from 1998 to 2003.

ISRAEL. To restrict the hunting of wildlife, Israel passed the Wildlife Protection Law in 1955, which later became the mechanism for meeting commitments under the **Convention on the International Trade in Endangered Species**. Israel passed its first laws for **national parks** and protected areas in 1963, updating these in 1992, 1998, and 2005. The government also created the Nature and Parks Protection Authority in 1998, and, as of 2015, it was responsible for more than 185 national parks and reserves. The Coastline Protection Law went into force in 2004, marking the first national framework to protect the coast.

In 1973, the government established the Environmental Protection Service to consolidate responsibility for environmental management and in 1988 created the Ministry of the Environment, which became the Ministry of Environmental Protection in 2006. A Greening Government initiative was started in the early 2000s to decrease waste in government offices.

In 1990, the **nongovernmental organization** Israel Union for Environmental Defense was founded to strengthen environmental legislation in Israel. Since the mid-2000s, the government has been aiming to increase the waste **recycling** rate. The framework for recycling was established through the 1993 Collection and Disposal of Waste for Recycling Law and developed through further legislation, including the 2001 Bottles and Beverage Container Deposit Law and a 2007 law for recycling vehicle **tires**. In 2007, an explosion at the Makhteshim Agan chemical plant in Ramat Hovav, an industrial zone and **hazardous waste** disposal site, sparked concerns over hazardous materials in the area.

A country with few energy sources, Israel is focused on researching and developing **solar energy**. Water resources are also scarce in Israel, motivating efforts to develop desalination and wastewater recycling technology. Management of fresh water is also linked to peace processes in Israel. In 1992, the Multilateral Working Group on Water Resources was created to advance the Middle East peace process. A 1994 Treaty of Peace with Jordan included water transfer quotas by Israel to Jordan, from the Yarmouk and Jordan Rivers and from the Sea of Galilee. The 1995 Agreement on Cooperation in Environmental Protection and Nature Conservation between Israel and Jordan (Environmental Agreement) also included water-sharing arrangements for the Jordan River.

IUCN. *See* INTERNATIONAL UNION FOR CONSERVATION OF NATURE (IUCN).

IVORY TRADE. The term *ivory* usually refers to elephant tusks but can also refer to the teeth and tusks of other animals (including hippopotamuses, walruses, warthogs, and whales). Ivory has a long history of use for carvings, jewelry, art, trophies, musical instruments, and signature seals. By the 1970s, elephant populations were at risk from overhunting and poaching for ivory, especially in places where hunters were using automatic weapons. In 1976, the **Convention on International Trade in Endangered Species of Wild Fauna and Flora (CITES)** listed Asian elephants in appendix I (species threatened with extinction), which bans international trade for commercial purposes. Throughout the 1980s, the much larger population of African elephants continued to decline, with legal hunters and poachers killing hundreds of thousands for the ivory trade. In 1989, CITES added African elephants to appendix I (effective January 1990). Partly in response to the now full ban on international trade in elephant ivory, trade in hippo ivory increased, and in 1995 CITES listed the common hippopotamus in appendix II (species at risk of extinction unless trade is controlled).

Between 5 and 10 million elephants roamed Africa in the 1930s. By 1977 the numbers were down to about 1.3 million. Twenty years later less than half of these remained. Still, the 10th CITES Conference in 1997 decided to shift the African elephant populations of Botswana, Namibia, and Zimbabwe from appendix I to appendix II—a decision that allowed trade in existing ivory stocks. In 1999, these states exported raw ivory to **Japan**, historically one of the largest importers, "on a onetime basis." In 2000, **South Africa**'s elephant population was also moved to appendix II. This is allowing for more opportunities to raise revenues, which supporters see as essential for protecting the remaining elephant herds. Critics counter, however, that lifting the universal ban on trade in elephant ivory allowed poaching to increase in places such as Zambia, **Kenya**, the Central African Republic, Mozambique, Ghana, and Congo, in part because of the difficulty of verifying the country of origin and legal status of traded ivory. In 2004, the parties to CITES agreed to an action plan to dismantle the unregulated trade in African ivory (at the time, of the approximately 40 countries with populations of wild elephants, only Angola was not a party to CITES; Angola joined in 2013). Today, many African countries—especially in southern Africa—do a better job of protecting savannah elephants. Still, every year poachers continue to kill tens of thousands of African elephants for ivory, especially across central and southern Africa.

J

JAPAN. Rapid economic growth after World War II left Japan heavily polluted by the 1960s. Beginning in the 1960s, partly in response to environmental scandals and citizen pressure, the government began regulating **pollution**. In the 1960s, an environmental office was created as part of the Ministry of Health and Welfare. The government also passed the Basic Law for Environmental Pollution Control in 1967. Its scope was fairly limited, however, only stating a need to aim for environmental protection consistent with maintaining a healthy economy. Also, there were no provisions to enforce the law. In 1970, however, the Japanese Diet held a special session—the Pollution Diet—that saw 14 laws passed to regulate specific forms of pollution. The new laws also made it a crime to spread pollution that damaged human health.

By the early 1970s, affected citizens were bringing pollution cases to the courts, where they won four flagship cases that increased pressure on the government to step in and regulate the environment. Known as the Big Four, these cases included three involving heavy metal poisoning (two about mercury and one about cadmium), while the fourth concerned asthma from sulfur dioxide and nitrogen dioxide. The environmental movement remained largely at the grassroots level, focusing on litigation, local assemblies, and local elections. Initially, business opposed environmental regulations, worrying that they would stall economic development, but it later switched tactics and cooperated with the government to do more to control pollution and promote energy efficiency. From the 1970s onward, the focus of Japanese environmental policy also began to move away from *kogai* (pollution) and toward *kankyo* (the environment).

Progress was dramatic. By the 1980s, Japan had gone from one of the world's most polluted countries to one of the cleanest in the developed world. Since then, Japan has continued to strengthen environmental regulations. In 1993, the Japanese Diet passed the Basic Environmental Law. The 1993 law brought together the environmental efforts of the government under one umbrella; previously these were dispersed throughout various government agencies. As required by the 1993 Environmental Law, in 1994, Japan started drafting the Basic Environmental Plan. In 2001, Japan's Environment Agency (created in 1971) became the Ministry of Environment. Japan has also hosted significant international environmental meetings, including the **climate change** negotiations for the **Kyoto Protocol** in 1997, the Third World Water Forum in Kyoto in 2003, and the adoption of the **Minamata Convention on Mercury** in 2013.

Meanwhile, since the late 1980s, the number of environmental **nongovernmental organizations (NGOs)** has been growing. A **Greenpeace** office was founded in 1989, and some older NGOs have been strengthening, such as the **World Wide Fund for Nature (WWF)**–Japan, founded in 1971, and **Friends of the Earth**, Japan, founded in 1980. The Japanese government has also become more willing to invite NGOs to participate in consultations and on decision-making bodies. Legislative changes, such as the 1998 Non-profit Organization Law, have also made it easier for NGOs to operate. Compared to the groups in Europe, **Australia**, and North America, however, Japan's NGOs still have smaller budgets, societal participation, and influence. Civil society input into environmentalism in Japan still tends to come more from grassroots citizen protests over particular environmental threats or problems, a tradition that goes back to at least the Meiji era (1868–1912) with protests over pollution from **mining**.

Over the past two decades Japan has been one of the world's environmental leaders for domestic **recycling**, waste disposal, and management of **greenhouse gases**. At the same time, however, on some issues—notably **whaling**, tropical **deforestation**, consumption of marine products, and trade in **endangered species**—Japan is still highly criticized by environmental groups such as Greenpeace. Japan has many environmental citizen groups, but compared to ones in Europe or North America, these rely less on formal structure and fund-raising campaigns and more on community participation. *See also* MINAMATA DISEASE.

JEVONS PARADOX. *See* REBOUND EFFECT.

K

KAZAKHSTAN. *See* ARAL SEA.

KELLY, PETRA (1947–1992). Petra Kelly was one of the founders of the West German Green Party in 1979, a party she described as a coalition of grassroots groups espousing nonviolent resistance to war and ecological destruction. She served as party chairperson from 1980 to 1982. In 1982, Kelly was awarded the Right Livelihood Award (sometimes called the Alternative Nobel Prize). The next year she was elected to the German Parliament, one of 28 Green members of Parliament elected that year. An author and prolific speaker, Kelly became an international figure over the next decade, working to integrate the concerns of ecology, peace, feminism, and human rights. She also helped to raise the worldwide profile of the German Green Party, with other green parties emulating its successful strategies and philosophies. In 1992, she was shot and killed in unclear circumstances. *See also* GERMANY; GREEN PARTY; SPAIN.

KENYA. Kenya puts considerable emphasis on managing **biodiversity**. This includes establishing **national parks**; most wildlife, however, live outside of these parks, so Kenyans have also been experimenting with promoting **ecotourism** and private initiatives to protect biodiversity. Efforts include reintroducing some species; for example, in 2001, the Kenya Wildlife Service relocated 56 elephants to the Meru National Park.

Pollution of freshwater from domestic, agricultural, and industrial sources is one of Kenya's most significant problems. Mombasa's sewer system, for example, is inadequate—with sludge from septic tanks and latrines flowing into local waterways. Major lakes such as Nakuru and Bogoria suffer from heavy metal poisoning (from industrial and agricultural runoff and sewage). Part of Lake Victoria in Kenyan territory—a crucial water resource for East Africa—is also polluted and suffers from invasive alien species.

The Kenyan Water Act of 2002 governs water management. Kenya also has a Water Resources Management Authority and a National Water Resource Management Strategy. The latest water strategy covers the period from 2012 to 2017 and among other aspects focuses on enhancing data collection and assessment and improving fresh-water access and management. In the past, to collect more water, the National Museums of Kenya introduced large-scale rainwater harvesting, even in the capital, Nairobi. In addition to domestic policies, Kenya, along with Uganda and Tanzania, also established the Lake Victoria Environmental Management Project (LVEMP) in 1995 to encourage **sustainable development** of the lake basin.

Kenya has also enacted the Environmental Management and Coordination Act in 1999, amended and updated over the years, including in 2015. This act sets guidelines for **environmental impact assessments** (EIAs), including provisions to take traditional knowledge into account and assess the impact of projects on local communities and cultures.

Kenya has been influential in developing global environmentalism. It was among the first countries to agree to "debt-for-nature" swaps in the late 1980s. The idea is to exchange canceled external debt for more conservation programs (thus reducing debt, which in turn reduces pressure to export natural resources to earn the foreign exchange necessary to service foreign debts). Kenya's **Green Belt Movement** and **Wangari Maathai** have also been at the forefront of innovative ideas for advancing environmentalism in the Third World.

KEYSTONE XL PIPELINE SYSTEM. *See* UNITED STATES.

KLEIN, NAOMI (1970–). Born in Montreal, Naomi Klein is **Canada**'s best-known anticapitalist writer and public intellectual. Her breakthrough book *No Logo* was published in 1999; a sweeping critique of the labor and environmental abuses of multinational corporations with global brands, it went on to sell more than a million copies. Her two other most influential books are *The Shock Doctrine* (2007), a frontal attack on the economics of neoliberalism, and *This Changes Everything* (2014), a book calling for the overthrow of capitalism to resolve the crisis of climate change. Her books have been translated into more than 30 languages. Over the past few years she has been focusing on raising global awareness of the threat of climate change for the poor and disenfranchised, including the release of a documentary of *This Changes Everything* in 2015. *See also* ADBUSTERS.

KOREA, NORTH. The government of the Democratic People's Republic of Korea (DPRK, or North Korea) has taken formal measures to protect the environment. For example, Cabinet Decisions 57 and 86 in 1972 and the Law on the Forest of DPR Korea of 1992 (revised in 1999) were adopted to restore degraded forests. The government has proclaimed 2 March as Tree Planting Day and developed the Ten-Year Plan for Afforestation/Reforestation. Other measures include the Law of the Land of 1977, the main legal framework for land management and **sustainable development** of land resources. The government also has laws to protect **biodiversity**, including the 1998 National Biodiversity Strategy and Action Plan of the DPR Korea as well as national public awareness campaigns to help implement environmental laws (such as the Land Development Campaign in the spring and autumn of 1996).

Another example of a formal government measure is the 1997 Law on Water Resource (amended in 1999) to protect water resources and promote sustainable development. The government also began a project in 2000 to build a canal between Gaecho and Taesong Lakes to help address water shortages for irrigation.

These formal government measures only reveal a small part of the story of environmentalism in North Korea. Grassroots environmentalism has little scope or influence in a country with a totalitarian-communist government poised for war. Predictably, environmental conditions are deteriorating in North Korea. The country suffers from increasingly severe droughts and shortages of fresh and clean water (industrialization has left many water sources polluted and depleted).

Air quality continues to worsen as the country relies on **coal** for its energy. Remaining forests and biodiversity are also under pressure from **deforestation**, forest fires, **logging**, insect damage, and encroaching farmland. Soil erosion is also getting worse, partly because of deforestation and partly because so much mountainous terrain has been converted into agricultural "land."

KOREA, SOUTH. The Japanese occupation (1910–1945) and the Korean War (1950–1953) devastated much of the natural environment in South Korea (officially, the Republic of Korea). Beginning in the 1960s, a central goal of government policy became rapid industrialization—with social and environmental concerns generally subordinate. Air quality in all major cities began to deteriorate; increasing numbers of people began to suffer chronic respiratory diseases. **Acid rain** became common. In 2003, the capital city of Seoul, for example, had the worst air quality among countries in the Organisation for Economic Co-operation and Development (OECD). Another serious problem by this time was water **pollution**, with industrial processes contaminating freshwater and maritime areas. More progress has been made on other environmental issues. For example, in 1985, South Koreans produced on average 2.2 kilograms of waste per day, compared to 1.0 kilogram in **Japan** and 0.9 kilogram in **Great Britain**. Ten years later, South Korea has halved per capita household waste.

South Korea's first environmental law was the 1961 New Forest Law to promote **reforestation**. The government soon passed the Anti-Public-Nuisance Control Law of 1963 (outlining goals for pollution controls). It did not create any administration or mechanisms to enforce these goals, however. A more far-reaching effort to improve environmental management began with the establishment of the Pollution Control Division within the Bureau of Sanitation of the Ministry of Health and Social Affairs in 1973. The first comprehensive legislation was the 1977 Environmental Preservation Act. The same year the government also passed the Marine Pollution Preservation Act. The administrative structure remained weak, but it would gradually strengthen over the next few decades.

To some extent these changes in the 1970s arose out of citizen activism, beginning with the 1966 anti–air pollution protests in Pusan around an **oil-fired power station**. Local residents were demanding financial compensation for damage to their properties and health rather than protesting about specific environmental concerns. Such activism increased in the 1970s, although it continued to focus on antipollution demonstrations, which tended to be local and temporary and was never able to organize effectively on a national level. The New Constitution of 1980 enshrined environmental protection as a right of citizens (Article 35). In 1986, the government passed the Solid Waste Management Act. During the 1980s, the government did take some concrete steps to improve environmental management, though it generally resisted implementing controls on industry or development. In 1990, the government created a Ministry of Environment (MoE).

Over the next few years major revisions were made to environmental law in South Korea, such as the Natural Environment Preservation Act and the Resource Recycling Act of 1992. Enforcement has been hampered, however, in part because Korean law does not permit litigation by citizens as a means of dispute resolution. Nevertheless, government support for environmental management has been slowly strengthening over the last four decades. Expenditures for pollution abatement and control, for example, have grown, both in total amount and as a percentage of gross domestic product. To address air pollution in Seoul, an "air-quality improvement plan" was put in place from 2005 to 2015 to improve vehicle, factory, and emission standards; the plan was enhanced and extended for the period 2015–2024.

KYOTO PROTOCOL TO THE UNITED NATIONS FRAMEWORK CONVENTION ON CLIMATE CHANGE. The Kyoto Protocol is the main legally binding international agreement to address **climate change**. Signatories settled on this protocol at the third session of the Conference of the Parties (COP3) of the **United Nations Framework Convention on Climate Change** (UNFCCC), held in Kyoto, **Japan**, in December 1997. (The nonbinding UNFCCC was signed at the **United Nations Conference on**

Environment and Development in 1992.) The rules did not allow the Kyoto Protocol to enter into force until at least 55 parties—accounting for at least 55 percent of the 1990 carbon dioxide emissions of signatories in Annex I (mostly developed countries)—had ratified it. This made it difficult for the agreement to go into force without the **United States**, which accounted for over 36 percent of these emissions. Nevertheless, the Kyoto Protocol did end up going into force in 2005 without support from the United States (which withdrew in 2001) after **Russia**, which accounted for 17.4 percent of 1990 emissions, ratified and pushed the total above 55 percent. By 2008 there were over 160 parties to the protocol, accounting for over 60 percent of the total emissions for Annex I countries.

The Kyoto Protocol required Annex I countries (which includes Russia) to reduce emissions of six **greenhouse gases**, in aggregate, by 5.2 percent below 1990 levels for the 2008–2012 commitment period. Specific targets varied. The European Union's target was 8 percent below 1990 levels, the U.S. target was 7 percent, and the target for Japan and **Canada** was 6 percent. Russia agreed to stabilize emissions at 1990 levels. **Australia**, however, was allowed to increase emissions by 8 percent above 1990 levels. Some developing countries, such as **India** and **China**, also agreed to voluntary, nonbinding reduction targets. In 2012 a second commitment period (ending in 2020) was agreed upon in Doha, Qatar (known as the Doha Amendment), but this is not yet in force under international law (although 55 states had ratified the amendment as of December 2015).

There were 192 parties to the Kyoto Protocol in 2016. States supporting the Kyoto Protocol, notably those in the European Union and Japan, see it as a significant step toward reducing greenhouse gases. More critical states, notably the United States under President George W. Bush from 2001 to 2009, have seen it as an ineffective instrument to deal with climate change, with the potential to damage economies (and thus lower governmental capacity to manage environmental affairs). In the end the United States was one of only a handful of countries to never ratify the Kyoto Protocol. Canada withdrew from the protocol in 2011 (effective as of 2012), although by then the Conservative government of Stephen Harper (2006–2015) was already ignoring its commitments under the amendment. Critics of the Kyoto Protocol have tended to call for a market approach, relying on better technologies rather than mandatory (and arbitrary) targets to reduce greenhouse gases. On the other hand, many **nongovernmental organizations (NGOs)** have been highly critical of relying on markets and technologies, seeing this approach as business as usual with a twist of environmentalism. Many NGOs have also been critical of the Kyoto Protocol, an agreement that many have argued was premised on insufficient emissions targets and inadequate penalties for noncompliance.

As temperatures rise and climate change intensifies, environmentalists (e.g., going into the 2015 Conference of the Parties of the United Nations Framework Convention on Climate Change in Paris, **France**) have been lobbying to build on the Kyoto Protocol to put in place an international treaty with more ambitious and binding commitments to reduce greenhouse gas emissions.

KYRGYZSTAN. *See* ARAL SEA.

Waste drums on a farm in Ontario, Canada, 2005.

Paddling from a canoe in Northern Ontario, 2003.

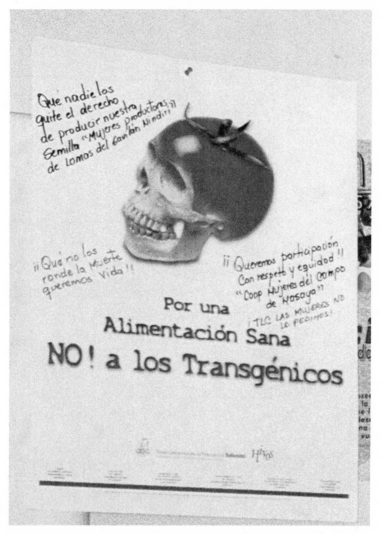

Poster to protest genetically modified maize at a women's cooperative, Nicaragua, 2005.

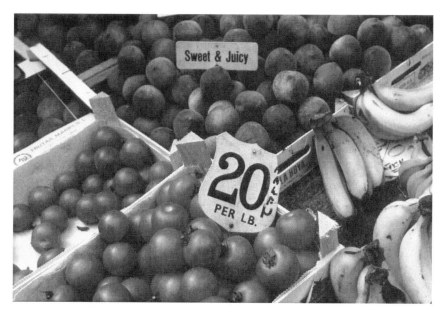

Fresh fruit and vegetable stand in London, England, 1991.

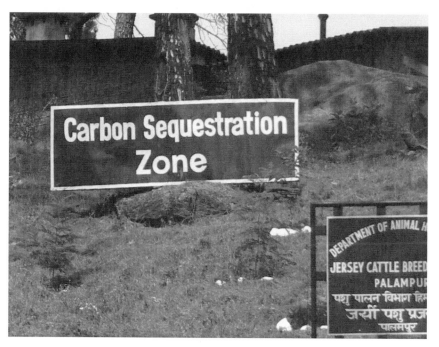

Himalayan town of Palampur, India, advertises a carbon sequestration zone, 2007.

A goat forages in plastic garbage in Conakry, Guinea, 1990.

Leaded gasoline for sale in one-liter vodka bottles, Guinea, 1990.

Beverage booth in Accra, Ghana, 2005.

A fossil-free rickshaw ride in Delhi, India, 2006.

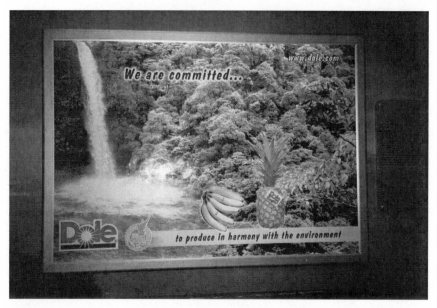

Advertisement for corporate social responsibility at the San José Airport, Costa Rica, 2005.

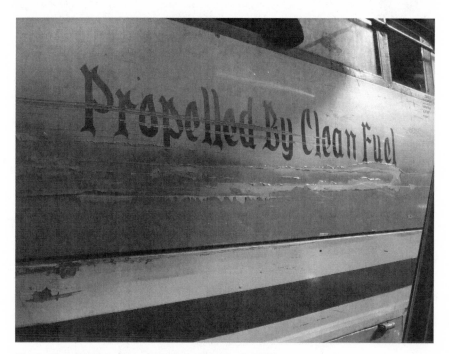

Bus in New Delhi, India, advertises clean fuel, 2006.

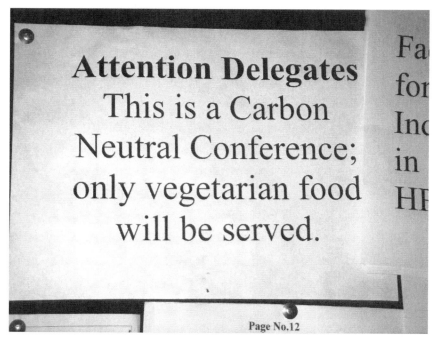

Attention Delegates
This is a Carbon
Neutral Conference;
only vegetarian food
will be served.

Fa
for
Inc
in
HF

Page No.12

Carbon-neutral climate-change conference in Palampur, India, 2007.

Clear-cut forest in Washington state near Mount Rainier, 2008.

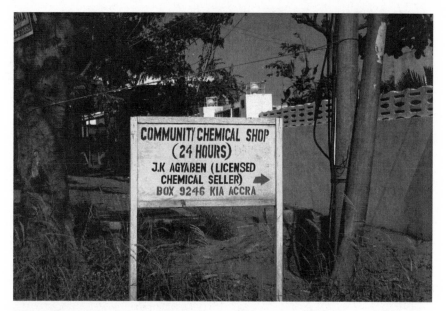

Community chemical shop sign in Accra, Ghana, 2005.

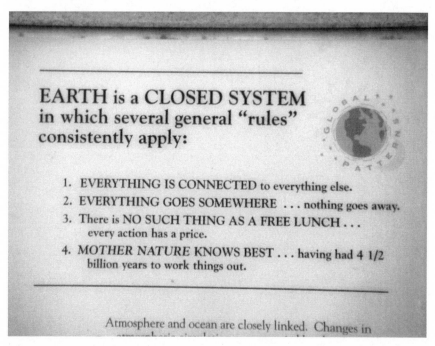

EARTH is a CLOSED SYSTEM in which several general "rules" consistently apply:

1. EVERYTHING IS CONNECTED to everything else.
2. EVERYTHING GOES SOMEWHERE ... nothing goes away.
3. There is NO SUCH THING AS A FREE LUNCH ... every action has a price.
4. MOTHER NATURE KNOWS BEST ... having had 4 1/2 billion years to work things out.

Atmosphere and ocean are closely linked. Changes in

Educational sign for ecological economics at Haystack Rock, Oregon coast, 2008.

Fair-trade coffee cooperative in Nicaragua, 2005.

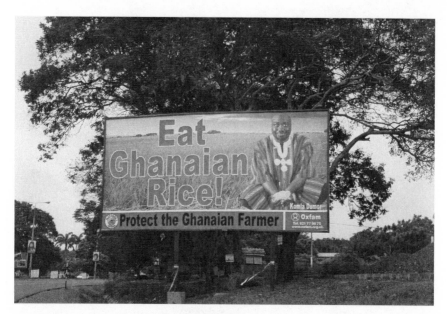

Advertising locally grown rice in Ghana, 2005.

Helltox insecticide in Guinea (probably containing DDT), 1989.

Litter and waste on Lake Nicaragua, Nicaragua, 2005.

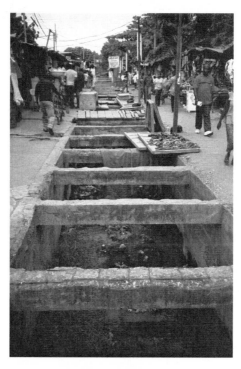

Open sewer at a market in Accra, Ghana, 2005.

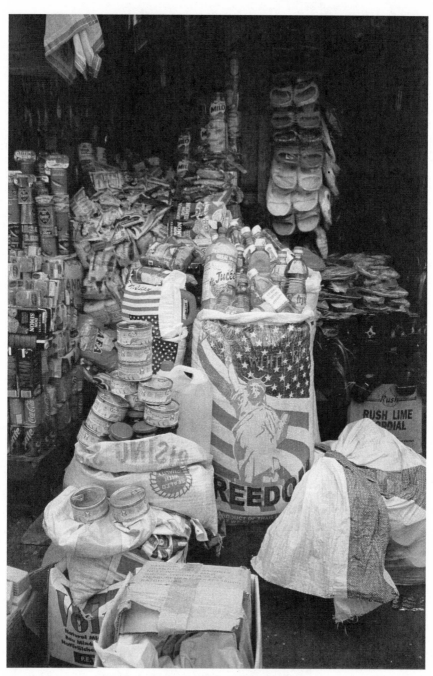

Market stand in Accra, Ghana, selling American rice, 2005.

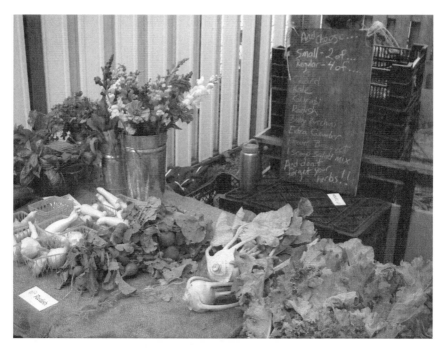

Local organic food in Ontario, Canada, 2008.

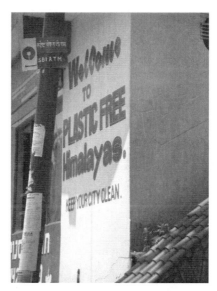

Sign reminding consumers of the ban on plastic shopping bags, on a mountain road near Dharamsala in Himachal Pradesh, India, 2007.

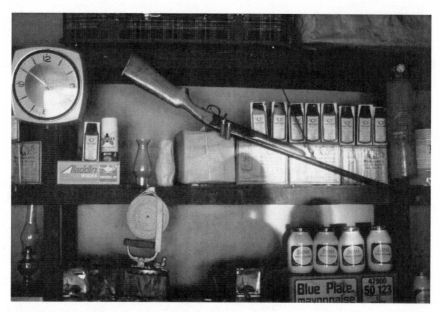

Rural store display in Guinea, 1990.

Factory emissions on a smoggy day near Hamilton, Ontario, Canada, 2006.

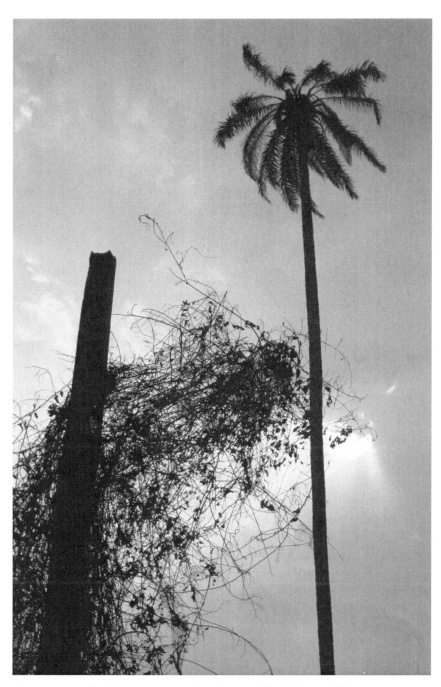

Tree burning after a fire clears a field in Guinea, West Africa, 1990.

Woman in Guinea displaying market goods, 1990.

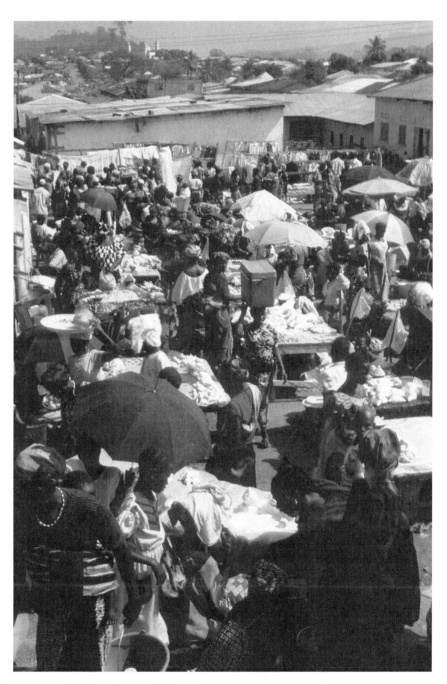

West African market in Guinea, 1990.

Bicycle taxis in Paris, France, 2008.

Clearing a farming field with fire in Guinea, 1990.

Car-free Mackinac Island, Michigan, 2007.

Recycle box for 3-D movie glasses, 2016.

Power lines from Bruce Nuclear Plant in Ontario, Canada, 2015.

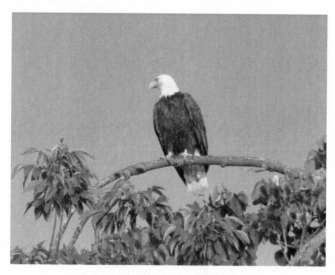

The eagles return to Bruce Peninsula, Ontario, Canada, 2014.

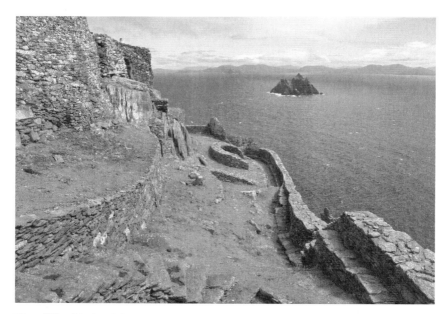

The cliffs of Ireland, 2015.

Farm enclosures in Ireland, 2015.

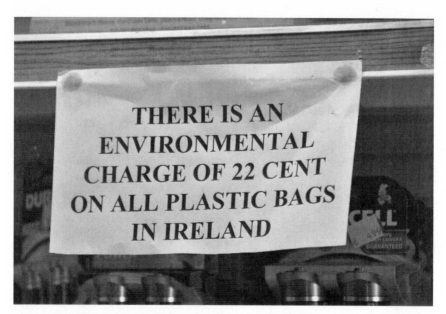

Plastic bag fee in Portmagee, Ireland, 2015.

Banana cultivation in Barbados, 2012.

Oil refinery in Come by Chance, Newfoundland, Canada, 2012.

Glacial retreat in the French Alps, 2013.

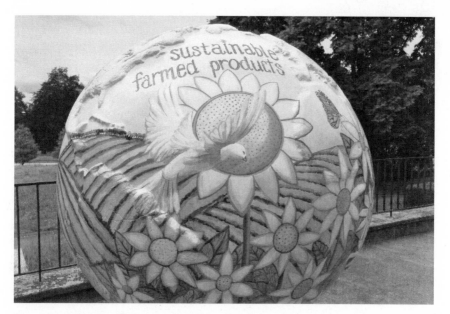

Promoting sustainable farmed products in Geneva, Switzerland, 2013.

L

LAKE BAIKAL. *See* SIBERIA.

LEADED GASOLINE. In 1921, a team of scientists led by **Thomas Midgley Jr.** discovered the value of putting tetraethyl lead into gasoline to reduce engine knock (or pinging) and thus increase the power and efficiency of the combustion engine in **automobiles.** A few scientists, such as Yandell Henderson at Yale University, called for precaution to prevail over profits, arguing that it was foolhardy to put a known poison into an increasingly common product. Still, after a brief sales pause from 1925 to 1926 to perform some rather perfunctory tests on the effects of leaded exhaust on laboratory animals, the leaded gasoline industry grew quickly. By the 1930s, 90 percent of the gasoline in the **United States** was leaded; by then, overseas markets were also developing.

Over the following decades few would question the safety of leaded gasoline until geochemist Clair Patterson (famous for dating the earth at 4.55 billion years old) published findings showing unnaturally high levels of lead in humans in the northern hemisphere. The cause, he argued, was primarily leaded gasoline, and he called for a quick phaseout. The subsequent phaseout was much slower than he was hoping, but, after many delays and setbacks, by the late 1980s the environmental movement in the United States had managed to phase out leaded gasoline. (This phaseout was spurred along by a growing body of scientific evidence of the harmful health effects, especially for children, of low but regular dosages of lead; it was aided as well by the U.S. government's decision, in an effort to improve air quality, to require all new cars sold after 1975 to have catalytic converters, which require unleaded gasoline to function properly.)

The phaseout of leaded gasoline in the United States did not include a phaseout of lead additive exports or overseas leaded gasoline facilities. Consumption of leaded gasoline in fact went up in many countries (especially in the Third World) as the U.S. lead additive industry searched for ways to regain lost revenue from declining sales in the United States (sales were also down in many other wealthy countries, such as **Japan** and **Canada**). By the end of the 1990s, for example, almost all of the gasoline in **sub-Saharan Africa** was still leaded. Following the 2002 **World Summit on Sustainable Development**, however, significant progress was made as a global environmental partnership involving the **United Nations Environment Programme**, the World Bank, aid institutions, governments, corporations, **nongovernmental organizations**, and local communities was created to accelerate change, so by 2006 sub-Saharan Africa became the first developing region to phase out leaded gasoline.

LEED (LEADERSHIP IN ENERGY AND ENVIRONMENTAL DESIGN). *See* GREEN ARCHITECTURE.

LEÓN SANTOS, JESÚS. *See* GOLDMAN ENVIRONMENTAL PRIZE.

LEOPOLD, ALDO (1887–1948). Born in Iowa, Aldo Leopold graduated from the forestry school at Yale University in 1909 and then joined the U.S. Forest Service in Arizona and New Mexico. Many consider Leopold the father of wildlife management in the **United States** (as well as a prominent advocate of environmental ethics). He influenced, for example, the 1924 decision to manage the Gila National Forest in New Mexico as a wilderness area (the first time the designation was made). In 1928, Leopold left the Forest Service to become an independent consultant; in 1933, he then joined the faculty at the University of Wisconsin–Madison as a chaired professor of game management in the Department of Agricultural Economics. That same year he published the first textbook on wildlife management. In 1935, Leopold helped found the **Wilderness Society** in the United States. That year he also bought a run-down farm, planted trees, and restored the prairie land; he then documented the changes in flora and fauna for a second book manuscript. He died just days after hearing that this manuscript was accepted for publication. The book, *A Sand County Almanac*, went on to sell millions of copies and shaped the emergence of the environmental movement in the 1950s and 1960s.

THE LIMITS TO GROWTH. The best-selling 1972 book *The Limits to Growth* brought worldwide attention to the idea that economic growth had limits because resources—and the earth itself—were finite. Authored by **Donella Meadows**, Dennis Meadows, Jørgen Randers, and William W. Behrens III, this book has sold 20–30 million copies. Using computerized modeling, the authors simulate future trends in industrialization, human population growth, natural resource depletion, malnutrition, and **pollution**. Based on these trends, the authors predicted that the earth's limits would be reached within 100 years. *Limits to Growth: The 30-Year Update* was published in 2004.

LIVING PLANET INDEX. Originally a collaborative project of the **United Nations Environment Programme**'s World Conservation Monitoring Centre and the **World Wide Fund for Nature/World Wildlife Fund (WWF)**, the Living Planet Index is now run by the WWF. It is a statistical measure of trends in global **biodiversity**, tracking thousands of vertebrate species (amphibians, birds, fish, mammals, and reptiles). It generates separate indices for freshwater, marine, and terrestrial species and then averages these into an aggregate index. The assumption is that even though vertebrates comprise just a fraction of species, trends here are telling for overall biodiversity. The index suggests that the biodiversity of natural ecosystems is crashing at unprecedented rates, with a decline from 1970 to 2010 of over 50 percent of the vertebrate populations studied. For many environmental **nongovernmental organizations**, measures such as this one are essential to counter the tendency of governments to measure (and thus understand) everything in economic terms—relying, for example, on measures such as gross domestic product.

LOMBORG, BJØRN (1965–). Bjørn Lomborg, as an associate professor in the Department of Political Science at the University of Aarhus, Denmark, rocketed to infamy among environmentalists with the 2001 English translation of his book *The Skeptical Environmentalist*. This book—with over 500 pages, reams of statistics, and nearly 3,000 footnotes—was hailed by the popular media as a groundbreaking refutation of environmentalism. It became a worldwide best seller, and Lomborg became a hero for those skeptical about the supposed "environmental crises" all around them. The statistical evidence, according to Lomborg, was irrefutable: the world was not running out of natural resources or energy, and the so-called environmental problems were more about media hype and nongovernmental antics than the "real state of the world."

Since 2001, Lomborg's career has been turbulent. Many ecologists roundly criticized *The Skeptical Environmentalist*, including in the well-known magazine *Scientific American*. As a worldwide backlash gained momentum, the Danish Committees on Scientific Dishonesty, under the Danish Ministry of Research and Information Technology, investigated and found that his book was "objectively dishonest" and "clearly contrary to the standards of good scientific practice" for knowingly selecting biased data. The ruling, however, also declared that because Lomborg was not a "scientist," the book was not a case of "scientific dishonesty." Lomborg filed a complaint about the handling of his case. The Ministry of Research determined that the Committees on Scientific Dishonesty did not properly document its findings and that the ruling was "dissatisfactory" and "emotional." Despite numerous critics, Lomborg continues to receive many honors and recognition. In 2004, *Time* magazine listed him as one of the world's 100 most influential people. In 2005, the magazines *Foreign Policy* and *Prospect* ranked him as the 14th most influential active public intellectual. In 2015 the government of **Australia** awarded him millions of dollars in funding to start a new research and policy center at the University of Western Australia, but after a public outcry the university and government withdrew their offers. *See also* CLIMATE CHANGE.

LONDON CONVENTION. *See* CONVENTION ON THE PREVENTION OF MARINE POLLUTION BY DUMPING OF WASTES AND OTHER MATTER.

LOVE CANAL. Love Canal, in Niagara Falls in the U.S. state of New York, was the site of one of the worst **hazardous waste** disasters of the 1970s. William T. Love began digging this canal at the beginning of the 20th century to install a hydroelectric facility between the upper and lower Niagara River. His project collapsed in 1910, however, and in the 1920s the now mile-long ditch became a municipal and chemical dumpsite. A few decades later, Hooker Chemical and Plastics Corporation (later Occidental Petroleum) bought the property, and by 1952, the firm had dumped over 20,000 tons of toxic wastes into the ditch (including at least 200 different chemicals, many carcinogenic).

In 1953, Hooker Chemical sold the land to the Niagara Falls Education Board for US$1. Shortly afterward the city of Niagara Falls began to build an elementary school on top of the site, and construction of a neighborhood began as well. By the 1970s, chemicals were seeping into yards and basements, with fumes and puddles of chemicals forming during heavy rains. Evidence began to mount of serious environmental and health harms, linking the site to birth defects, poisonings, and cancers. In 1978, faced with a grassroots movement generating nationwide publicity, the U.S. government evacuated homeowners closest to the site. Two years later, more families were relocated. That same year, the U.S. Congress created a superfund to make polluters more responsible for (and help finance) the cleanup of hazardous waste sites. Today, Love Canal is widely considered a seminal event for the **environmental justice** movement in the **United States**. *See also* ECO-FEMINISM.

LOVELOCK, JAMES (1919–). James Ephraim Lovelock is best known for developing the **Gaia Hypothesis**, which assumes that the earth is a living organism. Trained in chemistry, medicine, and biophysics, he has spent much of his working career as an independent scientist, visiting and teaching at various universities. In 1974, Lovelock was elected a fellow of **Great Britain**'s Royal Society. In 1990, he received the order of Commander of the Order of the British Empire. His career is an example of the influence of independent scientists and writers, who, especially after the 1960s, have been using the power of best-selling books and lecture tours to challenge the direction of global environmentalism with provocative ideas outside the mainstream of academia. In 2009 he published *The Vanishing Face of Gaia: The Final Warning*.

LOVINS, AMORY B. (1947–). Born in Washington, D.C., Amory Lovins is a consultant and experimental physicist with degrees from Harvard and Oxford Universities. In 2009, *Time* magazine ranked him among the world's 100 most influential thinkers for his work promoting the importance of economic efficiency and technology for improving environmental conditions. He is currently the chairman and chief scientist of the Rocky Mountain Institute, an entrepreneurial nonprofit organization that he founded in 1982 with his former wife, L. Hunter Lovins. The Rocky Mountain Institute focuses on advancing the efficiency and resource productivity of sectors such as **automobiles**, consumer goods retailing, construction, electricity, and water.

Lovins's many authored and coauthored books include *Winning the Oil Endgame: Innovation for Profits, Jobs, and Security* (2004); *The Natural Advantage of Nations: Business Opportunities, Innovation and Governance in the 21st Century* (2005); *Small Is Profitable: The Hidden Economic Benefits of Making Electrical Resources the Right Size* (2002); *Natural Capitalism: The Next Industrial Revolution* (2010, 10th anniversary edition); and *Reinventing Fire: Bold Business Solutions for the New Energy Era* (2011). He has received many awards and prizes, including a Right Livelihood Award (also called the Alternative Nobel Prize) in 1983, the Onassis Foundation's first DELPHI prize (one of the world's premier environmental awards) in 1989, and *Time* magazine's Heroes for the Planet Award in 2000.

M

MAATHAI, WANGARI MUTA (1940–2011). Born in **Kenya**, Wangari Maathai trained in biology and veterinary science before becoming a professor at the University of Nairobi in the 1970s. During her time as chair of the National Council of Women of Kenya (1981–1987), Maathai founded the **Green Belt Movement** to plant trees as a way to protect the environment, promote grassroots activism, and improve the lives of women. By the mid-1990s, this movement had already planted over 20 million trees; the number of trees planted across Africa was over 50 million by 2016. In 2004, Maathai was awarded the Nobel Peace Prize for her "contribution to **sustainable development**, democracy and peace," the first time the Norwegian Nobel Committee recognized local environmental activism as a means of enhancing world peace. Today, Maathai and the Green Belt Movement continue to inspire other grassroots environmental movements throughout the developing world. *See also* REFORESTATION.

MADRID PROTOCOL. *See* ANTARCTICA.

MALTHUS, THOMAS ROBERT (1766–1834). Born just south of London near Dorking, Surrey, Thomas Malthus studied mathematics at Cambridge University before being ordained as an Anglican parson. In 1805, he became a professor of political economy and history at the East India Company College in Hertfordshire (about 20 miles from central London). Today, Malthus's ideas continue to influence environmentalism through *An Essay on the Principle of Population*. First published in 1798, further editions would follow, with the sixth and final one appearing in 1826. This essay put forth a seemingly inevitable principle: Left unchecked, population increases exponentially. At the same time, food production can only increase arithmetically. Thus, without controls, the laws of math mean that famine will inevitably cause a dieback of an exploding human population. Today, environmentalists such as **Paul Ehrlich** who accept this logic are commonly called Malthusians or neo-Malthusians. *See also* GREEN REVOLUTION.

MALTHUSIANS. *See* MALTHUS, THOMAS ROBERT (1766–1834).

MANSER, BRUNO (1954–2000). Born in 1954 in Basel, Switzerland, Manser worked in the Swiss Alps before moving to Sarawak, Malaysia, in 1984. For the next six years he traveled with the nomadic Penan people, helping to organize protests against logging. In 1990, after years of evading authorities in Sarawak, who had declared him an enemy of the state, Manser returned to Europe, where he continued to publicize the plight of the Penan and the consequences of tropical logging for indigenous peoples. In 1992, he published the book *Voices from the Rainforest*. Manser also helped to found a nonprofit organization in Switzerland—Bruno Manser Fonds—which still advocates today for the Penan people and the forests of Sarawak.

An adept campaigner, Manser gained worldwide publicity with, for example, hunger strikes and parachute jumps. In one daring stunt in 1999, he entered Sarawak by paragliding onto the front lawn of the chief minister, a politician with close ties to the logging industry. Manser was promptly arrested and deported. The next year he illegally returned to the rain forests to again live with the Penan and has been missing since May 2000. He was officially declared missing and presumed dead in 2005. *See also* DEFORESTATION; ILLEGAL LOGGING.

MARINE PROTECTED AREAS (MPAs). Worldwide, more than 6,500 marine protected areas were in place in 2014. These include large lakes, seas, oceans, and **coral reefs** and cover a wide range of restrictions and rules for commercial use and ecological management, such as for **fishing** and tourism. MPAs covered more than 2 percent of ocean area in 2014. This percentage has been rising in recent years as governments establish larger and larger MPAs. The world's three largest noncontiguous ocean MPAs (between 1 and 1.3 million square kilometers in size) are the Pacific Remote Islands Marine National Monument (established in 2009 by the **United States** and extended in 2014), the Natural Park of the Coral Sea (established in 2012 by **France**), and the South Georgia and the South Sandwich Islands Marine Protected Area (established by **Great Britain** in the Southern Ocean in 2012). In 2015, Great Britain established the world's largest contiguous MPA: the **Pitcairn Marine Reserve**, covering 834,000 square kilometers. *See also* CONSERVATION INTERNATIONAL (CI).

MARINE STEWARDSHIP COUNCIL (MSC). Headquartered in London, the Marine Stewardship Council (MSC) is a nonprofit organization dedicated to the sustainable use of marine fisheries. Building on the example of the **Forest Stewardship Council (FSC)**, Unilever, the world's largest seafood buyer, and the **World Wide Fund for Nature/World Wildlife Fund (WWF)** established the MSC as a joint initiative in 1996. Unilever did this in part to protect declining fish stocks as well as to green its corporate image.

The MSC became a fully independent organization in 1999. It accredits independent certifiers to assess whether a fishery meets the MSC standard. Fisheries that do can put the MSC logo on their products to inform consumers. The standard requires sufficient fish stocks for a sustainable fishery as well as rules and procedures to minimize the impact of **fishing** on the marine environment (e.g., on seabirds and marine mammals).

As of 2015, around 250 fisheries producing more than 25,000 seafood products had been certified to the MSC environmental standard. Supporters see the MSC as a practical and effective way to move toward sustainable fishing. Critics see it as far too little, far too late, allowing a few consumers to feel responsible while industrial overfishing continues to deplete the oceans of commercial species like the northern cod (now endangered). *See also* ECO-CERTIFICATION; ECO-LABELING.

MARKET LIBERALISM. Advocates of market liberalism emphasize the value and efficiency of free markets, foreign direct investment, and technology transfers as ways of improving global environmental conditions. Policy prescriptions for developing countries include privatization, deregulation, and the signing of free trade agreements. Market liberals contest the claim of a "race to the bottom" in standards when multinational corporations invest in countries with less stringent environmental regulations. Instead, they claim that standards are more likely to ratchet up as multinational corporations bring more advanced technologies and management systems, producing not only for low-standard markets, but also exporting goods to high-standard markets (and thus needing to meet these higher regulatory requirements).

Market liberals do call for rules and institutional constraints for some issues, such as controlling the illegal trade in **endangered species**. But for real progress on most global environmental issues—such as **climate change**, **deforestation**, **mining**, and **fishing**—market liberals see market mechanisms coupled with light state regulations as the most effective way forward. More moderate market liberals also tend to support voluntary international certification agencies, such as the **Forest Stewardship Council** and the **Marine Stewardship Council**. *See also* BREAKTHROUGH INSTITUTE; CORPORATE SOCIAL RESPONSIBILITY (CSR); ECO-BUSINESS; ECO-MODERNISM.

MARRAKECH PROCESS. The Marrakech Process is designed to support consensus building and the development of a 10-Year Framework of Programmes for promoting sustainable consumption and production. It has three primary goals: to assist efforts to green national economies, to support more sustainable business practices, and to encourage consumers to live more sustainably. It aims to meet the objectives of the Johannesburg Plan of Action set out in the 2002 **World Summit on Sustainable Development**. The **United Nations Environment Programme** and UN Department of Economic and Social Affairs are the lead agencies; national governments, development-oriented agencies, and **nongovernmental organizations** are also key participants. Coming out of the Marrakech process, countries discussed a draft framework at the 19th session of the **UN Commission on Sustainable Development** in 2011.

MARSH, GEORGE PERKINS (1801–1882). George Perkins Marsh was multitalented: fluent in many languages, he was a congressman, a diplomat to Europe, a linguist, a manufacturer, a lawyer, a newspaper editor, a sheep farmer, a mill owner, a businessman, an inventor, and one of the founders of the Smithsonian Institution. Many consider him America's first environmentalist. Marsh was one of the first to argue that the collapse of past civilizations was partly because of environmental degradation. Foremost here was **deforestation**, which Marsh saw as contributing to significant secondary impacts such as soil erosion and water turbidity. His book *Man and Nature; or, Physical Geography as Modified by Human Action* (1864) provided the justification for the Forest Reserves Act, the foundational legislation for modern national forests in the **United States**. Marsh also argued that decisions need to account for the environmental consequences of actions, although he did advocate taming the wilderness and asserting human command over nature.

Man and Nature also inspired the Arbor Day movement in the United States during the late 1800s, a holiday set aside for planting trees (the first was in Nebraska on 10 April 1872, although the state did not proclaim Arbor Day a legal holiday until 1885, changing the date to 22 April).

MEADOWS, DONELLA (1941–2001). In 1968 Donella (Dana) Meadows received a Ph.D. from Harvard in biophysics. As part of an international research and policy group called the Club of Rome, she worked on the Massachusetts Institute of Technology team that programmed the computer model "World3." It simulated future trends for industrialization, population growth, natural resource depletion, malnutrition, and **pollution**. This was the basis for the book *The Limits to Growth* (1972), of which she was the lead author. This book predicted that, without significant changes, the earth would reach its limits within 100 years. In language accessible to the general public, it declared, "The most probable result will be a sudden and uncontrollable decline in both population and industrial capacity"—a conclusion appearing to verify the earlier ones of scholars such as **Paul Ehrlich**.

The Limits to Growth went on to sell 20–30 million copies in at least 37 languages. Many attacked it as exaggerated pseudoscience. Meadows, in her later speeches and writings, saw such vitriolic criticism as a result of the near religious belief in economic growth. In a work called *The Limits to Growth Revisited*, she summed up her frustrations as follows: "A book called *The Limits to Growth* could have been filled with nothing but blank pages, and some people would still have thought it was an anticapitalist plot or an anticommunist or an anti-Keynesian or an anti–Third World one. They never saw the book for its cover."

In 1981, she and her husband at the time—Dennis Meadows—founded the International Network of Resource Information Centers (INRIC) to promote the exchange of systems-oriented analysis and activism. In 1996, she founded the Sustainability Institute to research ecosystems and demonstrate ways of sustainable living—a **nongovernmental organization** she liked to call a "think-do-tank." Humbly, she often described herself as just a writer and a farmer, but many see her as a founding intellectual and activist of global environmentalism, along with prominent thinkers like **Rachel Carson**. From 1972 until her sudden death from meningitis, she taught environmental studies at Dartmouth College.

MELANESIA. The Melanesian islands are located northeast of **Australia** in the South Pacific. This region includes the countries of Papua New Guinea, the Solomon Islands, the Santa Cruz Islands, Vanuatu, New Caledonia, and Fiji. The islands are primarily volcanic and continental, and they are more amenable to human settlements than atolls and raised limestone islands, which are common in the South Pacific.

Principles of **sustainability** were common in the traditional practices and rules in Melanesian societies. Many societies depended on maritime resources vulnerable to overexploitation; moreover, many could not turn to the land for alternative food because of limited space and poor-quality soil for farming (one exception is Papua, the largest island in the region).

Today the Pacific island economies depend primarily on resource extraction (such as **logging**, **mining**, and **fishing**). Timber companies from Malaysia, for example, have operated significant logging operations in Papua New Guinea and the Solomon Islands, exporting logs and lumber to countries such as **Japan** and **China**. Papua New Guinea also has large copper and gold mines, while Fiji mines gold and New Caledonia holds large deposits of nickel and chromium. (The Solomon Islands and Vanuatu also contain bauxite, nickel, and copper, but so far these remain generally untapped). **Biodiversity** losses from mining, logging, and fishing are often significant, as a large percentage of plant and animal species are endemic to these islands.

Environmental policies using the language of **sustainable development** are now widespread across the Pacific island region. Implementation of environmental regulations is weak, however, throughout the entire region. Many factors explain this, including a lack of environmental monitoring capabilities and skilled practitioners, boom-and-bust resource economies, the burdens of servicing heavy foreign debts, political instability, and the power of multinational investors (known to bribe officials and smuggle out resources). Local and international **nongovernmental organizations** advocating for environmental protection have gained a higher profile in recent years, although these still wield relatively little influence.

At the same time, regional environmental cooperation in the South Pacific is strengthening, most notably with respect to the antinuclear movement and marine resource management. The South Pacific Regional Environment Programme (SPREP), emerging from a small program called the South Pacific Commission in the 1980s, is now an important intergovernmental organization aiming to protect and manage environmental and natural resources. It coordinates the implementation of regional treaties including the Convention for the Protection of the Natural Resources and Environment of the South Pacific Region (SPREP/Noumea Convention), the Convention on Conservation of Nature in the South Pacific (Apia Convention), and the Rarotonga South Pacific Nuclear Free Zone Treaty (NFZT). Meanwhile, regional organizations include the South Pacific Conference, the South Pacific Forum, the Forum Fisheries Agency, the Secretariat for the Pacific Community, the South Pacific Applied Geoscience Commission, and the Regional Seas Programme. The Strategic Action Programme for the International Waters of the Pacific Small Island Developing States was developed in 2001. In 2002, South Pacific states agreed as well to a Pacific Islands Regional Ocean Policy (PIROP).

MENDES, CHICO (1944–1988). Chico Mendes (Francisco Alves Mendes Filho) was a rubber tapper from the western Brazilian **Amazon**, working to extract rubber as well as to harvest nuts, fiber, and food. Using nonviolent techniques, he organized his fellow tappers in the 1970s and 1980s to defend the forests from destructive loggers and cattle ranchers clearing land for pasture. In 1985, with international support for his cause rising, he founded the National Council of Rubber Tappers. In 1988, the son of a cattle rancher assassinated Mendes, turning Mendes into a martyr for environmentalism. Seeing the global anger over his death also influenced the decision by the Brazilian government to offer to host the 1992 **United Nations Conference on Environment and Development** in Rio de Janeiro. In addition, the Brazilian government set aside an extractive forest reserve for rubber tappers. Today, the courage of Mendes continues to inspire peaceful movements against commercial logging and land clearing across the tropical world. *See also* BRAZIL; REFORESTATION.

MEXICO. From the 1940s to the 1980s, development in Mexico focused on industrialization and natural resource exports; environmental concerns were addressed mainly in the context of public health through the Health Secretariat. Constitutional reforms in the 1980s resulted in new administrative and judicial institutions for environmental protection. The Mexican government created the Secretaría de Desarrollo Urbano y Ecología (SEDUE, or Secretariat of Urban Development and Ecology) in 1982, passed new environmental laws in 1982 and 1988, and established its National Water Commission in 1989. Further structures were established in the early 1990s, including the National Ecology Institute, the attorney general for environmental protection, a National Water Law, and the Secretariat of Social Development (replacing SEDUE). In 2000, the Mexican government established the Secretariat of the Environment and Natural Resources to replace several earlier versions of environmental departments; it also transferred some resource responsibilities to the Secretariat of Agriculture, Livestock, Rural Development, Fisheries, and Food. In 2012 Mexico was hailed as the first developing country to pass "comprehensive" legislation to address its contributions to climate change. In 2015 Rafael Pacchiano Alamán of the Ecologist Green Party of Mexico was appointed as minister (secretary) of the Secretariat of Environment and Natural Resources.

Along with new legislation and structural reforms, the government has also been establishing voluntary regulation programs for industry. During the 1990s alone, Mexico created at least 10 programs, involving hundreds of firms. The central program, the National Environmental Auditing Program, also called the Clean Industry Program, was set up in 1992. It required firms to pay for independent third-party audits in exchange for a certificate to exempt them from regulatory inspections for two years (firms could also use the certificate for marketing). The program started with 77 participants; by 2005 it had over 3,000.

Mexico also has an active civil society promoting conservation and environmental protection. The Mexican Fund for the Conservation of Nature, established after the 1992 Earth Summit, is a private conservation organization initially under the auspices of the **World Wide Fund for Nature/World Wildlife Fund (WWF)**. It works collaboratively on environmental projects, including with the U.S. Agency for International Development (USAID) and the **Nature Conservancy**.

MIDGLEY, THOMAS, JR. (1889–1944). In 2003, Thomas Midgley Jr. was inducted into the American National Inventors Hall of Fame in Akron, Ohio. A prolific inventor, holding over 100 patents, Midgley is best remembered today for two discoveries with damaging ecological consequences lasting far past his lifetime. The first was his discovery in 1921 of the power of tetraethyl lead as an additive to reduce engine knock (the beginning of the **leaded gasoline** industry). The second was his 1928 discovery of a stable, nontoxic, and nonflammable refrigerant for refrigerators, the seemingly safe and innocuous chemical compounds called **chlorofluorocarbons (CFCs)**, which scientists, a half century later, discovered were depleting the ozone layer. *See also* OZONE DEPLETION.

MILLENNIUM DEVELOPMENT GOALS. Arising out of the **United Nation**'s Millennium Summit in 2000, the eight UN Millennium Development Goals were designed as a "blueprint" for states, UN agencies, and international development organizations. These included (all by 2015) reversing the spread of HIV/AIDS and malaria, halving extreme poverty and hunger, providing universal primary education, and achieving environmental **sustainability**. Some countries met some of the goals, but progress was halting and uneven across the majority of issues and countries. Most supporters now acknowledge that achieving all of these goals was impossible; still, the hope has always been that striving for them would inspire support for the world's poorest people.

MINAMATA CONVENTION ON MERCURY. Signed in 2013, the Minamata Convention is an international treaty to regulate the environmental and human health consequences of mercury. The name of the convention honors the history of Minamata, **Japan**, where in the 1950s and 1960s methyl mercury in the local seafood killed hundreds of residents as well as caused birth defects and long-term brain damage—what came to be known as "**Minamata disease**." The Minamata Convention aims to phase out the mining of mercury, including a ban on new mines. It also contains new regulations for controlling mercury air emissions and mercury pollution from artisanal gold mining. The Minamata Convention was not in force at the beginning of 2016. *See also* BASEL CONVENTION ON THE CONTROL OF TRANSBOUNDARY MOVEMENTS OF HAZARDOUS WASTES AND THEIR DISPOSAL; CONVENTION ON LONG-RANGE TRANSBOUNDARY AIR POLLUTION (CLRTAP); STOCKHOLM CONVENTION ON PERSISTENT ORGANIC POLLUTANTS.

MINAMATA DISEASE. Minamata disease, named after Minamata Bay in **Japan** where it was first officially "discovered" in villagers in 1956, is a neurological condition caused by methyl mercury poisoning. People in Minamata were poisoned after eating the local seafood, which was contaminated with methyl mercury discharged by the Chisso industrial plant upriver from Minamata Bay. In the 1950s and 1960s, hundreds of people were paralyzed and died, and hundreds more were born with birth defects and brain damage. In Japan, the publicity, lawsuits, and citizen protests in the 1960s and 1970s spurred an environmental cleanup as well as legislation to control industrial **pollution**. Globally, environmentalists continue to point to Minamata disease as an especially horrific example of the dangers of unregulated industrialization and uncontrolled economic growth. *See also* MINAMATA CONVENTION ON MERCURY.

MINDBOMBS. The term *mindbombs* was coined by **Robert "Bob" Hunter** to refer to activist campaigns that use the media to blast global consciousness with images, sounds, and language reflecting environmental values.

MINING. Minerals are a nonrenewable resource. Thus, to some degree, mining always damages the ecosystem. The environmental debate revolves around best practices: how to minimize consequences and when to close (or not begin) mining. Particular issues include water **pollution**, large volumes of waste, mine closure plans and site rehabilitation, energy use, toxic materials, and threats to **biodiversity**. Storing mine tailings is especially critical as these can contain heavy metals and poisons such as cyanide (used to extract gold). Mining can also create conflict within or between local communities, including indigenous groups, over access to surrounding natural resources and resulting wealth. One example is the conflict around diamond mining in Africa. Thus, many **nongovernmental organizations** call for extensive community consultation and participation in the environmental assessment of mining.

Currently, no comprehensive international agreement is in place for mining or mineral resources. The global mining industry has begun, however, to adopt voluntary codes of conduct under policies of **corporate social responsibility** as communities, governments, and environmental activists demand more accountability. Since 2000, many multinational mining companies, for example, have voluntarily followed the **United Nations Environment Programme (UNEP)** and the International Council on Mining and Metals' (ICMM's) "International Cyanide Management Code for the Manufacture, Transport, and Use of Cyanide in the Production of Gold." Similarly, since

2002 many multinational diamond miners follow an international voluntary certification system for "conflict diamonds" called the Kimberley Process Certification Scheme.

Such codes, however, tend to lack compliance mechanisms and allow nonsignatory companies to ignore them. Also, as mining often occurs in developing countries with less capacity to regulate industry, international mining companies tend to maintain lower standards here than at home. Again, various international initiatives are under way to address these double standards, such as enhancing local capacity with funding from institutions such as the World Bank.

MONTREAL PROTOCOL ON SUBSTANCES THAT DEPLETE THE OZONE LAYER. The 1987 Montreal Protocol is an international agreement to address stratospheric **ozone depletion**. The 1985 Vienna Convention for the Protection of the Ozone Layer was the framework for negotiating the Montreal Protocol. An Ozone Secretariat in Nairobi, **Kenya** (at the **United Nations Environment Programme**), is responsible for both the Vienna Convention and the Montreal Protocol.

The Montreal Protocol is one of the most successful international environmental agreements ever negotiated. Entering into force in 1989, it was quickly amended in 1990 and 1992 to make it even more comprehensive and now has had numerous revisions to improve and strengthen it. Financial assistance for phaseouts in developing countries was also made available through the Multilateral Fund for the Implementation of the Montreal Protocol (established in 1990). As of 2016, 197 parties had ratified the agreement, and, with high compliance levels, it has contributed to a worldwide phaseout of over 95 percent of ozone-depleting substances.

These ozone-depleting substances include **chlorofluorocarbons (CFCs)**, halons, carbon tetrachloride, methyl bromide, methyl chloroform, and hydrochlorofluorocarbons (HCFCs). Some significant problems still remain. For example, in some cases CFCs and HCFCs have been replaced by hydrofluorocarbons (HFCs), a **greenhouse gas** that contributes to **climate change**.

MUIR, JOHN (1838–1914). Born in Dunbar, Scotland, John Muir became a central figure in the history of American conservation. Muir saw creation and man as belonging to nature, rather than man presiding over nature. His critique of anthropocentrism was radical for the time of the industrial revolution of the 19th century, as was his call to protect nature for its own sake. A nature lover, Muir explored the North American and European wilderness, especially the southwest **United States**, writing and publishing naturalist articles in American literary magazines. Two of his best-known campaigns were in California, for the Sierra Nevada and Yosemite National Park. His

Sierra campaign led to the founding of the **Sierra Club** in 1892 (he was president until his death). Muir is also credited with influencing President Theodore Roosevelt's conservation programs and the **national parks** movement.

N

NAESS, ARNE. *See* DEEP ECOLOGY.

NANOTECHNOLOGY. Engineering nanomaterials are one of the newer technologies to spark intense debates between those who see them as a way to improve quality of life and those who call for more precaution to account for the uncertainty of long-term environmental consequences. Critics are calling for a range of measures: from consumer labeling to complete bans. Nanomaterials are tiny engineered substances—from just 1 to 100 nanometers in size. Engineering something so small is hard to even imagine: one nanometer equals a mere billionth of a meter (it takes 100,000 nanometers to reach the diameter of a human hair). Scientists are now able to arrange metals and other compounds the size of a nanometer into shapes that often look like rods or spheres, thus creating stronger and more durable materials with innovative properties.

The nanotechnology industry is rapidly expanding, and countless consumer products now contain nanomaterials, including food, food packaging, cosmetics, wrinkle-free clothing, stain-resistant fabric, sunscreen, cleaning products, and tennis rackets. Critics worry that these tiny nanomaterials will escape into the environment as products break down and then leach into tissues, cell membranes, and food chains, perhaps acting in ways similar to carcinogens like asbestos. At a minimum, critics are calling for a **precautionary approach** as the industry incorporates nanotechnology into consumer products worth trillions of dollars. This would avoid risking a repeat of past ecological disasters where technologies were introduced into the global environment without adequate understanding or government regulations, such as the use of lead in gasoline in the 1920s and **chlorofluorocarbons (CFCs)** in refrigerators in the 1930s. *See also* LEADED GASOLINE.

NARMADA DAM. The Narmada Dam project, also called the Narmada Valley project, involves building a series of large, medium, and small hydroelectric dams on the Narmada River and its tributaries in **India**. Prime Minister Jawaharlal Nehru floated the idea in the 1940s, but it did not take hold until the late 1970s as the country looked for ways to produce electricity and irrigate drought-prone areas. In the 1980s, increasing numbers of environmental and human rights groups opposed construction. Facing a growing backlash, in 1990 the World Bank withdrew from the project. The Indian government has persisted, however, and the project continued to move ahead even in the face of ongoing grassroots protests and worldwide criticism. After decades of controversy, the largest of the dams—the Sardar Sarovar Dam—became operational in 2006, and despite ongoing disputes, the government authorized another height increase in 2014. *See also* THREE GORGES DAM.

NATIONAL AUDUBON SOCIETY. The National Audubon Society is an American nonprofit environmental organization dedicated to conserving natural ecosystems, focusing in particular on protecting and studying birds in natural habitats. Established in 1905 from local Audubon clubs that emerged in the late 1800s, it is one of the world's oldest conservation organizations. The society is named in honor of John James Audubon, an ornithologist who painted, described, and cataloged the birds of North America. Today, the Audubon Society has hundreds of thousands of members across hundreds of local chapters in the **United States**. Members participate in public education and advocacy to promote nature conservation. Local chapters organize bird-watching and conservation activities. Audubon also works with a network of partner organizations to protect birds and nature in other countries. It is an example of the ongoing global influence of the earliest wave of U.S. environmentalism.

NATIONAL PARKS. As of 2015, about 15 percent of the earth's land area (including inland waters) was set aside for environmental protection as nature reserves, parks, wildlife refuges, or wilderness. The definitions of national parks, reserves, and sanctuaries vary across countries and regions, however, and there are considerable differences in the degree of "legal protection," even across the most vulnerable tundra, deserts, and rain forests. Moreover, especially in the developing world, enforcement is often weak, and many national parks and nature reserves regularly experience **illegal logging**, **mining**, and poaching. In contrast, some conservation biologists see a need to set aside and fully protect at least 20 percent of the earth's land area to preserve global **biodiversity**.

NATURAL GAS. Natural gas is the world's third-largest energy source, after **oil** and **coal**. Since the mid-1960s production and consumption of natural gas have been slowly edging upward. Most analysts predict that levels will continue to rise over the next 30 years as governments and corporations seek out less carbon-polluting alternatives to oil and coal.

The development of the natural gas industry in the first half of the 20th century took place mostly in the **United States**, with North America's share of the global consumption of natural gas sitting at 90 percent in 1950. Today, however, North America accounts for less than one-quarter of global consumption, with countries such as **Russia**, **China**, and **Iran**, as well as countries in the European Union, now significant consumers. To diversify its energy portfolio, Japan invested in natural gas and became the largest importer of liquefied natural gas (natural gas that is liquefied to reduce its volume) by the end of the 1970s. Russia and the United States are currently the largest producers of natural gas and have the largest reserves.

Natural gas is often called "clean" because it releases less pollutants and carbon dioxide than oil for the same amount of energy. However, methane—a byproduct of producing natural gas—is a **greenhouse gas** with more than 20 times the warming effects of carbon dioxide.

NATURAL RESOURCES DEFENSE COUNCIL (NRDC). Founded in 1970 by law students and attorneys working in the **United States**, the Natural Resources Defense Council (NRDC) has been especially influential in drafting, shaping, and changing environmental laws in the United States. Today, with over one million members and a staff of hundreds of lawyers, scientists, and policy analysts, NRDC is involved in a wide range of campaigns, including ones regarding **climate change**, environmental health, **China**, toxic chemicals, oceans, and wildlife.

NATURE CONSERVANCY. Founded in 1951 in the **United States** (with roots going back to 1915), the Nature Conservancy uses a nonconfrontational approach to promote conservation of plants, animals, and nature. Its primary strategy is to acquire land by direct purchase or through land management agreements, leases, and easements. Today, with more than one million members, it has managed to set aside millions of hectares of land in the United States, **Canada**, Latin America, the Caribbean, and many other parts of the world. It directly manages thousands of nature preserves.

A secondary strategy to protect **biodiversity** was its Natural Heritage Inventory Program (started in 1974), a scientific database of rare and **endangered species** and ecosystems, which employed hundreds of scientists and information managers. In 2000, this program was turned into the Association for Biodiversity Information, a nonprofit conservation organization later renamed NatureServe (headquartered in Arlington, Virginia). Today, Nature-Serve coordinates a network of natural heritage programs/biological invento-ries. By sharing objective scientific data on biodiversity with all stakeholders (such as governments, indigenous groups, conservation organizations, corpo-rations, and the general public), NatureServe tries to ensure informed deci-sions regarding the impacts of development on endangered species and eco-systems.

NAURU. Nauru is a small island country situated between **Australia** and Hawaii. Nauru, like its nearest neighboring country of Banaba, was rich in natural phosphate at the beginning of the 20th century. Australia was the first to mine and export Nauruan phosphate to fertilize its sprawling farmlands. By the time Nauru gained independence in 1968, one-third of the country had been strip-mined. The postcolonial government of Nauru, however, contin-ued to mine the phosphate at a furious rate, and by the mid-1970s Nauru ranked second in the world in per capita income. But the foundations of this wealth were unsustainable, and Nauru's phosphate **mining** industry col-lapsed as accessible supplies ran out.

For ecologists Carl McDaniel and John Gowdy, as with the history of **Easter Island**, Nauru is a "parable" of the global unsustainability of capital-ism. Nauru's only bank has been closed; its 10,000 citizens have some of the world's highest rates of diabetes, obesity, smoking, and alcoholism; and a primary source of the government's income now derives from serving as an Australian detention camp for asylum seekers caught en route to Australia. *See also* ECOLOGICAL IMPERIALISM.

NEW CALEDONIA. *See* MELANESIA.

NEW ZEALAND. New Zealand contains a large number of unique native species. Environmental problems include **biodiversity** loss, soil erosion (50 percent of land area shows some signs), **deforestation** (less than one-quarter of original indigenous forest cover was left by the early 1980s), and waste management.

Land and forest degradation dates back to the resource industries and farming practices of the earliest European settlers. A tradition of conserva-tion, however, also dates back to these colonial days, as administrators put in place policies to protect the scenic beauty and manage resources more effi-ciently and effectively. The Forests Act of 1874—to deal with deforesta-tion—was later repealed because of worries it would hamper economic de-velopment. Other acts were soon passed, however, including the State Forests Act of 1885 and the Land Act of 1892 (to preserve government-owned land). The first **national park** was created in 1887, the second in

1900. Many acts would follow over the next century, including the Soil Conservation and Rivers Control Act of 1941 (dealing with erosion and flooding), the Nature Protection Council in 1950, and the Water and Soil Conservation Act of 1967.

The modern environmental movement began in the 1960s with growing grassroots support to better protect and manage the environment. The Values Party (created in 1972) was one of the first green parties globally. Key issues over the next few decades included air **pollution** and public health, the use of Lake Manapouri (in the late 1960s) to produce hydroelectric power, a plan to clear-cut 340,000 hectares of forest in South Island (abandoned in 1975 after a public outcry), and French nuclear testing in the Pacific (which hit the news worldwide after the sinking of the *Rainbow Warrior* in 1985).

Institutional reforms in the 1980s altered the framework for environmental protection. Key among these was the reconstitution of local government and the increasing acceptance of economic incentives and market instruments as tools to implement policy. As a result, local areas have taken on an increasingly important role in environmental management. The city of Christchurch, for example, declared itself a "Clean Air Zone," with the local government investing to control air pollution from open fires (the devastating earthquake of 2011 has required a major rebuilding of Christchurch). Also important in New Zealand was the initiation of the Resource Management Law Reform in 1988, leading to the Resource Management Act of 1991. This act incorporates a principle of **sustainability** and brings together most of the previous environmentally related legislation (replacing 57 existing laws and reducing 800 units of government to 93).

Other important changes since then include the New Zealand Forest Accord of 1991, which was signed by major forest companies and environmental groups. Industry agreed to no longer replace indigenous forests with exotic plantations; environmentalists agreed to support exotic forests as an alternative to logging of native forests.

Today, New Zealand has 14 national parks as well as scores of forest and conservation parks, leaving around 30 percent of its total land area under some form of protection. The Green Party of Aotearoa New Zealand, founded in 1990, has also been one of the world's more successful environmentally oriented political parties. In 2016, it held 14 seats in New Zealand's Parliament, making it the country's third-largest political party.

NIGERIA. In 1977, the Nigerian government created the state-run Nigerian National Petroleum Corporation. In recent years Nigeria has been Africa's largest **oil** producer and one of the world's biggest exporters of crude oil, with the vast majority of its export revenues coming from oil.

The oil industry has been a major source of environmental degradation and human rights violations in Nigeria. For example, in the early 1990s, the Movement for the Survival of the Ogoni People (MOSOP) led a nonviolent campaign against environmental damage from multinational oil companies, especially Shell Oil, in the Niger Delta. After large protests in 1993, Shell suspended operations; then in 1995, to the outrage of human rights and environmental groups worldwide, the government executed a founding member of MOSOP, **Ken Saro-Wiwa**, along with eight others. Since then the struggle against oil production in the Niger Delta has been ongoing, with some tactics now becoming violent, including kidnappings and militant take-overs of facilities by rebel groups such as the Movement for the Emancipation of the Niger Delta.

Over the last two decades the Nigerian government has reorganized its bureaucracy to support more **sustainable development**. It established a Federal Environmental Protection Agency in 1988, which was later replaced by the Federal Ministry of the Environment in 2000. Jurisdiction over environmental regulation also falls under state control, and in the mid-1990s each state established a state environmental protection agency. Nigeria also participates in regional environmental initiatives. It helped to create the Niger River Commission (CFN, or Commission du Fleuve Niger) in 1964 and the subsequent Niger Basin Authority (ABN, or l'Autorité du Bassin du Niger) in 1980. In 1968, it also joined the African Convention on the Conservation of Nature and Natural Resources.

Highly affected by **desertification**, Nigeria started the Arid Zone Afforestation Project (AZAP) in 1976. It ratified the **United Nations Convention to Combat Desertification** in 1997 and created the Department of Drought and Desertification Amelioration in the Ministry of the Environment in 2000. **Nongovernmental organizations** have also been active in promoting forest conservation. For example, the Forestry Association of Nigeria initiated a National Tree Planting Campaign in 1970; in 1982, the Nigerian Conservation Foundation was formed to promote conservation (in particular forest resources).

NIMBY. An acronym meaning "not in my backyard," NIMBY describes a common sentiment within many communities that opposes locating certain kinds of projects nearby on environmental and safety grounds—such as garbage dumps, incinerators, freeways, and power plants—while supporting (or at least accepting) that the project may need to go ahead in someone else's backyard. For some analysts, this helps to explain why environmental conditions are often worse in communities with more minorities or higher rates of poverty, as NIMBYism tends to shift costs onto the least powerful groups in society.

NONGOVERNMENTAL ORGANIZATIONS (NGOs). Over the past few decades nongovernmental organizations, or NGOs, have been driving agents of environmental action and education. As more groups were emerging and strengthening in the 1960s and 1970s in countries like the **United States** and **Great Britain**, environmental NGOs began to spread into both developing and developed countries, from **India, Kenya, Mexico,** and the **Philippines** to **Australia, Finland, Japan,** and **Spain,** and today these NGOs exist in every country, covering just about every environmental issue.

The organizational characteristics of environmental NGOs range from leaderless movements and loose networks (e.g., **Critical Mass,** the **Earth Liberation Front,** and **Reclaim the Streets**) to highly ordered and structured organizations (e.g., the **Nature Conservancy**). The focus, tactics, and mandates vary considerably, too, from organizations established to protect individual species (e.g., **Brazil**'s Tartarugas Marinhas, or Sea Turtles organization) or sectors (e.g., forestry, with the **Forest Stewardship Council,** the **Programme for the Endorsement of Forest Certification,** and the **Sustainable Forestry Initiative**), to groups pushing for environmental laws and regulations for broad issues (e.g., **Environmental Defense Fund** and the **Natural Resources Defense Council**), to those advocating conservation and large-scale environmental action (e.g., the **World Wide Fund for Nature/ World Wildlife Fund**). Some are primarily think tanks with a focus on research (e.g., **Resources for the Future**); others work as advocates, consultants, and lobbyists (e.g., the **World Resources Institute** and the **Sierra Club**); others focus on activism over social media (e.g., **SumOfUs**); and others focus on grassroots action (e.g., **Food Not Bombs** and the **Green Belt Movement**). NGOs also span from local and national groups (e.g., the U.S.-based **National Audubon Society** and **Wilderness Society**) to international organizations and networks (e.g., the **International Union for Conservation of Nature, Greenpeace,** and the **Third World Network**), as well as everything in between.

Some organizations that started as local or national efforts have expanded their activities to address global issues (e.g., **Conservation International** and **Friends of the Earth,** both of which began in the United States). Changes in government or government policies have allowed NGOs to emerge in some countries, such as Mikhail Gorbachev's glasnost policy in **Russia,** the fall of the Soviet Union, and **China**'s shift toward a more open economy in the mid-1990s. NGO networks also span national borders, with many working on regional or international issues, and with many in developed countries supporting and funding efforts for conservation in developing countries. Examples of this include Norway's Bellona Foundation, which advocates for better nuclear waste management in Russia.

Some NGOs oppose and take direct action against governments and corporations (e.g., **Earth First!**, the Earth Liberation Front, and the **Animal Liberation Front**), while others cooperate in formal and informal partnerships (e.g., the **Marine Stewardship Council**, the **Roundtable on Sustainable Palm Oil**, and the **Singapore** Environment Council). A few NGOs arise out of the business world itself, such as the **World Business Council for Sustainable Development**. These alliances between NGOs and industry have contributed to developing environmental laws, **eco-certification** programs, voluntary environmental initiatives, **corporate social responsibility**, and protected areas; some activists, however, see many of these efforts as **greenwash** that does little to advance true environmental protection. *See also* CENTER FOR INTERNATIONAL ENVIRONMENTAL LAW (CIEL); COALITION FOR ENVIRONMENTALLY RESPONSIBLE ECONOMIES (CERES); ENVIRONMENTAL INVESTIGATION AGENCY (EIA); INTERNATIONAL INSTITUTE FOR ENVIRONMENT AND DEVELOPMENT (IIED); INTERNATIONAL INSTITUTE FOR SUSTAINABLE DEVELOPMENT (IISD); INTERNATIONAL ORGANIZATION FOR STANDARDIZATION (ISO) 14000, 14001, AND 26000; INTERNATIONAL SOCIETY FOR ECOLOGICAL ECONOMICS (ISEE); RAINFOREST ACTION NETWORK (RAN); UNION OF CONCERNED SCIENTISTS; WILDLIFE CONSERVATION SOCIETY; WORLDWATCH INSTITUTE; WWOOF.

NORWAY. *See* BRUNDTLAND, GRO HARLEM (1939–); WHALING.

NUCLEAR POWER/ENERGY. A highly controversial form of energy, nuclear power is billed by some as a "green" and "sustainable" energy source, while others label it a "dangerous" and "costly" (economically and environmentally) option. It is created by extracting energy from atomic nuclei of uranium atoms, using nuclear fission (the most common method), nuclear fusion, or radioactive decay. The heat produced by splitting the atoms converts water into steam, which then spins a turbine or generator to produce electricity. Nuclear power accounted for around one-tenth of the world's total electricity production in 2015.

Advocates of nuclear energy stress its potential to reduce air **pollution** and **greenhouse gas** emissions (thus mitigating **climate change**). They also argue that with proper procedures and safety protocols, it is possible to isolate and safely store the small amount of remaining nuclear waste. Critics counter by raising safety and environmental concerns about the production of nuclear power, as well as the disposal of radioactive waste, pointing to accidents such as the 1979 **Three Mile Island nuclear accident** in the **United States**, the 1986 **Chernobyl nuclear meltdown** in the Ukraine (at the time, part of the Soviet Union), and the meltdown at the Fukushima Daiichi nuclear power facility in 2011. Environmentalists have organized large protests against nuclear power, such as those in **France** in the 1970s and Germany in 2011. Most **green parties**, too, oppose nuclear technology. Several **nongovernmental organizations**, including **Greenpeace**, also campaign actively against nuclear power. Nuclear power generation often sparks particularly strong reactions because of its close association for many people with nuclear weapons.

The siting of nuclear reactors and waste disposal facilities reveals a **NIMBY** (not in my backyard) attitude in many communities; some citizens are willing to tolerate (or even support) the idea of using nuclear power but are reluctant to bear the risks themselves. The input of uranium for power generation also raises environmental concerns, as open-pit **mining** is often used to extract the ore, which tends to be found in low concentrations (**Canada**, **Australia**, and Kazakhstan accounted for around two-thirds of the world's uranium production in 2014).

Early international agreements to address nuclear issues include the 1960 Paris Convention on Third Party Liability in the Field of Nuclear Energy and the 1963 Vienna Convention on Civil Liability in the Field of Nuclear Energy. More recent agreements on nuclear issues include the 1994 Convention on Nuclear Safety, the 1996 Comprehensive Nuclear Test Ban Treaty, and the 1997 Convention on Supplementary Compensation for Nuclear Damage. *See also* CONVENTION ON THE CONSERVATION OF ANTARCTIC MARINE LIVING RESOURCES (CCAMLR); RUSSIA.

O

OCCUPY MOVEMENT. The Occupy Movement emerged in 2011 out of Occupy Wall Street. Occupy Wall Street was an idea of Kalle Lasn and his anticonsumerist **Adbusters** team. Using the Twitter hashtag #OccupyWall-Street, Lasn and his team called on fellow activists to "occupy" Wall Street in New York City's Zuccotti Park to protest global inequality, overconsumption, corporate greed, and environmental decay. Lasn chose September 17 as the start date: his mother's birthday.

Adbusters' idea was to launch a spontaneous, leaderless uprising of radical environmentalists, disenfranchised labor, and angry youth; Adbusters made no attempt to lead or control the gathering. The refrain of Occupy Wall Street—"We are the 99 percent"—grabbed the world's attention, and by the end of October, as many as a 1,000 other "occupations" across 80 or so countries were under way—what journalists and activists were now calling the "Occupy Movement." Protestors across the world were calling for less inequality, hierarchy, exploitation, and destruction. By this point, however, state police and secret services were cracking down, recording, threatening, arresting, and jailing protestors. The initial great strength of the movement—leaderless spontaneity without specific demands—became a weakness under harsh government treatment and with the passage of time, and by the end of 2011 the movement had waned. *See also* NONGOVERNMENTAL OR-GANIZATIONS (NGOs); RECLAIM THE STREETS (RTS).

OCCUPY WALL STREET. *See* OCCUPY MOVEMENT.

OCEAN ACIDIFICATION. The oceans absorb around one-third of anthropogenic carbon emissions. Oceans are becoming more acidic as carbonic acid forms (seen in falling levels of hydrogen ion concentration, known as pH levels). More acidic water is bleaching **coral reefs**, altering shell formation, and disturbing natural food cycles in the oceans. In the lead-up to the 21st Conference of the Parties of the **United Nations Framework Convention on Climate Change** in Paris, **France**, in 2015, scientists, activists, and some states called for more attention to ocean acidification during the negotiations. *See also* CLIMATE CHANGE; MARINE PROTECTED AREAS (MPAs).

OIL. As the world's largest source of energy, oil—its production and consumption—dominates current transportation, industrial, and agricultural systems. The oil industry represents a powerful economic sector and is a valuable export commodity for many countries, including Angola, **Argentina**, **Canada**, Iraq, **Iran**, **Nigeria** (Africa's largest oil producer), Norway, **Russia**, Saudi Arabia, Venezuela, and the United Arab Emirates. Demand for energy is unlikely to decrease—the Energy Information Administration of the **United States** projects that global energy demand will continue to rise steadily into the near future—and most analysts project that oil consumption will increase significantly unless major advances occur in **renewable energy** technology and incentives shift the world economy away from its current dependence on fossil fuels. Environmental concerns and energy security could encourage such a shift. **Sweden**, for example, has announced bold plans to phase out oil, substantially increasing the government's budget for solar energy, including again in 2016. In 2015, **Costa Rica** managed to rely exclusively on renewable energy for more than two months in a row.

Many environmental **nongovernmental organizations (NGOs)**, such as the **Rainforest Action Network** (with its Freedom from Oil Campaign) and **Greenpeace**, see reducing oil consumption as essential to preventing a global environmental disaster. Along with emissions from **coal** and **natural gas**, **greenhouse gas** emissions from burning oil as gasoline in automobiles and in industrial production contribute significantly to **climate change**; some groups focus on encouraging public transit and cycling (e.g., **Critical Mass**) and reducing the dominance of cars in cities (e.g., **Reclaim the Streets**), while others promote new technology, such as **hybrid automobiles**.

Oil spills from transportation and storage facilities also cause environmental degradation, with notable examples including the grounding of the *Torrey Canyon* in 1967, the *Exxon Valdez* **oil spill** in 1989, the controversy over the decommissioning of the *Brent Spar* in 1995, and the spilling of millions of barrels of oil into the Gulf of Mexico following an explosion on BP's *Deepwater Horizon* oil rig in 2010. Activists have pushed to hold corporations accountable for oil spills and dumping, as with the efforts of Pablo Fajardo Mendo and Luis Yanza in Ecuador, who were among the winners of the **Goldman Environmental Prize** in 2008. Oil exploration also poses environmental risks to sensitive ecosystems, and some international steps have been taken to protect particularly vulnerable regions. The Environmental Protocol to the Antarctic Treaty (the Madrid Protocol), for example, stopped oil and mineral exploration in **Antarctica**. Oil is also one of the six most critical environmental problems in the **Arctic**, as identified by the Arctic Council (created in 1996 by **Finland**, **Canada**, Denmark, Iceland, Norway, **Russia**, Sweden, and the United States).

The oil crisis of the 1970s spurred efforts to promote energy efficiency, leading to developments in **green architecture** and **eco-efficiency** to conserve resources. Prices of oil have been volatile, rising and falling sharply many times over the past half century. Some environmentalists see high oil prices as a positive trend that could lead to less dependence on oil; some encourage **carbon taxes** as part of a strategy to increase consumer prices further.

Initially seen by some environmentalists as a "silver bullet," replacing oil with **biofuels** has become one of the most contentious strategies to reduce the global dependence on oil. Many are now concerned with the consequences for food prices for the world's poorest people. Also, the greenhouse gas emission reductions from biofuels depend on production methods and land conversion that may cause **deforestation** of primary forests as countries such as **Indonesia** develop even more palm oil plantations. *See also* CUBA; PEAK OIL; SIBERIA; STRONG, MAURICE (1929–2015).

ORGANIC FOOD. Sales of organic food have been rising steadily in North America and Europe as consumers look for healthy ways to avoid pesticides, **synthetic chemicals**, and **genetically modified organisms**. Definitions of *organic* vary considerably, even within countries. The U.S. Department of Agriculture's National Organic Program, for example, allows for three other uses of organic besides "100 percent organic." Retailers can label products "organic" when at least 95 percent of the ingredients are organic, they can use the phrase "made with organic ingredients" when the product contains at least 70 percent organic ingredients and no sulfites, and they can use the term "organic" when listing ingredients for products made with less than 70 percent organic ingredients.

In recent years sales of organic fruits and vegetables have been doing especially well in Europe and North America; although rising, sales of organic meat comprise a tiny portion of the total meat market (for example, well under 1 percent in the **United States**). *See also* COFFEE; CUBA; WWOOF.

OUTER SPACE. By definition, outer space is beyond the earth's atmosphere. No clear physical boundary exists, however, between the atmosphere and outer space. A common demarcation is the altitude limit of aircrafts, but some use the term to refer to space beyond the range of satellite orbits. For environmentalism, outer space represents a particular type of global commons, where the resource is not consumed but rather accessed and explored, primarily with technology.

The principle of national sovereignty has never been applied to outer space—significantly, for example, the **United States** did not claim territorial sovereignty over the moon in 1969. The main international organization for space law is the **United Nations** and its Committee on the Peaceful Uses of Outer Space (COPUOS), which became a permanent body of the UN General Assembly in 1959. The United Nations Office for Outer Space Affairs (UNOOSA) assists this committee and serves as its secretariat.

Five treaties govern outer space: the 1967 Treaty on Principles Governing the Activities of States in the Exploration and Use of Outer Space, Including the Moon and Other Celestial Bodies (the Outer Space Treaty); the 1968 Agreement on the Rescue of Astronauts, the Return of Astronauts and the Return of Objects Launched into Outer Space (the Rescue Agreement); the 1972 Convention on International Liability for Damage Caused by Space Objects (the Liability Convention); the 1975 Convention on Registration of Objects Launched into Outer Space (the Registration Convention); and the 1979 Agreement Governing the Activities of States on the Moon and Other Celestial Bodies (the Moon Agreement).

For global environmentalism, the picture of the earth from outer space has reinforced the image of the planet as fragile and interconnected. It remains a powerful symbol for global environmental consciousness. One of the most famous pictures was taken by astronauts Neil Armstrong, Michael Collins, and Edwin (Buzz) Aldrin on their way to the moon in 1969.

OZONE DEPLETION. In 1970, Paul Crutzen of the Max Planck Institute for Chemistry in Mainz, **Germany**, raised the possibility that nitrogen oxides from fertilizers and supersonic aircraft might be harming the ozone layer 20–50 kilometers above the earth. In 1974, Mario J. Molina and F. Sherwood Rowland put forth the theory that **chlorofluorocarbons (CFCs)** might be drifting into the stratosphere, breaking apart, and causing a chain reaction that would deplete the ozone layer. Molina and Rowland stressed that this would have catastrophic consequences, as the ozone layer is necessary to protect against the harmful effects of ultraviolet radiation from the sun. All three would go on to win the 1995 Nobel Prize in Chemistry.

Today, many see the global effort to phase out ozone-depleting substances as one of the greatest success stories of global environmentalism. Nevertheless, most scientists still expect that it will take another half century or so for the ozone layer to recover to 1980 levels. *See also* MIDGLEY, THOMAS, JR. (1889–1944); MONTREAL PROTOCOL ON SUBSTANCES THAT DEPLETE THE OZONE LAYER.

P

PALM OIL. Production of palm oil went up fourfold from 1995 to 2015, and analysts predict demand will continue to rise over the next few decades. Particularly in Asia and Africa, palm oil is widely used for cooking and deep frying. Common as well in processed food, cereals, bread, cosmetics, and personal care products, in some supermarkets, half of all packaged and processed products contain palm oil. More than four-fifths of the world's palm oil was coming from **Indonesia** and Malaysia in 2015, where, especially in Indonesia, growers of oil palms (the source of palm oil) have a long history of burning down degraded rain forests to fertilize the nutrient-poor soil (e.g., the **Indonesian forest fires of 1997–1998**). The burning of trees, coal seams, and peat lands in Indonesia routinely produces a choking haze of soot that reaches across Malaysia and **Singapore** and into the **Philippines**. Land-use shifts and **deforestation** made Indonesia the world's fifth-biggest emitter of greenhouse gases in 2014.

Nongovernmental organizations such as the **World Wide Fund for Nature/World Wildlife Fund (WWF)**, **Greenpeace**, the **Rainforest Action Network (RAN)**, and **SumOfUs** are all campaigning against palm oil with links to deforestation; in 2004, the WWF helped to establish the primary certification organization for palm oil, the **Roundtable on Sustainable Palm Oil**. Greenpeace, RAN, and SumOfUs have all pressured palm oil buyers—such as Unilever, Nestlé, Procter & Gamble, and Pepsi—to only source "sustainable" and "responsible" palm oil as part of an overall commitment to "zero deforestation."

PANARCHY. Lance H. Gunderson and **C. S. Holling** developed the term *panarchy* to advance the theory of ecosystem change. It combines the words *Pan*, the ancient Greek god of nature, and *hierarchy*. They used the term to avoid the colloquial understanding of hierarchy, which suggests a rigid, top-down approach, and create a framework for analyzing changing hierarchical systems (including within and across nature, societies, and institutions) with constantly adaptive cycles of growth, accumulation, restructuring, and renewal. An example of panarchy within society might occur when a community advocacy group manages to catalyze cycles of adaptive change across organizations until a full-scale societal change comes about.

PAPUA NEW GUINEA. *See* MELANESIA.

PARIS AGREEMENT. *See* UNITED NATIONS FRAMEWORK CONVENTION ON CLIMATE CHANGE (UNFCCC).

PASSENGER PIGEON. The passenger pigeon was once the most common bird in eastern North America, with perhaps as many as five billion birds at the peak. Hunted for food, the number of passenger pigeons declined steadily during the 19th century, then began falling sharply from about 1870 to 1890. The last passenger pigeon died in a Cincinnati zoo in 1914. Within the environmental movement, the extinction of the passenger pigeon remains a common example (sometimes told as a metaphor) of the potential devastating environmental damage that can be caused by unthinking development.

PBDEs. *See* POLYBROMINATED DIPHENYL ETHERS (PBDEs).

PEAK OIL. American geophysicist Marion King Hubbert (1903–1989) developed the idea of peak **oil**. In 1949, he calculated the total world oil supply and consumption. In 1956, presenting his findings as a bell-shaped curve, he predicted that in the **United States**, oil production would peak and subsequently fall between 1966 and 1972. This did occur in the early 1970s, although since then ensuing oil discoveries and new technologies have allowed for more oil output than Hubbert was expecting. Later, Hubbert predicted that global oil production would peak in the 1990s, lecturing and writing on how societies needed to prepare for life after petroleum. Inadequate data, flaws in his method, and miscalculating the potential of untapped and unmapped reserves explain this inaccurate and pessimistic prediction.

Others have picked up where Hubbert left off, and although this remains a contentious way of analyzing oil supplies, today a wide range of estimates exist for the date when global oil production will peak. Some see this as occurring before 2025, others expect it before 2030, and still others see 2050 as a reasonable date. For critics of this kind of analysis, the inaccurate estimates for global oil supplies demonstrate the tendency of many environmentalists to underestimate the potential for new knowledge and technologies to find or increase the supplies of so-called nonrenewable resources. For many environmentalists, this analysis reveals a disturbing trend toward ever-higher consumption of fossil fuels (with ever-higher emissions of **greenhouse gases**) and confirms the need to move quickly toward developing clean alternative energy (such as **solar power** and **wind power**).

PERSISTENT ORGANIC POLLUTANTS (POPs). Persistent organic pollutants are a large group of mostly **synthetic chemicals**. The **United Nations Environment Programme** has targeted the so-called dirty dozen for global phaseout. These include four originating mainly from industrial processes—polychlorinated biphenyls (PCBs), hexachlorobenzene (HCB), dioxins, and furans—and eight used primarily as pesticides: **dichlorodiphenyltrichloroethane (DDT)**, toxaphene, mirex, heptachlor, chlordane, aldrin, endrin, and dieldrin. The **Stockholm Convention on Persistent Organic Pollutants**, adopted in 2001 and in force since 2004, is the primary international legal mechanism for phasing these out (with 179 parties as of 2015).

Air and water currents can transport POPs far away from their emission source. Many POPs travel as well through a process of repeated evaporation and redeposit known as the "grasshopper effect." POPs also tend to build up in animals and plants, a process called bioaccumulation. That property of POPs also leads to an increase in the concentration of chemicals higher up in the food chain, a process called biomagnification. Environmentalist **Rachel Carson** was one of the first to recognize the potential effects of POPs in wildlife and people, which include reproductive and immune system disorders, neurological and developmental effects, and some cancers.

THE PHILIPPINES. Management of natural resources and the environment is fragmented in the Philippines, with responsibilities split between the national government and local government units. At the national level, responsibility is centered in the Department of Environment and Natural Resources, which oversees the Environmental Management Bureau, the Forest Management Board, the Parks and Wildlife Bureau, the Department of Energy, and the National Water Resources Board.

The presidency of Ferdinand Marcos (1965–1986) did pass some environmental legislation—including the 1976 Water Code of the Philippines, the 1977 Philippine Environmental Policy, and the 1978 Environmental Impact Assessment System—but pervasive corruption contributed to weak environmental regulation, destructive logging and land use, extensive **deforestation**, and severe soil erosion. In 1989, following devastating floods, the government banned timber exports; however, **illegal logging** was still widespread, and rates of deforestation and land degradation stayed high, contributing to more natural disasters, such as mudslides in 2003 on the island of Leyte.

The 1989 Philippine Strategy for Sustainable Development was put in place in 1989, and the Philippine Council for Sustainable Development (PCSD) was created in 1992 following the **United Nations Conference on Environment and Development**. In 1996, the government also established a national Agenda 21 to support the implementation of **Agenda 21** from this summit (although this has not been very effective). The Civil Society Counterpart Council for Sustainable Development was formed in 2001 as the nongovernmental equivalent to the government's PCSD.

The Philippines is one of the world's **biodiversity** hot spots. In an effort to protect this, it ratified the **Convention on International Trade in Endangered Species** in 1981 and the **Convention on Biological Diversity** in 1993. It also created the National Integrated Protected Areas System Act in 1992.

Garbage is one of the biggest urban environmental problems in the Philippines. The government passed the Ecological Solid Waste Management Act in 2000. However, the disposal and **recycling** infrastructure remains inadequate. In 2001, for example, President Gloria Arroyo declared a state of emergency in Metro Manila because of its mounting garbage crisis. Air **pollution** is another serious problem in cities such as Manila. The government did pass the Clean Air Act in 1999, and in 2003 it both required emission testing for motor vehicles registration and established hydrocarbon emission standards for motorcycles and tricycles. Since then, the Department of Environment and Natural Resources has stressed the value of better maintenance of vehicles, educating and encouraging owners, for example, with a "National Check Your Car Day" in 2014 and 2015 (offering free emission testing). However, many residents still live in conditions with unhealthy outdoor and indoor air (as well as inadequate sewage and unsafe water).

The Philippines has a vibrant civil society, with active environmental **nongovernmental organizations**. These include the Legal Rights and Natural Resources Center (a member of **Friends of the Earth** International), which started in 1988, and the Fund for Nature of the Philippines, which became a member of the **World Wide Fund for Nature/World Wildlife Fund (WWF)** in 1997. The WWF has been involved in the Philippines since 1969, when it funded efforts to protect the Philippine eagle. Eagle conservation was promoted by the Monkey-Eating Eagle Conservation Program, established in 1969. The program lost traction but was sustained by Peace Corps volunteers from the **United States** and rekindled in 1987, when it became the Philippine Eagle Foundation. The Philippines was also the first country in Asia to participate in a WWF debt-for-nature swap, in 1988.

PHOSPHATE. *See* NAURU.

PHOTOVOLTAIC ENERGY. *See* SOLAR POWER/ENERGY.

PINCHOT, GIFFORD (1865–1946). Born in Connecticut, Gifford Pinchot was the first chief of the **United States** Forest Service from 1905–1910. He was a pioneer in the American movement to conserve and manage forests, including playing a leading role in developing a national forest policy and promoting more efficient use of forest resources. He later served as governor of Pennsylvania (1923–1927 and 1931–1935). *See also* ECO-FORESTRY; WISE USE MOVEMENT.

PITCAIRN MARINE RESERVE. In 2015, **Great Britain** established the Pitcairn Marine Reserve in the middle of the Pacific Ocean. Covering 834,000 square kilometers (320,000 square miles), it is the world's largest contiguous marine reserve, linking the islands around Pitcairn Island, which sits more than 5,500 kilometers from **New Zealand**. Great Britain's jurisdiction in what is one of the most remote places on earth goes back to Fletcher Christian who, after leading the mutiny on the HMS *Bounty* in 1789, fled with a group of Tahitians to Pitcairn Island in 1790. A small colony of 50 or so people still live on Pitcairn, including descendants of the mutineers. Satellites will scan for any illegal **fishing** in the Pitcairn Marine Reserve, with the landing ports of trawlers notified if activities look suspicious. The Pitcairn Marine Reserve is part of a broader trend in ocean conservation toward establishing massive contiguous and noncontiguous **marine protected areas**.

PLASTIC. Plastics are made of petroleum and **natural gas**, both nonrenewable resources. Consumer and industrial uses vary from building material to packaging for goods and food to medical equipment. A common classification system to assist with disposal and **recycling** of consumer plastics is to number them from one to seven according to resin type (developed by the Society of the Plastics Industry in the **United States**). Recycled plastic is turned into many products, including pillow stuffing, plastic lumber, textiles, and drainage pipes.

Plastics do not easily degrade, a characteristic that concerns many in the environmental movement. Some plastic debris can photodegrade (break down into small pellets after extended exposure to sunlight), but most does not biodegrade (decompose into organic matter through bacterial digestion). Caught in ocean gyres, two regions of the Pacific Ocean now swirl with millions of tons of plastic: the so-called **Eastern Garbage Patch** off the coast of Hawaii and the smaller Western Garbage Patch off the coast of **Japan** (together covering a massive area of the Pacific). Plastic can harm marine life as it enters the food chain (plastic polymers effectively absorb toxic compounds such as **dichlorodiphenyltrichloroethane [DDT]** and polychlorinated biphenyls [PCBs], which act as endocrine disruptors to species that consume them).

Plastic production, which rose fourfold between 1980 and 2010, is continuing to rise steadily. By 2016 scientists were estimating that at least five trillion pieces of plastic were in the oceans, with millions of tons of plastic flowing in each year. Environmentalists see so much plastic—and the chemicals leaching out—as a threat to human health. One of the worries is phthalates, which are used as plasticizers (softeners) in polyvinyl chloride (PVC) products. In advance of conclusive scientific evidence, for example, the European Union has banned the use of certain phthalates in toys and child-care articles since 1999. Incineration of PVC is also the largest contributor of chlorine into incinerators, which produces significant dioxin emissions. Another worry for human health is **bisphenol A (BPA)**, a chemical that seems to mimic the female hormone estrogen and is common in everything from hard, clear plastic bottles to the lining in canned foods to dental sealants. *See also* OIL.

POLLUTER PAYS PRINCIPLE. The polluter pays principle is a principle incorporated into international environmental law and regulatory policies to allocate the cost of environmental damage to those who cause that damage. It relies on markets to achieve better environmental outcomes, where users and producers of products and activities that impose environmental costs on society bear responsibility for those costs (either voluntarily or through government incentives and penalties).

The principle has been adopted into the environmental policies of the Organisation for Economic Co-operation and Development, the European Community, **Vietnam**, and other countries, as well as integrated into international commitments, such as the declaration at the 1992 Rio Summit, which states that "national authorities should endeavour to promote the internalization of environmental costs and the use of economic instruments, taking into account the approach that the polluter should, in principle, bear the cost of **pollution**, with due regard to the public interest and without distorting international trade and investment."

Its application can include legal penalties for those who cause environmental degradation through industrial and business activities (such as requiring companies to pay for the restoration of rivers downstream from factories or for the cleanup of oil spills) and requirements that producers of goods take responsibility for end-of-life products (part of **extended product responsibility**). Applying the polluter pays principle promotes **environmental justice** by placing the costs of environmental degradation on those benefiting from polluting activities, and it encourages economic efficiency by internalizing the costs of pollution into the production process. *See also* BASEL

CONVENTION ON THE CONTROL OF TRANSBOUNDARY MOVE-
MENTS OF HAZARDOUS WASTES AND THEIR DISPOSAL; CON-
VENTION ON THE PREVENTION OF MARINE POLLUTION BY
DUMPING OF WASTES AND OTHER MATTER; FRANCE; GERMA-
NY; SWEDEN.

POLLUTION. A broad term, *pollution* encompasses many forms of contamination, degradation, and modification of natural and built environments.
Pollution of natural environments is often described by its location: for example, air pollution (indoor, outdoor, and transboundary), water pollution
(fresh water or ocean), and land pollution. It is also described by its form
(e.g., **smog**, **oil** spills, **plastics**, and **persistent organic pollutants**), by its
severity (e.g., garbage versus toxic or **hazardous wastes**), or by its cause
(e.g., industry, **automobiles**, and **mining**). The impacts of pollution are
equally far ranging and may include degrading habitats, which can threaten
biodiversity and harm vulnerable and **endangered species** (including **coral
reefs**). It can also affect human health, causing negative impacts on resources
and sectors that support human lives and livelihoods (e.g., **fishing**), as well
as contribute to **climate change**.

Many **nongovernmental organizations**, including **Greenpeace** and **Resources for the Future**, focus their activities on reducing or controlling
pollution. Public awareness, changes in behavior such as **recycling** and minimizing consumption, and corporate accountability for cleaner production
methods and **eco-efficiency** are all potential ways to reduce pollution.

Most countries, including **Canada**, **India**, **South Korea**, and **Taiwan**,
among many others, have passed legislation to control air and water pollution. However, even with regulations, many countries—such as **Chile**, **China**, and **Iran**—are still plagued by problems, especially in urban areas. Air
pollution is particularly bad in megacities in developing countries, where, for
example, many automobiles do not have catalytic converters and two-stroke
scooters and motorcycles are common. Forest fires (both intentional and
wild) can also contribute to air pollution; countries such as **Indonesia**, Malaysia, and **Singapore** are particularly affected by forest fires and have negotiated a transboundary haze treaty in an effort to tackle the problem.

Many international agreements also focus on reducing pollution, including
the **Convention on Long-Range Transboundary Air Pollution
(CLRTAP)**, the **Convention on the Prevention of Marine Pollution by
Dumping of Wastes and Other Matter**, and the **Basel Convention on the
Control of Transboundary Movements of Hazardous Wastes and Their
Disposal**. Market-based instruments, such as **carbon taxes** and **emissions
trading**, are also becoming an increasingly common means to address pollu-

tion; these types of policies follow the **polluter pays principle**, which allocates the costs of environmental damage to those who benefit from the activities that cause the pollution.

Delegates at the 1972 **United Nations Conference on the Human Environment** in **Sweden** coined the term *the pollution of poverty*, describing the role they attributed to underdevelopment and poverty in causing environmental degradation. The concept of **sustainable development** arose in response to this (and to broader concerns about poverty and environmental degradation). However, some environmental economists warn that during the early stages of economic development, pollution tends to intensify (see, for example, the **environmental Kuznets curve**). The **Green Revolution** is one example of where increased production and economic growth in agriculture led to increased pollution, as the development came with intensified use of pesticides and fertilizers. Some environmentalists advocate for development strategies that strive to avoid the pollution that tends to accompany rapid industrialization. *See also* ACID RAIN; ARCTIC; EASTERN GARBAGE PATCH; *EXXON VALDEZ* OIL SPILL; FRANCE; GERMANY; HYBRID AUTOMOBILES.

POLYBROMINATED DIPHENYL ETHERS (PBDEs). Polybrominated diphenyl ethers, or PBDEs, are put into consumer items as flame retardants and are now common in pillows, mattresses, rugs, curtains, TVs, and computers. Heralded as an advance in consumer safety in the 1970s, PBDEs raised few environmental or health concerns until scientists in **Sweden** set off alarms in the late 1990s after discovering that PBDEs in human breast milk seemed to be rising in some populations. Tests now confirm that these chemicals, with a chemical structure similar to polychlorinated biphenyls (PCBs) (some call them "chemical cousins") are somehow migrating from these products into people—not, apparently, mainly through food, as with other **persistent organic pollutants** such as dioxins or PCBs, but by collecting in homes, particularly in air and household dust.

Residents of the **United States** appear to have the world's highest levels of PBDEs (followed by Canadians). Tests around the year 2005 showed that residents of North America have 10–40 times higher PBDE levels than residents of **Japan** or Europe. Environmentalists are now campaigning to ban PBDEs, as laboratory experiments on animals suggest that they can cause hyperactivity, attention deficit, and low sperm counts. Medical researchers also worry that PBDEs may mimic and interfere with human hormones (such as thyroid hormones) and may damage brain development, even in only trace amounts.

Progress toward eliminating PBDEs is occurring. The Swedish company IKEA was one of the first companies to ban them. Many European governments have now taken steps to eliminate two of the worst formulations of

PBDEs: those common in mattresses and those in computer housings and monitors. Some states in the United States have done the same. Over the past decade, the U.S. Environmental Protection Agency has also been working with major producers such as DuPont to phase PBDEs out voluntarily. Some U.S. manufacturing and retail firms have also taken steps to stop using PBDEs, such as the computer company Dell.

POLYCHLORINATED BIPHENYLS (PCBs). *See* PERSISTENT ORGANIC POLLUTANTS (POPs).

PRECAUTIONARY APPROACH/PRINCIPLE. Following a precautionary approach requires a strategy to allow science enough time to investigate uncertainties and anticipate risks, while giving policy makers enough clout to prevent risky decisions in the pursuit of profits and markets (such as putting tetraethyl lead into gasoline to create **leaded gasoline**). Such an approach includes a duty of care, where the burden of proof about harm rests with those proposing to introduce a substance into the environment. Other caveats may also surround and either enhance or detract from the power of this principle. For example, Principle 7 of the **United Nations Global Compact** refers to the definition of a precautionary approach from the Rio Declaration from the 1992 **United Nations Conference on Environment and Development**, which stresses the need to apply precaution according to state "capabilities" and with "cost-effective measures."

PRESERVATION. The concept of preservation developed in the **United States** in the 19th century to convey the idea of protecting nature for its own sake (in contrast to conservation, which at the time put more emphasis on caring for nature for economic or leisure reasons). Many associate the preservation movement with the American naturalist **John Muir** (1838–1914), the founder of the **Sierra Club**, although other forces were important, too, such as a growing outdoor movement among upper- and middle-class Americans. Preservationists in the United States were able to mobilize to save some of the California redwoods; they also contributed to the establishment of state and **national parks**, such as Yellowstone National Park (1872) and Yosemite National Park (1890).

PRODUCT STEWARDSHIP. Product stewardship is a voluntary industry strategy to mitigate the negative environmental and health impacts of products (usually chemicals) throughout their life cycle, including research, manufacturing, transportation, storage, consumption, and disposal. Other goals include reducing corporate liability, preventing negative publicity, and earning public trust, as well as preempting legislation. First established by Dow

Chemical in 1972, product stewardship is an example of a market-based instrument for environmentalism, where industries self-regulate to internalize some of the costs of **pollution** to promote **sustainable development** and **corporate social responsibility**. As part of a product stewardship strategy, companies sometimes agree to accept back a dangerous product for **recycling**. One high-profile product stewardship program is **Responsible Care**, established in the 1980s by the chemical industry. Critics see the voluntary nature of product stewardship as insufficient, lacking in accountability, and often ineffective without government regulation to enforce and audit implementation. *See also* EXTENDED PRODUCER/PRODUCT RESPONSIBILITY (EPR).

PROGRAMME FOR THE ENDORSEMENT OF FOREST CERTIFICATION (PEFC). Launched in 1999 by representatives from 11 European countries, the Programme for the Endorsement of Forest Certification (PEFC) Council is a nonprofit **nongovernmental organization** that aims to provide "an assurance mechanism to purchasers of wood and paper products that they are promoting the sustainable management of forests." PEFC is a global umbrella organization comprising dozens of independent national forest certification systems. **Canada** and the **United States** joined in 2001. As of 2016, more than 260 million hectares of forest were PEFC certified. Supporters see this as part of a global movement to develop environmental markets, providing consumers with independent guarantees of **sustainability**. Critics worry that the standards are too low; for example, the program permits logging in old-growth and other forest areas with high ecological value. *See also* ECO-CERTIFICATION; SUSTAINABLE FORESTRY INITIATIVE (SFI).

PROXIMITY PRINCIPLE. *See* BASEL CONVENTION ON THE CONTROL OF TRANSBOUNDARY MOVEMENTS OF HAZARDOUS WASTES AND THEIR DISPOSAL.

R

RAINBOW WARRIOR. The *Rainbow Warrior* was one of the vessels that **Greenpeace** International planned to use to disrupt French nuclear tests in the South Pacific in July 1985. Docked at Auckland Harbor in **New Zealand** on 10 July 1985, the ship sank after two devices exploded on board. One of the crew—a Netherlands national—drowned. Five days later, two agents of the Directorate General of External Security, a branch of the French Ministry of Defense, were arrested in New Zealand. The chief justice of the High Court of New Zealand would later sentence each for manslaughter and willful damage. The killing strained relations between New Zealand and **France**; worldwide, the sinking of the *Rainbow Warrior* became a symbol of the courage of environmentalists and a sign of the brutality of those working to subvert the movement. Today, a ship named the *Rainbow Warrior* continues to ply the world's oceans on behalf of the Greenpeace cause.

RAIN FOREST. *See* DEFORESTATION.

RAINFOREST ACTION NETWORK (RAN). Founded in 1985 by Randall Hayes, the central goal of the Rainforest Action Network (RAN) is to protect rain forests and the rights of those living in these forests, although recently it has also been campaigning to halt **climate change**. Its primary tactic involves direct-action campaigns targeting specific corporations, with the aim of changing purchasing or other behavior.

The first successful campaign was a 1987 boycott of the restaurant chain Burger King, which stopped importing "rain forest beef"—cattle raised on pastures created from cleared rain forests—after sales dropped by more than 10 percent. Other campaigns over the past few decades have included the Old Growth Campaign (to protect old-growth forests from logging), the Freedom from Oil Campaign (to reduce **oil**-related conflicts, decrease oil dependence in the **United States**, and mitigate climate change by working with the auto industry to increase fuel efficiency and reduce **greenhouse gases**), and the Conflict Palm Oil Campaign (to pressure companies into only buying **palm oil** certified as not contributing to **deforestation**, the clearing of peat lands, human rights abuses, or community conflict). The Old Growth Campaign influenced the purchasing policies of some major retailers, including Kinko's, Home Depot, and Lowe's, all of which committed to stop buying or selling products made from old-growth timber. RAN's Freedom from Oil Campaign targeted the Ford Motor Company, among other major multinational companies. The Conflict Palm Oil Campaign influenced the purchasing policies of a large number of companies, including Hershey's, Nestlé, Kellogg's, Mars, and General Mills (with many agreeing to only purchase palm oil certified by the **Roundtable on Sustainable Palm Oil**).

RAMOS, ROSA HILDA. *See* GOLDMAN ENVIRONMENTAL PRIZE.

RAMSAR CONVENTION ON WETLANDS. *See* CONVENTION ON WETLANDS OF INTERNATIONAL IMPORTANCE ESPECIALLY AS WATERFOWL HABITAT.

REBOUND EFFECT. Sometimes labeled the Jevons paradox, within environmentalism the rebound effect posits that the seeming ecological gains from integrating new technologies, improving energy and natural resource efficiencies, or reducing waste can be misleading, as firms and consumers may behave differently or invest savings in new ventures or new purchases, rebounding to produce equally great, if not greater, overall problems for **sustainability**. Calling this the Jevons paradox comes from an 1865 book, *The Coal Question*, by William Stanley Jevons, who showed how the increasing efficiency of steam engines did not cause **coal** consumption to decline but instead to rise as new incentives came into play to find new uses. Since Jevons, researchers have documented many examples of the rebound effect across energy and natural resources systems as well as within communities of consumers. Much of the debate, however, remains confined to academic journals and scholarly conferences, while considerable differences exist in interpreting the relative significance of the rebound effect. Some **nongovernmental organizations** continue to campaign to bring these effects to light, with proposals, for example, to tax energy savings to try to prevent the rebound effect from increasing overall energy consumption. But **corporate social responsibility** and governmental programs to promote **sustainable development** tend to downplay—or basically ignore—the possibility of rebound effects.

RECLAIM THE STREETS (RTS). Relying on grassroots and spontaneous organization and espousing a principle of nonviolence, Reclaim the Streets (RTS) involves protests opposing corporate capitalism (usually with a specific focus on the societal and environmental damage from the increasing dependency on **automobiles**). It first emerged in London in 1991 as part of a direct-action movement against automobiles in **Great Britain**.

This group disbanded, but another reemerged in 1994 in the "Battle for Claremont Road," also known as the "No M11" campaign, to protest plans to demolish a residential street in East London to build a thoroughfare. Protestors occupied every vacant house on the street, then turned the neighborhood into a street party. Although this did not stop construction of the thoroughfare, RTS became famous for its street parties—or political raves. Street Party 1 (1995) was held in Camden Town. Street Party 2 (1995) was held at the Angel, Islington (north London). Street Party 3 (July 1996) was much bigger, occupying a stretch of motorway in west London, with over 7,000 participants. Organizers pulled these protests off by using tight security, with only a handful of people knowing a party's location ahead of time.

Shortly after Street Party 3, chapters of RTS began to emerge in the **United States**, with the first in San Francisco when RTS/Bay Area held a street party on Berkeley's Telegraph Avenue in 1998. Today, although the group has done little to slow the growing global dependency on the automobile as the primary form of transportation, this diffuse movement has spread around the world, with occasional protests occurring in, for example, **Australia**, **Canada**, **Finland**, **India**, Ireland, and **Mexico**. *See also* GUERRILLA GARDENING.

RECYCLING. Recycling is a waste management strategy to reprocess used materials into new products, thus reducing the amount of waste. Proponents contend that it is more ecologically benign than landfills and incineration, depleting fewer resources. Also, it can generate economic benefits, including funds for municipalities from sales, job creation, and new markets from product innovation.

Modern household recycling started in the late 1960s in response to concerns about social equity and **pollution**. Community groups ran early facilities, selling collected materials back to manufacturers. In Western societies, curbside recycling was spreading by the late 1980s. Reasons for these programs vary, but common ones are rising landfill costs, public opposition to incineration and new landfills, escalating amounts of garbage, and strengthening public support for environmentalism. Recycling in industrial processes also occurs, where one industry's waste stream becomes a raw material for a different industry.

Today, recycling has turned into billion-dollar businesses in many countries, with the global recycling trade alone heading toward $1 trillion in value. Some environmentalists criticize recycling for not challenging unsustainable patterns of production and consumption. Others stress that it is at best only a partial solution to the environmental consequences of rising consumption. Often, for example, breaking materials down and remanufacturing them requires chemical and energy inputs and releases toxins. It is common as well to reinforce recycled content with new materials. Most environmentalists, however, support recycling, although many propose a "3-R" waste management hierarchy: reduce, reuse, and, as a last resort, recycle. *See also* DEEP ECOLOGY; EXTENDED PRODUCER/PRODUCT RESPONSIBILITY (EPR); GLASS; PLASTIC; PRODUCT STEWARDSHIP; TIRES.

REES, WILLIAM. *See* ECOLOGICAL FOOTPRINT.

REFORESTATION. Forestation includes both afforestation and reforestation. Afforestation involves establishing forest cover in areas without a recent history of forests. Reforestation involves reestablishing forests on degraded forestlands or in areas where forests grew in more recent times. In developed countries, replanting efforts over the last few decades have allowed the total area of temperate forests to expand, although afforested and reforested areas are often less complex forest ecosystems (including many monoculture plantations). Intense logging, fires, and land clearing in developing countries, however, have left tropical **deforestation** rates far exceeding any gains from afforestation and reforestation. Still, reforestation can provide many benefits in developing countries—for example, slowing soil erosion and **desertification** and providing people with wood and fuel—and it has been an effective strategy for some community-based environmental movements, such as the **Green Belt Movement** in **Kenya**. Growing forests also sequester carbon, and many see reforestation as both a feasible and valuable way to reduce **greenhouse gases** and address **climate change**. *See also* ILLEGAL LOGGING.

RENEWABLE ENERGY. Renewable energy is, in theory, from inexhaustible sources, unlike, for example, energy from finite sources such as **fossil fuels**. This includes **solar energy**; **wind energy**; **geothermal energy**; wave, tidal, and ocean thermal energy; hydroelectricity; and biomass.

Except for hydroelectricity and biomass, in practice, these energy sources are often expensive, unreliable, or available only on a small scale. Worldwide, renewable energy supplies less than one-fifth of the world's total primary energy. Developing countries currently account for three-quarters of renewable energy use globally, principally in the form of biomass or hydropower.

Countries such as Austria, **Canada**, **New Zealand**, Switzerland, and **Sweden** currently derive over 50 percent of their electricity production from renewables. A few countries, such as Paraguay, Iceland, Nepal, Mozambique, the Democratic Republic of Congo, **Costa Rica**, and Norway obtain the majority of their energy needs from renewable energy. The sustainable energy movement, including environmentalists like **Amory B. Lovins**, is calling for more efforts to develop renewable energies such as wind and solar power to address threats like **climate change**. *See also* BRAZIL; HYBRID AUTOMOBILES; PHOTOVOLTAIC ENERGY; THREE GORGES DAM.

RESOURCES FOR THE FUTURE (RFF). Founded in 1952, Resources for the Future (RFF) is a nonprofit and nonaligned organization based in Washington, D.C. It was the first think tank in the **United States** to focus solely on environmental, energy, and natural resource issues. Today, it contributes in particular to demonstrating the value of economic tools for developing effective policy for exploiting and conserving natural resources. Many RFF researchers hold doctorate degrees in economics, but staff expertise also includes engineering, law, ecology, city planning, and public policy. Current research efforts concentrate on **biodiversity**, **climate change**, **deforestation**, **pollution** control (including air), land and water use, **hazardous waste**, energy policy, and environmental issues in developing countries.

RESPONSIBLE CARE. A voluntary commitment by the chemical industry to environmental and social responsibility, Responsible Care is an environmental management system for chemicals. Companies that commit must continuously improve the health, safety, security, and environmental performance of chemical operations as well as respond to public concerns about the safe management of chemicals. It encourages companies to go above and beyond government requirements. Goals include improving chemical processes, practices, and procedures; reducing waste, accidents, incidents, and emissions; and developing reliable communication with the public. Standards comprise Codes of Management Practice addressing **product steward-ship**, community awareness and emergency response, employee health and safety, process safety, and **pollution** prevention. Companies undergo a third-party independent audit for a Responsible Care Management System (RCMS) standard or an integrated standard such as the RC14001 American standard (which provides joint certification with the **International Organization for Standardization [ISO] 14001**).

Launched in **Canada** in 1985 by the Canadian Chemical Producers' Association (spurred in part by the chemical accident in 1984 in **Bhopal, India**), by 2015, Responsible Care had been adopted in 60 countries. It is one of the largest and most successful voluntary **corporate social responsibility** initiatives. In 2005, the International Council of Chemical Associations created a Responsible Care Global Charter to encourage adoption of national Responsible Care programs and to advance the global chemical industry's commitment to **sustainable development** consistent with the environmental principles of the **United Nations Global Compact**. Participation is mandatory for membership in many national chemical industry associations, such as the Canadian Chemical Producers' Association and the American Chemistry Council (formerly the Chemical Manufacturers' Association). *See also* CORPORATE SOCIAL RESPONSIBILITY (CSR); ECO-CERTIFICATION.

RIKHVANOVA, MARINA. *See* GOLDMAN ENVIRONMENTAL PRIZE.

RIO SUMMIT. *See* UNITED NATIONS CONFERENCE ON ENVIRONMENT AND DEVELOPMENT (UNCED).

ROUNDTABLE ON SUSTAINABLE PALM OIL (RSPO). Founded in 2004, the nongovernmental Roundtable on Sustainable Palm Oil certifies responsible and sustainable palm oil production. Clearing for oil palms, the source of **palm oil**, is a leading cause of tropical **deforestation**, particularly in Malaysia and **Indonesia**, which together produce more than four-fifths of the world's palm oil. The **World Wide Fund for Nature/World Wildlife Fund (WWF)** took the lead on setting up the RSPO, cooperating with producers (e.g., the Malaysian Palm Oil Association), buyers (e.g., the British-Dutch firm Unilever), and other stakeholders. RSPO had grown from 10 founding members to more than 1,700 members by 2015, bringing together growers, processors, investors, buyers, manufacturers, venders, and **nongovernmental organizations**. RSPO audits growers and processors, verifying compliance on a range of standards, including land-clearing practices, pesticide management, and greenhouse gas emissions.

Supporters see the RSPO as offering incentives for corporations and governments to avoid illegal and destructive land clearing by reducing demand for palm oil grown on deforested land while increasing demand for certified palm oil. Critics of the RSPO claim that poor environmental and social practices within the global palm oil industry remain common, and plantation owners still routinely burn down tropical forests to plant oil palms. The WWF has remained largely supportive of RSPO, although the NGO is pressing for tougher guidelines and better monitoring of standards. *See also* ECO-CERTIFICATION; INDONESIAN FOREST FIRES, 1997–1998.

RUSSIA. A tradition of natural history and nature protection societies was in place prior to the 1917 Russian Revolution; in that year, for example, a Conservation Conference to discuss the establishment of **national parks** was held in Petrograd. Still, the 1920s is sometimes called the golden age for Russian environmentalism as the new Soviet Union (USSR, or Union of Soviet Socialist Republics, 1922–1991) put in place legislation to support *zapovedniki*, or protected areas, first set up in the 1890s. These were similar to national parks in the **United States**, although locations were selected more for ecological criteria.

The Soviet Union's First Five-Year Plan of 1929–1933, however, ended this wave of environmentalism, increasing timber production and altering production methods in agriculture and industry. In the 1930s and 1940s, the state did not allow intellectual or political dissent; conservationists were labeled un-Marxist and antirevolutionary. By the end of the 1950s, the protected area had decreased from 12.5 million to 1.5 million hectares. Joseph Stalin's death in 1953 did little to change Soviet environmentalism; not until the 1970s did environmental writings appear in newspapers and magazines. During this time the extent of protected areas also began to rise again. But it was not until Mikhail Gorbachev's glasnost that environmental critics and the environmental movement began to gain strength.

Among the many environmental problems of the Soviet Union were the eutrophication of Lake Baikal caused by the effluents of a paper mill; the accident at the **Chernobyl** nuclear plant in 1986; nuclear contamination from the nuclear arms race; air **pollution** in industrial cities; and lead, carbon monoxide, and nitrogen oxide pollution from traffic. In Central Asia, the **Aral Sea**, once the world's fourth-largest lake, shrank by half by the early 1990s as authorities diverted its inflows to agriculture and hydroelectricity.

The breakup of the Soviet Union in 1991 contributed to an economic crisis in the Russian Federation. This added to environmental pressures, especially on water and air quality and **hazardous waste** management.

President Mikhail Gorbachev's glasnost policy mandating a more open and transparent government allowed many environmental **nongovernmental organizations (NGOs)** and civil society groups to form. For example, the Socio-Ecological Union, founded in 1988, persisted after the fall of the Soviet Union and now operates as a network of hundreds of NGOs across the former Union of Soviet Socialist Republics. Other environmental groups also began to take shape and gain more influence in the 1990s. For example, the Ecojuris Institute of Environmental Law was founded in 1991 as Russia's first public-interest environmental law firm. By 1998, it had won a Supreme Court case brought against several government proposals, including for development in protected forest areas. Other groups have had some notable achievements, too. For example, the government created a national park to protect the Siberian tiger in 2007, in part because of advocacy and pressure by the **World Wide Fund for Nature/World Wildlife Fund (WWF)** and other environmental groups.

Official political participation by environmental activists started in 1991 with the founding of the Interregional Green Party, which started as a local political party in Leningrad (St. Petersburg). In 2005, this party became Zelenaya Alternativa (GROZA), or Green Alternative, a national political movement but not a political party. The political **green party** of Russia, the Russian Ecological Party, or the Greens, was started as the Constructive Ecological Party in 1992.

In 2000, environmental responsibilities were transferred from the State Committee for Environmental Protection to the Natural Resources Ministry. Some environmental NGOs like **Greenpeace** saw this as a troubling move, since the Natural Resources Ministry is focused on resource extraction rather than conservation.

Nuclear waste and safety has been a major issue in Russia. A European Commission program to improve nuclear safety across the former Soviet Union, the Technical Assistance to the Commonwealth of Independent States (TACIS) Programme, was launched in 1991. The program was revised in 1998 following a slow start, highlighted by incidents such as an explosion at a plutonium-processing facility in Tomsk in 1993. Russia was also criticized following a 1996 exposé on nuclear waste from a nuclear submarine base in the **Arctic**, by Alexander Nikitin (a Russian environmentalist and winner of the 1997 **Goldman Environmental Prize**) and the Bellona Foundation (an NGO from Norway).

Russia suffers from many other environmental problems as well. The country has the world's largest **natural gas** reserves as well as substantial **coal** and **oil** reserves. Several ships caught in 2007 in a storm in the straits between the Azov and Black Seas spilled oil, sulfur, and other toxic materials. Around that time, the WWF and others were also raising concerns over environmental damage in Chechnya, following many years of conflict over demands for independence. Environmental concerns in the area include chemical and radioactive pollution, leaking oil pipelines, inadequate sewerage systems that cause water contamination, and **illegal logging**.

In 1997, Russia joined the Group of Eight (G8); its presidency in 2006 was focused, in part, on energy. Also in 1997, Russia signed an Agreement on Partnership and Cooperation with the European Union (EU), which includes environmental cooperation concerns. Environmental issues were included in subsequent Russia-EU agreements, including the EU-Russia Strategic Partnership and the EU-Russia Common Economic Space road map. Notably, in 2005, Russia ratified the **Kyoto Protocol**, a landmark event, as it allowed the protocol to enter into force (it needed at least 55 countries contributing at least 55 percent of 1990 **greenhouse gas** emissions).

Over the past decade, however, President Vladimir Putin, to some extent during his first tenure as president (2000–2008), but even more so since starting his second formal tenure in 2012, has been progressively cracking down on civil society dissent, including criticism and challenges from environmental groups. New legislation in 2012 (along with later amendments) requires any Russian NGO with a link to a foreign organization (e.g., funding or partnerships), or any NGO with "political" goals, to register as a "foreign agent." Since 2012, this so-called foreign agents law, along with more repressive responses to environmental campaigns from 2012 to 2016, has weakened Russia's environmental movement, especially those with ties to international environmental campaigns and organizations. *See also* FISHING; NUCLEAR POWER/ENERGY; SEALING; SIBERIA.

S

SANTA CRUZ ISLANDS. *See* MELANESIA.

SANTOS, FELICIANO DOS. *See* GOLDMAN ENVIRONMENTAL PRIZE.

SARO-WIWA, KEN (1941–1995). Kenule (Ken) Beeson Saro-Wiwa was a Nigerian public servant, environmentalist, television producer, and author (with more than two dozen books). The son of a chief of the Ogoni people, in 1990, he helped found the Movement for the Survival of the Ogoni People (MOSOP) to fight with nonviolent tactics for social and ecological justice (especially against the multinational **oil** companies). MOSOP was popular among the Ogoni; for example, more than half of the 500,000 Ogoni people showed up at one protest in 1993. Saro-Wiwa was particularly critical of the oil company Shell and **Nigeria**'s military dictatorship for destroying the environment and threatening the survival of the Ogoni people.

In 1993, four chiefs, including Saro-Wiwa's brother-in-law and a founding member of MOSOP, were murdered during a riot in Ogoni. In October 1995, Saro-Wiwa and eight others were sentenced to hang for inciting the murders. Human rights and environmental groups, along with many governments, condemned the ruling. To the surprise of many observers, despite the international backlash Saro-Wiwa was executed in November 1995, creating an even greater storm of worldwide anger at Nigeria's dictator, General Sani Abacha, as well as at Shell. Today, Saro-Wiwa is honored worldwide as an example of the bravery necessary for environmentalism in corrupt and repressive states propped up by profit-seeking multinational corporations. Worldwide tributes to his courage and commitment marked the 20th anniversary of his execution in November 2015.

SCHOPS, IGNACE. *See* GOLDMAN ENVIRONMENTAL PRIZE.

SCHUMACHER, E. F. (1911–1977). Born in Bonn, **Germany**, Ernst Friedrich (Fritz) Schumacher left Germany in 1936 for **Great Britain** (where earlier he had been a Rhodes Scholar at Oxford University) to escape Nazism. Unable to find work in his field, he became a farm laborer before being interned for three months during World War II as an enemy alien. Returning to the farm after his internment, Schumacher began to write on the economic prerequisites for lasting peace in Europe. Having gained British citizenship in 1946, he then became an economic advisor to—and was a member of—the British Control Commission, which worked to rebuild the German economy. In the 1950s and 1960s, he was chief economic advisor to the British National Coal Board. In 1955, he traveled to Burma for the **United Nations**, a trip that would inspire his writings on what he called "Buddhist economics," where priority is put on improving human lives, with local economies producing goods from local resources for local needs. After a trip to **India** in 1961, Schumacher pioneered the idea of intermediate or appropriate technology, arguing that simpler technologies that match the scale of community life were often more efficient and environmentally suitable in rural developing areas. He brought all of these ideas together into his best-selling 1973 book, *Small Is Beautiful: Economics as If People Matter*, which to this day remains highly influential among those who argue for the localization of economies to advance sustainability. *See also* ECOLOGICAL ECONOMICS.

SEA SHEPHERD CONSERVATION SOCIETY. *See* WATSON, PAUL (1950–).

SEALING. As early as 5000 BC, native people were hunting seals in what is now Atlantic **Canada**. European settlers have hunted harp seals for over 300 years off the coast of Newfoundland and in the Gulf of St. Lawrence. Countries involved over the centuries include **Russia**, **Great Britain**, Norway, Canada, and the **United States**, mostly sealing in Canadian waters but also in the White and Baltic Seas, the North Pacific, and the Sub-**Antarctic** Islands. Already, by the end of the 19th century, a dozen species of seals were on the verge of extinction.

Environmentalists and animal rights activists began to protest the hunting of harp seals in eastern Canada in the 1960s, saying it was cruel and unsustainable. Protestors objected in particular to the "slaughter" of "baby" whitecoats—harp pups between 6 and 12 days old—usually killed with several blows to the skull with a wooden bat or hooked gaff.

Facing a global outcry, the Canadian federal government began to regulate harvesting and impose quotas. But the antisealing campaign continued to gain ground in the 1970s as environmental groups such as **Greenpeace** joined forces with animal rights groups such as the International Fund for

Animal Welfare (IFAW). The activists were creative and bold, confronting hunters and cuddling whitecoats in front of millions of television viewers. During the 1970s, activists became better organized, fund-raising for million-dollar budgets, filling conventions with snow-white balloons, and handing politicians petitions with thousands of pages of signatures calling for an end to the hunt.

Over time, activists began to focus on disrupting import markets in Europe (the primary market for white fur coats). This strategy eventually produced a dramatic victory when, in 1983, the European Community imposed a two-year ban on the import of whitecoat pelts. The ban was renewed in 1985 and, with an antisealing campaign to boycott Canadian fish products growing in Europe and the United States, the Canadian government banned the hunt for whitecoats in 1987, in effect ending Canada's commercial seal hunt.

This did not last, however. In the mid-1990s, the Canadian government began to increase the allowable catch for seals older than 12 days, provide subsidies, and develop new markets. Although it was still illegal to kill whitecoats and only small boats and locals could harvest the older seals, the Canadian government was effectively reopening the commercial hunt. By the mid-2000s, commercial sealers were landing over 320,000 harp seals, larger than the hunts of the 1970s and 1980s. The activists returned—angry and vocal—but struggled to gain the same influence as in the mid-1990s, partly because the primary markets for seal fur coats had shifted to **China** and Russia. Since 2009, however, as prices and demand have fallen for seal products, total annual commercial catch levels have dropped below 100,000 harp seals, with only 35,000 landed in 2015, even though the Canadian government's official "allowable catch" is 400,000 harp seals.

SHALE GAS. *See* NATURAL GAS.

SHALLOW ECOLOGY. *See* DEEP ECOLOGY.

SHIVA, VANDANA (1952–). Born in Dehradun, **India**, Vandana Shiva trained as a physicist, receiving a doctorate from the University of Western Ontario in 1978 with a dissertation title of "Hidden Variables and Non-locality in Quantum Theory." Returning to India, Shiva did research for the Indian Institute of Management on technology, science, and environmental policy. In 1982, she moved back to her hometown to set up her Research Foundation for Science, Technology and Ecology. Since that time she has become one of the world's leading environmental writers and campaigners on issues of **biodiversity, genetically modified organisms (GMOs),** food security, and gender. She helped found the movement Navdanya to protect the diversity of food sources, promote organic farming, and advocate for the rights of farmers in India. She was also a leader in the Neem Campaign and Basmati Campaign, which strove to prevent biopiracy (the appropriation of the rights of indigenous peoples over knowledge, generally using patents). Her books include *The Violence of the Green Revolution*, *Monocultures of the Mind*, *Staying Alive*, *Biopiracy: The Plunder of Nature and Knowledge*, *Soil Not Oil: Environmental Justice in an Age of Climate Crisis*, and *Ecofeminism* (with Maria Mies).

SIBERIA. Strictly speaking, Siberia only encompasses the region extending east of the Ural Mountains up to the western border of the Russian Far East, which is geographically and economically distinct (mountainous and more sparsely populated). Both regions, however, are generally grouped into what is called Siberia. For centuries this remote and expansive region has been a source of natural resources, and the priorities of faraway governments have tended to override local efforts to promote conservation or sustainable production.

Today, the region continues to supply the global economy with natural resources. It contains vast **oil** and **natural gas** reserves, for example, the eastern Siberian gas fields in Yakutia and around the Lena River and the oil and gas fields under Sakhalin Island in the Far East. It also has deep mineral stores, especially in the Far East. Timber is equally vast, with the forests of Siberia and the Far East containing a vast wood supply.

This richness in natural resources has affected the environment in many ways, often negatively. Waterways, such as the Ob River, are contaminated; in many cities, such as Kemerovo Oblast in the southwest, residents suffer from high rates of bronchial asthma and lung cancer. **Deforestation** rates are also some of the world's highest. Water and soil quality are much better in the Far East, but even here environmental degradation is severe in many of the places with open-pit **mining**. The region also suffers from the legacy of nuclear testing, radioactive waste storage, and plutonium mining during the era of the Soviet Union from 1922 to 1991.

Environmental activism in Siberia existed throughout the Soviet period but was particularly influential during the years of Nikita Khrushchev (1953–1964), following his "opening" of the political system. Students and scientists were at the core of this activism. One example is the Kedrograd movement in the late 1950s to protect Siberian pine forests. Led by students from the Leningrad forestry academy, it proposed harvesting forest resources without damaging the trees. A second example was the scientific movement in the 1960s to protect Lake Baikal, a **United Nations Educational, Scientific and Cultural Organization (UNESCO)** World Heritage Site and the world's oldest and deepest freshwater lake, from industrial waste, air **pollution**, deforestation, and plans to divert flows for agriculture and hydroelectricity. Today, local environmentalists are joined by international campaigners from groups such as **Greenpeace**, with, for example, campaigns to save the boreal forests from logging. *See also* GOLDMAN ENVIRONMENTAL PRIZE; RUSSIA; SIBERIAN PERMAFROST.

SIBERIAN PERMAFROST. Around 50 billion metric tons of methane—about one-sixth of the total stored on land—sits in the northeast Siberian ice complex. Melting permafrost in **Siberia** is now releasing this methane, which has about 20 times the greenhouse effect of carbon dioxide. Some ecologists worry that this is producing a self-reinforcing feedback, with warmer conditions producing more methane and more methane accelerating the process of warming. *See also* CLIMATE CHANGE.

SIERRA CLUB. The Sierra Club is one of the oldest and largest grassroots environmental organizations in the **United States**. Cofounded in 1892 by preservationist **John Muir**, who became its first president, the Sierra Club originally focused on preserving the forests and ecosystems of the Sierra Nevada. Today, it campaigns on a range of issues, from protecting national forests and marine **biodiversity** to promoting **environmental justice**, sustainable consumption, population management, and responsible trade. Headquartered in San Francisco, it has a lobbying office in Washington, D.C. (since 1963), as well as many state and regional offices. It has hundreds of thousands of members in local chapters throughout the United States as well as an affiliate Sierra Club of **Canada**. Members receive the magazine *Sierra*. *See also* NONGOVERNMENTAL ORGANIZATIONS (NGOs); PRESERVATION.

SIMON, JULIAN (1932–1998). Simon was a professor of business administration at the University of Maryland and a senior fellow at the Cato Institute. One of his best-known books is *The Ultimate Resource* (1981). Writers such as Simon—and more recently **Bjørn Lomborg**—have challenged the pessimistic prediction of a looming "global crisis" common among environmentalists. For these optimists, history is defined primarily by social and economic progress. This history confirms the fallacy of believing in limits to growth, as efficiency gains from ingenuity and technology can in fact allow economic growth to continue forever. Thus, for Simon the current trajectory toward better standards of living can, with balanced responses to the alarmism of environmentalism, also continue indefinitely. Simon's publications have stirred a hornet's nest of environmental critics. His defenders respond by pointing to global trends over the last century, like longer life expectancies and higher per capita incomes.

SINGAPORE. A small island state with few natural resources, Singapore has a strong administrative framework for environmental governance and legislation. Following independence from Malaysia in 1965 (a short-lived arrangement replacing British rule in 1963), the government created its Ministry of the Environment in 1972. In 2004, this became the Ministry of the Environment and Water Resources (MEWR) with control over the National Environment Agency and the Public Utilities Board. The **National Parks** Board oversees several hundred parks and gardens in the country, along with three nature reserves and one wetland reserve. In 1998, the Interagency Committee on Energy Efficiency was created; it was restructured as the National Energy Efficiency Committee in 2001, then as the National Climate Change Committee in 2006 when Singapore acceded to the **Kyoto Protocol**.

Singapore gives particular attention to developing water technology, first experimenting with water **recycling** in 1974. High costs precluded significant progress until the late 1990s, however, when the Public Utilities Board started the Singapore Water Reclamation Study (known as the NEWater Study).

Nongovernmental organizations tend to cooperate closely with government agencies in Singapore. The National Council on the Environment, created in 1990 and renamed the Singapore Environment Council (SEC) in 1995, works with the government to coordinate environmental action. For example, the SEC administers the Singapore Green Labelling Scheme (SGLS), an **eco-labeling** program created in 1992 by the Ministry of the Environment.

Singapore is active in promoting cooperative environmental management in the Asia-Pacific region. It is the headquarters of the Asia-Pacific Centre for Environmental Law, established in 1996 by the National University of Singapore's Faculty of Law, the Commission on Environmental Law of the **International Union for Conservation of Nature (IUCN)**, and the **United Nations Environment Programme**. In 2002, the nongovernmental Environmental Challenge Organisation (ECO) Singapore was founded to support environmental movements in Singapore. It also acts as the Secretariat for the Asia Youth Environmental Network and helped to found the Asia-Europe Meeting (ASEM) Youth Network for Sustainable Development.

Singapore has some of the world's strictest environmental regulations for **automobiles** and industry (both for waste and emissions). In recent years, however, during drier months, a smoky haze from forest fires in **Indonesia** has been drifting over Singapore (as well as Malaysia and **Thailand**) and causing unhealthy levels of air **pollution**; in an effort to stop this, in 2003 Singapore ratified the ASEAN Agreement on Transboundary Haze Pollution. Since then, however, haze over Singapore has been an ongoing problem. To promote sustainable sourcing practices and weaken demand for products contributing to peat-land fires and deforestation in Indonesia, the Singapore

Green Labelling Scheme has encouraged companies to sign a "Haze Declaration," affirming that they would only purchase wood products from "sustainable sources." By November 2015, 145 companies had made this pledge. *See also* INDONESIAN FOREST FIRES, 1997–1998.

SINGER, PETER (1946–). Born in **Australia**, philosopher Peter Albert David Singer was educated at the University of Melbourne and Oxford University. Since 1999, he has been Ira W. DeCamp Professor of Bioethics at Princeton University; since 2005, he has also held a Laureate Professorship at the University of Melbourne. His book *Animal Liberation* (1975) has been especially influential among those critical of the anthropocentrism of modern environmentalism. He is also considered a leading intellectual within the animal rights movement, although his controversial arguments have angered many people, such as advocates for the disabled. In 2015 he published the book *The Most Good You Can Do: How Effective Altruism Is Changing Ideas about Living Ethically*, arguing for the value of "effective altruism" (rational rather than emotional charitable giving) as a way of stimulating positive social and political change.

SMOG. Combining the words *smoke* (especially from burning **coal**) and *fog*, the word *smog* became common after a London newspaper quoted Dr. Henry Antoine Des Voeux in 1905 describing the London fog as "smog." Today, smog refers more generally to air **pollution** hanging over cities as a thick haze. First World cities with heavy traffic and a natural tendency to trap pollution—such as London and Los Angeles—still regularly experience smog. On the one hand, air quality in much of the First World tends to be improving with stricter controls on **automobile** and industrial emissions. On the other hand, smog remains severe and is worsening in many cities of the Third World, for example, Beijing, Mexico City, Santiago, and Tehran. **India** is facing an especially grave air-quality crisis, with the World Health Organization declaring cities such as Delhi, Patna, Gwalior, Raipur, and Karachi some of the world's most polluted in 2015. Globally, every year outdoor air pollution continues to cause millions of people to die prematurely. *See* CHILE.

SOLAR POWER/ENERGY. Solar power arises from solar heat and photovoltaic energy. Along with wind energy, solar electricity is one of the fastest-growing forms of renewable energy. The vast majority comes from photovoltaic energy; solar thermal power plants, most in the First World, produce the rest. Solar collectors can also generate heat and hot water for domestic use, common, for example, in **Israel**, Turkey, and Greece.

The capacity to generate solar electricity has been rising steadily over the last decade. In 2006 **Germany** was leading production, followed by **Japan** and the **United States**. By the beginning of 2015, Germany was still leading in solar power capacity, but by then **China** and **Taiwan** (combined) had climbed to second in the world. Many analysts predict that solar electricity will continue to grow as a source of power, especially as countries such as China invest in solar technologies and power generation.

Photovoltaic energy occurs by converting light directly into electricity. In 1839, French physicist Edmund Becquerel was the first to note the photoelectric effect. Albert Einstein won the Nobel Prize in 1921 for his theories explaining this effect, the basis of modern photovoltaic technology. In 1954, Bell Laboratories developed a silicon photovoltaic cell able to convert enough sunlight to power electrical equipment. The United States space program would later develop photovoltaic cells to power satellites.

Photovoltaic technology involves significant investment and operating costs as a commercial renewable energy source. Some environmentalists see this as a potential solution to provide a limitless source of environmentally friendly energy for the billions of people who currently live in areas without access to electricity. Doubters worry that it is too expensive and unreliable (due to the seasonal nature of sunshine and the difficulty of storage) to power the transportation and agriculture infrastructure necessary for reasonable standards of living in these places. Currently, photovoltaic solar energy only accounts for a small portion of the world's energy supply, and the focus of industry is on improving the technology to reduce its cost. *See also* RENEWABLE ENERGY.

SOLOMON ISLANDS. *See* MELANESIA.

SOUTH AFRICA. In 1981, the South African government put in place its National Conservation Strategy. The National Parks Act had already been passed in 1926; as of 2016, there were 19 **national parks** (e.g., the Kgalagadi Transfrontier Park and the Kruger National Park) managed under the Department of Environmental Affairs. Much greater environmental issues, however, include **deforestation**, **mining** degradation, population pressures, scarce water resources, invasive species, and a severe HIV/AIDS epidemic (one of the worst in the world).

Marked by the policy of apartheid from 1948 to 1994, South Africa established a new constitution in 1996 under President Nelson Mandela, which includes the right to water in the bill of rights. The 1997 National Water Policy and 1998 Water Act emphasized **sustainability** and equity, establishing a water tribunal for dispute resolution and water rights based on permits. In 1997, the government ratified the **Convention to Combat Desertifica-**

tion, which led to a National Action Programme. In 2001, the government introduced a Free Basic Water policy, which gave each household the right to safe and free water each month. In the mid-2000s, South Africa became, according to the **United Nations** Human Development Report for 2006, one of only a few countries to spend less on its military than on water and sanitation.

South Africa is one of the world's largest producers of platinum, gold, and chromium. Diamonds are also important to its economy. In light of concerns over conflict diamonds, the Kimberley Process was started in South Africa in 2000 to create an international certification scheme for rough diamonds.

South Africa has also played an influential role in advancing global environmentalism. The Wildlife and Environment Society of South Africa was founded in 1926 and became one of the founding members of the **International Union for Conservation of Nature (IUCN)**. The **World Summit on Sustainable Development** was held in Johannesburg in 2002 as a follow-up to the Earth Summit held in Rio de Janeiro in 1992.

South Africa also contains some of the world's largest nature reserves. Poaching and illegal activities, however, have long plagued these parks. In 2013, a group, comprised mostly of women, set up the Black Mamba Anti-Poaching Unit to try to better protect one of the reserves: the Olifants West Region of Balule Nature Reserve, a section of South Africa's Greater Kruger National Park. Unarmed, and relying mostly on education, spot-checking, and tracking, this small unit has been highly successful, reducing the poaching of rhinos and the illegal hunting of bushmeat. In recognition, the UN presented the Black Mamba Anti-Poaching Unit with a 2015 UN Champion of the World award.

SOUTH PACIFIC REGIONAL ENVIRONMENT PROGRAMME (SPREP). *See* MELANESIA.

SOVIET UNION. *See* RUSSIA.

SPACESHIP EARTH. The metaphor of spaceship earth became popular in the 1960s as a way to emphasize the need to respect resource limits and care for operating systems to enable the earth to continue to support life as it journeys through space and time. Pictures of the earth from space, in particular ones as astronauts went to the moon in the late 1960s, brought home for many people the vulnerability of life on a small planet swirling through a vast universe. Since then the image of the earth from space has been a core symbol of environmentalism, appearing on everything from books to T-shirts to websites. For some people it continues to evoke the need to care for and respect the interconnected life systems of a "spaceship earth." *See also* BOULDING, KENNETH E. (1910–1993).

SPAIN. Spain's first **national parks** law was passed in 1916 and was replaced with new laws to protect national spaces in 1957, 1975, and 1989. As of 2016, the country had 15 national parks, setting up a new parks network in 2007. The Ministry of Rural, Marine, and Natural Environments is the government department responsible for environmental management.

The Confederation of the Greens, Spain's **green party**, was founded in 1984. **Petra Kelly**, a founder of the German Green Party, was instrumental in its formation; she convened a meeting of Spanish environmental activists in the early 1980s, which led to the Manifesto of Tenerife and the party's creation. Spain also has active **nongovernmental organizations** for the environment, including Amigos de la Tierra España, created in 1979 as part of **Friends of the Earth** International.

Although it is a party to the **Kyoto Protocol**, Spain has struggled to meet its commitments to reduce **greenhouse gas** emissions below 1990 levels. A new national **climate change** adaptation plan was approved in 2006; however, significant challenges face the country, including severe droughts that have undermined hydroelectricity generation, and as of 2016 Spain's greenhouse gas emissions far exceeded 1990 levels.

Genetically modified organisms (GMOs) have evoked mixed responses in Spain. In 2005, Spain became the only European Union country to allow commercial genetically modified corn crops (since then a few other EU countries have allowed limited production). Although some areas of Spain have declared themselves "GMO-free zones," in 2015 Spain was the EU's only significant producer of genetically modified crops; the country, however, is still far behind world GM crop producers such as the **United States**, **Brazil**, **Argentina**, **India**, **Canada**, and **China**.

STEADY-STATE ECONOMY. Economist **Herman Daly** developed the notion of a steady-state economy, building on philosopher John Stuart Mill, who imagined economies becoming mature and one day reaching a steady state. For Daly, in a steady-state economy the inflow and outflow of people and capital are constant at levels sufficient for a satisfying and sustainable life. This does not necessarily mean zero growth in the gross national product, as it is not defined in these terms, but it does require a rate of throughput of matter and energy that is as low as possible.

Such an economy, Daly argues, would not harm the global environment yet would still allow societies to develop and improve human well-being. He has published many articles and books explaining his vision, including *To-*

ward a Steady-State Economy in 1973 (edited), *Steady-State Economics: The Economics of Biophysical Equilibrium and Moral Growth* in 1977, and *Economics, Ecology, Ethics: Essays toward a Steady-State Economy* in 1980 (edited). In 2011 he published (along with the ecological economist Joshua Farley) the second edition of his textbook, *Ecological Economics: Principles and Applications*.

STOCKHOLM CONFERENCE. *See* UNITED NATIONS CONFERENCE ON THE HUMAN ENVIRONMENT.

STOCKHOLM CONVENTION ON PERSISTENT ORGANIC POLLUTANTS. The Stockholm Convention was adopted in 2001 and entered into force in 2004 (90 days after the 50th ratification). As of 2015, there were 179 parties. The convention involves multiple strategies for controlling **persistent organic pollutants (POPs)**, toxic chemicals that persist in the environment, accumulate in the fatty tissue of living organisms, and biomagnify through food chains. It covers 12 of the worst POPs arising from pesticides, industrial chemicals, combustion, and incineration. Research over the last few decades has found that the "dirty dozen" (which includes **dichlorodiphenyltrichloroethane [DDT]**, polychlorinated biphenyls [PCBs], dioxins, and furans) can, among other things, cause cancer as well as damage liver, nervous, and reproductive systems in wildlife and people. The Stockholm Convention seeks to ban and restrict intentional production of POPs, minimize and eventually eliminate unintentional POPs, manage and dispose of stockpiles safely, control imports and exports of POPs, promote technologies and practices to replace existing POPs, and prevent the creation of new POPs. The rules allow for some exemptions, for example, allowing DDT for disease control until effective replacements become available as well as allowing PCBs in electrical transformers and other equipment until 2025.

Environmentalists have been campaigning to ban these chemicals since the 1960s—spurred in part by **Rachel Carson**'s influential critique of DDT in her book *Silent Spring*. In the 1990s, the Inuit people became an influential moral force in the environmental movement, advocating for an international environmental treaty against POPs. These pollutants move on wind and water currents. They also migrate though food chains and as fish, birds, animals, and people travel. In a process sometimes called the "grasshopper effect," POPs can also travel through the atmosphere by a repeated (often seasonal) process of evaporation, deposit, evaporation, and deposit, one that tends to settle POPs in colder climates. The result is that places like the **Arctic** now contain significant amounts of POPs even though the origins are primarily in distant lands, from incinerators in **Japan** to smokestacks in **Mexico**. Tests show, for example, worrying levels of POPs in the blood and breast milk of

Inuit women, a fact many advocates of bans and phaseouts see as unfair, unjust, and, for a few, even an environmental violation of human rights. *See also* CANADA; CONVENTION ON LONG-RANGE TRANSBOUNDARY AIR POLLUTION (CLRTAP); VIETNAM.

STRONG, MAURICE (1929–2015). Born in **Canada**, Maurice Strong was one of the most influential organizing figures behind the globalization of modern environmentalism. In 1966, he went from president of the Power Corporation of Canada to head of Canada's External Aid Office (which became the Canadian International Development Agency). From 1970 to 1972, Strong served as secretary general of the **United Nations Conference on the Human Environment** before becoming the first executive director of the **United Nations Environment Programme** in 1973. He returned to Canada to serve as president of the **oil** company Petro-Canada from 1976 to 1978, then as chairman of the International Energy Development Corporation and the Canada Development Investment Corporation in the first half of the 1980s. A member of the **World Commission on Environment and Development** from 1983 to 1987, Strong also became an undersecretary general of the **United Nations** in 1985. After that, he once again became secretary general of a major international environmental conference, this time the 1992 **United Nations Conference on Environment and Development**. In 1995, Strong was appointed as a senior advisor to the president of the World Bank, then, before stepping aside, as a senior advisor to Secretary General Kofi Annan on UN reforms and as a UN envoy to **North Korea**.

SUB-SAHARAN AFRICA. The region of sub-Saharan Africa, lying south of the Sahara desert, comprises 49 countries. Since the 1980s, much of this region has been in financial, social, and environmental turmoil. There are many reasons, which vary from place to place, but generally these include the legacy of colonialism, **ecological imperialism**, boom-and-bust resource economies, unemployment, AIDS, rapid population growth, wars, droughts, and crop failures. Today, with two-thirds of people in this region relying on natural resources and agriculture for income, it contains the highest proportion of poor people among major world regions.

Just about every ecosystem in this region is in crisis. It suffers from some of the world's highest rates of **deforestation, desertification, biodiversity** loss, and soil erosion. Enforcement of conservation and wildlife is inconsistent, and poaching and **illegal logging** are rampant. Low-technology industry, old transportation systems, and weak enforcement of environmental regulations have left the air in many cities dirty and dangerous; water and sewage systems in many places are unsanitary, too. The need for wood and animal waste for domestic cooking is also degrading forests and contributing to unhealthy indoor air.

At the same time, community environmentalism is strong in some areas. Two examples among many are **Wangari Maathai**'s **Green Belt Movement** to plant trees in **Kenya** and the activities of **Ken Saro-Wiwa** in **Nigeria**. In recent years, the region has also had notable environmental achievements, such as phasing out **leaded gasoline** in just four years following the 2002 **World Summit on Sustainable Development** in Johannesburg, **South Africa** (becoming the world's first developing region to accomplish this).

Two-thirds of the African continent is desert or drylands, and governments in Africa see desertification as one of the most significant environmental stresses. African states were instrumental in establishing the 1994 **United Nations Convention to Combat Desertification in Countries Experiencing Serious Drought and/or Desertification, Particularly in Africa** (which entered into force in 1996 and as of 2016 had 196 parties to the agreement).

SUMOFUS. Founded in 2011 by Taren Stinebrickner-Kauffman, SumOfUs is an advocacy group using social media to unite consumers and activists into campaigns to pressure multinational corporations into more responsible and sustainable practices. Calling itself a "global movement," SumOfUs covers environmental, labor, and community issues, generally targeting well-known brands. It has run campaigns, for instance, to push Kellogg's, McDonald's, and Pepsi into reforming their purchasing policies for **palm oil**. Tactics include "subvertising," such as a mock commercial linking Doritos chips to the death of orangutans and **deforestation** in **Indonesia** and Malaysia.

SumOfUs is one of many new environmental advocacy organizations that do organizing online—through Facebook (since 2004), YouTube (since 2005), Twitter (since 2006), Tumblr (since 2007), Instagram (since 2010), and Snapchat (since 2011)—to "shame" and "expose" poor environmental and social practices by global brands (e.g., Nestlé, Nike, and Starbucks) and big-box retailers (e.g., Walmart, Office Depot, and Home Depot). Partly in response, these companies are increasingly saying they have turned a corner, with some even claiming to be "**sustainability**" leaders, pointing to governments as the true "laggards." Under the rubric of **corporate social responsibility**, these companies are setting sweeping "aspirational" goals, such as "zero deforestation," "100 percent recycling," and "zero carbon footprints." To some extent such pledges are little more than traditional **greenwash**, primarily aiming to enhance corporate images and advance public relations. Yet these corporate responses also reflect a shift in corporate strategy toward using sustainability policies and tools to pursue traditional business gains:

finding savings and efficiencies to increase profits, sales, and growth. *See also* ECO-BUSINESS; NONGOVERNMENTAL ORGANIZATIONS (NGOs).

SUSTAINABILITY. The most common governmental understanding of sustainability comes from the 1987 **World Commission on Environment and Development**'s report, *Our Common Future* (also known as the Brundtland Commission, after the chair, **Gro Harlem Brundtland**). The Brundtland Commission framed sustainability as "**sustainable development**," defining it as "development that meets the needs of the present without compromising the ability of future generations to meet their own needs." At a general level the idea of sustainability is aiming to balance environmental, social, and economic systems, with the overall goal of maintaining resilience, balance, and the integrity of all three. The concept of sustainability is highly contested, however, with varying definitions in economics, business, politics, and across the environmental movement. More human-centric ways to understand sustainability focus on maintaining in perpetuity steady growth in the prosperity of humanity. More biocentric ways focus on retaining the capacity of the earth to sustain all life forms in ever-adapting and constantly interacting ecological systems.

Since the mid-2000s the corporate world has increasingly come to embrace "sustainability" as its primary word to describe **corporate social responsibility** programs. The understanding of sustainability among multinational corporations has a strong business focus, with programs and policies aiming to reduce waste, enhance manufacturing efficiencies, and access increasingly scarce high-quality natural resource inputs (e.g., cocoa to make chocolate). Some observers even see these companies as progressively taking control of the discourse of sustainability, turning the concept into "**eco-business**" to gain traditional competitive advantages, such as lowering costs, controlling supply chains, and driving competitors out of business. This corporate shift toward employing the discourse of sustainability has also contributed to more environmental NGOs partnering on programming and fundraising with multinational corporations, such as the **World Wide Fund for Nature/World Wildlife Fund (WWF)**'s partnership with Coca-Cola since 2007.

SUSTAINABLE DEVELOPMENT. The idea of sustainable development can be traced back to the Cocoyoc Declaration, issued in 1974 at a symposium on development and environment hosted by the **United Nations Environment Programme** and the United Nations Conference on Trade and Development in Cocoyoc, **Mexico**. However, the World Conservation Strategy of 1980, published by the **International Union for Conservation of**

Nature (IUCN), is commonly credited with launching the term into the international vocabulary. The publication of the 1987 **World Commission on Environment and Development** report, *Our Common Future* (also known as the Brundtland Report, after its chair **Gro Harlem Brundtland**), brought it to the center of environmental debate. The commission defined sustainable development as "development that meets the needs of the present without compromising the ability of future generations to meet their own needs." This definition was central to the discussions at the 1992 **United Nations Conference on Environment and Development (UNCED)**. Afterward, the United Nations Commission on Sustainable Development (UNCSD) was established to ensure effective follow-up of the conference's resolutions. Sustainable development defined in this way would then shape the mandate and goals of the 2002 **World Summit on Sustainable Development** in Johannesburg, **South Africa**.

Today, this definition remains the most common one among governments, business, and intergovernmental agencies. Here, because poverty is identified as a major cause of environmental degradation, economic growth remains necessary. The main approaches to achieve this form of sustainable development are market-based instruments, for example, green taxes, tradable emissions permits, **eco-business**, and **eco-efficiency**.

The term as defined by the Brundtland Commission has many critics. Some contend the concept is ambiguous or vague; others see it as a clever way to legitimize the status quo of continued growth and overconsumption. Ecological economists such as **Herman Daly** and **Robert Costanza** commonly point to what they see as a contradiction in this definition, arguing that infinite economic growth is physically impossible in a closed ecosystem with finite resources and that true sustainable development requires "development without growth." *See also* SUSTAINABILITY.

SUSTAINABLE FOREST MANAGEMENT. Today, many see sustainable forest management as the forestry component of **sustainable development**. It has a long history, however, going back over a century to the idea of managing a forest in a way that ensures a **sustainable yield** of timber. More recent understandings of sustainable forest management tend to put more weight on nontimber products and services as well as protecting water supplies, **biodiversity**, soil quality, cultural sites, and the well-being of indigenous peoples. Two examples of international initiatives to support sustainable forest management are the International Tropical Timber Organization Guidelines and the **Forest Stewardship Council** Principles and Criteria. *See also* CANADIAN STANDARDS ASSOCIATION, CSA Z809; DEFORESTATION; ECO-FORESTRY; ILLEGAL LOGGING; SUSTAINABLE FORESTRY INITIATIVE (SFI).

SUSTAINABLE FORESTRY INITIATIVE (SFI). The Sustainable Forestry Initiative (SFI) program, established in 1994 by the American Forest and Paper Association, is a voluntary certification standard to promote **sustainable forest management** and responsible purchasing practices. In 2007, the SFI became a fully independent organization. A board of directors—with representatives from industry, landowners, communities, environmental groups, academia, and the public sector—governs the SFI standard. It now has international recognition through the international **Programme for the Endorsement of Forest Certification (PEFC)** schemes. It is an example of a worldwide trend over the last few decades toward increasing numbers of environmental labeling and certification schemes for forest products. The best-known international program is the **Forest Stewardship Council**.

SUSTAINABLE YIELD. A sustainable yield is the rate one can harvest without harming the capacity of the ecosystem to regenerate the same amount in the future. The idea—what some call the maximum sustainable yield—is a common organizing principle for environmental management of renewable resources like forests and fisheries. In forestry, for example, it is the basis for determining guidelines such as the annual allowable cut. Supporters see this as a sensible way to supply resources without damaging ecosystems; however, critics see it as unachievable in practice and thus argue that it ends up justifying unsustainable production and overconsumption. *See also* DEFORESTATION; ILLEGAL LOGGING; SUSTAINABLE FOREST MANAGEMENT.

SUZUKI, DAVID (1936–). Born in Vancouver, **Canada**, David T. Suzuki is professor emeritus at the University of British Columbia and cofounder of the David Suzuki Foundation. He is one of the world's best-known environmental writers (with over 40 books), activists, and radio and TV personalities (since 1979 hosting the Canadian Broadcasting Corporation's *The Nature of Things with David Suzuki*). For many environmentalists, his career is a prime example of the power of the popular media to translate academic research into a language able to change global environmental consciousness, an idea dating back to the emergence of **Greenpeace** in Vancouver during the 1970s.

SWAMPY (DANIEL HOOPER) (1974–). Daniel Hooper, nicknamed "Swampy," rose to fame in the mid-1990s after a protest against yet another new highway through the British countryside. For years activists had been camping along the route, living in tree houses and chaining themselves to concrete blocks. Then a group including Swampy pioneered a new form of environmental resistance by digging and hiding in tunnels under the excavation site. It would take a week for the British government to find and evict these protestors, with the press relishing in their efforts to dodge radar and diggers. The 22-year-old Swampy was the last to come out, becoming an instant celebrity **eco-warrior**. Afterward, he would appear in tabloids and fashion shots and on television celebrity panels, and, along with a second tunnel protest to prevent a new runway at the Manchester airport, he managed to bring an intense media spotlight on road building in **Great Britain** in the late 1990s. Many environmentalists still see Swampy as a hero of the direct nonviolent action movement, although he is no longer an active protestor. Critics, however, commonly deride him as a joke, an example of how the media tends to give far too much coverage to the silly antics of a few outliers in the environmental movement.

SWEDEN. The Ministry of the Environment is the central agency in charge of the environment, climate, and energy issues in Sweden. The Swedish Environmental Protection Agency, which reports to the Ministry of the Environment, was established in 1967. The Swedish Environment Party/**Green Party**, Miljöpartiet de Gröna, was founded in 1981, first winning seats in Parliament in 1988. In 2016 the party held 25 parliamentary seats as well as four seats in the European Parliament. Environmental legislation in Sweden is coordinated through the 1999 Environmental Code, which includes, among other things, a **precautionary principle** and a **polluter pays principle**.

Sweden has been influential in advancing global environmentalism. In 1972, Stockholm hosted the **United Nations Conference on the Human Environment**, which among many accomplishments launched the **United Nations'** first **World Environment Day**. Since then, Sweden has also moved forward negotiations for environmental agreements, such as the 2001 **Stockholm Convention on Persistent Organic Pollutants**.

Sweden has an active civil society around environmentalism. For example, in the late 1960s, soil scientist Dr. Svante Odén helped to raise public awareness about **acid rain** in Sweden. In 1982, the Swedish **nongovernmental organization** Secretariat on Acid Rain was founded as a partnership including **Friends of the Earth**, Sweden; the Swedish Society for Nature Conservation; and the **World Wide Fund for Nature (WWF)**–Sweden. Sweden is also home to several environmental research institutions, including the International Institute of Ecological Economics (Beijer Institute), established in 1977; the Stockholm Environment Institute, founded in 1989; and the Stockholm International Water Institute, created in 1991.

In recent years the government has been focusing on promoting **renewable energy**. A **carbon tax** on "domestic travel fuels" (**oil, coal, natural gas**, and so on) was put in place in 1991 and increased in both 1997 and 2007. In 2003, the government introduced Tradable Green Certificates for renewables in electricity production; in 2005, it set a target of 3 percent for renewable fuels in transportation; and in 2006, it announced ambitious plans to aspire to phase out oil consumption. To move along this aspirational goal, the government has been ramping up budgetary expenditures on solar energy, doing so again in 2016.

SYNTHETIC CHEMICALS. Synthetic chemistry started in European laboratories seeking to make anesthetics and disinfectants in the mid-19th century. **Dichlorodiphenyltrichloroethane (DDT)**, for example, was discovered in 1874 but not developed as a pesticide until 1939. At the turn of the 20th century, the production of **oil**-based dyes in **Germany** led the way for the commercialization of synthetic chemicals. Between 50,000 and 100,000 new chemicals were brought into commercial production after the synthetic chemical revolution of World War II. Production kept increasing, and by the end of the 20th century, around 18 million synthetic substances were known to science. Today, thousands of new synthetic substances are created every year, with multinational companies like Dow and DuPont in lead roles. Among the chemicals currently in use, only a small number have complete toxicological profiles. More than 500 different synthetic chemicals have now been found in human blood, body fat, and breast milk.

Many people believe synthetic chemicals have contaminated the planet, contributing to illness and death in humans and other species. One of the best-known critiques of synthetic chemicals—in particular DDT—is **Rachel Carson**'s 1962 book, *Silent Spring*. A number of environmental disasters are also associated with synthetic chemicals, including tragedies such as **Love Canal** and **Bhopal**. Many of these chemicals are persistent, reactive, and oil soluble, allowing them to enter and travel up the food chain through processes known as bioaccumulation and biomagnification. The class of synthetic chemicals with such properties is generally called **persistent organic pollutants**. Another well-known class of synthetic chemicals is **chlorofluorocarbons (CFCs)**, the primary cause of **ozone depletion**. *See also* BISPHENOL A (BPA); HAZARDOUS WASTE; ORGANIC FOOD; POLYBROMINATED DIPHENYL ETHERS (PBDEs).

T

TAIWAN. The issues of environmental protection and public health are closely tied in Taiwan, with the Environmental Protection Bureau emerging in 1979 out of the Department of Environmental Health, which the Department of Health set up in 1971. Prior to that, municipal units managed environmental issues. The city of Taipei, for example, integrated its Municipal Cleaning Unit and Sewage Treatment Commission with its Department of Environmental Cleaning in 1968 to manage waste, air, and water **pollution**.

Taiwan established the Environmental Protection Agency in 1987. Since then, it has managed to improve air quality through a mix of policies, such as mandatory use of unleaded gasoline and controls on vehicles and industrial emissions. Nevertheless, a high population density, industrial activity, two-stroke motorcycles and scooters, and dust and pollution from mainland **China** mean residents still suffer from significant exposure to air pollutants. China sees Taiwan as part of its official territory, and thus Taiwan is in an unusual international position. It follows the guidelines of many environmental treaties, such as the **Basel Convention**, the **Montreal Protocol**, and the **Kyoto Protocol**, but is not an official signatory. Taiwan introduced a green building **eco-certification** system in 1999, which is similar to the LEED (Leadership in Energy and Environmental Design) green building rating system in the **United States** and **Japan**'s CASBEE (Comprehensive Assessment System for Building Environmental Efficiency) certification scheme.

The 1980s and 1990s saw many environmental **nongovernmental organizations** emerge in Taiwan, including the Environmental Quality Protection Foundation (1984), the Taiwan Christian Ecological Center (1992), Wetlands Taiwan (1994), the Taiwan Business Council for Sustainable Development (1995), and the Society of Wilderness (1996). The Wild at Heart Legal Defense Association was created in 2003 to provide legal advice on environmental issues; in 2005, it was involved in several cases, including one to stop a hydroelectric power plant because of an incomplete **environmental impact assessment** and falsified data, and another to indict the Taiwan Cement Corporation for illegal dumping of waste **oil**.

199

In 2014, explosions of natural gas pipelines in the Taiwanese city of Kaohsiung killed 32 people and injured hundreds. The subsequent public outcry energized civil society demands for greater environmental accountability, stricter safety standards, stronger controls over petrochemical corporations, and more governmental transparency. In 2014 the Green Party Taiwan (founded in 1996) won two seats in local elections; as of the beginning of 2016, however, the party did not hold any seats in the Taiwanese legislature. *See also* GREEN ARCHITECTURE.

TAJIKISTAN. *See* ARAL SEA.

TASMANIA WILDERNESS SOCIETY. *See* WILDERNESS SOCIETY.

THAILAND. Thailand has an especially long history of forest management. The Royal Forest Department was created in 1897, and all forests were declared government property in 1899. The Forest Act was passed in 1941 (updating the 1913 Forest Protection Act), and the Forest Industry Organization was created in 1956. The 1960s saw the establishment of protected areas, with the 1960 Wildlife Protection and Preservation Act, the 1961 National Park Act, and the 1964 National Forest Reserve Act. At the same time, however, **deforestation** increased, and replanting and silvicultural practices in logged areas were poor. Political instability after a military coup in 1976 also contributed to deforestation, as forests were cleared to fight rebel groups. Following severe flooding and subsequent landslides in southern Thailand, the government banned commercial logging in natural forests in 1989.

Rapid industrialization and intensive resource consumption over the last few decades have put intense pressure on Thailand's environment. In response, several Thai environmental **nongovernmental organizations** were established in the late 1980s and early 1990s, including the Thailand Environment Institute, which focuses on conservation and environmental certification. Over the years the Thai Green Coalition acted as a political advocacy organization for environmental issues; however, Thailand did not officially have a political **green party** until the former head of the National Parks, Wildlife and Plant Conservation Department registered the Thai Forest Land Reclamation Party formed in 2012. Several important pieces of environmental legislation also passed in the early 1990s, including the Enhancement and Conservation of National Environment Quality Act, an amended Navigation in Thai Waterways Act, the Forest Plantation Act, and the Wild Animals Reservation and Protection Act. Thailand also managed to phase out **leaded gasoline** by 1995, although large numbers of old vehicles, forest fires, factories, and power plants all mean that air quality, particularly in urban areas such as Bangkok, remains poor. The Asian financial crisis of 1997–1998 also hit the economy hard, adding pressures to earn foreign exchange by exporting natural resources and agricultural products; the 2004 tsunami, which killed thousands of people, added further to the hardships of life in many coastal and island communities.

For genetically modified crops, the reception has been mixed in Thailand. In 1995, the government allowed **genetically modified** crops in research settings, but in 2001 it put in place a temporary ban on these field trials to ensure that proper safeguards were in place. The lifting of this ban in 2007 resulted in a court case against the government. Today, Thailand both has GMO-free zones and grows small amounts of GM produce.

Thailand also participates in many regional and international environmental agreements, including the ASEAN Agreement on Transboundary Haze Pollution (in force from 2003), the **Kyoto Protocol**, the **Convention on Biological Diversity**, the Convention on Migratory Species, and the **Convention on International Trade in Endangered Species**. Although Thailand (like **China** and Malaysia) is making increasing efforts to join international agreements and improve environmental management at home, Thai companies continue to disrupt the environment of neighboring countries such as Burma (Myanmar), for example, by logging old-growth forests and importing timber from unsustainable sources.

THIRD WORLD NETWORK (TWN). An international network of nonprofit **nongovernmental organizations** founded in 1984, the Third World Network (TWN) publishes books and articles, organizes conferences, and facilitates dialogues with international negotiators and processes on issues relating to development and South-North relations. With an international secretariat in Penang (Malaysia), it also has offices in Delhi (**India**), Montevideo (Uruguay), Geneva, and Accra (Ghana). For environmentalism, it has been an influential voice in raising the profile of critical nongovernmental perspectives from within developing countries on issues such as trade, foreign debt, intellectual property rights, **climate change**, biosafety, and human rights.

THOREAU, HENRY DAVID (1817–1862). Born in Concord, Massachusetts, the philosopher and author Henry David Thoreau is best remembered among environmentalists for his poetry and contributions to the fields of ecology and environmental history. After graduating from Harvard University and running a school in Concord, Massachusetts, with his older brother John from 1838 to 1841, he moved in with his mentor, Ralph Waldo Emerson, as a live-in handyman. During this time, Thoreau published his first poems in the transcendentalist journal *The Dial*. In 1845, he convinced

Emerson to allow him to build a small cabin on Emerson's property in the woods at Walden Pond, where he wrote his first book, *A Week on the Concord and Merrimack Rivers*. Thoreau began his second book, *Walden*, while there, and, inspired by spending a night in jail for refusing to pay a poll tax, he also wrote one of his most famous works, *Civil Disobedience* (originally published as *Resistance to Civil Government*).

THREE GORGES DAM. The Three Gorges Dam, located in the upper Yangtze River of **China**, was the world's largest hydroelectric dam when it was fully completed in 2012. It was designed to generate over 80 billion kilowatt-hours of electricity annually—about 10 percent of China's total capacity when construction began in 1994. Many environmentalists and human rights advocates (as well as a few members of the National People's Congress) have opposed the dam. Filling the gigantic reservoir (which began in 2003) required relocating 1–2 million people. It entailed, too, the loss of 30,000 hectares of agricultural land. Supporters see this project as **sustainable development**—as a way to produce **renewable energy** and replace **coal** burning in steam power plants. Critics counter that the costs for local peoples and ecologies outweigh the benefits for generating cleaner electricity. *See also* NARMADA DAM.

THREE MILE ISLAND NUCLEAR ACCIDENT. The partial meltdown of a core reactor in 1979 at the Three Mile Island Nuclear Generating Station in Harrisburg, Pennsylvania, remains the biggest accident in commercial nuclear history in the **United States**. The release of radioactivity did not lead to the immediate deaths of any workers or residents in the area; along with television crews, President Jimmy Carter even visited the control room during the crisis to show it was safe. Still, the accident—caused by maintenance, operational, design, and response errors—undermined American public confidence and strengthened environmental opposition to **nuclear power**. This would reinforce the earlier trend in the United States during the 1970s to scale back plans to expand nuclear power. The cleanup operation at Three Mile Island did not end until December 1993, costing nearly US$1 billion. *See also* CHERNOBYL NUCLEAR MELTDOWN.

TIPPING POINT. The tipping point, in ecological terms, occurs when the process of steady change in an ecosystem (for example, a decline in the numbers of a particular species) suddenly begins to accelerate into an uncontrollable change (for example, extinction of a species). This idea is common among those environmentalists who call for tough measures to prevent seemingly separate environmental "problems"—from **deforestation** to **desertification** to **endangered species** to overfishing to **mining** to **climate change** to

ozone depletion to **persistent organic pollutants**—from aggregating to a point that tips the earth into a global crisis beyond the capacity of humanity to control. (This is not the same meaning as in the best-selling book by Malcolm Gladwell, *The Tipping Point*, published in 2000, which uses the phrase to explain social epidemics.)

TIRES. Decades ago, the **United States** had stockpiled and junked as many as 2–3 billion truck and car tires. Tires are difficult to bury in landfills because they work their way back to the surface, and many of these became health and environmental threats. Tire fires are also difficult to extinguish and can last a long time, releasing toxic pollutants. Notable tire fires in U.S. history include a seven-million-tire fire in Virginia in 1983 and a tire fire that lasted 30 days in California in 1999. Thirty years ago, very few tires were recycled in the United States. Today, around 90 percent are ground down and recycled (or repurposed), and tire stockpiles are now smaller and better managed (although fires do sometimes still break out). **Recycling** programs turn the used tires into fuel, sports surfaces, rubber products, and rubberized asphalt.

Global figures on the number of tires in landfills are difficult to calculate, but most environmentalists see this as an increasing environmental threat in developing countries without the capacity to recycle and monitor landfills (and as car sales soar). In 2012, for example, a stockpile of five million tires caught fire in Kuwait. Besides generating toxic fires, tire stockpiles in the developing world are also breeding grounds for pests (rodents) and diseases, as tires hold water and protect insects (such as mosquitoes) from spraying programs. *See also* AUTOMOBILES.

TOLBA, MOSTAFA KAMAL (1922–). Born in Zifta, Egypt, Mostafa Kamal Tolba graduated from Cairo University in 1943 and received a Ph.D. from Imperial College in 1948. He became internationally known, first as the head of Egypt's delegation at the 1972 **United Nations Conference on the Human Environment** and later as the executive director of the **United Nations Environment Programme (UNEP)** from 1976 to 1992. Tolba was instrumental during the negotiations over the **Montreal Protocol on Substances That Deplete the Ozone Layer**, personally negotiating with delegations to ensure that a treaty was reached. After leaving the UNEP, in 1994 he started the International Center for Environment and Development (ICED), a **nongovernmental organization** that funded environmental projects in the Third World.

TORREY CANYON. The *Torrey Canyon*, a 974-foot (297-meter) **oil** tanker flying a Liberian flag to take advantage of lower taxes, wages, and shipping standards was carrying millions of gallons of crude oil when on 18 March 1967 it ran aground on Pollard's Rock, part of the Seven Stones reef near Cornwall, **Great Britain**. Owned by Barracuda Tanker Corporation, a subsidiary of the Union Oil Company of California, and chartered by British Petroleum, it was the largest recorded shipwreck to date. Attempts to salvage and refloat the tanker using tugs and air compressors were unsuccessful. The tanker broke into pieces and more oil tanks ruptured, causing several oil slicks. The standard practice at the time was to disperse spilled oil with detergent, but the amount of oil overwhelmed this approach, so the British government chose to burn the oil off and sink the tanker by dropping bombs and using other weapons. When the oil spill reached the shoreline of Great Britain, it stretched 260 square miles (or roughly 670 square kilometers). The number of seabirds killed was probably around 15,000. The disaster drew worldwide publicity to the ecological dangers of shipping oil on the high seas, spurring the growing global environmental movement in the late 1960s. *See also EXXON VALDEZ* OIL SPILL.

TOURISM. *See* ECOTOURISM.

TRAGEDY OF THE COMMONS. Garrett Hardin's article "The Tragedy of the Commons" is one of the most influential articles in the evolution of environmentalism. Published in *Science* in 1968, it tells the story of access to and the collapse of the English commons as an analogy to access and collapse of shared spaces in modern times, such as the high seas, atmosphere, and unregulated forests. It is, Hardin reasoned, in the rational self-interest of a herder to breed and graze as many animals as possible on a pasture "open to all." Adding one more animal enhances a herder's personal wealth far more than it degrades the pasture for his herd. Not adding another animal to conserve the grazing land will merely penalize this herder as others add animals instead. Over time, without preventative measures, the logic of each person pursuing such private gain will destroy the pasture.

This same logic and process, Hardin surmised, is true in all commons with rising populations and unrestricted access. "Ruin is the destination toward which all men rush," he wrote, "each pursuing his own best interest in a society that believes in the freedom of the commons. Freedom in a commons brings ruin to all." The only way to prevent this collapse, he concluded, is "mutual coercion, mutually agreed upon by the majority of the people affected." To this day Hardin's metaphor continues to hold great sway among environmentalists, who see the pursuit of self-interest (state, corporate, and personal) and open access to common spaces as a core cause of the global ecological crisis. It is also frequently invoked by those who call for a world government to solve crises like **climate change**.

TURKMENISTAN. *See* ARAL SEA.

U

UNION OF CONCERNED SCIENTISTS. Founded in 1969, the Union of Concerned Scientists is a nonprofit organization based in the **United States**. It grew out of a 1968 statement of concern by faculty at the Massachusetts Institute of Technology, including the heads of the biology, chemistry, and physics departments, who were calling for "more responsible exploitation of scientific knowledge" and admonishing governments (especially the U.S. government) for "an intention to enlarge further our immense destructive capabilities." Signatories wanted to "convey to our students the hope that they will devote themselves to bringing the benefits of science and technology to mankind and to ask them to scrutinize the issues raised here before participating in the construction of destructive weapons systems."

Today, with hundreds of thousands of members, the organization aims to combine citizen action with reliable and independent scientific knowledge to promote cleaner and safer environments. Recently, it has been active around issues such as global security, air quality, **climate change**, clean energy, food, clean vehicles, **palm oil**, and invasive species.

UNITED NATIONS. The United Nations is the core institution for organizing and coordinating global environmental action among states. Among countless meetings and conferences, four stand out: the 1972 **United Nations Conference on the Human Environment**, the 1992 **United Nations Conference on Environment and Development**, the 2002 **World Summit on Sustainable Development**, and the United Nations Conference on Sustainable Development in 2012. The UN also houses organizations responsible for supporting and improving global environmental management. The **United Nations Environment Programme (UNEP)**, which was established following the 1972 UN Conference on the Human Environment, has the most direct mandate. But many others also influence global, national, and local environmental management, including the UN Development Programme (UNDP), the UN Food and Agriculture Organization (FAO), and the UN Population Fund (formerly the **United Nations Fund for Population Activities**). The UN also cooperates closely with powerful organizations such as the World

Bank, the International Monetary Fund (IMF), and the **Global Environment Facility (GEF)** (which has three implementing agencies: the World Bank, the UNDP, and the UNEP).

The UN also plays a key role in defining terms and setting agendas for international environmental negotiations and management. In 1983, for example, the UN convened the **World Commission on Environment and Development**, which in 1987 would put forth a definition of **sustainable development** that to this day still guides most of the world's environmental policies (defined as "development that meets the needs of the present without compromising the ability of future generations to meet their own needs"). The UN also strives to raise environmental awareness through activities such as **World Environment Day** (held every year on 5 June).

UN environmental agreements are also the basis of many of the international rules governing environmental management. Some of the hundreds of agreements include the UN Framework Convention on Climate Change and the **Kyoto Protocol to the United Nations Framework Convention on Climate Change**; the UN **Convention on International Trade in Endangered Species of Wild Fauna and Flora (CITES)**; the **United Nations Convention to Combat Desertification in Countries Experiencing Serious Drought and/or Desertification, Particularly in Africa**; the Ramsar Convention on Wetlands; the **Convention on Biological Diversity**; and the **Stockholm Convention on Persistent Organic Pollutants**. *See also* WORLD CHARTER FOR NATURE.

UNITED NATIONS COMMISSION ON SUSTAINABLE DEVELOP-MENT. *See* SUSTAINABLE DEVELOPMENT.

UNITED NATIONS CONFERENCE ON ENVIRONMENT AND DE-VELOPMENT (UNCED). The United Nations Conference on Environment and Development (UNCED) was held in Rio de Janeiro (**Brazil**) in June 1992 on the 20th anniversary of the **United Nations Conference on the Human Environment** (Stockholm). Commonly known as the Rio or Earth Summit, it was the largest **United Nations** conference to date, with 178 national delegations, over 1,400 officially accredited **nongovernmental organizations**, and 117 heads of state participating. The Canadian **Maurice Strong** was again secretary general of the conference (as he was for the 1972 conference in Stockholm). Another 17,000 people also attended a parallel nongovernmental forum.

The official conference produced two documents of particular note: the Rio Declaration on Environment and Development and **Agenda 21** (a 300-page action plan for **sustainable development**). The Rio Declaration lays out 27 principles on the rights and responsibilities of states for environment and development, placing more emphasis on the right to develop than was the case with the Declaration on the Human Environment adopted at the 1972 Stockholm Conference. Rio also opened two conventions for signature: the **United Nations Framework Convention on Climate Change** and the **Convention on Biological Diversity**. As well, it issued a nonbinding statement of principles for forest management after efforts to sign a legally binding forest treaty failed. Finally, it created the United Nations Commission on Sustainable Development to monitor and evaluate the progress of meeting the objectives set out at Rio.

The 1992 Rio Summit brought global environmentalism to the top of the agendas of world leaders. As at the 1972 conference, contentious debates occurred over the links between environmental change, development, poverty, and South-North inequities. In the end most states endorsed the definition of sustainable development put forth in 1987 by the **World Commission on Environment and Development**: "development that meets the needs of the present without compromising the ability of future generations to meet their own needs." Over the following decades, this concept (and compromise), which assumes that more economic growth is compatible with a better global environment, shifted global environmentalism into a more cooperative stance with corporations and economic interests. The **World Summit on Sustainable Development**, held 10 years later in Johannesburg, **South Africa**, further ensured the supremacy of this concept. This was followed 10 years later by the 2012 United Nations Conference on Sustainable Development in Rio de Janeiro, **Brazil**—a conference designed to move along global implementation of sustainable development, but one that many environmentalists have come to see as contributing to a frustratingly slow process of reforms.

UNITED NATIONS CONFERENCE ON THE HUMAN ENVIRONMENT. The United Nations Conference on the Human Environment, held in June 1972 in Stockholm, **Sweden**, was the first international environmental conference for state officials. **Maurice Strong**, a Canadian businessman and environmentalist, was secretary general of the conference, commonly called the Stockholm Conference. About 1,200 people attended, with delegates from 113 countries and two heads of government: Olof Palme (Sweden) and Indira Gandhi (**India**). The communist bloc boycotted the conference, however, to protest the exclusion of East Germany. Three nongovernmental conferences ran parallel to the official one: the Environment Forum (with **United Nations** support), the People's Forum, and the Dai Dong Independent Conference on the Environment (held the week before the official one).

The Stockholm Conference revealed fundamental differences between environmentalism in developed and developing countries. Developing countries were wary that "northern" concerns over **pollution** and nature conservation would trump far greater environmental problems arising from poverty and underdevelopment. "Southern" delegates coined the phrase *the pollution of poverty*, an idea that still runs strong in environmentalism in the developing world. Tensions between the North and South arose too over responsibility, financing, and the inequalities of global capitalism.

The conference produced a Declaration on the Human Environment (including 26 principles), an Action Plan (with 109 recommendations), and a Resolution on Institutional and Financial Arrangements. All of these were nonbinding on signatory states. Significantly, these documents protected the principle of state sovereignty and the right of states to control domestic resources. They did so, however, while recognizing the competing interests of developed and developing countries as well as the responsibility of all states to consider cross-border environmental damage.

The conference did not produce many concrete environmental commitments by states. It did set the stage, though, for further state negotiations as an increasingly significant source of global environmentalism. In addition, it led to the United Nations General Assembly establishing the **United Nations Environment Programme**, which opened in 1973 with its headquarters in Nairobi, **Kenya**, with Maurice Strong as its first executive director.

UNITED NATIONS CONVENTION ON THE LAW OF THE SEA (UNCLOS). Adopted in 1982, the Law of the Sea Treaty—officially the Third United Nations Convention on the Law of the Sea (UNCLOS), after two previous agreements from 1958 and 1960—provides a legal framework for governing the oceans. UNCLOS III, or LOST as some critics call it, took 15 years to negotiate. The process started in 1967 after the Maltese ambassador to the **United Nations** called for an international agreement to protect the oceans. The treaty did not enter into force until 1994, with a subsequent implementation agreement added in 1996. The convention had 167 parties as of 2015. It replaced the previous Law of the Sea treaties: the Convention on the Territorial Sea and Contiguous Zone, the Convention on the Continental Shelf, the Convention on the High Seas, and the Convention on Fishing and Conservation of Living Resources of the High Seas.

UNCLOS includes dispute resolution mechanisms, where states failing to resolve contentious issues independently must choose among the International Tribunal for the Law of the Sea, the International Court of Justice, or one of two arbitration tribunals established through the convention. Key provisions of UNCLOS include the establishment of exclusive economic zones (EEZs), regulations over continental shelves, deep seabed **mining**, and rules concerning marine scientific research. EEZs give coastal states rights over resources (from fish to **oil**) in the waters or ocean floor 200 miles from the shoreline. **Climate change** will challenge some of these resource claims as rising sea levels alter EEZs. *See also* FISHING.

UNITED NATIONS CONVENTION TO COMBAT DESERTIFICA-TION IN COUNTRIES EXPERIENCING SERIOUS DROUGHT AND/ OR DESERTIFICATION, PARTICULARLY IN AFRICA. The **United Nations Conference on Environment and Development (UNCED)** first initiated negotiations for a treaty on **desertification** in 1972. In 1977, a UN Conference on Desertification agreed on a Plan of Action to Combat Desertification; however, by the early 1990s, the **United Nations Environment Programme** had concluded that this was insufficient and the problem was intensifying. The UN Convention to Combat Desertification (UNCCD) was adopted in 1994 (entering into force in 1996). There were 196 parties to the UNCCD in 2016. Although the convention addresses land degradation globally, it has a specific focus on Africa because two-thirds of the continent is desert or drylands, while three-quarters of its agricultural drylands were already degraded to some extent by the mid-1990s. The Regional Implementation Annex for Africa provides a framework for UNCCD activities in Africa.

The UNCCD established two new partnerships in 2008: one with the UN Economic Commission for Africa, for issues including financing and capacity building, and the other for a science program—the Oasis Challenge Program.

The **United Nations** also works to raise awareness of desertification more generally. The year 2006 was the UN's International Year of Deserts and Desertification, and the honorary spokesperson for the year was the Kenyan environmental activist **Wangari Maathai** (1940–2011), a Nobel Peace Prize winner (2004) and leader of the **Green Belt Movement**. *See also* SUB-SAHARAN AFRICA.

UNITED NATIONS EDUCATIONAL, SCIENTIFIC AND CULTU-RAL ORGANIZATION (UNESCO). The **United Nations** Educational, Scientific and Cultural Organization seeks to identify natural and cultural heritage sites of exceptional value around the world, working to preserve and protect these with the assistance of national governments (including emergency assistance to sites in danger). It is guided by the international Convention Concerning the Protection of the World Cultural and Natural Heritage (adopted in 1972), which arose from the merging of two separate, though related, movements: preserving cultural sites and conserving nature. By 2016 UNESCO had listed more than 650 biosphere reserves across 120 countries.

UNITED NATIONS ENVIRONMENT PROGRAMME (UNEP). The United Nations Environment Programme, or UNEP, was set up following the 1972 **United Nations Conference on the Human Environment** with headquarters in Nairobi, **Kenya**, and a global network of regional offices. Responsibility for environmental governance is dispersed throughout the **Unit-**

ed **Nations**, although the UNEP is the primary environmental agency. Its initial mandate was to educate, inspire, and enable; in the 1990s, it expanded to facilitate coherent implementation of **sustainable development**. It is primarily funded by governments but also receives funding from **nongovernmental organizations** and businesses. **Maurice Strong** was the first executive director; Achim Steiner has been the executive director since 2006 (after several renewals, his term is set to expire in June 2016).

Most analysts agree that the UNEP has been successful in establishing a strong base of environmental information and coordinating international environmental negotiations and conventions on issues such as **climate change**, **ozone depletion**, and **biodiversity**. Critics stress that its mandate is too vague, with a weak political and financial base compared to other UN agencies, in part because back in 1972 some states worried that it might constrain economic growth, consumption, and development.

UNITED NATIONS FRAMEWORK CONVENTION ON CLIMATE CHANGE (UNFCCC). The United Nations Framework Convention on Climate Change was opened for signature at the 1992 **United Nations Conference on Environment and Development** held in Rio de Janeiro, **Brazil**; it entered into force in 1994. Designed to slow rising temperatures and mitigate climate change, this convention did not specify actions but rather established a "framework" for working toward more specific and binding commitments under international law.

At the third session of the Conference of the Parties in 1997 in Kyoto, **Japan**, negotiating states agreed to a binding protocol to the UNFCCC: the **Kyoto Protocol to the United Nations Framework Convention on Climate Change**. The Kyoto Protocol set different national emission reduction targets for so-called Annex I countries (developed economies, including **Russia**). It came into force in 2005 without the ratification of the **United States**—an outcome most negotiators thought was highly unlikely given that the United States was the world's leading emitter of **greenhouse gases**. For the first commitment from 2008 to 2012, the protocol aimed to reduce the combined emissions of six greenhouse gases by 5.2 percent below 1990 levels. Specific targets varied widely, however, with, for instance, the European Union agreeing to reduce emissions 8 percent *below* 1990 levels and **Australia** agreeing to limit emissions to no more than 8 percent *above* 1990 levels.

In 2009, state leaders and negotiators met in Copenhagen, Denmark, at the 15th Conference of the Parties to the UNFCCC. Ambitions were high, with many civil society groups and state delegates calling for a new, binding international agreement to replace the Kyoto Protocol. In the end, however, states could not pull this off, and although organizers tried to highlight areas of unanimity (e.g., on the need to reduce greenhouse gases) and the creativity of many proposals, most observers saw the Copenhagen Conference as a failure.

By 2012 many states had not met their commitments under the Kyoto Protocol. (The United States never ratified the agreement, while **Canada** formally withdrew.) By then more and more climate experts were calling for much greater reductions in greenhouse gas emissions to avoid cataclysmic warming and mass extinctions. That year in Doha, Qatar, negotiators agreed to a second commitment period (ending in 2020) for the UNFCCC's Kyoto Protocol (called the Doha Amendment). Going into the 21st Conference of the Parties to the UNFCCC in 2015 in Paris, **France**, however, the Doha Amendment was not yet in force, although some ratifying states were none-theless promising to meet their commitments.

The Paris Climate Change Conference was held from 30 November to 11 December 2015. Once again, demands were high for a new (and ambitious) binding international agreement on climate change (including replacing the commitments under the Kyoto Protocol). Negotiations among the representatives from 195 countries were tense and difficult; coalitions of representatives formed and shifted across a host of proposals, including, among many other issues, emission targets, temperature-rise limits, financing, loss and liability claims, forestry and land use, and tracking and ratcheting-up processes. In the end an agreement was reached, a feat political leaders around the world hailed as a historic turning point in the multilateral processes to mitigate and adapt to climate change.

The Paris Agreement calls for a rapid peaking of greenhouse gas emissions, still aiming to halt warming to no more than 2 degrees Celsius above preindustrial levels, but adding a new aspirational target of 1.5 degrees Celsius. With these targets in mind, the Paris Agreement calls on leading economies to reduce national emissions and shift to renewable and clean energy. National reduction commitments, however, are nonbinding and vary widely across developed and developing countries. The consensus to support a non-binding agreement arose in part because U.S. negotiators insisted (the majority of U.S. senators had said they would not ratify a binding agreement; however, the U.S. president has the authority to enact a nonbinding agreement). Although targets are nonbinding, states did agree to track and report on emission reductions every five years, as well as to work on ratcheting up commitments over time (presumably as progress reports are reviewed and compared).

Some analysts see the voluntary nature of the Paris Agreement as severely undermining its capacity to decarbonize the world economy and move toward zero net emissions. But others see this as a necessary compromise to ensure U.S. participation as well as to develop a fully global response to climate change, including within emerging economies such as **China, India,**

Brazil, and Russia. Also vital for gaining support for the Paris Agreement among developing countries was the creation of a global financing mechanism for climate change mitigation and **adaptation** in poorer countries, which by 2020 will offer a minimum of $100 million a year in funding. Support will include extending alternative energy technologies (**solar power** and **wind power**) as well as expanding programs such as Reduced Emissions through Avoided **Deforestation** and Degradation (REDD) + Conservation (REDD+). Arguably, however, this financial gain for developing countries is partially (and perhaps largely) offset by the exclusion of any mechanism within the Paris Agreement for poor countries to make claims for losses and damages as temperatures warm, storms intensify, species die off, and seas rise.

UNITED NATIONS FUND FOR POPULATION ACTIVITIES (UNFPA). Since at least 1798, the year the first edition of *An Essay on the Principle of Population* by **Thomas Malthus** was published, analysts have been worrying about the consequences of the escalating size of the world's human population. By the 1960s, when **Paul Ehrlich** wrote his best-selling book *The Population Bomb*, many were projecting social and environmental catastrophe unless measures were put in place to slow the growth of the human population (then at over three billion and rising fast). To assist national efforts to understand and manage population growth, the **United Nations** created the Fund for Population Activities in 1969 (renamed the UN Population Fund in 1987, although it kept the acronym UNFPA). Today, the UNFPA remains the world's largest source of international financing for population programs (both governmental and nongovernmental), with a mandate that includes expanding reproductive choices for individuals and couples as well as working with governments to reduce poverty and promote **sustainable development**.

Despite declining birthrates in many prosperous places and despite the efforts of organizations such as the UNFPA, some environmentalists—for example, a faction of the **Sierra Club** in the **United States**—continue to express alarm about the growing world population (now at 7.4 billion and growing quickly). Yet many in the environmental movement no longer focus on population growth and instead concentrate on how to best promote sustainable development for a population heading toward 10 billion by around the year 2050.

UNITED STATES. Government efforts in the United States to conserve natural resources go back to the earliest colonial settlements. In 1626, for instance, Plymouth Colony passed an ordinance to regulate the timber industry. By the mid-1800s, the public was taking an interest in conservation:

George Perkins Marsh, for example, published *Man and Nature* in 1864, which called for protection of songbirds and prevention of soil erosion. The U.S. Commission of Fish and Fisheries was founded in 1871—the first federal agency tasked with conservation of a particular natural resource. Rapid urbanization and industrial growth from 1870 to 1900 caused some serious environmental problems, including water contamination, unsanitary waste disposal, and air **pollution**, prompting civil society groups to emerge around various environmental issues.

A movement to preserve natural areas also gained strength in the 1800s, with public activism leading to the establishment of Yellowstone National Park in 1872, Sequoia and Kings Canyon and Yosemite Parks in 1890, and Mount Rainier National Park in 1899. This process continued with the Forest Reserve Act of 1891. A true "environmental" movement was emerging by the turn of the 20th century, with markers such as the founding of the **Sierra Club** in 1892 by **John Muir**. It was broadly split into two submovements: preservationists (wanting to preserve wilderness areas) and conservationists (wanting to exploit natural resources more sustainably).

Conservationists began to emerge as the dominant camp in the early 1900s. A number of prominent conservation organizations were created in this period: the **National Audubon Society** in 1905, the National Parks Association (now called the National Parks Conservation Association) in 1919, and the Izaak Walton League in 1922. Simultaneously, municipal governments began to introduce regulations to tackle pollution and protect public health, dealing with issues such as sanitation, waste removal, exposure to hazardous substances in workplaces, and so on. The role of the federal government in conservation grew during the Great Depression, with projects such as the Tennessee Valley Authority (1933) and the Soil Conservation Service (1935) (now called the Natural Resources Conservation Service), both of which provided work to unemployed young men.

After World War II ended in 1945, the focus of U.S. environmentalism began to shift away from how to best exploit natural resources and toward more active measures to preserve land for recreational purposes. Environmental problems became a major national issue in the 1960s, with best-selling books such as **Rachel Carson**'s *Silent Spring* (1962) and **Paul Ehrlich**'s *The Population Bomb* (1968) and high-profile environmental disasters such as the **oil** spills off the coast of Santa Barbara, California, in January and February 1969. The federal government passed major environmental legislation during this time, including the first Clean Air Act (1963), the Water Quality Act (1965), the Endangered Species Preservation Act (1966) (an amendment later changed its name to the Endangered Species Conservation Act), and the National Environmental Policy Act (NEPA) (1970). In this same period, membership in environmental **nongovernmental organizations (NGOs)** grew quickly (tenfold for the Sierra Club between 1952 and 1969 alone).

Environmentalism continued to strengthen during the 1970s, although not at the fast pace of the 1960s, as other matters, including the oil crisis (1973–1974, 1979–1980), took center stage. The Environmental Protection Agency (EPA) was created in 1970, and Congress passed a number of new bills, such as the Marine Mammal Protection Act (1972) and the Resource Conservation and Recovery Act (1976). At times events did drag environmental issues to the top of the political agenda, most notably after the **Three Mile Island nuclear accident** in 1979.

The 1980s saw the beginning of an antienvironmental backlash. In 1981, the new administration of Ronald Reagan cut the EPA's budget, personnel, and powers to enforce regulations. This administration then pursued an active and effective policy of obstruction, aiming to weaken governmental regulation generally and environmental regulation in particular. While the Democratic Congress succeeded in blocking Reagan's broader environmental agenda, he was successful in using his discretionary powers as chief executive to weaken regulatory activity throughout the government (the principal strategy was to appoint individuals supporting his environmental agenda to upper- and mid-level positions in the bureaucracy).

The presidency of George H. W. Bush (1989–1993) was less hostile to environmental regulations than his predecessor, presiding over the emergence of the 1990 Clean Air Act Amendments and the 1992 Energy Policy Act, two major pieces of legislation. The early 1990s also saw global environmental problems such as **climate change** and **biodiversity** rise to the top of the world agenda (as the 1992 **United Nations Conference on Environment and Development** shows). The Bill Clinton/**Al Gore** administration came to power with strong environmental credentials, but congressional resistance stymied many initiatives during the administration's two terms. Congress, for example, defeated Clinton's proposal to change public lands policies (with the aid of congressional Democrats from western states). The 1995–1996 Republican Congress led by Newt Gingrich was especially hostile to any sort of government regulation. It cut EPA and Interior Department budgets and attempted to change a number of environmental laws, although President Clinton vetoed these attempts. Eventually, the antienvironmentalism of Congress over this time prompted a public backlash (for example, the largest environmental NGOs gathered signatures in support of an Environmental Bill of Rights, which they presented to Congress and the White House). Republicans decided to tone down the efforts to reform environmental policy during the rest of Clinton's term, but congressional resistance continued to prevent significant progress on strengthening environmental measures.

The presidency of George W. Bush returned Republican antiregulatory sentiment to the White House. Democratic control of the Senate in 2001–2002 frustrated early efforts at deregulation. The administration seized on the rolling blackouts in California in early 2001 as an excuse to create a new national energy plan, which relaxed environmental regulations and spurred exploration for energy resources in public lands.

Federal-state relations, fragmented political institutions, and formal division of power across the legislative, executive, and judicial branches of government in the United States makes the formation and implementation of environmental regulations more complex than in many countries. Most federal environmental laws since 1970, for example, require or permit implementation by the states. Also, localism, interest groups, and "horse-trading" in Congress, along with the powers of committees, subcommittees, and particular members of Congress, can further complicate environmental decision making. Because a comparatively high number of points in the policy process exist where actors can block or veto an initiative, broad-based coalitions are often necessary to push through new legislation. The bureaucracy—with the EPA as a lead agency, but with dozens of federal agencies with responsibilities over aspects of environmental protection and health—can again make for a very tangled regulatory structure around environmental management.

The judicial branch also influences environmental regulation through its power to interpret legislation and ensure compliance by federal agencies (courtesy of the Administrative Procedures Act of 1946). Litigation has been a crucial tool in the politics of environmental regulation—environmental organizations, businesses, and federal agencies have all gone to court when other avenues failed to produce results. In the 1970s, judicial decisions tended to advance the environmental movement's agenda. After the mid-1980s, however, the courts became less friendly to environmental concerns, in part due to judicial appointments by Republican presidents.

Since 2009, the administration of President Barack Obama has seen a resurgence of environmental interest, although to a lesser extent action, as differences within the Democratic Party and strong opposition from Republicans in Congress thwart Obama's initiatives. Those calling for greater environmental controls on oil production, for instance, gained supporters after an explosion at BP's *Deepwater Horizon* oil rig spilled millions of barrels of oil into the Gulf of Mexico in 2010. Those calling for stronger action to address climate change gained strength after hurricane Sandy flooded large parts of New York and New Jersey in 2012. Those calling for stronger measures to conserve fresh water gained strength as droughts swept across parts of the country, including severe dry weather and forest fires in California in 2014 and 2015. Those calling for more vigilance on **automobile** companies gained supporters after the EPA discovered in 2015 that Volkswagen had added software into its diesel cars to falsify emission test readings (as emission levels for these cars were far above the allowable European and U.S. standards).

In his second term, President Obama also took up the cause of climate change, negotiating a joint agreement with **China** to lower emissions and describing climate change at the 2014 New York Summit on Climate Change as an "urgent and growing threat" that is going to "define the contours of this century more dramatically than any other." Following years of lobbying and pressure by environmental groups, in 2015 President Obama rejected the proposal for a fourth phase of the Keystone XL Pipeline system, a project that would have allowed the Canadian province of Alberta to transport large volumes of "tar sands" oil to U.S. refineries. *See also* EARTH FIRST!; ECOLOGICAL FOOTPRINT; EMISSIONS TRADING; ENVIRONMENTAL DEFENSE FUND (EDF); *EXXON VALDEZ* OIL SPILL; GREEN PARTY; LEADED GASOLINE; LOVE CANAL; OCCUPY MOVEMENT; ORGANIC FOOD; POLYBROMINATED DIPHENYL ETHERS (PBDEs); PRESERVATION; WISE USE MOVEMENT.

UZBEKISTAN. *See* ARAL SEA.

V

VIETNAM. The Vietnam War (1959–1975) caused extensive environmental damage to Vietnam's countryside. The use of herbicides, including the dioxin-containing Agent Orange, by the **United States** defoliated vast areas of forests, destroyed rice crops, and polluted food chains.

Additional land degradation and high rates of **deforestation** followed free market reforms by the Communist Party in the mid-1980s to promote rapid agricultural and industrial growth. Since the early 1990s, however, environmental management of forests, land, and water has been improving. With support from the **Global Environment Facility** and the United Nations Development Programme, the government conducted a Protected Areas for Resource Conservation landscape ecology pilot project from 1999 to 2004. To coordinate river development, flood control, and information sharing, Cambodia, Lao PDR, **Thailand**, and Vietnam created the Mekong River Commission in 1995, replacing the former Committee for Coordination of Investigations of the Lower Mekong Basin (founded in 1957), which had a rocky history through wars in the region. In 1999, Vietnam also passed a law on water resource management with a **polluter pays principle** (although the government has struggled to implement it). Other specific initiatives also began in the 1990s. In 1992, the Cat Loc Rhino Sanctuary (part of the Cat Tien National Park since 1998) was set up to protect forests for the critically endangered Javan rhino. Various groups, including the **World Wide Fund for Nature/World Wildlife Fund (WWF)**, also began working to protect the forested border region of Cambodia, Vietnam, and Lao PDR, especially for elephants, rhinos, and tigers.

Vietnam's Ministry of Natural Resources and Environment was created in 2002, along with its National Strategy for Environmental Protection. Vietnam's environmental problems remain serious, including **air pollution**, garbage, chemical contamination, deforestation, and **biodiversity** loss. Since the mid-2000s, however, the government has strengthened its **environmental impact assessments**, adopted the Rio Earth Summit Agenda 21 Strategy for Sustainable Development (in 2004), put in place a new national **biodiversity** action plan, promoted greater energy efficiency, implemented measures to improve waste and water management, and enhanced reporting and monitoring requirements for industry. In 2012 the government introduced its "National Strategy for Environmental Protection until 2020 and Vision toward 2030" to extend the legal basis for managing environmental issues.

At an international level, Vietnam has ratified the **Stockholm Convention on Persistent Organic Pollutants** and taken steps to better manage the disposal of polychlorinated biphenyl, or PCBs. Regarding international efforts to protect the ozone layer, Vietnam was still using **ozone-depleting** substances (for insulation foam, refrigerators, air conditioners, and fire extinguishers for industrial uses) in the mid-2000s, but since then it has made steady progress to phase out **chlorofluorocarbons (CFCs)** and halons, with, for example, the government banning the import of CFCs in 2010.

VOLUNTARY SIMPLICITY. Voluntary simplicity is a loosely organized social movement that, among other things, calls for decreasing consumption in order to live at a more environmentally friendly scale. It is also referred to as simple living, downshifting, downsizing, or simplifying. Core values include material simplicity, appropriate living, ecological awareness, and consuming a fair earth share. The phrase is commonly credited to Richard Gregg (from his 1936 essay, "The Value of Voluntary Simplicity"). The movement, however, traces its roots to much earlier, starting with the teachings of Buddha, Christ, and Muhammad, and later to people like **Henry David Thoreau**, Ralph Waldo Emerson, and **Mahatma Gandhi**. In the **United States** the idea of voluntary simplicity spread organically through the 1980s, gaining particular attention in the late 1990s after a series of major American newspapers ran articles on the idea. *See also* ECOLOGICAL FOOTPRINT.

W

WARD, BARBARA (1914–1981). A British economist and author, Barbara Ward influenced the early discussion around the concept and definition of **sustainable development**. In 1971, she founded the **International Institute for Environment and Development (IIED)**; after retiring as Schweitzer Professor of Economic Development from Columbia University, Ward served as president of IIED from 1973 and chair from 1980. One of her most influential books was *Only One Earth* (coauthored with René Dubos), prepared for the 1972 **United Nations Conference on the Human Environment**.

WATER. *See* ANTARCTICA; ARAL SEA; AUSTRALIA; BANGLADESH; CHINA, PEOPLE'S REPUBLIC OF; HYDROELECTRICITY; ISRAEL; NARMADA DAM; POLLUTION; THREE GORGES DAM; UNITED STATES.

WATSON, PAUL (1950–). Born in Toronto, **Canada**, Paul Watson was an early (and some would say a founding) member of **Greenpeace**. Before long, however, he was at odds with the philosophy of "bearing witness," instead arguing for direct action against whaling and sealing. In 1977 he cofounded the Earthforce Environmental Society to stop whaling and sealing. In 1979 he captained the *Sea Shepherd* to the ice floes off the Magdalen Islands in Canada's Gulf of St. Lawrence, confronting sealers and spray-painting white pups with red dye to destroy the pelts (this did not hurt the pups as they molt within a few weeks). Off Portugal later that year, Watson rammed and severely damaged the *Sierra*, a whaling ship he described as a "notorious prolific pirate whaler."

In 1981 Watson renamed his organization the Sea Shepherd Conservation Society, and for the next 30 years he sailed the seas more than 200 times to take direct action to save whales, seals, dolphins, and sharks. Although arrested and charged many times with scuttling and boarding ships and destroying nets and equipment, he has never been convicted of any serious charges. After skipping bail in Germany in 2012 while facing Interpol notices for extradition to Costa Rica and Japan, he sailed for a while as a fugitive before moving in 2013 to the U.S. state of Vermont and then later to Paris, **France**, where he is working to resolve his legal situation (as of 2015, Interpol still considers him a "wanted person").

WATT-CLOUTIER, SHEILA (1953–). *See* CANADA.

WHALING. Hunting whales for oil and food has a long history, from the Inuit to the Europeans to the Japanese. This disparate hunt, however, did not begin to threaten the survival of whale populations until the 19th and 20th centuries as harvesting became increasingly efficient. The first treaty to manage whaling went into effect in 1931, but this did little to halt the declining populations as whalers continued to take tens of thousands of whales a year. The International Whaling Commission (IWC) was formed in 1946, but again the number of whales continued to decline. In the mid-1960s, **Japan** was still hunting close to 27,000 whales a year, and whale meat was the most consumed type of meat in the country.

Animal rights and environmental activists began to campaign to save whales in the 1960s and 1970s. Groups such as **Greenpeace** went to sea to thwart whalers. Greenpeace also employed media "**mindbombs**" to change global consciousness about the worth of a "whale," using images and metaphors to reimagine a whale from an animal for food and oil to a sentient, majestic creature too beautiful to harm. Activists also lobbied states, including those with no history of whaling. With whale numbers continuing to fall, in 1982 the IWC shifted away from trying to manage whales sustainably and declared a moratorium on commercial whaling, effective in the 1985–1986 season. It was supposed to be a temporary moratorium, lifted once the IWC approved the Revised Management Procedure, but the IWC was never able to agree on new procedures, and it has turned into a de facto permanent ban.

Today, the IWC allows limited whaling for indigenous communities (such as the Inuit in Greenland) and for scientific research, but it continues to ban commercial whaling. The debate about the merits of the ban is ongoing in the IWC. In 2006, a resolution was put forth at the IWC to resume commercial whaling, but it did not achieve the necessary three-quarters majority to pass. Critics, in particular Japan and Norway, argue that the moratorium is too blunt, ignoring the fact that not all whale species are threatened, and accuse the IWC of caving in to the sentimentality of the Greenpeace mind-set. Pro-whaling states estimate, for example, that the population of minke whales in the southern oceans is high enough to sustain some commercial operations, although estimates of the population size are highly contested. Many anti-whaling countries inside the IWC have shifted away from environmental arguments and toward ethical ones to uphold the moratorium.

Despite the IWC moratorium, some countries, notably Japan, Norway, and Iceland, continue to hunt whales. Japan relies on the clause allowing scientific research to continue to hunt hundreds of whales a year (which, under IWC rules, the country must process and distribute as meat). Norway also hunts hundreds of whales every year under IWC rules that allow a country to not comply if it registers an objection to a rule; Iceland relies on a similar argument to justify its hunt, having quit and rejoined the IWC with a "reservation." Commercial whalers have killed tens of thousands of whales since the 1986 IWC moratorium. The commercial whaling that remains, however, is currently not the biggest threat to the survival of whales; rather, it is the disturbance of their habitats from things like **persistent organic pollutants** and **climate change**.

WILDERNESS SOCIETY. Two separate environmental organizations operate under this name, one in the **United States**, the other in **Australia**. The Wilderness Society (U.S.) focuses on science, analysis, and advocacy to protect and restore wilderness areas in the United States. Founded in 1935 with the assistance of conservationists such as **Aldo Leopold**, the organization was instrumental in passing the 1964 U.S. Wilderness Act. Indeed, the organization's executive secretary, Howard Zahniser, was the primary author of the act.

The Wilderness Society (Australia) is a national organization based in communities. It advocates protecting and restoring wilderness and natural areas in Australia. It began in 1976 as the Tasmania Wilderness Society, changing its name in 1984 after a successful campaign to save the Franklin River in Tasmania. It now has campaign centers in every state of Australia. The organization claims that its work since 1976 has protected millions of hectares of land from development and degradation. *See also* NONGOVERNMENTAL ORGANIZATIONS (NGOs).

WILDLIFE CONSERVATION SOCIETY. Headquartered at the Bronx Zoo in New York City, the Wildlife Conservation Society has been working to conserve wildlife and wilderness since 1895. One of the first conservation organizations in the **United States**, today the society operates in scores of countries across Africa, Asia, and North and Latin America to conserve everything from tigers to butterflies. *See also* NONGOVERNMENTAL ORGANIZATIONS (NGOs).

WILSON, EDWARD O. (1929–). Born in Alabama in 1929, Edward O. Wilson is currently Pellegrino University Research Professor Emeritus at Harvard University. At age 13 he discovered the first known colony of fire ants in the **United States** and went on to become one of the world's leading authorities on ants. After uncovering how ants communicate, Wilson became a highly controversial scientist when he began to extend his conclusions about the behavior of ants to the behavior of humans. He is well known, too, for his scholarly and popular contributions to environmental writings, including his research on conservation and species extinctions. Indicative of Wilson's influence are his more than 75 international awards, including the U.S. National Medal of Science and two Pulitzer Prizes for *On Human Nature* (1978) and *The Ants* (1990). *Time* magazine named Wilson one of America's 25 Most Influential People in 1995. He remains a highly active and influential scholar. In 2012 he published *The Social Conquest of Earth*; in 2014 he published yet another award-winning book, *The Meaning of Human Existence*.

WIND POWER/ENERGY. Wind power from turbines is a **renewable energy** that does not emit carbon dioxide or other **greenhouse gases**. Since the 1990s, wind and **solar power** have been two of the fastest-growing energy sectors. Global wind power capacity from 1992 to 2003 alone increased 16 times; by 2007, it had more than doubled again. Nearly three-quarters of this capacity was installed in Europe. By then wind power was providing 20 percent of electricity in Denmark and 5 percent in **Germany** and **Spain**. The German state of Schleswig-Holstein was meeting 30 percent of its energy needs with wind power.

Since then the capacity of wind power has continued to expand. By 2014 total global wind power capacity was five times higher than it had been in 2006. In Denmark, wind power in 2014 supplied around 40 percent of the country's total energy needs. Since the mid-2000s, **China** has been a leader in wind power. In 2006, China had relatively little wind power capacity; in 2010, China surpassed the **United States** as the world's leading wind power country. From 2010 to 2014, China's wind capacity continued to expand rapidly, more than doubling, leaving China accounting for nearly one-third of the world's wind power capacity in 2014. In 2015 wind power was supplying 3–4 percent of global electricity; the International Energy Agency sees the potential for this to increase to as much as 18 percent by 2050.

Many in the environmental movement see wind power as one of the most effective ways to move away from a dependence on fossil fuels; however, others (including many outside the movement) oppose expanding capacity because, among other things, turbines kill birds, destroy the visual landscape, and generate noise. In **Great Britain**, for example, a protest movement against wind power has been bolstered by the Country Guardian, an antiwind lobby group founded in 1991. Globally, environmentalists are split, with groups such as **Greenpeace** and **Friends of the Earth** supporting wind power and defending government wind policies often in the face of local antiwind lobbies in the affected communities. *See also* CLIMATE CHANGE; PEAK OIL.

WISE USE MOVEMENT. Used in 1910 by **Gifford Pinchot** to describe his understanding of scientific natural resource management, since the late 1980s the phrase *wise use* in the **United States** has become associated with a loose grassroots movement including farmers, loggers, miners, and property owners who oppose the mainstream environmental movement (in particular, the tendency to create public lands for conservation). Many in the wise use movement, especially political and religious conservatives, see environmental advocacy groups as too "radical," with hidden agendas to exaggerate problems and take over land; instead, they advocate private property and environmental resources going to benefit locals (who, by living off the land, are true "environmentalists"). Ron Arnold, executive vice president of the Center for the Defense of Free Enterprise, has been a critical influence in promoting the wise use movement in the United States.

WORLD BUSINESS COUNCIL FOR SUSTAINABLE DEVELOPMENT (WBCSD). First established as the Business Council for Sustainable Development (BCSD) in 1991 by Swiss industrialist Stephan Schmidheiny to participate in the 1992 **United Nations Conference on Environment and Development**, the council merged with the World Industry Council on the Environment in 1995 to become the World Business Council for Sustainable Development (WBCSD). Today, the World Business Council works to promote the role of business in achieving **sustainable development**, promoting the green image of big business while also supporting efforts to promote **corporate social responsibility**. Its main approaches to sustainable development are **eco-efficiency**, **eco-business**, global market liberalization, and **industry self-regulation**. It also works with an international network of corporate and **nongovernmental organization** partners, including the **United Nations Environment Programme** and environmental groups such as the **World Wide Fund for Nature/World Wildlife Fund (WWF)**. The WBCSD has been active in international environmental policy, such as negotiating the **Kyoto Protocol** and subsequent **climate change** agreements, advocating flexible, market-based instruments.

Activist groups such as **Greenpeace**, Corporate Watch, and **SumOfUs** see the WBCSD as little more than big **greenwash**. Still, it has gained legitimacy as the voice of big business for international environmental discussions and is a sign of the trend over the last two decades to include big business as an active participant in the global environmental movement.

WORLD CHARTER FOR NATURE. Adopted by the **United Nations** in 1982, the World Charter for Nature lays out "general principles," "functions," and "implementation" for judging and guiding human interaction with nature. Principle 1, for example, states, "Nature shall be respected and its essential processes shall not be impaired." Although this document has not translated into many specific and concrete changes, it is an important symbolic declaration of the significance of environmentalism within the United Nations.

WORLD COMMISSION ON ENVIRONMENT AND DEVELOP-MENT. The World Commission on Environment and Development was established in 1983 by the **United Nations** General Assembly. Chaired by Norwegian prime minister **Gro Harlem Brundtland**, it presented its report *Our Common Future* (commonly called the Brundtland Report) to the UN General Assembly in 1987. To this day its definition of **sustainable development**—"development that meets the needs of the present without compromising the ability of future generations to meet their own needs"—remains the consensus one for the international community of states and national governments. Most businesses also accept this definition. Many environmental **nongovernmental organizations** also accept it, although more radical groups see it as a disastrous compromise, allowing business as usual to brand the pursuit of profit, economic growth, and development with the word *sustainable*. More specifically, some groups contest the logical policy arising from the conclusions of the World Commission on Environment and Development: that economic growth is necessary to alleviate poverty (and because poverty causes environmental degradation, the pursuit of growth can solve environmental problems).

WORLD CONSERVATION UNION. *See* INTERNATIONAL UNION FOR CONSERVATION OF NATURE (IUCN).

WORLD ENVIRONMENT DAY. The **United Nations** General Assembly established World Environment Day in 1972 to mark the opening of the **United Nations Conference on the Human Environment**. The **United Nations Environment Programme (UNEP)** was entrusted with its commemoration. Every year, on 5 June, countries around the world now celebrate World Environment Day to focus attention on the need for collective political action to tackle environmental problems. It provides an opportunity for people across different cultures to raise ecological awareness with fun activities such as street rallies, green concerts, and tree planting. It also provides an opportunity to encourage states to sign and ratify international environmental agreements and for state leaders to announce new environmental policies or agencies.

Each year a different city hosts the global celebrations, working with the UNEP to choose a theme. In 2006, the international celebrations for World Environment Day were held in Algeria, with the theme "Don't Desert Drylands!" In 2007, Environment Day was hosted by **Norway**, with the slogan "Melting Ice—a Hot Topic?" The theme for 2008 in Wellington, **New Zealand**, was "Kick the Habit! Towards a Low Carbon Economy." The theme in 2013, in Mongolia, was "Think. Eat. Save." The theme in 2014, in Barbados, was "Raise Your Voice Not the Sea Level." The theme in 2015, in Italy, was "Seven Billion Dreams. One Planet. Consume with Care." The first theme was a saying still well known among environmentalists: "Only One Earth."

WORLD RESOURCES INSTITUTE (WRI). Founded in 1982, the World Resources Institute (WRI) was set up to conduct independent and scientific policy research and analysis on global environmental change and natural resource management. Nonprofit and nongovernmental, WRI was specifically *not* an activist organization like **Greenpeace** or the **World Wide Fund for Nature/World Wildlife Fund (WWF)**. Its goal was to ensure that its research was hard hitting and accurate about the changing state of the world's environment, but also politically practical about the development needs of growing human populations so that policy makers found the research—and recommendations—relevant. The founding president was James Gustave Speth (serving until 1993), who later went on to become dean at the School of Forestry and Environmental Studies, Yale University, from 1999 to 2009. The president of WRI in 2016 was Andrew Steer, an economist who was previously at the World Bank (joining WRI as president in 2012). *See also* INTERNATIONAL INSTITUTE FOR ENVIRONMENT AND DEVELOPMENT (IIED).

WORLD SUMMIT ON SUSTAINABLE DEVELOPMENT. The World Summit on Sustainable Development, held in 2002 in Johannesburg, **South Africa**, was an even larger international environmental conference than the **United Nations Conference on Environment and Development (UNCED)** held in Rio de Janeiro 10 years earlier. Over 180 countries sent representatives, although only about 100 heads of state came, fewer than at Rio. In total, there were more than 10,000 delegates, at least 8,000 civil society representatives and 4,000 members of the press, as well as thousands of ordinary citizens. Popularly called Rio+10 or the Johannesburg Summit, it evaluated the progress of **sustainable development** since UNCED. Its mandate also included setting clearer targets to implement the Rio goals.

The two most important publications from the Johannesburg Summit were the Johannesburg Declaration on Sustainable Development (a summary of challenges and general commitments) and the Johannesburg Plan of Implementation to meet these. Both of these are nonbinding agreements. As during the negotiations for the Rio Conference, the most contentious and least settled issue remained financing for sustainable development. Some analysts see the Johannesburg Summit as a success, focusing states on global environmental problems and advancing implementation of sustainable development through voluntary partnerships with corporations and **nongovernmental organizations**. Others see it as an outright failure, just another example of too much rhetoric and not enough action or money. The reality is somewhere in between, with the Johannesburg Summit adding yet another layer of common understanding to international efforts to advance environmentalism globally.

WORLDWATCH INSTITUTE. Founded by Lester Brown in 1974, who served as president for 25 years, the Worldwatch Institute (based in Washington, D.C.) conducts independent research on **sustainability** and social justice. It is funded by donations from private foundations and individuals, as well as by the sale of its research and some government grants.

Worldwatch focuses on analyzing environmental, social, and economic trends from a global and interdisciplinary perspective. It is especially well known for its annual State of the World reports (first launched in 1984). The 2015 State of the World is titled *About Confronting Hidden Threats to Sustainability*. Critics, such as **Bjørn Lomborg**, argue that such "research" is creating a misleading statistical database of the state of the global environment in order to justify and publicize their research. Supporters within the environmental movement see Worldwatch as an essential source of cutting-edge statistics and projections, less encumbered by the conservative tendencies and technical language typical of much of the peer-reviewed scientific literature.

WORLD WIDE FUND FOR NATURE/WORLD WILDLIFE FUND (WWF). Founded in 1961 as the World Wildlife Fund, the international headquarters of the World Wide Fund for Nature (WWF) is in Gland, Switzerland (the organization now tends to just use the acronym WWF, since the organizations in **Canada** and the **United States** did not join the rest of the world in 1986 in changing the name to the World Wide Fund for Nature). The original vision was to raise funds for conservation, working in partnership with the **International Union for Conservation of Nature (IUCN)**. Its mission was to conserve **biodiversity**, promote sustainable use of renewable natural resources, and reduce **pollution** and wasteful consumption. It began to develop its own agenda during the 1960s, moving away from partnerships with the IUCN.

Today, the WWF has millions of regular supporters worldwide and operates across scores of countries. Its guiding principles are to remain nonpolitical, global, independent, and scientific, building partnerships with local communities, governments, and business. Its work is geared toward conservation projects, including funding thousands of projects, fieldwork, research, policy advice, education, and raising public awareness. It has a reputation within the environmental movement for its partnerships with business (with some seeing these as practical and successful and others as a sellout). It helped launch, for example, the **Forest Stewardship Council** in 1993, the Marine Stewardship Council in 1996, and the Roundtable on Sustainable Palm Oil in 2004. Local WWF branches also develop independent partnerships. In the past, WWF-**Sweden** has cooperated with the multinational food firm Tetra Pak on responsible wood purchases and **climate change** policies. WWF-India has cooperated with the Austrian crystal firm Swarovski to establish a wetlands visitor center in the Keoladeo National Park in **India**. And WWF-Denmark has cooperated with the pharmaceutical firm Novo Nordisk to reduce carbon dioxide emissions. The U.S. branch of the WWF has a long-standing partnership with Coca-Cola to support water governance and polar bear conservation (extended in 2013 to last until at least 2020). The U.S. WWF also designates firms that give them "$1 million or more" as "Million Dollar Pandas"; as of 2016, this included Coca-Cola, Domtar, Avon, Bank of America, and Gap.

WWOOF. World Wide Opportunities on Organic Farms, or WWOOF, is a network of national organizations that link travelers wanting to volunteer on organic farms (or smallholdings and gardens) in exchange for food and accommodation. Beginning in **Great Britain** in 1971, it has evolved into a global "WWOOFing" movement, building worldwide networks of "WWOOFers" and farmers around a common vision of sustainable living and traveling.

YANZA, LUIS. *See* GOLDMAN ENVIRONMENTAL PRIZE.

Bibliography

CONTENTS

INTRODUCTION

Thomas Malthus's *Essay on the Principle of Population* (1798) was one of the earliest and most influential publications on environmentalism. Over the next century and a half, many other influential books were published from time to time, such as Henry David Thoreau's *Walden* (1884) and Aldo Leopold's *A Sand County Almanac* (1949). After the late 1960s, books and articles on environmentalism began to appear with increasing frequency. Today, it is close to impossible to keep up with this ever-expanding academic literature, which spans almost every discipline—including anthropology, architecture, economics, environmental studies, biology, geography, history, human ecology, international relations, law, medicine, occupational health, philosophy, planning, political science, psychology, and sociology.

Many of the most influential books have been lasting best sellers, crossing disciplines and reaching readers within government and the general public. These include Rachel Carson's *Silent Spring* (1962), Paul Ehrlich's *The Population Bomb* (1968), Donella Meadows et al.'s *Limits to Growth* (1972), E. F. Schumacher's *Small Is Beautiful* (1973), and James Lovelock's books *Gaia* (1979) and *The Ages of Gaia* (1995). A few articles, too, have had stunning intellectual reach, such as Garrett Hardin's "The Tragedy of the Commons" (1968), which drew an analogy of access and historical collapse of the English commons with access and future collapse of modern-day commons (such as the atmosphere or high seas). Now one of the most cited articles of all time, scholars continue to debate the merits of Hardin's analysis in "The Tragedy of the Commons," with some seeing much value (e.g., Marvin Soroos, 2005) and others, notably Elinor Ostrom (e.g., in her 1990 book *Governing the Commons*), questioning the logic and accuracy of Hardin's parable.

The debates over the "tragedy of the commons" comprise just a small portion of a vast literature shaping the direction and understanding of environmentalism. Although many overlaps exist, one reasonable way to divide this literature is into six broad categories: global environmentalism, national environmentalism, specific environmental issues, environmental ethics and philosophies, environmental events and influential people, and Internet resources on environmentalism.

Within global environmentalism, many research tracts exist, with varying contributions to knowledge. Most of this research assumes that environmentalism is a progressive force of global change. A small subset, however, is highly critical, arguing that the research tends to exaggerate environmental problems (often presenting unreliable statistics to "confirm" crises) by underestimating the benefits of technology, ingenuity, capitalism, free markets, and economic growth (e.g., Phillips, 2015). In recent years, Bjørn Lomborg has been leading the critical charge since publishing his best seller, *The Skeptical Environmentalist* (2001). But he is following in the footsteps of others, such as the economist Julian Simon, who published, for example, *The Ultimate Resource* in 1981, and journalist Gregg Easterbrook, who published the best seller *A Moment on the Earth* in 1995.

For those who believe a global environmental crisis looms (or is already here), much of the literature includes an analysis of the consequences of globalization and global capitalism—with many works focusing on particular aspects, such as the impact of the politics and economics of growth, poverty, consumption, trade, multinational corporations, corporate greenwash, financing, and debt. Typical of the books highly critical of the consequences of the globalization of capitalism are Hilary French's *Vanishing Borders* (2000) and Peter Newell's *Globalization and the Environment* (2012). Some of these books see potential good from economic globalization, such as Arthur Mol's *Globalization and Environmental Reform* (2001), but most, such as Gustave Speth's *The Bridge at the Edge of the World* (2008) and Naomi Klein's *This Changes Everything* (2014), see a need for an overhaul of the world economy. Other writers concentrate on particular aspects of globalizing capitalism, such as economic growth (e.g., Herman Daly's *Beyond Growth*, 1996; Richard Heinberg's *The End of Growth*, 2011; and Samuel Alexander's *Prosperous Descent*, 2015); consumption (e.g., my book *The Shadows of Consumption*, 2008, and Justin Lewis's *Beyond Consumer Capitalism*, 2013); the claims of corporate social responsibility (e.g., my book with Jane Lister, *Eco-Business*, 2013); the principle of sufficiency (e.g., Thomas Princen's *The Logic of Sufficiency*, 2005, and Samuel Alexander's *Sufficiency Economy*, 2015); poverty (e.g., Jack Hollander's *The Real Environmental Crisis*, 2003); trade (e.g., Eric Neumayer's *Greening Trade and Investment*, 2001); multinational corporations (e.g., Christopher Wright and Daniel Nyberg's *Climate Change, Capitalism, and Corporations*, 2015); and Third World debt (e.g., Susan George's *The Debt Boomerang*, 1992).

A second significant strand of the literature on global environmentalism analyzes the contributions of international agreements, international organizations, nongovernmental organizations, grassroots activism, and shifting forms of global governance more generally. Specialists on global negotiations, such as Pamela Chasek (e.g., *Earth Negotiations*, 2001) and Oran Young (e.g., *International Cooperation*, 1994), have advanced our understanding of why and how international environmental norms and rules form, strengthen, and change. Recently, many of these specialists have been working in particular to evaluate the effectiveness of environmental agreements (e.g., Edward Miles et al., *Environmental Regime Effectiveness*, 2001, and Oran Young, *Institutional Dynamics*, 2010). Other researchers have analyzed the consequences of organizations such as the World Bank (e.g., Tamar Gutner's *Banking on the Environment*, 2002, and Susan Park's *World Bank*

Group Interactions with Environmentalists, 2010) and nongovernmental organizations such as Greenpeace, the World Wide Fund for Nature/World Wildlife Fund (WWF), and Friends of the Earth (e.g., Paul Wapner's *Environmental Activism and World Civic Politics*, 1996; Brian Doherty and Timothy Doyle's *Environmentalism, Resistance and Solidarity*, 2013; and *NGO Diplomacy*, 2007, edited by Michele Betsill and Elisabeth Corell).

An even larger number of books and articles in this second strand of literature are now analyzing the nature and influence of emerging forms of global environmental governance. Those focusing more on government-based governance include Walter Baber and Robert Bartlett's *Consensus and Global Environmental Governance* (2015); Frank Biermann's *Earth System Governance* (2014); Ken Conca's *An Unfinished Foundation* (2015); Victor Galaz's *Global Environmental Governance, Technology and Politics* (2014); Thomas Hale, David Held, and Kevin Young's *Gridlock* (2013); and Sikina Jinnah's *Post-Treaty Politics* (2014). Those focusing more on market-based governance include Graeme Auld's *Constructing Private Governance* (2014); Benjamin Cashore, Graeme Auld, and Deanna Newsom's *Governing through Markets* (2004); Robert Falkner's *Business Power and Conflict in International Environmental Politics* (2008); Doris Fuchs's *Understanding Business Power in Global Governance* (2005); Jessica Green's *Rethinking Private Authority* (2014); and Aseem Prakash and Matthew Potoski's *The Voluntary Environmentalists* (2006).

A third strand of the literature on global environmentalism brings in analyses of issues such as history, security, justice, and science to further probe the nature of environmentalism (and ideas such as sustainability and sustainable development). The collection of books is diverse here, including ones like Ramachandra Guha's *Environmentalism* (2000); Thomas Homer-Dixon's *Environment, Scarcity and Violence* (1999); Andrew Dobson's *Justice and the Environment* (1998); and Stephen Bocking's *Nature's Experts* (2004). The analysis of the concept of sustainability is particularly rich and includes Jeremy Caradonna's *Sustainability* (2014); Simon Dresner's *The Principles of Sustainability* (2008); Andrés Edwards's *Thriving beyond Sustainability* (2010); Neil Harrison's *Sustainable Capitalism and the Pursuit of Well-Being* (2014); Melissa Leach, Ian Scoones, and Andy Stirling's *Dynamic Sustainabilities* (2010); Donella Meadows's *Thinking in Systems* (2008); Peter Nemetz's *Business and the Sustainability Challenge* (2013); Paul Robbins's *Political Ecology* (2011); Margaret Robertson's *Sustainability* (2014); and Leslie Thiele's *Sustainability* (2013).

There is also an impressive literature in this third strand on the varieties and shifting nature of environmentalism more generally. A few notable examples are John Cianchi's *Radical Environmentalism* (2015), Rob Nixon's *Slow Violence and the Environmentalism of the Poor* (2011), my 2014 book *Protest Inc.* with Genevieve LeBaron, Adrian Parr's *Hijacking Sustainability*

(2012), Ramachandra Guha and Joan Martínez-Alier's *Varieties of Environmentalism* (1997), Donald Liddick's *Eco-Terrorism* (2006), Joan Martínez-Alier's *The Environmentalism of the Poor* (2004), Carolyn Merchant's *Radical Ecology* (2005), and Thomas Rudel's *Defensive Environmentalists and the Dynamics of Global Reform* (2014).

Another large body of literature on environmentalism focuses on particular countries or regions. This literature commonly refers to, or is relevant for, understanding global change, but its primary contribution is to understand the nature of environmentalism within particular cultures, political systems, or economic structures. This includes studies comparing histories and policies, as well as ones examining specific places such as Africa (e.g., Gregory Maddox's 2006 book *Sub-Saharan Africa* and Knut Nustad's 2015 book *Creating Africas*); Antarctica and the Arctic (e.g., Marla Cone's 2005 book *Silent Snow*); the Asia-Pacific (e.g., for China, Elizabeth Economy's 2004 book *The River Runs Black* and Judith Shapiro's 2016 book *China's Environmental Challenges*); Europe (e.g., Matthew Auer's 2005 book *Restoring Cursed Earth*, on Eastern Europe and Russia); Latin America (e.g., Kathryn Hochstetler and Margaret Keck's 2007 book *Greening Brazil*); the Middle East (e.g., Mostafa Dolatyar and Tim Gray's 2000 book *Water Politics in the Middle East*); North America (e.g., Robert Gottlieb's 2005 book *Forcing the Spring*); and Oceania (e.g., Judith Bennett's 2000 book *Pacific Forest*). The literature on the United States and Western Europe is particularly extensive here, although in the interests of balanced coverage, the following bibliography only provides a sampling.

Much of this global and national literature involves case studies of particular environmental problems. The most extensive body of writing is on climate change, with the amount of research now increasing rapidly (e.g., Harriet Bulkeley et al.'s *Transnational Climate Change Governance* in 2014; David Ciplet, J. Timmons Roberts, and Mizan R. Khan's *Power in a Warming World* in 2015; and Nicholas Stern's *Why Are We Waiting?* in 2015). Many books and articles have also been written on air pollution, food, forest management, and ozone depletion. But the coverage of many other issues is extensive, too, including automobiles, biodiversity, endangered species, energy, hazardous chemicals and waste, oceans, persistent organic pollutants, urbanization, water, and whaling (see the bibliography for a sampling). Much of this broader literature also weaves in arguments and concepts from environmental ethics and particular environmental philosophies (e.g., Peter Wenz's 2001 book *Environmental Ethics Today*), although some of this literature is distinct, as is true for many of the bibliographies and autobiographies of environmentalists and the histories of particular environmental disasters (again, see the bibliography for examples).

Popular journals such as *Scientific American* have published some of the most influential environmental thinking (for example, the debate in 1993 between Herman Daly and Jagdish Bhagwati over the environmental consequences of trade). The journal *Nature* has also published articles with profound impacts on global environmental relations—for example, the 1974 article by Mario J. Molino and F. Sherwood Rowland that would lead to an international agreement to ban chlorofluorocarbons (CFCs) and other ozone-depleting substances. A diverse range of other professional journals also publish articles more specifically on environmental problems and the meaning and significance of environmentalism itself. These include *Climate Policy*, *Ecological Economics*, *Environment*, *Environment and Planning (A, B, C, D)*, *Environment and Urbanization*, *Environmental Ethics*, *Environmental History*, *Environmental Politics*, *Environmental Values*, *Global Environmental Change—Human and Policy Dimensions*, *Global Environmental Politics*, the *Journal of Environment and Development*, the *Journal of Environmental Planning and Management*, and *Organization & Environment*.

The Internet, however, holds a significant and growing amount of the world's environmental research, scientific databases, advocacy networks, and knowledge exchanges. As an inexpensive and fast way to reach readers in a large number of countries, over the last decade this has become the primary place that nongovernmental organizations publish and archive information. Increasingly, governments, corporations, and the United Nations are also turning to the Internet to disseminate up-to-date information (and sometimes to counter nongovernmental and academic criticism). Academics still tend to publish first and foremost in peer-reviewed university presses and academic journals, but even here the Internet is becoming increasingly important as e-publishing gains ground on standard publishing practices. As computers become cheaper and as the Internet extends further into more developing countries, more and more information is also appearing on grassroots environmentalism in even the remotest regions of the earth. The list of Internet resources at the end of this bibliography provides a sampling of the very best websites for a range of environmental issues (from air pollution to whaling). It provides as well the websites of many of the international environmental agreements, as these are useful sources of scientific and consensus-based statistics. Finally, it provides the website addresses for over 50 nongovernmental environmental groups and international agencies, as these contain more up-to-date and detailed information about grassroots and global environmental initiatives than is possible to obtain from reading books or articles.

DIRECTORIES, REFERENCE WORKS, STATISTICS, AND JOURNALS

Directories and Reference Works

Allaby, Michael A., ed. *The Oxford Dictionary of Ecology*. 4th ed. Oxford: Oxford University Press, 2010.

Atkinson, Giles, Simon Dietz, Eric Neumayer, and Matthew Agarwala, eds. *Handbook of Sustainable Development*. 2nd ed. Cheltenham, England: Edward Elgar, 2014.

Betsill, Michele M., Kathryn Hochstetler, and Dimitris Stevis, eds. *Advances in International Environmental Politics*. 2nd ed. New York: Palgrave Macmillan, 2014.

Collin, P. H. *Dictionary of Environment & Ecology*. 5th ed. London: Bloomsbury, 2009.

Daniels, Tom. *The Environmental Planning Handbook for Sustainable Communities and Regions*. 2nd ed. Chicago: APA Planners Press, 2014.

Dauvergne, Peter, ed. *Environmental Politics*. Cheltenham, England: Edward Elgar, 2013.

————, ed. *Handbook of Global Environmental Politics*. Cheltenham, England: Edward Elgar, 2012.

Dryzek, John S., and David Schlosberg, eds. *Debating the Earth: The Environmental Politics Reader*. 2nd ed. Oxford: Oxford University Press, 2005.

Grafton, R. Quentin, Harry W. Nelson, N. Ross Lambie, and Paul R. Wyrwoll. *A Dictionary of Climate Change and the Environment*. Cheltenham, England: Edward Elgar, 2012.

Krech, Shepard, III, J. R. McNeill, and Carolyn Merchant, eds. *Encyclopedia of World Environmental History*. New York: Routledge, 2003.

Martínez-Alier, Joan, and Roldan Muradian, eds. *Handbook of Ecological Economics*. Cheltenham, England: Edward Elgar, 2015.

Park, Chris, and Michael Allaby. *A Dictionary of Environment and Conservation*. 2nd ed. Oxford: Oxford University Press, 2013.

Pattberg, Philipp H., and Fariborz Zelli. *Encyclopedia of Global Environmental Governance and Politics*. Cheltenham, England: Edward Elgar, 2015.

Reisch, Lucia A., and John Thøgersen. *Handbook of Research on Sustainable Consumption*. Cheltenham, England: Edward Elgar, 2015.

Robinson, Nicholas A., Wang Xi, Lin Harmon, and Sarah Wegmueller, eds. *Dictionary of Environmental and Climate Change Law*. Cheltenham, England: Edward Elgar, 2013.

Saunier, Richard E., and Richard A. Meganck. *Dictionary and Introduction to Global Environmental Governance*. 2nd ed. London: Earthscan, 2009.

Schreurs, Miranda, and Elim Papadakis. *Historical Dictionary of the Green Movement*. Lanham, Md.: Scarecrow Press, 2007.

Stokke, Olav Schram, and Øystein B. Thommessen, eds. *Yearbook of International Co-operation on Environment and Development*. London: Earthscan, 2003.

Thai, Khi V., Dianne Rahm, and Jerrell D. Coggburn, eds. *Handbook of Globalization and the Environment*. Boca Raton, Fla.: CRC Press, 2007.

Trzyna, Thaddeus C., and Julie Didion, eds. *World Directory of Environmental Organizations*. 6th ed. London: Earthscan, 2001.

Wells, Edward R., and Alan M. Schwartz. *Historical Dictionary of North American Environmentalism*. Lanham, Md.: Scarecrow Press, 1997.

Wijen, Frank, Kees Zoeteman, and Jan Pieters, eds. *A Handbook of Globalisation and Environmental Policy*. 2nd ed. Cheltenham, England: Edward Elgar, 2012.

Statistics

Sacquet, Anne-Marie. *World Atlas of Sustainable Development: Economic, Social and Environmental Data*. London: Anthem Press, 2005.

United Nations Development Programme, United Nations Environment Programme, World Bank, and World Resources Institute. *World Resources 2005: The Wealth of the Poor: Managing Ecosystems to Fight Poverty*. Washington, D.C.: World Resources Institute, 2005.

United Nations Environment Programme. *UNEP Yearbook 2014*. Nairobi, Kenya: United Nations Environment Programme, 2014.

World Bank. *The Little Green Data Book 2010*. Washington, D.C.: World Bank, 2010.

———. *World Development Indicators 2015*. Washington, D.C.: World Bank Publications, 2015.

———. *World Development Report 2013: Jobs*. Washington, D.C.: World Bank Publications, 2013.

———. *World Development Report 2014: Risk and Opportunity*. Washington, D.C.: World Bank Publications, 2014.

———. *World Development Report 2015: Mind, Society, and Behavior*. Washington, D.C.: World Bank Publications, 2015.

World Resources Institute. *Earth Trends*. 2015. http://earthtrends.wri.org (accessed 16 November 2015).

———. *World Resources Report 2013–2015: Creating a Sustainable Food Future*. Washington, D.C.: World Resources Institute, 2015.

Worldwatch Institute. *State of the World 2014: Governing for Sustainability.* Washington, D.C.: Island Press, 2014.

————. *State of the World 2015: Confronting Hidden Threats to Sustainability.* Washington, D.C.: Island Press, 2015.

Journals

Climate Policy (Elsevier). Focuses on climate change.

Ecological Economics (Elsevier). The journal of the International Society for Ecological Economics.

Environment (Heldref). Analyzes the interface of environment and development.

Environment and Planning A (Pion). Interdisciplinary research on urban and regional environmental issues.

Environment and Planning B—Planning & Design (Pion). Publishes research on formal methods, models, and theories with a focus on the built environment of cities and regions.

Environment and Planning C—Government and Policy (Pion). Interdisciplinary research with a focus on governments and policy from an international perspective.

Environment and Planning D—Society and Space (Pion). Interdisciplinary research with a focus on the interrelationship of social and spatial issues.

Environment and Urbanization (Sage). Analyzes urban and environmental issues, especially in Africa, Asia, and Latin America.

Environmental Ethics (Center for Environmental Philosophy). Interdisciplinary research on philosophical aspects of environmental issues.

Environmental History (co-published by the Forest History Society and the American Society for Environmental History in association with History Cooperative). Publishes historical research on human interactions with the natural world.

Environmental Politics (Taylor & Francis). Concentrates on environmental movements, political parties, and environmental policy.

Environmental Values (White Horse Press). Provides research on values, environmental policy, and current and future conditions for people and other species.

Global Environmental Change—Human and Policy Dimensions (Elsevier). Interdisciplinary research on global environmental change, covering issues such as economics, equity, health, public policy, risk, science, and international relations.

Global Environmental Politics (MIT Press). Analyzes the connections between political forces and environmental change, particularly the consequences of local-global interactions.

Journal of Environment and Development (Sage). Concentrates on analyses of sustainable development and public policy, including local, regional, and international case studies.

Journal of Environmental Planning and Management (Taylor & Francis). Concentrates on planning and management of the environment.

Organization & Environment: International Journal for Ecosocial Research (Sage). Publishes research on connections between the natural environment and formal and informal organizational patterns.

GLOBAL ENVIRONMENTALISM (GENERAL WORKS)

Corporate Social Responsibility

Bhattacharya, C. B., Sankar Sen, and Daniel Korschun. *Leveraging Corporate Responsibility: The Stakeholder Route to Maximizing Business and Social Value*. Cambridge: Cambridge University Press, 2011.

Cramer, Aron, and Z. Karabell. *Sustainable Excellence: The Future of Business in a Fast-Changing World*. Emmaus, Penn.: Rodale, 2010.

Dauvergne, Peter, and Jane Lister. *Eco-Business: A Big-Brand Takeover of Sustainability*. Cambridge, Mass.: MIT Press, 2013.

Hawken, Paul, Amory B. Lovins, and L. Hunter Lovins, *Natural Capitalism: The Next Industrial Revolution*. 10th anniversary ed. (with a new introduction). New York: Routledge, 2010.

Humes, Edward. *Force of Nature: The Unlikely Story of Wal-Mart's Green Revolution*. New York: HarperCollins, 2011.

Laszlo, Chris, and Nadya Zhexembayeva. *Embedded Sustainability: The Next Big Competitive Advantage*. Sheffield, England: Greenleaf, 2011.

Lozano, Josep M., Laura Albareda, Tamyko Ysa, Heike Roscher, and Manila Marcuccio. *Governments and Corporate Social Responsibility: Public Policies beyond Regulation and Voluntary Compliance*. New York: Palgrave Macmillan, 2008.

Marcus, Alfred A. *Innovations in Sustainability: Fuel and Food*. Cambridge: Cambridge University Press, 2015.

McElhaney, Kellie. *Just Good Business: The Strategic Guide to Aligning Corporate Responsibility and Brand*. San Francisco, Calif.: Berrett-Koehler, 2008.

Visser, Wayne. *The Age of Responsibility: CSR 2.0 and the New DNA of Business*. Chichester, England: Wiley, 2011.

Werther, William, and David Chandler. *Strategic Corporate Social Responsibility: Stakeholders in a Global Environment*. Thousand Oaks, Calif.: Sage, 2010.

Critiques of Environmentalism

Bailey, Ronald, ed. *Global Warming and Other Eco-Myths: How the Environmental Movement Uses False Science to Scare Us to Death*. Roseville, Calif.: Forum, 2002.

Driessen, Paul. *Eco-Imperialism: Green Power, Black Death*. Bellevue, Wash.: Free Enterprise Press, 2003.

Easterbrook, Gregg. *A Moment on the Earth: The Coming Age of Environmental Optimism*. New York: Penguin, 1995.

Lomborg, Bjørn. *Cool It: The Skeptical Environmentalist's Guide to Global Warming*. New York: Knopf, 2007.

———. *The Skeptical Environmentalist: Measuring the Real State of the World*. Cambridge: Cambridge University Press, 2001.

MacDonald, Christine Catherine. *Green, Inc.: An Environmental Insider Reveals How a Good Cause Has Gone Bad*. Guilford, CT: Lyons Press, 2008.

Moore, Patrick. *Confessions of a Greenpeace Dropout: The Making of a Sensible Environmentalist*. Revised and updated. Vancouver, BC: Beatty Street Publishing, 2010.

Nordhaus, Ted, and Michael Shellenberger. *Break Through: From the Death of Environmentalism to the Politics of Possibility*. Boston, Mass.: Houghton Mifflin, 2007.

Phillips, Leigh. *Austerity Ecology & the Collapse-Porn Addicts: A Defence of Growth, Progress, Industry and Stuff*. Alresford, England: Zero Books, 2015.

Simon, Julian L. *Population Matters*. New Brunswick, N.J.: Transaction Publishers, 1990.

———. *The Ultimate Resource*. Princeton, N.J.: Princeton University Press, 1981.

———. *The Ultimate Resource 2*. Princeton, N.J.: Princeton University Press, 1996.

Stirling, M. David. *Green Gone Wild: Elevating Nature above Human Rights*. Bellevue, Wash.: Merril Press, 2008.

Degrowth, Sufficiency, and Steady-State Economics

Alexander, Samuel. *Collected Essays*. Vol. 1, *Prosperous Descent: Crisis as Opportunity in an Age of Limits*. Melbourne, Australia: Simplicity Institute, 2015.

———. *Collected Essays*. Vol. 2, *Sufficiency Economy: Enough, for Everyone, Forever*. Melbourne, Australia: Simplicity Institute, 2015.

D'Alisa, Giacomo, Federico Demaria, and Giorgos Kallis, eds. *Degrowth: A Vocabulary for a New Era*. New York: Routledge, 2015.

Daly, Herman. *Beyond Growth: The Economics of Sustainable Development*. Boston, Mass.: Beacon, 1996.

———. *Steady-State Economics: The Economics of Biophysical Equilibrium and Moral Growth*. San Francisco, Calif.: W. H. Freeman, 1977.

Daly, Herman, and John Cobb Jr. *For the Common Good: Redirecting the Economy toward Community, the Environment, and a Sustainable Future*. Boston, Mass.: Beacon Press, 1996.

Dietz, Robert, and Daniel W. O'Neill. *Enough Is Enough: Building a Sustainable Economy in a World of Finite Resources*. San Francisco, Calif.: Berrett-Koehler, 2013.

Heinberg, Richard. *The End of Growth: Adapting to Our New Economic Reality*. Gabriola Island, B.C.: New Society Publishers, 2011.

Jackson, Tim. *Prosperity without Growth: Economics for a Finite Planet*. London: Earthscan, 2009.

Latouche, Serge. *Farewell to Growth*. Cambridge: Polity, 2009.

Princen, Thomas. *The Logic of Sufficiency*. Cambridge, Mass.: MIT Press, 2005.

———. *Treading Softly: Paths to Ecological Order*. Cambridge, Mass.: MIT Press, 2010.

Discount Retailing

Andersen, Michael Moesgaard, and Flemming Poulfelt. *Discount Business Strategy: How the New Market Leaders Are Redefining Business Strategy*. Chichester, England: Wiley, 2006.

Brunn, Stanley D., ed. *Wal-Mart World: The World's Biggest Corporation in the Global Economy*. New York: Routledge, 2006.

Cline, Elizabeth L. *Over-Dressed: The Shockingly High Cost of Cheap Fashion*. New York: Portfolio/Penguin, 2012.

Fishman, Charles. *The Wal-Mart Effect: How the World's Most Powerful Company Really Works—and How It's Transforming the American Economy*. New York: Penguin, 2006.

Laird, Gordon. *The Price of a Bargain*. Toronto, Ont.: McClelland & Stewart, 2009.

Lichtenstein, Nelson. *The Retail Revolution: How Wal-Mart Created a Brave New World of Business*. New York: Henry Holt, 2009.

Mitchell, Stacy. *Big-Box Swindle*. Boston, Mass.: Beacon, 2006.

Shell, Ellen Ruppel. *Cheap: The High Cost of Discount Culture*. New York, Penguin, 2009.

Eco-Consumerism and Eco-Products

Bartley, Tim, Sebastian Koos, Hiram Samel, Gustavo Setrini, and Nik Summers. *Looking Behind the Label: Global Industries and the Conscientious Consumer*. Bloomington: Indiana University Press, 2015.

Boström, Magnus, and Mikael Klintman. *Eco-Standards, Product Labelling and Green Consumerism*. New York: Palgrave Macmillan, 2008.

Conroy, Michael. *Branded! How the Certification Revolution Is Transforming Global Corporations*. Gabriola Island, B.C.: New Society Publishers, 2007.

Divinney, Tim, Pat Auger, and Giana Eckhardt. *The Myth of the Ethical Consumer*. Cambridge: Cambridge University Press, 2010.

Harrison, Rob, Terry Newholm, and Deirdre Shaw. *The Ethical Consumer*. Thousand Oaks, Calif.: Sage, 2005.

Henderson, Hazel. *Ethical Markets: Growing the Green Economy*. White River Junction, Vt.: Chelsea Green, 2006.

Honey, Martha. *Ecotourism and Certification Setting Standards in Practice*. Washington, D.C.: Island Press, 2002.

Micheletti, Michele. *Political Virtue and Shopping: Individuals, Consumerism and Collective Action*. New York: Palgrave Macmillan, 2003.

Stolle, Dietlind, and Michele Micheletti. *Political Consumerism: Global Responsibility in Action*. Cambridge: Cambridge University Press, 2015.

Eco-Efficiency and Ecological Modernization

Bailey, Ronald. *The End of Doom: Environmental Renewal in the Twenty-First Century*. New York: Thomas Dunne Books, 2015.

Curran, Giorel. *Sustainability and Energy Politics: The Promises of Ecological Modernisation and Corporate Social Responsibility*. New York: Palgrave Macmillan, 2015.

DeSimone, Livio, and Frank Popoff, with the World Business Council for Sustainable Development. *Eco-Efficiency: The Business Link to Sustainable Development*. Cambridge, Mass.: MIT Press, 1997.

McDonough, William, and Michael Braungart. *Cradle to Cradle: Remaking the Way We Make Things*. New York: North Point, 2002.

———. *The Upcycle: Beyond Sustainability—Designing for Abundance*. New York: North Point, 2013.

Mol, Arthur P. J. *Globalization and Environmental Reform: The Ecological Modernization of the Global Economy*. Cambridge, Mass.: MIT Press, 2001.

Mol, Arthur P. J., David A. Sonnenfeld, and Gerty Spaargaren, eds. *The Ecological Modernisation Reader: Environmental Reform in Theory and Practice*. New York: Routledge, 2009.

World Business Council for Sustainable Development. *Eco-Efficiency: Creating More Value with Less Impact*. Geneva, Switzerland: World Business Council for Sustainable Development, 2000.

Economic Growth, Population, and Consumption

Bakan, Joel. *Childhood Under Siege: How Big Business Targets Your Children*. New York: Simon & Schuster, 2011.

Cohen, Maurie J., and Joseph Murphy. *Exploring Sustainable Consumption: Environmental Policy and the Social Sciences*. Oxford: Pergamon, 2001.

Crocker, David A., and Toby Linden, eds. *Ethics of Consumption: The Good Life, Justice, and Global Stewardship*. Lanham, Md.: Rowman & Littlefield, 1998.

Dauvergne, Peter. *The Shadows of Consumption: Consequences for the Global Environment*. Cambridge, Mass.: MIT Press, 2008.

Davidson, Eric A. *You Can't Eat GNP: Economics as If Ecology Mattered*. Cambridge, Mass.: Perseus Publishing, 2000.

Ehrlich, Paul R. *The Population Bomb*. New York: Sierra Club-Ballantine, 1968.

Ehrlich, Paul R., and Anne H. Ehrlich. *One with Nineveh: Politics, Consumption, and the Human Future*. Washington, D.C.: Island Press, 2004.

Escobar, Arturo. *Encountering Development: The Making and Unmaking of the Third World*. Princeton, N.J.: Princeton University Press, 1995.

Gerth, Karl. *As China Goes, So Goes the World: How Chinese Consumers are Transforming Everything*. New York: Hill & Wang/Farrar, Straus & Giroux, 2010.

Guha, Ramachandra. *How Much Should a Person Consume? Environmentalism in India and the United States*. Berkeley: University of California Press, 2006.

Hardin, Garrett. *Living within Limits: Ecology, Economics, and Population Taboos*. Oxford: Oxford University Press, 2000.

Jha, Raghbendra, and K. V. Bhanu Murthy. *Environmental Sustainability: A Consumption Approach*. New York: Routledge, 2006.

Kuznets, Simon. "Economic Growth and Income Inequality." *American Economic Review* 45, no. 1 (1955): 1–28.

Lange, Hellmuth, and Lars Meier. *The New Middle Classes: Globalizing Lifestyles, Consumerism, and Environmental Concern*. Dordrecht, Netherlands: Springer, 2009.

Leonard, Annie. *The Story of Stuff: The Impact of Overconsumption on the Planet, Our Communities, and Our Health—And How We Can Make It Better*. New York: Free Press, 2010.

Lewis, Justin. *Beyond Consumer Capitalism: Media and the Limits of Imagination*. Cambridge: Polity, 2013.

Malthus, Thomas Robert. *Essay on the Principle of Population*. London: J. Johnson, 1798. Electronic Scholarly Publishing Project, http://www.esp.org/books/malthus/population/malthus.pdf (accessed 16 November 2008).

Meadows, Donella H. "The Limits to Growth Revisited." In *The Cassandra Conference: Resources and the Human Predicament*, edited by Paul Ehrlich and John P. Holdren, 257–70. College Station: Texas A&M University Press, 1993.

Meadows, Donella H., Dennis L. Meadows, William W. Behrens, and Jørgen Randers. *The Limits to Growth*. New York: The Club of Rome, 1972.

Meadows, Donella H., Dennis L. Meadows, and Jørgen Randers. *Beyond the Limits: Confronting Global Collapse, Envisioning a Sustainable Future*. White River Junction, Vt.: Chelsea Green, 1992.

Micheletti, Michele, Andreas Follesdal, and Dietlind Stolle, eds. *Politics, Products, and Markets: Exploring Political Consumerism Past and Present*. New Brunswick, N.J.: Transaction Publishers, 2004.

Myers, Norman, and Jennifer Kent. *The New Consumers: The Influence of Affluence on the Environment*. Washington, D.C.: Island Press, 2004.

Porritt, Jonathon. *Capitalism as If the World Matters*. London: Earthscan, 2007.

Princen, Thomas, Michael Maniates, and Ken Conca, eds. *Confronting Consumption*. Cambridge, Mass.: MIT Press, 2002.

Rapley, John. *Understanding Development: Theory and Practice in the Third World*. Boulder, Colo.: Lynne Rienner, 2002.

Sachs, Wolfgang. *Planet Dialectics: Explorations in Environment and Development*. London: Zed Books, 1999.

Schor, Juliet. *The Overspent American: Upscaling, Downshifting, and the New Consumer*. New York: Basic Books, 1998.

Schor, Juliet B., and Douglas B. Holt, eds. *The Consumer Society Reader*. New York: New Press, 2000.

Southerton, Dale, Heather Chappells, and Bas Van Vliet, eds. *Sustainable Consumption: The Implications of Changing Infrastructures of Provision*. Cheltenham, England: Edward Elgar, 2004.

Vale, Robert, and Brenda Vale, eds. *Living within a Fair Share Ecological Footprint*. New York: Routledge, 2013.

Vogel, David. *Trading Up: Consumer and Environmental Regulation in a Global Economy*. Cambridge, Mass.: Harvard University Press, 1995.

Wackernagel, Mathis, and William Rees. *Our Ecological Footprint: Reducing Human Impact on the Earth*. Gabriola Island, B.C.: New Society Publishers, 1996.

Wheeler, Kathryn, and Miriam Glucksmann. *Household Recycling and Consumption Work: Social and Moral Economies*. New York: Palgrave Macmillan, 2015.

Woollard, Robert F., and Aleck S. Ostry, eds. *Fatal Consumption: Rethinking Sustainable Development*. Vancouver, B.C.: University of British Columbia Press, 2000.

Ecological Imperialism

Crosby, Alfred W. *Ecological Imperialism: The Biological Expansion of Europe, 900–1900*. New ed. Cambridge: Cambridge University Press, 2004.

Grove, Richard. *Green Imperialism: Colonial Expansion, Tropical Island Edens and the Origins of Environmentalism, 1600–1860*. Cambridge: Cambridge University Press, 1995.

Hornberg, Alf, J. R. McNeill, and Joan Martínez-Alier, eds. *Rethinking Environmental History: World-System History and Global Environmental Change*. Lanham, Md.: AltaMira Press, 2007.

Kirch, Patrick V., and Jean-Louis Rallu, eds. *The Growth and Collapse of Pacific Island Societies: Archaeological and Demographic Perspectives*. Honolulu: University of Hawaii Press, 2007.

Petras, James, and Henry Veltmeyer. *Extractive Imperialism in the Americas: Capitalism's New Frontier*. Boston, Mass.: Brill Academic Publishers, 2015.

———. *Globalization Unmasked: Imperialism in the 21st Century*. London: Zed Books, 2001.

Trigger, Bruce G. *The Children of Aataentsic: A History of the Huron People to 1660*. 1976; Montreal: McGill-Queen's University Press, 1987.

Film and Media

Brereton, Pat. *Hollywood Utopia: Ecology in Contemporary American Cinema*. Bristol, England: Intellect Books, 2005.

Cubitt, Sean. *EcoMedia*. Amsterdam, Netherlands: Rodopi, 2005.

Gustafsson, Tommy, and Pietari Kääpä, eds. *Transnational Ecocinema: Film Culture in an Era of Ecological Transformation*. Bristol, England: Intellect Books, 2013.

Ingram, David. *Green Screen: Environmentalism and Hollywood Cinema*. Exeter, England: University of Exeter Press, 2004.

Ivakhiv, Adrian J. *Ecologies of the Moving Image: Cinema, Affect, Nature.* Waterloo, Ont.: Wilfrid Laurier University Press, 2013.

Lu, Sheldon H., and Jiayan Mi. *Chinese Ecocinema: In the Age of Environmental Challenge.* Hong Kong: Hong Kong University Press, 2010.

Murray, Robin L., and Joseph K. Heumann. *Ecology and Popular Film: Cinema on the Edge.* Albany: State University of New York Press, 2009.

Rust, Stephen, Salma Monani, and Sean Cubitt. *Ecocinema Theory and Practice.* New York: Routledge, 2013.

———, eds. *Ecomedia: Key Issues.* New York: Routledge, 2015.

Taylor, Bron, ed. *Avatar and Nature Spirituality.* Waterloo, Ont.: Wilfrid Laurier University Press, 2013.

Weik von Mossner, Alexa, ed. *Moving Environments: Affect, Emotion, Ecology, and Film.* Waterloo, Ont.: Wilfrid Laurier University Press, 2014.

Willoquet-Maricondi, Paula, ed. *Framing the World: Explorations in Ecocriticism and Film.* Charlottesville: University of Virginia Press, 2010.

Financing and Debt

Ganzi, John, Frances Seymour, and Sandy Buffett, with Navroz Dubash. *Leverage for the Environment: A Guide to the Private Financial Services Industry.* Washington, D.C.: World Resources Institute, 1998.

George, Susan. *The Debt Boomerang.* London: Pluto, 1992.

———. *A Fate Worse than Debt.* London: Penguin, 1988.

Gutner, Tamar L. *Banking on the Environment: Multilateral Development Banks and Their Environmental Performance in Central and Eastern Europe.* Cambridge, Mass.: MIT Press, 2002.

Malbasic, Ivona, and Jozsef Feiler, eds. *Heavy Footprint: The World Bank and Environment in Europe and Central Asia.* Budapest, Hungary: CEE Bankwatch Network, 2000.

McQueen, Mike, and Ed McMahon. *Land Conservation Financing.* Washington, D.C.: Island Press, 2013.

Rich, Bruce. *Mortgaging the Earth: The World Bank, Environmental Impoverishment, and the Crisis of Development.* London: Earthscan, 1994.

Roodman, David Malin. *The Natural Wealth of Nations: Harnessing the Market for the Environment.* New York: Norton, 1998.

Schmidheiny, Stephan, and Federico Zorraquín. *Financing Change: The Financial Community, Eco-efficiency, and Sustainable Development.* Cambridge, Mass.: MIT Press, 1996.

Global Ecological Crisis

Diamond, Jared M. *Collapse: How Societies Choose to Fail or Succeed.* Rev. ed. New York: Penguin, 2011.

———. *Guns, Germs, and Steel: The Fates of Human Societies.* New York: Norton, 1999.

Gore, Al. *An Inconvenient Truth: The Planetary Emergency of Global Warming and What We Can Do about It.* New York: Rodale Books, 2006.

Higgs, Kerryn. *Collision Course: Endless Growth on a Finite Planet.* Cambridge, Mass.: MIT Press, 2014.

McDaniel, Carl N., and John M. Gowdy. *Paradise for Sale: A Parable of Nature.* Berkeley: University of California Press, 2000.

McKibben, Bill. *Eaarth: Making a Life on a Tough New Planet.* New York: Times Books, 2010.

———. *The End of Nature.* New York: Random House, 2006.

Ophuls, Patrick. *Plato's Revenge: Politics in the Age of Ecology.* Cambridge, Mass.: MIT Press, 2011.

Wilson, Edward O. *The Future of Life.* New York: Knopf, 2002.

Wright, Ronald. *A Short History of Progress.* Toronto, Ont.: House of Anansi Press, 2004.

Global Environmental Governance

Adeel, Zafar, ed. *East Asian Experience in Environmental Governance: Response in a Rapidly Developing Region.* Tokyo: United Nations University Press, 2003.

Auld, Graeme. *Constructing Private Governance: The Rise and Evolution of Forest, Coffee, and Fisheries Certification.* New Haven, Conn.: Yale University Press, 2014.

Ayre, Georgina, and Rosalie Callway, eds. *Governance for Sustainable Development: A Foundation for the Future.* London: Earthscan, 2005.

Baber, Walter F., and Robert V. Bartlett. *Consensus and Global Environmental Governance: Deliberative Democracy in Nature's Regime.* Cambridge, Mass.: MIT Press, 2015.

Badenoch, Nathan. *Transboundary Environmental Governance: Principles and Practice in Mainland Southeast Asia.* Washington, D.C.: World Resources Institute, 2002.

Bernstein, Steven, and Louis W. Pauly, eds. *Global Liberalism and Political Order: Toward a New Grand Compromise?* Albany: State University of New York Press, 2007.

Biermann, Frank. *Earth System Governance: World Politics in the Anthropocene.* Cambridge, Mass.: MIT Press, 2014.

Biermann, Frank, and Steffen Bauer, eds. *A World Environmental Organization: Solution or Threat for Effective International Environmental Governance?* Aldershot, England: Ashgate, 2005.

Biermann, Frank, and Philipp Pattberg, eds. *Global Environmental Governance Reconsidered.* Cambridge, Mass.: MIT Press, 2012.

Bruch, Carl, Wole Coker, and Chris VanArsdale. *Breathing Life into Fundamental Principles: Implementing Constitutional Environmental Protections in Africa.* Washington, D.C.: World Resources Institute, 2001.

Chambers, W. Bradnee, and Jessica F. Green, eds. *Reforming International Environmental Governance: From Institutional Limits to Innovative Reforms.* Tokyo: United Nations University Press, 2005.

Chasek, Pamela, ed. *The Global Environment in the Twenty-First Century: Prospects for International Cooperation.* New York: United Nations University Press, 2000.

Conca, Ken. *An Unfinished Foundation: The United Nations and Global Environmental Governance.* Oxford: Oxford University Press, 2015.

Falkner, Robert. *Business Power and Conflict in International Environmental Politics.* New York: Palgrave Macmillan, 2008.

Fuchs, Doris. *Understanding Business Power in Global Governance.* Baden-Baden, Germany: Nomos, 2005.

Galaz, Victor. *Global Environmental Governance, Technology and Politics: The Anthropocene Gap.* Cheltenham, England: Edward Elgar, 2014.

Glasbergen, Peter, Frank Biermann, and Arthur P. J. Mol, eds. *Partnerships, Governance and Sustainable Development.* Cheltenham, England: Edward Elgar, 2007.

Green, Jessica F. *Rethinking Private Authority: Agents and Entrepreneurs in Global Environmental Governance.* Princeton, N.J.: Princeton University Press, 2014.

Haas, Peter M., Robert O. Keohane, and Marc A. Levy, eds. *Institutions for the Earth: Sources of Effective International Environmental Protection.* Cambridge, Mass.: MIT Press, 1993.

Hale, Thomas, David Held, and Kevin Young. *Gridlock: Why Global Cooperation Is Failing Just When We Need It Most.* Cambridge: Polity, 2013.

Hardin, Garrett. "Extensions of 'The Tragedy of the Commons.'" *Science* 280 (1 May 1998): 682–83.

———. "The Tragedy of the Commons." *Science* 162 (1968): 1243–48.

Hempel, Lamont C. *Environmental Governance: The Global Challenge.* Washington, D.C.: Island Press, 1996.

Higgins, Vaughan, and Geoffrey Lawrence, eds. *Agricultural Governance: Globalization and the New Politics of Regulation.* New York: Routledge, 2005.

Jasanoff, Sheila, and Marybeth Long Martello, eds. *Earthly Politics: Local and Global in Environmental Governance*. Cambridge, Mass.: MIT Press, 2004.

Jinnah, Sikina. *Post-Treaty Politics: Secretariat Influence in Global Environmental Governance*. Cambridge, Mass.: MIT Press, 2014.

Jordan, Andrew, Rüdiger K. W. Wurzel, and Anthony R. Zito, eds. *New Instruments of Environmental Governance? National Experiences and Prospects*. London: Frank Cass, 2003.

Kanie, Norichika, and Peter M. Haas, eds. *Emerging Forces in Environmental Governance*. Tokyo: United Nations University Press, 2004.

Krasner, Stephen D. *International Regimes*. Ithaca, N.Y.: Cornell University Press, 1983.

Le Prestre, Philippe G., ed. *Governing Global Biodiversity: The Evolution and Implementation of the Convention on Biological Diversity*. Aldershot, England: Ashgate, 2002.

Lipschutz, Ronnie D. *Global Environmental Politics: Power, Perspectives, and Practice*. Washington, D.C.: CQ Press, 2003.

Lipschutz, Ronnie D., with Judith Mayer. *Global Civil Society and Global Environmental Governance*. Albany: State University of New York Press, 1996.

Oberthür, Sebastian, and Thomas Gehring, eds. *Institutional Interaction in Global Environmental Governance: Synergy and Conflict among International and EU Policies*. Cambridge, Mass.: MIT Press, 2006.

Ostrom, Elinor. *Governing the Commons: The Evolution of Institutions for Collective Action*. Cambridge: Cambridge University Press, 1990.

Park, Jacob, Ken Conca, and Matthias Finger, eds. *The Crisis of Global Environmental Governance: Towards a New Political Economy of Sustainability*. New York: Routledge, 2008.

Soroos, Marvin. "Garrett Hardin and Tragedies of Global Commons." In *Handbook of Global Environmental Politics*, edited by Peter Dauvergne, 35–50. Cheltenham, England: Edward Elgar, 2005.

Spaargaren, Gert, Arthur P. J. Mol, and Frederick H. Buttel, eds. *Governing Environmental Flows: Global Challenges to Social Theory*. Cambridge, Mass.: MIT Press, 2006.

Speth, James Gustave, and Peter Haas. *Global Environmental Governance*. Washington, D.C.: Island Press, 2006.

Steinberg, Paul F. *Who Rules the Earth? How Social Rules Shape Our Planet and Our Lives*. Oxford: Oxford University Press, 2015.

Tilwell, Matthew, and Richard Tarasofsky. *Towards Coherent Environmental and Economic Governance: Legal and Practical Approaches to MEA-WTO Linkages*. Gland, Switzerland: WWF, 2001.

Vogler, John. *The Global Commons: Environmental and Technological Governance*. 2nd ed. Chichester, England: Wiley, 2000.

Weale, Albert, et al. *Environmental Governance in Europe: An Ever Closer Ecological Union?* Oxford: Oxford University Press, 2000.

Whiteside, Kerry H. *Precautionary Politics: Principle and Practice in Confronting Environmental Risk.* Cambridge, Mass.: MIT Press, 2006.

Young, Oran R., ed. *Global Governance: Drawing Insights from the Environmental Experience.* Cambridge, Mass.: MIT Press, 1997.

———. *Institutional Dynamics: Emergent Patterns in International Environmental Governance.* Cambridge, Mass.: MIT Press, 2010.

———. *International Governance: Protecting the Environment in a Stateless Society.* Ithaca, N.Y.: Cornell University Press, 1994.

Global Environmental Politics

Axelrod, Regina S., and Stacy D. VanDeveer, eds. *The Global Environment: Institutions, Law, and Policy.* 3rd ed. Washington, D.C.: CQ Press, 2014.

Chasek, Pamela S., David L. Downie, and Janet Welsh Brown. *Global Environmental Politics.* 6th ed. Boulder, Colo.: Westview, 2013.

Clapp, Jennifer, and Peter Dauvergne. *Paths to a Green World: The Political Economy of the Global Environment.* 2nd ed. Cambridge, Mass.: MIT Press, 2011.

Conca, Ken, and Geoffrey D. Dabelko, eds. *Green Planet Blues: Critical Perspectives on Global Environmental Politics.* 5th ed. Boulder, Colo.: Westview, 2014.

Death, Carl, ed. *Critical Environmental Politics.* New York: Routledge, 2013.

DeSombre, Elizabeth R. *The Global Environment and World Politics.* 2nd ed. London: Continuum, 2007.

Falkner, Robert. *The Handbook of Global Climate and Environment Policy.* New York: Wiley-Blackwell, 2013.

Harris, Paul G. *Routledge Handbook of Global Environmental Politics.* New York: Routledge, 2013.

Kütting, Gabriela, ed. *Global Environmental Politics: Concepts, Theories and Case Studies.* New York: Routledge, 2010.

Mitchell, Ronald B. *International Politics and the Environment.* Thousand Oaks, Calif.: Sage, 2009.

Nicholson, Simon, and Paul Wapner, eds. *Global Environmental Politics: From Person to Planet.* New York: Routledge, 2014.

Nicholson, Simon, and Sikina, Jinnah, eds. *New Earth Politics.* Cambridge, Mass.: MIT Press, 2016.

O'Neill, Kate. *The Environment and International Relations.* 2nd ed. Cambridge: Cambridge University Press, 2017.

Globalization

Carrier, James G., ed. *Confronting Environments: Local Understanding in a Globalizing World*. Walnut Creek, Calif.: AltaMira Press, 2003.

French, Hilary. *Vanishing Borders: Protecting the Planet in the Age of Globalization*. New York: Norton, 2000.

Hirst, Paul, and Grahame Thompson. *Globalization in Question*. 3rd ed. Cambridge: Polity, 1999.

Jorgenson, Andrew, and Edward Kick, eds. *Globalization and the Environment*. Boston, Mass.: Brill, 2006.

Kütting, Gabriela. *Globalization and the Environment: Greening Global Political Economy*. Albany: State University of New York Press, 2004.

Leichenko, Robin M., and Karen L. O'Brien. *Environmental Change and Globalization: Double Exposures*. New York: Oxford University Press, 2008.

Mander, Jerry, and Victoria Tauli-Corpuz, eds. *Paradigm Wars: Indigenous Peoples' Resistance to Globalization*. New expanded ed. San Francisco, Calif.: Sierra Club Books, 2006.

McKibbin, Bill. *Deep Economy: The Wealth of Communities and the Durable Future*. New York: Times Books, 2007.

Newell, Peter. *Globalization and the Environment: Capitalism, Ecology and Power*. Cambridge: Polity, 2012.

Paavola, Jouni, and Ian Lowe, eds. *Environmental Values in a Globalising World: Nature, Justice and Governance*. New York: Routledge, 2005.

Ritzer, George, and Paul Dean. *Globalization: A Basic Text*. Chichester, England: Wiley, 2015.

Speth, James Gustave, ed. *Worlds Apart: Globalization and the Environment*. Washington, D.C.: Island Press, 2003.

Vertovec, Steven, and Darrell A. Posey, eds. *Globalization, Globalism, Environment, and Environmentalism: Consciousness of Connections*. New York: Oxford University Press, 2003.

Histories

Adams, William M. *Against Extinction: The Story of Conservation*. London: Earthscan, 2004.

Beckert, Sven. *Empire of Cotton: A Global History*. New York: Knopf, 2015.

Bocking, Stephen. *Ecologists and Environmental Politics: A History of Contemporary Ecology*. New Haven, Conn.: Yale University Press, 1997.

Brenton, Tony. *The Greening of Machiavelli: The Evolution of International Environmental Politics*. London: Royal Institute of International Affairs, 1994.

Caldwell, Lynton Keith. *International Environmental Policy: From the Twentieth to the Twenty-First Century.* Durham, N.C.: Duke University Press, 1996.

Diamond, Jared M. *Collapse: How Societies Choose to Fail or Succeed.* New York: Viking, 2005.

Guha, Ramachandra. *Environmentalism: A Global History.* New York: Longman, 2000.

Haq, Gary, and Alistair Paul. *Environmentalism since 1945.* New York: Routledge, 2011.

MacDonald, Gordon J. "Environment: Evolution of a Concept." *Journal of Environment & Development* 12, no. 2 (June 2003): 151–76.

Macekura, Stephen J. *Of Limits and Growth: The Rise of Global Sustainable Development in the Twentieth Century.* Cambridge: Cambridge University Press, 2015.

Marsh, George Perkins. *Man and Nature; or, Physical Geography as Modified by Human Action.* New York: Scribner, 1864.

Mauch, Christof, Nathan Stoltzfus, and Douglas R. Weiner, eds. *Shades of Green: Environmental Activism around the Globe.* Lanham, Md.: Rowman & Littlefield, 2006.

McNeill, J. R. *Something New Under the Sun: An Environmental History of the Twentieth-Century World.* New York: Norton, 2001.

McNeill, J. R., and Erin Stewart Mauldin, eds. *A Companion to Global Environmental History.* New York: Wiley-Blackwell, 2015.

Peterson del Mar, David. *Environmentalism.* 2nd ed. New York: Routledge, 2011.

Ponting, Clive. *A Green History of the World: The Environment and the Collapse of Great Civilizations.* 1st American ed. New York: St. Martin's, 1992.

Radkau, Joachim. *The Age of Ecology: A Global History.* Translated by Patrick Camiller. Cambridge: Polity, 2014.

International Organizations

Fox, Jonathan A., and L. David Brown, eds. *The Struggle for Accountability: The World Bank, NGOs, and Grassroots Movements.* Cambridge, Mass.: MIT Press, 1998.

Goldman, Michael. *Imperial Nature: The World Bank and Struggles for Social Justice in the Age of Globalization.* New Haven, Conn.: Yale University Press, 2005.

Kelly, Trish. *The Impact of the WTO: The Environment, Public Health and Sovereignty.* Cheltenham, England: Edward Elgar, 2007.

Le Prestre, Philippe. *The World Bank and the Environmental Challenge.* Selinsgrove, Pa.: Susquehanna University Press, 1989.

Park, Susan. *World Bank Group Interactions with Environmentalists: Changing International Organisation Identities.* Manchester, England: Manchester University Press, 2010.

Rao, P. K. *The World Trade Organization and the Environment.* London: Macmillan, 2000.

Rechkemmer, Andreas, ed. *UNEO: Towards an International Environment Organization: Approaches to a Sustainable Reform of Global Environmental Governance.* Baden-Baden, Germany: Nomos, 2005.

Sampson, Gary P. *The WTO and Sustainable Development.* Tokyo: United Nations University Press, 2005.

Sampson, Gary, and John Whalley, eds. *The WTO, Trade, and the Environment.* Cheltenham, England: Edward Elgar, 2005.

Schmeier, Susanne. *Governing International Watercourses: River Basin Organizations and the Sustainable Governance of Internationally Shared Rivers and Lakes.* New York: Routledge, 2013.

Young, Zoe. *A New Green Order: The World Bank and the Politics of the Global Environment Facility.* London: Pluto Press, 2003.

Justice

Adamson, Joni, Mei Mei Evans, and Rachel Stein, eds. *The Environmental Justice Reader: Politics, Poetics, & Pedagogy.* Tucson, Ariz.: University of Arizona Press, 2002.

Ammons, Elizabeth, and Modhumita Roy, eds. *Sharing the Earth: An International Environmental Justice Reader.* Athens: University of Georgia Press, 2015.

Anand, Ruchi. *International Environmental Justice: A North-South Dimension.* Aldershot, England: Ashgate, 2004.

Anguelovski, Isabelle. *Neighborhood as Refuge: Community Reconstruction, Place Remaking, and Environmental Justice in the City.* Cambridge, Mass.: MIT Press, 2014.

Bauer, Joanne, ed. *Forging Environmentalism: Justice, Livelihood, and Contested Environments.* Armonk, N.Y.: M. E. Sharpe, 2006.

Brechin, Steven, Peter Wilshusen, Crystal Fortwangler, and Patrick West, eds. *Contested Nature: Promoting International Biodiversity with Social Justice in the Twenty-First Century.* Albany: State University of New York Press, 2003.

Bullard, Robert D., ed. *The Quest for Environmental Justice: Human Rights and the Politics of Pollution.* San Francisco, Calif.: Sierra Club Books, 2005.

Carmin, JoAnn, and Julian Agyeman, eds. *Environmental Inequalities beyond Borders: Local Perspectives on Global Injustices*. Cambridge, Mass.: MIT Press, 2011.

Cole, Luke W., and Sheila R. Foster. *From the Ground Up: Environmental Racism and the Rise of the Environmental Justice Movement*. New York: New York University Press, 2001.

Dobson, Andrew. *Justice and the Environment: Conceptions of Environmental Sustainability and Dimensions of Social Justice*. Oxford: Oxford University Press, 1998.

Faber, Daniel, ed. *The Struggle for Ecological Democracy: Environmental Justice Movements in the United States*. New York: Guilford, 1998.

Hampson, Ren Osler, and Judith Reppy, eds. *Earthly Goods: Environmental Change and Social Justice*. Ithaca, N.Y.: Cornell University Press, 1996.

Hofrichter, Richard, ed. *Toxic Struggles: The Theory and Practice of Environmental Justice*. Salt Lake City: University of Utah Press, 2002.

Konisky, David M., ed. *Failed Promises: Evaluating the Federal Government's Response to Environmental Justice*. Cambridge, Mass.: MIT Press, 2015.

Low, Nicholas, and Brendan Gleeson. *Justice, Society and Nature: An Exploration of Political Ecology*. New York: Routledge, 1998.

Malin, Stephanie A. *The Price of Nuclear Power: Uranium Communities and Environmental Justice*. New Brunswick, N.J.: Rutgers University Press, 2015.

Mutz, Kathryn M., Gary C. Bryner, and Douglas S. Kenney. *Justice and Natural Resources: Concepts, Strategies, and Applications*. Washington, D.C.: Island Press, 2001.

Ottinger, Gwen, and Benjamin R. Cohen, eds. *Technoscience and Environmental Justice: Expert Cultures in a Grassroots Movement*. Cambridge, Mass.: MIT Press, 2011.

Pellow, David Naguib. *Garbage Wars: The Struggle for Environmental Justice in Chicago*. Cambridge, Mass.: MIT Press, 2007.

Robertson, Christina, and Jennifer Westerman, eds. *Working on Earth: Class and Environmental Justice*. Reno: University of Nevada Press, 2015.

Sandler, Ronald, and Phaedra C. Pezzullo, eds. *Environmental Justice and Environmentalism: The Social Justice Challenge to the Environmental Movement*. Cambridge, Mass.: MIT Press, 2007.

Schlosberg, David. *Environmental Justice and the New Pluralism: The Challenge of Difference for Environmentalism*. Oxford: Oxford University Press, 2002.

Shiva, Vandana. *Soil Not Oil: Environmental Justice in an Age of Climate Crisis*. Reprint ed. Berkeley, Calif.: North Atlantic Books, 2015.

Stein, Rachel, ed. *New Perspectives on Environmental Justice: Gender, Sexuality, and Activism*. New Brunswick, N.J.: Rutgers University Press, 2004.

Taylor, Dorceta. *Toxic Communities: Environmental Racism, Industrial Pollution, and Residential Mobility*. New York: New York University Press, 2014.

Timmons, Roberts J., and Bradley C. Parks. *A Climate of Injustice: Global Inequality, North-South Politics, and Climate Policy*. Cambridge, Mass.: MIT Press, 2007.

Localization and Simplicity Movements

Dawson, Jonathan. *Ecovillages: New Frontiers for Sustainability*. Foxhole, England: Green Books, 2006.

De Young, Raymond, and Thomas Princen, eds. *The Localization Reader: Adapting to the Downshift*. Cambridge, Mass.: MIT Press, 2012.

Elgin, Duane. *Voluntary Simplicity: Toward a Way of Life That Is Outwardly Simple, Inwardly Rich*. 2nd ed. New York: HarperCollins, 2010.

Grisby, Mary. *Buying Time and Getting By: The Voluntary Simplicity Movement*. Albany: State University of New York Press, 2004.

Hines, Colin. *Localization: A Global Manifesto*. London. Earthscan, 2000.

Kaufman, Frederik A. *Foundations of Environmental Philosophy: A Text with Readings*. Boston, Mass.: McGraw-Hill, 2003.

Litfin, Karen T. *Ecovillages: Lessons for Sustainable Community*. Cambridge: Polity, 2013.

Schumacher, E. F. *Small Is Beautiful: Economics as If People Mattered*. New York: Harper & Row, 1973.

Multinational Corporations

Anderson, Sarah, and John Cavanagh. *Top 200: The Rise of Corporate Global Power*. Washington, D.C.: Institute for Policy Studies, 1999.

Barnet, Richard J., and John Cavanagh. *Global Dreams: Imperial Corporations and the New World Order*. New York: Simon & Schuster, 1994.

Beder, Sharon, *Global Spin: The Corporate Assault on Environmentalism*. Rev. ed. Foxhole, England: Green Books, 2002.

Bruno, Kenny, and Joshua Karliner. *Earthsummit.biz: The Corporate Takeover of Sustainable Development*. Oakland, Calif.: Food First Books, 2002.

Esty, Daniel C., and Andrew S. Winston. *Green to Gold: How Smart Companies Use Environmental Strategy to Innovate, Create Value, and Build Competitive Advantage*. New Haven, Conn.: Yale University Press, 2006.

Garcia-Johnson, Ronie. *Exporting Environmentalism: U.S. Multinational Chemical Corporations in Brazil and Mexico*. Cambridge, Mass.: MIT Press, 2000.

Gedicks, Al. *Resource Rebels: Native Challenges to Mining and Oil Corporations*. Boston, Mass.: South End Press, 2001.

Greer, Jed, and Kenny Bruno. *Greenwash: The Reality behind Corporate Environmentalism*. Penang, Malaysia: Third World Network, 1997.

Hay, Bruce L., Robert N. Stavins, and Richard H. K. Vietor, eds. *Environmental Protection and the Social Responsibility of Firms*. Washington, D.C.: RFF Press, 2005.

Holme, Richard, and Phil Watts. *Corporate Social Responsibility: Making Good Business Sense*. Geneva, Switzerland: World Business Council for Sustainable Development, 2000.

Johnstone, Nick, ed. *Environmental Policy and Corporate Behaviour*. Cheltenham, England: Edward Elgar, 2007.

Kamieniecki, Sheldon. *Corporate America and Environmental Policy: How Often Does Business Get Its Way?* Stanford, Calif.: Stanford University Press, 2006.

Karliner, Joshua. *The Corporate Planet: Ecology and Politics in the Age of Globalization*. San Francisco, Calif.: Sierra Club, 1997.

Korten, David C. *The Post-Corporate World: Life after Capitalism*. San Francisco, Calif.: Berrett-Koehler, 1999.

———. *When Corporations Rule the World*. 3rd ed. San Francisco, Calif.: Berrett-Koehler, 2015.

Leighton, Michelle, Naomi Roht-Arriaza, and Lyuba Zarsky. *Beyond Good Deeds: Case Studies and a New Policy Agenda for Corporate Accountability*. Berkeley, Calif.: Nautilus Institute, 2002.

Levy, David L., and Peter J. Newell, eds. *The Business of Global Environmental Governance*. Cambridge, Mass.: MIT Press, 2005.

Oreskes, Naomi, and Erik M. Conway. *Merchants of Doubt: How a Handful of Scientists Obscured the Truth on Issues from Tobacco Smoke to Global Warming*. London, Bloomsbury, 2010.

Pearson, Charles, ed. *Multinational Corporations, the Environment, and the Third World*. Durham, N.C.: Duke University Press, 1987.

Prakash, Aseem. *Greening the Firm: The Politics of Corporate Environmentalism*. Cambridge: Cambridge University Press, 2000.

Prakash, Aseem, and Matthew Potoski. *The Voluntary Environmentalists: Green Clubs, ISO 14001, and Voluntary Regulations*. Cambridge: Cambridge University Press, 2006.

Rowell, Andrew. *Green Backlash: Global Subversion of the Environment Movement*. New York: Routledge, 1996.

Schmidheiny, Stephan, with Business Council for Sustainable Development. *Changing Course: A Global Business Perspective on Development and the Environment*. Cambridge, Mass.: MIT Press, 1992.

Utting, Peter, and Jennifer Clapp, eds. *Corporate Accountability and Sustainable Development*. Oxford: Oxford University Press, 2008.

Watts, Phil, and Richard Holme. *Corporate Social Responsibility: Meeting Changing Expectations*. Geneva, Switzerland: World Business Council for Sustainable Development, 1999.

Wright, Christopher, and Daniel Nyberg. *Climate Change, Capitalism, and Corporations: Processes of Creative Self-Destruction*. Cambridge: Cambridge University Press, 2015.

Negotiations and Agreements

Agarwal, Anil, Sunita Narain, and Anju Sharma, eds. *Green Politics: Global Environmental Negotiations 1*. New Delhi: Centre for Science and Environment, 1999.

Chasek, Pamela. *Earth Negotiations: Analyzing Thirty Years of Environmental Diplomacy*. Tokyo: United Nations University Press, 2001.

Davenport, Deborah Saunders. *Global Environmental Negotiations and U.S. Interests*. New York: Palgrave Macmillan, 2006.

Downie, Christian. *The Politics of Climate Change Negotiations: Strategies and Variables in Prolonged International Negotiations*. Cheltenham, England: Edward Elgar, 2014.

Hatch, Chris, ed. *Environmental Policymaking: Assessing the Use of Alternative Policy Instruments*. Albany: State University of New York Press, 2005.

Kanie, Norichika, and Steinar Andresen. *Improving Global Environmental Governance: Best Practices for Architecture and Agency*. New York: Routledge, 2015.

Kutney, Gerald. *Carbon Politics and the Failure of the Kyoto Protocol*. New York: Routledge, 2015.

Kütting, Gabriela. *Environment, Society and International Relations: Towards More Effective International Environmental Agreements*. New York: Routledge, 2000.

Miles, Edward L., Arild Underdal, Steinar Andresen, Jørgen Wettestad, Jon Birger Skjærseth, and Elaine M. Carlin. *Environmental Regime Effectiveness: Confronting Theory with Evidence*. Cambridge, Mass.: MIT Press, 2001.

Oberthür, Sebastian, and Hermann E. Ott. *The Kyoto Protocol: International Climate Policy for the 21st Century*. Dordrecht, Netherlands: Springer, 1999.

Pinguelli-Rosa, Luiz, and Mohan Munasinghe, eds. *Ethics, Equity, and International Negotiations on Climate Change*. Cheltenham, England: Edward Elgar, 2002.

Sjöstedt, Gunnar, and Ariel Macaspac Penetrante, eds. *Climate Change Negotiations: A Guide to Resolving Disputes and Facilitating Multilateral Cooperation*. New York: Routledge, 2015.

Stokke, Olav Schram, Jon Hovi, and Geir Ulfstein, eds. *Implementing the Climate Regime: International Compliance*. London: Earthscan, 2005.

Susskind, Lawrence, and Saleem H. Ali. *Environmental Diplomacy: Negotiating More Effective Global Agreements*. 2nd ed. Oxford: Oxford University Press, 2015.

Tolba, Mostafa K., with Iwona Rummel-Bulska. *Global Environmental Diplomacy: Negotiating Environmental Agreements for the World, 1973–1992*. Cambridge, Mass.: MIT Press, 1998.

Victor, David, Kal Raustiala, and Eugene Skolnikoff, eds. *The Implementation and Effectiveness of International Environmental Commitments: Theory and Practice*. Cambridge, Mass.: MIT Press, 1998.

Weiss, Edith Brown, and Harold K. Jacobson, eds. *Engaging Countries: Strengthening Compliance with International Environmental Accords*. Cambridge, Mass.: MIT Press, 1998.

Wettestad, Jörgen. *Designing Effective Environmental Regimes: The Key Conditions*. Cheltenham, England: Edward Elgar, 1999.

Young, Oran R., ed. *The Effectiveness of International Environmental Regimes: Causal Connections and Behavioral Mechanisms*. Cambridge, Mass.: MIT Press, 1999.

———. *Institutional Dynamics: Emergent Patterns in International Environmental Governance*. Cambridge, Mass.: MIT Press, 2010.

———. *International Cooperation: Building Regimes for Natural Resources and the Environment*. Ithaca, N.Y.: Cornell University Press, 1989.

Nongovernmental Organizations and Activism

Betsill, Michele M., and Elisabeth Corell, eds. *NGO Diplomacy: The Influence of Nongovernmental Organizations in International Environmental Negotiations*. Cambridge, Mass.: MIT Press, 2007.

Boli, John, and George M. Thomas. *Constructing World Culture: International Nongovernmental Organizations since 1875*. Stanford, Calif.: Stanford University Press, 1999.

Curran, Giorel. *21st Century Dissent: Anarchism, Anti-Globalization and Environmentalism*. New York: Palgrave Macmillan, 2006.

Dale, Stephen. *McLuhan's Children: The Greenpeace Message and the Media*. Toronto, Ont.: Between the Lines, 1996.

Dauvergne, Peter. *Environmentalism of the Rich*. Cambridge, Mass.: MIT Press, 2016.

Dauvergne, Peter, and Genevieve LeBaron. *Protest Inc.: The Corporatization of Activism*. Cambridge: Polity, 2014.

Doherty, Brian, and Timothy Doyle, *Environmentalism, Resistance and Solidarity: The Politics of Friends of the Earth International*. Basingstoke, England: Palgrave Macmillan, 2013.

Fernandez, Luis A. *Policing Dissent: Social Control and the Anti-Globalization Movement*. New Brunswick, N.J.: Rutgers University Press, 2008.

Fisher, Julie. *Nongovernments: NGOs and the Political Development of the Third World*. West Hartford, Conn.: Kumarian Press, 1997.

Graham, Kevin. *Contemporary Environmentalists*. New York: Facts on File, 1996.

Hironaka, Ann, *Greening the Globe: World Society and Environmental Change*. Cambridge: Cambridge University Press, 2014.

Keck, Margaret E., and Kathryn Sikkink. *Activists beyond Borders: Advocacy Networks in International Politics*. Ithaca, N.Y.: Cornell University Press, 1998.

Mauch, Christof, Nathan Stoltzfus, and Douglas R. Weiner, eds. *Shades of Green: Environmental Activism around the Globe*. Lanham, Md.: Rowman & Littlefield, 2006.

Nelson, Paul J. *The World Bank and Nongovernmental Organizations: The Limits of Apolitical Development*. London: Macmillan, 1995.

Oberthür, Sebastian, Matthias Buck, Sebastian Müller, Stefanie Pfahl, Richard G. Tarasofsky, Jacob Werksman, and Alice Palmer. *Participation of Non-Governmental Organisations in International Environmental Governance*. Berlin: Ecologic Institute, 2002.

Potter, David, ed. *NGOs and Environmental Policies: Asia and Africa*. London: Frank Cass, 1996.

Potter, Will. *Green Is the New Red: An Insider's Account of a Social Movement under Siege*. San Francisco, Calif.: City Lights Books, 2011.

Princen, Thomas, and Matthias Finger, eds. *Environmental NGOs in World Politics: Linking the Local and the Global*. New York: Routledge, 1994.

Richey, Lisa Ann, and Stefano Ponte. *Brand Aid: Shopping Well to Save the World*. Minneapolis: University of Minnesota Press, 2011.

Rudel, Thomas K. *Defensive Environmentalists and the Dynamics of Global Reform*. Cambridge: Cambridge University Press, 2014.

Saunders, Clare. *Environmental Networks and Social Movement Theory*. London: Bloomsbury, 2013.

Starr, Amory, Luis A. Fernandez, and Christian Scholl. *Shutting Down the Streets: Political Violence and Social Control in the Global Era*. New York: New York University Press, 2011.

Taylor, Bron Raymond, ed. *Ecological Resistance Movements: The Global Emergence of Radical and Popular Environmentalism.* Albany: State University of New York Press, 1995.

Taylor, J. Gary, and Patricia J. Scharlin. *Smart Alliance—How a Global Corporation and Environmental Activists Transformed a Tarnished Brand.* New Haven, Conn.: Yale University Press, 2004.

Tesh, Sylvia Noble. *Environmental Activists and Scientific Proof.* Ithaca, N.Y.: Cornell University Press, 2000.

Wall, Derek. *Babylon and Beyond: The Economics of Anti-Capitalist, Anti-Globalist and Radical Green Movements.* London: Pluto Press, 2005.

Wapner, Paul. *Environmental Activism and World Civic Politics.* Albany: State University of New York Press, 1996.

Zelko, Frank. *Make It a Green Peace! The Rise of Counterculture Environmentalism.* Oxford: Oxford University Press, 2013.

Political Economy

Andrews-Speed, Philip, Raimund Bleischwitz, Tim Boersma, Corey Johnson, Geoffrey Kemp, and Stacy D. VanDeveer. *Want, Waste, or War? The Global Resource Nexus and the Struggle for Land, Energy, Food, Water and Minerals.* New York: Routledge, 2015.

Bates, Robert H. *Open-Economy Politics: The Political Economy of the World Coffee Trade.* Princeton, N.J.: Princeton University Press, 1997.

Boyce, James K. *The Political Economy of the Environment.* Cheltenham, England: Edward Elgar, 2002.

Bridge, Gavin, and Philippe Le Billon. *Oil.* Cambridge: Polity, 2012.

Byrne, John, Leigh Glover, and Cecilia Martínez, eds. *Environmental Justice: Discourses in International Political Economy.* New Brunswick, N.J.: Transaction, 2002.

Gonzalez, George A. *Corporate Power and the Environment: The Political Economy of U.S. Environmental Policy.* Lanham, Md.: Rowman & Littlefield, 2001.

Hall, Derek. *Land.* Cambridge: Polity, 2013.

Klein, Naomi. *This Changes Everything: Capitalism vs. the Climate.* New York: Simon & Schuster, 2014.

Speth, James Gustave. *The Bridge at the Edge of the World: Capitalism, the Environment, and Crossing from Crisis to Sustainability.* New Haven, Conn.: Yale University Press, 2008.

Stavins, Robert N., ed. *The Political Economy of Environmental Regulation.* Cheltenham, England: Edward Elgar, 2004.

Stevis, Dimitris, and Valerie Assetto, eds. *The International Political Economy of the Environment: Critical Perspectives*. Boulder, Colo.: Lynne Rienner, 2001.

Talbot, John M. *Grounds for Agreement: The Political Economy of the Coffee Commodity Chain*. Lanham, Md.: Rowman & Littlefield, 2004.

Young, Oran R. *Natural Resources and the State: The Political Economy of Resource Management*. Ithaca, N.Y.: Cornell University Press, 1981.

Poverty

Bass, Stephen, et al., eds. *Reducing Poverty and Sustaining the Environment: The Politics of Local Engagement*. London: Earthscan, 2005.

Dellink, Rob B., and Arjan Ruijs, eds. *Economics of Poverty, Environment and Natural-Resource Use*. Dordrecht, Netherlands: Springer, 2008.

Dulal, Hari Bansha, ed. *Poverty Reduction in a Changing Climate*. Lanham, Md.: Lexington Books, 2015.

Hollander, Jack M. *The Real Environmental Crisis: Why Poverty, Not Affluence, Is the Environment's Number One Enemy*. Berkeley: University of California Press, 2003.

Johnson, Pierre Marc, Karel Mayrand, and Marc Paquin, eds. *Governing Global Desertification: Linking Environmental Degradation, Poverty, and Participation*. Aldershot, England: Ashgate, 2006.

Middleton, Neil, and Phil O'Keefe. *Rio Plus Ten: Politics, Poverty and the Environment*. London: Pluto Press, 2003.

Moellendorf, Darrel. *The Moral Challenge of Dangerous Climate Change: Values, Poverty, and Policy*. Cambridge: Cambridge University Press, 2014.

World Bank. *Poverty and Environment: Understanding Linkages at the Household Level*. Washington, D.C.: World Bank, 2007.

Science and Environmentalism

Bocking, Stephen. *Nature's Experts: Science, Politics, and the Environment*. New Brunswick, N.J.: Rutgers University Press, 2004.

Dessler, Andrew E., and Edward A. Parson. *The Science and Politics of Global Climate Change: A Guide to the Debate*. Cambridge: Cambridge University Press, 2006.

Dimitrov, Radoslav S. *Science and International Environmental Policy: Regimes and Nonregimes in Global Governance*. Lanham, Md.: Rowman & Littlefield, 2006.

Ehrlich, Paul R., and Anne H. Ehrlich. *Betrayal of Science and Reason: How Anti-Environmental Rhetoric Threatens Our Future*. Washington, D.C.: Island Press, 1996.

Harrison, Neil E., and Gary C. Bryner, eds. *Science and Politics in the International Environment*. Lanham, Md.: Rowman & Littlefield, 2004.

Jasanoff, Sheila. *Science and Public Reason*. Reprint ed. New York: Routledge, 2013.

Layzer, Judith A. *The Environmental Case: Translating Values into Policy*. 4th ed. Washington, D.C.: CQ Press, 2015.

Litfin, Karen T. *Ozone Discourse: Science and Politics in Global Environmental Cooperation*. New York: Columbia University Press, 1994.

Rockwood, Larry L., Ronald E. Stewart, and Thomas Dietz. *Foundations of Environmental Sustainability: The Co-Evolution of Science and Policy*. New York: Oxford University Press, 2007.

Young, Christian C. *The Environment and Science: Social Impact and Interaction*. Santa Barbara, Calif.: ABC-CLIO, 2005.

Security

Ali, Saleem H., ed. *Peace Parks: Conservation and Conflict Resolution*. Cambridge, Mass.: MIT Press, 2007.

Barbier, Edward B. *Nature and Wealth: Overcoming Environmental Scarcity and Inequality*. New York: Palgrave Macmillan, 2015.

Barnett, Jon. *The Meaning of Environmental Security: Environmental Politics and Policy in the New Security Era*. New York: Zed Books, 2001.

Brauch, Hans Günter, et al., eds. *Globalization and Environmental Challenges: Reconceptualizing Security in the 21st Century*. Hexagon Series on Human and Environmental Security and Peace 3. Berlin: Springer-Verlag, 2008.

Chalecki, Elizabeth L. *Environmental Security: A Guide to the Issues*. Westport, Conn.: Praeger, 2013.

Conca, Ken, and Geoffrey D. Dabelko, eds. *Environmental Peacemaking*. Washington, D.C.: Woodrow Wilson Center Press, 2003.

Dalby, Simon. *Environmental Security*. Minneapolis: University of Minnesota Press, 2002.

———. *Security and Environmental Change*. Cambridge: Polity, 2013.

Detraz, Nicole. *Environmental Security and Gender*. New York: Routledge, 2014.

Diehl, Paul F., and Nils Petter Gleditsch, eds. *Environmental Conflict*. Boulder, Colo.: Westview, 2001.

Floyd, Rita, and Richard Matthew, eds. *Environmental Security: Approaches and Issues*. New York: Routledge, 2013.

Homer-Dixon, Thomas F. *Environment, Scarcity and Violence*. Princeton, N.J.: Princeton University Press, 1999.

————. *The Ingenuity Gap: Facing the Economic, Environmental, and Other Challenges of an Increasingly Complex and Unpredictable World*. New York: Knopf, 2000.

Hough, Peter. *Environmental Security: An Introduction*. New York: Routledge, 2014.

Jeffery, Roger, and Baskar Vira, eds. *Conflict and Cooperation in Participatory Natural Resource Management*. Basingstoke, England: Palgrave, 2001.

Lal, Rattan, et al. *Food Security and Environmental Quality in the Developing World*. Boca Raton, Fla.: Lewis Publishers/CRC Press, 2003.

Manwaring, Max G., ed. *Environmental Security and Global Stability: Problems and Responses*. Lanham, Md.: Lexington Books, 2002.

McDonald, Bryan L. *Food Security*. Cambridge: Polity, 2010.

Naylor, Rosalind, ed. *The Evolving Sphere of Food Security*. Oxford: Oxford University Press, 2014.

Ophuls, William. *Ecology and the Politics of Scarcity: Prologue to a Political Theory of the Steady State*. San Francisco, Calif.: W. H. Freeman, 1973.

Page, Edward A., and Michael Redclift, eds. *Human Security and the Environment: International Comparisons*. Cheltenham, England: Edward Elgar, 2002.

Peluso, Nancy Lee, and Michael Watts, eds. *Violent Environments*. Ithaca, N.Y.: Cornell University Press, 2001.

Pirages, Dennis, and Ken Cousins, eds. *From Resource Scarcity to Ecological Security: Exploring New Limits to Growth*. Cambridge, Mass.: MIT Press, 2005.

Posluszna, Elzbieta. *Environmental and Animal Rights Extremism, Terrorism, and National Security*. Oxford: Butterworth-Heinemann, 2015.

Rothe, Delf. *Securitizing Global Warming: A Climate of Complexity*. New York: Routledge, 2015.

Sachs, Wolfgang, ed. *Global Ecology: A New Arena of Political Conflict*. London: Zed Books, 1993.

Shiva, Vandana. *The Violence of the Green Revolution*. London: Zed Books, 1992.

Suliman, Mohamed, ed. *Ecology, Politics and Violent Conflict*. London: Zed Books, 1999.

Watson, Iain, and Chandra Lal Pandey, eds. *Environmental Security in the Asia-Pacific*. New York: Palgrave Macmillan, 2015.

Sustainability and Sustainable Development

Agyeman, Julian, Robert Bullart, and Bob Evans, eds. *Just Sustainabilities: Development in an Unequal World*. London: Earthscan, 2003.

Baker, Susan. *Sustainable Development*. 2nd ed. New York: Routledge, 2016.

Bigg, Tom, ed. *Survival for a Small Planet: The Sustainable Development Agenda*. London: Earthscan, 2004.

Bryner, Gary C. *Gaia's Wager: Environmental Movements and the Challenge of Sustainability*. Lanham, Md.: Rowman & Littlefield, 2001.

Caradonna, Jeremy L. *Sustainability: A History*. Oxford: Oxford University Press, 2014.

Dresner, Simon. *The Principles of Sustainability*. 2nd ed. London: Earthscan, 2008.

Edwards, Andrés R. *The Sustainability Revolution: Portrait of a Paradigm Shift*. Gabriola Island, B.C.: New Society Publishers, 2005.

———. *Thriving beyond Sustainability: Pathways to a Resilient Society*. Gabriola Island, B.C.: New Society Publishers, 2010.

Ehrenfield, John R. *Sustainability by Design: A Subversive Strategy for Transforming Our Consumer Culture*. New Haven, Conn.: Yale University Press, 2008.

Fredericks, Sarah E. *Measuring and Evaluating Sustainability: Ethics in Sustainability Indexes*. New York: Routledge, 2015.

Green, Jessica F., and W. Bradnee Chambers, eds. *The Politics of Participation in Sustainable Development Governance*. Tokyo: United Nations University Press, 2006.

Harcourt, Wendy. *Feminist Perspectives on Sustainable Development*. London: Zed Books, 1994.

Harrison, Neil E. *Sustainable Capitalism and the Pursuit of Well-Being*. New York: Routledge, 2014.

Johnston, Josee, Michael Gismondi, and James Goodman, eds. *Nature's Revenge: Reclaiming Sustainability in an Age of Corporate Globalization*. Peterborough, Ont.: Broadview Press, 2006.

Keiner, Marco, ed. *The Future of Sustainability*. Dordrecht, Netherlands: Springer, 2006.

Kelly, Petra. *Fighting for Hope*. Translated by Marianne Howarth. London: Chatto & Windus, 1984.

Leach, Melissa, Ian Scoones, and Andy Stirling. *Dynamic Sustainabilities: Technology, Environment, Social Justice*. London: Earthscan, 2010.

Meadows, Donella H. *Thinking in Systems: A Primer*. Edited by Diana Wright of the Sustainability Institute. White River Junction, Vt.: Chelsea Green, 2008.

Munasinghe, Mohan, and Rob Swart. *Primer on Climate Change and Sustainable Development: Facts, Policy Analysis, and Applications.* Cambridge: Cambridge University Press, 2005.

Nemetz, Peter N. *Business and the Sustainability Challenge: An Integrated Perspective.* New York: Routledge, 2013.

Parr, Adrian. *Hijacking Sustainability.* Cambridge, Mass.: MIT Press, 2012.

Pearce, David, and Jeremy Warford. *World without End: Economics, Environment and Sustainable Development.* New York: Oxford University Press, 1993.

Redclift, Michael, ed. *Sustainability: Critical Concepts in the Social Sciences.* New York: Routledge, 2005.

Robbins, Paul. *Political Ecology.* 2nd ed. New York: Wiley-Blackwell, 2011.

Robertson, Margaret. *Sustainability: Principles and Practice.* New York: Routledge, 2014.

Rogers, Peter P., Kazi F. Jalal, and John A. Boyd. *An Introduction to Sustainable Development.* London: Earthscan, 2007.

Strachan, Janet R., et al. *The Plain Language Guide to the World Summit on Sustainable Development.* London: Earthscan, 2005.

Sukhbir, Sandhu, Stephen McKenzie, and Howard Harris, eds. *Linking Local and Global Sustainability.* Dordrecht, Netherlands: Springer, 2014.

Thiele, Leslie. *Sustainability.* Cambridge: Polity, 2013.

World Commission on Environment and Development. *Our Common Future.* Oxford: Oxford University Press, 1987.

Trade

Anderson, Terry L., and Donald R. Leal. *Free Market Environmentalism for the Next Generation.* New York: Palgrave Macmillan, 2015.

Bhagwati, Jagdish. "The Case for Free Trade." *Scientific American*, November 1993, 42–49.

Burtless, Gary, Robert Z. Lawrence, Robert E. Litan, and Robert J. Shapiro. *Globaphobia: Confronting Fears about Open Trade.* Washington, D.C.: Brookings Institution Press, 1998.

Copeland, Brian R., and M. Scott Taylor. *Trade and the Environment: Theory and Evidence.* Princeton, N.J.: Princeton University Press, 2013.

Daly, Herman E. "The Perils of Free Trade." *Scientific American*, November 1993, 50–57.

De Schutter, Olivier. *Trade in the Service of Sustainable Development: Linking Trade to Labour Rights and Environmental Standards.* Oxford: Hart Publishing, 2015.

Deere, Carolyn L., and Daniel C. Esty, eds. *Greening the Americas: NAF-TA's Lessons for Hemispheric Trade*. Cambridge, Mass.: MIT Press, 2002.

Esty, Daniel C. *Greening the GATT: Trade, Environment, and the Future*. Washington, D.C.: Institute for International Economics, 1994.

Gallagher, Kevin P. *Free Trade and the Environment: Mexico, NAFTA and Beyond*. Stanford, Calif.: Stanford University Press, 2004.

Hogenboom, Barbara. *Mexico and the NAFTA Environment Debate: The Transnational Politics of Economic Integration*. Utrecht, Netherlands: International Books, 1998.

Krueger, Jonathan. *International Trade and the Basel Convention*. London: Earthscan, 1999.

Krut, Riva, and Harris Gleckman. *ISO 14001: A Missed Opportunity for Global Sustainable Industrial Development*. London: Earthscan, 1998.

Low, Patrick. *International Trade and the Environment*. Washington, D.C.: World Bank, 1992.

Minter, Adam. *Junkyard Planet: Travels in the Billion-Dollar Trash Trade*. London: Bloomsbury, 2013.

Mukhopadhyay, Kakali, and Paul J. Thomassin. *Economic and Environmental Impact of Free Trade in East and South East Asia*. Dordrecht, Netherlands: Springer, 2010.

Neumayer, Eric. *Greening Trade and Investment: Environmental Protection without Protectionism*. London: Earthscan, 2001.

Steinberg, Richard, ed. *The Greening of Trade Law: International Trade Organizations and Environmental Issues*. Lanham, Md.: Rowman & Littlefield, 2002.

Thoyer, Sophie, and Benoît Martimort-Asso, eds. *Participation for Sustainability in Trade*. Aldershot, England: Ashgate, 2007.

Tussie, Diana, ed. *The Environment and International Trade Negotiations: Developing Country Stakes*. Basingstoke, England: Macmillan, 2000.

NATIONAL ENVIRONMENTALISM

Comparative Histories and Policies

Adams, W. M. *Green Development: Environment and Sustainability in a Developing World*. 3rd ed. New York: Routledge, 2008.

Araya, Daniel, ed. *Smart Cities as Democratic Ecologies*. New York: Palgrave Macmillan, 2015.

Bryant, Raymond, and Sinéad Bailey. *Third World Political Ecology*. New York: Routledge, 1997.

Burchell, Jon. *The Evolution of Green Politics: Development and Change within European Green Parties.* London: Earthscan, 2002.

Cass, Loren R. *The Failures of American and European Climate Policy: International Norms, Domestic Politics, and Unachievable Commitments.* Albany: State University of New York Press, 2006.

Chatterjee, Pratap, and Matthias Finger. *The Earth Brokers: Power, Politics and World Development.* New York: Routledge, 1994.

Connelly, James, and Graham Smith. *Politics and the Environment: From Theory to Practice.* 2nd ed. New York: Routledge, 2003.

de Bruijn, Theo, and Vicky Norberg-Bohm, eds. *Industrial Transformation: Environmental Policy Innovation in the United States and Europe.* Cambridge, Mass.: MIT Press, 2005.

Desai, Uday. *Environmental Politics and Policy in Industrialized Countries.* Cambridge, Mass.: MIT Press, 2002.

Doyle, Timothy. *Environmental Movements in Minority and Majority Worlds: A Global Perspective.* 2nd ed. New Brunswick, N.J.: Rutgers University Press, 2005.

Dryzek, John, David Downs, Christian Hunold, Hans-Kristian Hernes, and David Schlosberg. *Green States and Social Movements: Environmentalism in the United States, United Kingdom, Germany, and Norway.* New York: Oxford University Press, 2003.

Duit, Andreas, ed. *State and Environment: The Comparative Study of Environmental Governance.* Cambridge, Mass.: MIT Press, 2014.

Elliott, Lorraine. *The Global Politics of the Environment.* 2nd ed. New York: New York University Press, 2004.

Gahrton, Per. *Green Parties, Green Future: From Local Groups to the International Stage.* London: Pluto Press, 2015.

Gillespie, Alexander. *Waste Policy: International Regulation, Comparative and Contextual Perspectives.* Cheltenham, England: Edward Elgar, 2015.

Griffiths, Tom, and Libby Robin, eds. *Ecology and Empire: Environmental History of Settler Societies.* Edinburgh, Scotland: Keele University Press, 1997.

Grundmann, Reiner. *Transnational Environmental Policy: Reconstructing Ozone.* New York: Routledge, 2001.

Hardoy, Jorge E., Diana Mitlin, and David Satterthwaite. *Environmental Problems in Third World Cities.* New York: Routledge, 2011.

Harrington, Winston, Richard D. Morgenstern, and Thomas Sterner, eds. *Choosing Environmental Policy: Comparing Instruments and Outcomes in the United States and Europe.* Washington, D.C.: Resources for the Future, 2004.

McBeath, Jerry, and Jonathan Rosenberg. *Comparative Environmental Politics.* Dordrecht, Netherlands: Springer, 2006.

Miller, Marian A. L. *The Third World in Global Environmental Politics.* Boulder, Colo.: Lynne Rienner, 1995.

Muller-Rommel, Ferdinand, and Thomas Poguntke, eds. *Green Parties in National Governments.* London: Frank Cass, 2002.

Nagel, Stuart S., ed. *Environmental Policy and Developing Nations.* Jefferson, N.C.: McFarland, 2002.

Peritore, N. Patrick. *Third World Environmentalism: Case Studies from the Global South.* Gainesville: University Press of Florida, 1999.

Schreurs, Miranda A. *Environmental Politics in Japan, Germany, and the United States.* Cambridge: Cambridge University Press, 2002.

Slovic, Scott, Swarnalatha Rangarajan, and Vidya Sarveswaran, eds. *Ecocriticism of the Global South.* Lanham, Md.: Lexington Books, 2015.

Steel, Brent, Richard Clinton, and Nicholas Lovrich. *Environmental Politics and Policy: A Comparative Approach.* New York: McGraw-Hill, 2003.

Steinberg, Paul F., and Stacy D. VanDeveer. *Comparative Environmental Politics: Theory, Practice, and Prospects.* Cambridge, Mass.: MIT Press, 2012.

Vig, Norman J., and Michael G. Faur, eds. *Green Giants? Environmental Policies of the United States and the European Union.* Cambridge, Mass.: MIT Press, 2004.

Weidner, Helmut, and Martin Jänicke, eds. *Capacity Building in National Environmental Policy: A Comparative Study of 17 Countries.* Dordrecht, Netherlands: Springer, 2002.

Wurzel, Rüdiger K. W. *Environmental Policy-Making in Britain, Germany and the European Union: The Europeanisation of Air and Water Pollution Control.* Manchester, England: Manchester University Press, 2002.

Africa

Adams, Jonathan S., and Thomas O. McShane. *The Myth of Wild Africa: Conservation without Illusion.* Berkeley: University of California Press, 1996.

Bassett, Thomas J., and Donald Crummey. *African Savannas: Global Narratives and Local Knowledge of Environmental Change.* Oxford: James Currey, 2003.

Broch-Due, Vigdis, and Richard A. Schroeder, eds. *Producing Nature and Poverty in Africa.* Uppsala, Sweden: Nordic Africa Institute, 2000.

Caminero-Santangelo, Byron. *Different Shades of Green: African Literature, Environmental Justice, and Political Ecology.* Charlottesville: University of Virginia Press, 2014.

Clapp, Jennifer. *Adjustment and Agriculture in Africa: Farmers, the State, and the World Bank in Guinea.* New York: St. Martin's, 1997.

Davies, Jonathan. *Conservation and Sustainable Development: Linking Practice and Policy in Eastern Africa.* New York: Routledge, 2012.

Dibie, Robert, ed. *Non-Governmental Organizations and Sustainable Development in Sub-Saharan Africa.* Lanham, Md.: Lexington Books, 2007.

Etemire, Uzuazo. *Law and Practice on Public Participation in Environmental Matters: The Nigerian Example in Transnational Comparative Perspective.* New York: Routledge, 2015.

Fabricius, Christo, and Eddie Koch, with Hector Magome and Steven Turner, eds. *Rights, Resources and Rural Development: Community-Based Natural Resource Management in Southern Africa.* London: Earthscan, 2004.

Hasler, Richard. *Agriculture, Foraging and Wildlife Resource Use in Africa: Cultural and Political Dynamics in the Zambezi Valley.* London: Kegan Paul, 1995.

Hughes, David McDermott. *From Enslavement to Environmentalism: Politics on a Southern African Frontier.* Seattle: University of Washington Press, 2008.

Keeley, James, and Ian Scoones. *Understanding Environmental Policy Processes: Cases from Africa.* London: Earthscan, 2003.

Leach, Melissa, and Robin Mearns. *The Lie of the Land: Challenging Received Wisdom on the African Environment.* Westport, Conn.: Greenwood, 1996.

Low, Pak Sum, ed. *Climate Change and Africa.* Cambridge: Cambridge University Press, 2005.

Maddox, Gregory. *Sub-Saharan Africa: An Environmental History.* Santa Barbara, Calif.: ABC-CLIO, 2006.

Martin, Glen. *Game Changer: Animal Rights and the Fate of Africa's Wildlife.* Berkeley: University of California Press, 2012.

Nelson, Fred, ed. *Community Rights, Conservation and Contested Land: The Politics of Natural Resource Governance in Africa.* New York: Routledge, 2012.

Nest, Michael. *Coltan.* Cambridge: Polity, 2011.

Nustad, Knut G. *Creating Africas: Struggles over Nature, Conservation and Land.* London: Hurst, 2015.

Reid, Robin S. *Savannas of Our Birth: People, Wildlife, and Change in East Africa.* Berkeley: University of California Press, 2012.

Smillie, Ian. *Diamonds.* Cambridge: Polity, 2014.

Antarctica and the Arctic

Bargagli, Roberto. *Antarctic Ecosystems: Environmental Contamination, Climate Change, and Human Impact.* Dordrecht, Netherlands: Springer, 2005.

Cone, Marla. *Silent Snow: The Slow Poisoning of the Arctic.* New York: Grove Press, 2005.

Elliott, Lorraine. *International Environmental Politics: Protecting the Antarctic.* London: Macmillan, 1994.

Gjørv, Gunhild Hoogensen, and Dawn Bazely, eds. *Environmental and Human Security in the Arctic.* New York: Routledge, 2013.

Herber, Bernard P. *Protecting the Antarctic Commons: Problems of Economic Efficiency.* Tucson: Udall Center for Studies in Public Policy, University of Arizona, 2007.

Huettmann, Falk, ed. *Protection of the Three Poles.* Dordrecht, Netherlands: Springer, 2012.

Jensen, Leif Christian, and Geir Hönneland. *Handbook of the Politics of the Arctic.* Cheltenham, England: Edward Elgar, 2015.

Jorgensen, Dolly, and Sverker Sorlin. *Northscapes: History, Technology, and the Making of Northern Environments.* Vancouver, B.C.: University of British Columbia Press, 2014.

Joyner, Christopher C. *Governing the Frozen Commons: The Antarctic Regime and Environmental Protection.* Columbia: University of South Carolina Press, 1998.

McMonagle, Robert J. *Caribou and Conoco: Rethinking Environmental Politics in Alaska's ANWAR and Beyond.* Lanham, Md.: Lexington Books, 2008.

Mikkelsen, Aslaug, and Oluf Langhelle, eds. *Arctic Oil and Gas: Sustainability at Risk?* New York: Routledge, 2008.

Osherenko, Gail, and Oran R. Young. *The Age of the Arctic: Hot Conflicts and Cold Realities.* Cambridge: Cambridge University Press, 2005.

Shadian, Jessica M. *The Politics of Arctic Sovereignty: Oil, Ice, and Inuit Governance.* New York: Routledge, 2015.

Stone, David P. *The Changing Arctic Environment: The Arctic Messenger.* Cambridge: Cambridge University Press, 2015.

Triggs, Gillian, and Anna Riddell, eds. *Antarctica: Legal and Environmental Challenges for the Future.* London: British Institute of International and Comparative Law, 2007.

Wadhams, P., J. A. Dowdeswell, and A. N. Schofield, eds. *The Arctic and Environmental Change.* Amsterdam: Gordon & Breach, 1996.

Wenzel, George. *Animal Rights, Human Rights Ecology, Economy and Ideology in the Canadian Arctic.* London: Belhaven Press, 1991.

Wynn, Graeme. *Canada and Arctic North America: An Environmental History.* Santa Barbara, Calif.: ABC-CLIO, 2007.

Young, Oran R. *Creating Regimes: Arctic Accords and International Governance.* Ithaca, N.Y.: Cornell University Press, 1998.

Young, Oran R., and Gail Osherenko, eds. *Polar Politics: Creating International Environmental Regimes*. Ithaca, N.Y.: Cornell University Press, 1993.

Asia-Pacific

Ako, Rhuks. *Environmental Justice in Developing Countries: Perspectives from Africa and Asia-Pacific*. New York: Routledge, 2013.

Ananta, Aris, Armin Bauer, and Myo Thant, eds. *The Environments of the Poor in Southeast Asia, East Asia and the Pacific*. Singapore: Institute of Southeast Asian Studies, 2013.

Barrett, Brendan F. D., ed. *Ecological Modernization and Japan*. New York: Routledge Curzon, 2005.

Broad, Robin, with John Cavanagh. *Plundering Paradise: The Struggle for the Environment in the Philippines*. Berkeley: University of California Press, 1993.

Broadbent, Jeffrey. *Environmental Politics in Japan: Networks of Power and Protest*. Cambridge: Cambridge University Press, 1998.

Bryant, Raymond L. *The Political Ecology of Forestry in Burma, 1824–1994*. London: Hurst, 1997.

Clifford, Mark L. *The Greening of Asia: The Business Case for Solving Asia's Environmental Emergency*. New York: Columbia University Press, 2015.

Day, Kristen A., ed. *China's Environment and the Challenge of Sustainable Development*. London: M. E. Sharpe, 2005.

Economy, Elizabeth C. *The River Runs Black: The Environmental Challenge to China's Future*. Ithaca, N.Y.: Cornell University Press, 2004.

Fahn, James David. *A Land on Fire: The Environmental Consequences of the Southeast Asian Boom*. Boulder, Colo.: Westview, 2003.

Filho, Walter Leal, ed. *Climate Change in the Asia-Pacific Region*. Dordrecht, Netherlands: Springer, 2015.

Fulda, Andreas, ed. *Civil Society Contributions to Policy Innovation in the PR China: Environment, Social Development and International Cooperation*. New York: Palgrave Macmillan, 2015.

Gallagher, Kelly Sims. *China Shifts Gears: Automakers, Oil, Pollution, and Development*. Cambridge, Mass.: MIT Press, 2006.

Hasegawa, Koichi. *Constructing Civil Society in Japan: Voices of Environmental Movements*. Melbourne, Australia: Trans Pacific, 2004.

Imura, Hidefumi, and Miranda A. Schreurs. *Environmental Policy in Japan*. Washington, D.C.: Edward Elgar and the World Bank, 2005.

Kalland, Arne, and Gerard Persoon, eds. *Environmental Movements in Asia*. Richmond, England: Curzon Press, 1998.

Lamb, David. *Regreening the Bare Hills: Tropical Forest Restoration in the Asia-Pacific Region*. Dordrecht, Netherlands: Springer, 2011.

Lee, Yok-Shiu F., and Alvin Y. So, eds. *Asia's Environmental Movements: Comparative Perspectives*. Armonk, N.Y.: M. E. Sharpe, 1999.

Lye, Lin-Heng, Victor R. Savage, Kua Harn Wei, Chou Loke-Ming, and Tan Puay-Yok, eds. *Sustainability Matters: Environmental and Climate Changes in the Asia-Pacific*. Singapore: World Scientific Publishing, 2015.

Ma, Xioaying. *Environmental Regulation in China: Institutions, Enforcement, and Compliance*. Lanham, Md.: Rowman & Littlefield, 1998.

Manton, Michael, and Linda Anne Stevenson. *Climate in Asia and the Pacific: Security, Society and Sustainability*. Dordrecht, Netherlands: Springer, 2014.

Matsumura, Hiroshi. *Japan and the Kyoto Protocol: Conditions for Ratification*. London: Royal Institute of International Affairs Energy and Environment Programme, 2000.

McKean, Margaret A. *Environmental Protest and Citizen Politics in Japan*. Berkeley: University of California Press, 1981.

Merson, John, and Rosie Cooney. *Conservation in a Crowded World: Case Studies from the Asia-Pacific*. Sydney, Australia: University of New South Wales, 2012.

Mitsuhashi, Tadahiro. *Environment in Japan*. Tokyo: Foreign Press Center, Japan, 2001.

Najam, Adil, ed. *Environment, Development and Human Security: Perspectives from South Asia*. Lanham, Md.: University Press of America, 2003.

O'Rourke, Dara. *Community-Driven Regulation: Balancing Development and the Environment in Vietnam*. Cambridge, Mass.: MIT Press, 2004.

Shapiro, Judith. *China's Environmental Challenges*. 2nd ed. Cambridge: Polity, 2016.

Stolz, Robert. *Bad Water: Nature, Pollution, and Politics in Japan, 1870–1950*. Durham, N.C.: Duke University Press, 2014.

Putra, Nur Azha, and Eulalia Han. *Governments' Responses to Climate Change: Selected Examples from Asia Pacific*. Dordrecht, Netherlands: Springer, 2014.

Europe

Andonova, Liliana B. *Transnational Politics of the Environment: The European Union and Environmental Policy in Central and Eastern Europe*. Cambridge, Mass.: MIT Press, 2004.

Auer, Matthew R. *Restoring Cursed Earth: Appraising Environmental Policy Reforms in Eastern Europe and Russia*. Lanham, Md.: Rowman & Littlefield, 2005.

Barry, John, Brian Baxter, and Richard Dunphy, eds. *Europe, Globalization and Sustainable Development*. New York: Routledge, 2004.

Beatley, Timothy. *Green Urbanism: Learning from European Cities*. Washington, D.C.: Island Press, 2000.

Bomberg, Elizabeth. *Green Parties and Politics in the European Union*. New York: Routledge, 1998.

Burchell, Jon. *The Evolution of Green Politics: Development and Change within European Green Parties*. New York: Routledge, 2014.

Carmin, JoAnn, and Stacy D. VanDeveer, eds. *EU Enlargement and the Environment: Institutional Change and Environmental Policy in Central and Eastern Europe*. New York: Routledge, 2005.

Carter, F. W., and David Turnock. *Environmental Problems of East Central Europe*. New York: Routledge, 2002.

Dawson, Jane I. *Eco-Nationalism: Anti-Nuclear Activism and National Identity in Russia, Lithuania, and Ukraine*. Durham, N.C.: Duke University Press, 1996.

Eder, Klaus, and Maria Kousis, eds. *Environmental Politics in Southern Europe: Actors, Institutions, and Discourses in a Europeanizing Society*. Dordrecht, Netherlands: Kluwer Academic, 2001.

Grant, Wyn, Duncan Matthews, and Peter Newell. *The Effectiveness of European Union Environmental Policy*. London: Macmillan Press, 2000.

Hunter, Janet R., and Zachary A. Smith, eds. *Protecting Our Environment: Lessons from the European Union*. Albany: State University of New York Press, 2005.

Jordan, Andrew, ed. *Environmental Policy in the European Union*. 2nd ed. London: Earthscan, 2005.

Jordan, Andrew, and Duncan Liefferink, eds. *Environmental Policy in Europe: The Europeanization of National Environmental Policy*. New York: Routledge, 2004.

Korppoo, Anna, Jacqueline Karas, and Michael Grubb, eds. *Russia and the Kyoto Protocol: Opportunities and Challenges*. London: Chatham House, 2006.

McCormick, John. *Environmental Policy in the European Union*. Basingstoke, England: Palgrave, 2001.

Moe, Arild, and Kristian Tangen. *The Kyoto Mechanisms and Russian Climate Politics*. London: Royal Institute of International Affairs, 2000.

Oldfield, Jonathan D. *Russian Nature: Exploring the Environmental Consequences of Societal Change*. Burlington, Vt.: Ashgate, 2006.

Pereira, Henrique M., and Laetitia Navarro. *Rewilding European Landscapes*. Dordrecht, Netherlands: Springer, 2015.

Prendiville, Brendan. *Environmental Politics in France.* Boulder, Colo.: Westview, 1994.

Rootes, Christopher, ed. *Environmental Protest in Western Europe.* Oxford: Oxford University Press, 2003.

Rüdiger, K. W. Wurzel, Anthony R. Zito, and Andrew J. Gordon. *Environmental Governance in Europe: A Comparative Analysis of New Environmental Policy Instruments.* Cheltenham, England: Edward Elgar, 2014.

Saska, Petrova. *Communities in Transition: Protected Nature and Local People in Eastern and Central Europe.* Burlington, Vt.: Ashgate, 2014.

Uekötter, Frank. *The Greenest Nation? A New History of German Environmentalism.* Cambridge, Mass.: MIT Press, 2014.

Weibust, Inger, and James Meadowcroft, eds. *Multilevel Environmental Governance: Managing Water and Climate Change in Europe and North America.* Cheltenham, England: Edward Elgar, 2015.

Weiner, Douglas R. *A Little Corner of Freedom: Russian Nature Protection from Stalin to Gorbachev.* Berkeley: University of California Press, 1999.

Wiener, Jonathan B., Michael D. Rogers, James K. Hammitt, and Peter H. Sand, eds. *The Reality of Precaution: Comparing Risk Regulation in the United States and Europe.* New York: Routledge, 2013.

Zito, Anthony. *Creating Environmental Policy in the European Union.* Basingstoke, England: Palgrave, 2000.

Latin America

Blackman, Allen, Rebecca Epanchin-Niell, Juha Siikamäki, and Daniel Velez-Lopez. *Biodiversity Conservation in Latin America and the Caribbean: Prioritizing Policies.* New York: Routledge, 2014.

Campbell, Jeremy. *Conjuring Property: Speculation and Environmental Futures in the Brazilian Amazon.* Seattle: University of Washington Press, 2015.

Carruthers, David V., ed. *Environmental Justice in Latin America: Problems, Promise, and Practice.* Cambridge, Mass.: MIT Press, 2008.

Collinson, Helen, ed. *Green Guerrillas: Environmental Conflicts and Initiatives in Latin America and the Caribbean.* London: Latin America Bureau, 1996.

Edwards, Guy, and J. Timmons Roberts. *A Fragmented Continent: Latin America and the Global Politics of Climate Change.* Cambridge, Mass.: MIT Press, 2015.

García-Guadilla, María-Pilar. *Environmental Movements, Politics, and Agenda 21 in Latin America.* Geneva, Switzerland: United Nations Research Institute for Social Development, 2005.

Hall, Anthony. *Forests and Climate Change: The Social Dimensions of REDD in Latin America*. Cheltenham, England: Edward Elgar, 2012.

Hochstetler, Kathryn, and Margaret E. Keck. *Greening Brazil: Environmental Activism in State and Society*. Durham, N.C.: Duke University Press, 2007.

Jenkins, Rhys, ed. *Industry and the Environment in Latin America*. New York: Routledge, 2000.

Koont, Sinan. *Sustainable Urban Agriculture in Cuba*. Gainesville: University Press of Florida, 2011.

Mathews, Andrew S. *Instituting Nature: Authority, Expertise, and Power in Mexican Forests*. Cambridge, Mass.: MIT Press, 2011.

O'Toole, Gavin. *Environmental Politics in Latin America and the Caribbean: Introduction*. Liverpool: Liverpool University Press, 2014.

Roberts, J. Timmons, and Nikki Demetria Thanos. *Trouble in Paradise: Globalization and Environmental Crises in Latin America*. New York: Routledge, 2003.

Silvius, Kirsten M., Richard E. Bodmer, and Jose M. V. Fragaso, eds. *People in Nature: Wildlife Conservation in South and Central America*. New York: Columbia University Press, 2005.

Sklair, Leslie. *Assembling for Development*. San Diego: University of California, Center for U.S.-Mexican Studies, 1993.

Steinberg, Paul F. *Environmental Leadership in Developing Countries: Transnational Relations and Biodiversity Policy in Costa Rica and Bolivia*. Cambridge, Mass.: MIT Press, 2001.

Striffler, Steve. *In the Shadows of State and Capital: The United Fruit Company, Popular Struggle, and Agrarian Restructuring in Ecuador, 1900–1995*. Durham, N.C.: Duke University Press, 2002.

Striffler, Steve, and Mark Moberg, eds. *Banana Wars: Power, Production, and History in the Americas*. Durham, N.C.: Duke University Press, 2003.

Utting, Peter, ed. *The Greening of Business in Developing Countries*. London: Zed Books, 2002.

West, Sarah Elizabeth. *Environmental Issues in Latin America and the Caribbean*. Dordrecht, Netherlands: Springer, 2005.

Middle East

Adaman, Fikret, and Murat Arsel, eds. *Environmentalism in Turkey: Between Democracy and Development?* Hampshire, England: Ashgate, 2005.

Allan, Tony. *The Middle East Water Question: Hydropolitics and the Global Economy*. London: I. B. Tauris, 2000.

Barnes, Jessica. *Cultivating the Nile: The Everyday Politics of Water in Egypt*. Durham, N.C.: Duke University Press, 2014.

Davis, Diana K., and Edmund Burke III, eds. *Environmental Imaginaries of the Middle East and North Africa*. Athens: Ohio University Press, 2011.

Dolatyar, Mostafa, and Tim S. Gray. *Water Politics in the Middle East*. New York: St. Martin's, 2000.

Foltz, Richard C., ed. *Environmentalism in the Muslim World*. New York: Nova Science Publishers, 2005.

Hillstrom, Kevin, and Laurie Collier Hillstrom. *Africa and the Middle East: A Continental Overview of Environmental Issues*. Santa Barbara, Calif.: ABC-CLIO, 2003.

Jabbra, Joseph G., and Nancy Walstrom Jabbra. *Challenging Environmental Issues: Middle Eastern Perspectives*. Leiden, Netherlands: Brill, 1997.

Orenstein, Daniel E., Alon Tal, and Char Miller. *Between Ruin and Restoration: An Environmental History of Israel*. Pittsburgh: University of Pittsburgh Press, 2013.

Sowers, Jeannie L. *Environmental Politics in Egypt: Activists, Experts, and the State*. New York: Routledge, 2014.

Starr, Joyce, and Daniel Stoll. *The Politics of Scarcity: Water in the Middle East*. Boulder, Colo.: Westview, 1988.

Tal, Alon. *Pollution in a Promised Land: An Environmental History of Israel*. Berkeley: University of California Press, 2002.

North America

Altamirano-Jiménez, Isabel. *Indigenous Encounters with Neoliberalism: Place, Women, and the Environment in Canada and Mexico*. Vancouver, B.C.: University of British Columbia Press, 2013.

Berry, Evan. *Devoted to Nature: The Religious Roots of American Environmentalism*. Berkeley: University of California Press, 2015.

Black, Brian. *Nature and the Environment in Twentieth-Century American Life*. Westport, Conn.: Greenwood, 2006.

Boyd, David R. *Cleaner, Greener, Healthier: A Prescription for Stronger Canadian Environmental Laws and Policies*. Vancouver, B.C.: University of British Columbia Press, 2016.

DeSombre, Elizabeth R. *Domestic Sources of International Environmental Policy: Industry, Environmentalists, and U.S. Power*. Cambridge, Mass.: MIT Press, 2000.

Gottlieb, Robert. *Forcing the Spring: The Transformation of the American Environmental Movement*. Rev. ed. Washington, D.C.: Island Press, 2005.

Harrison, Kathryn. *Passing the Buck: Federalism and Canadian Environmental Policy*. Vancouver, B.C.: University of British Columbia Press, 1996.

Kline, Benjamin. *First Along the River: A Brief History of the U.S. Environmental Movement*. 4th ed. Lanham, Md.: Rowman & Littlefield, 2011.

Leopold, Aldo. *A Sand County Almanac*. New York: Oxford University Press, 1949.

Lifset, Robert D. *Power on the Hudson: Storm King Mountain and the Emergence of Modern American Environmentalism*. Pittsburgh: University of Pittsburgh Press, 2014.

Mart, Michelle. *Pesticides, a Love Story: America's Enduring Embrace of Dangerous Chemicals*. Lawrence: University Press of Kansas, 2015.

McKenzie, Judith. *Environmental Politics in Canada: Managing the Commons into the Twenty-First Century*. Don Mills, Ont.: Oxford University Press, 2002.

O'Connor, Ryan. *The First Green Wave: Pollution Probe and the Origins of Environmental Activism in Ontario*. Vancouver, B.C.: University of British Columbia Press, 2014.

Porter, Joy. *Native American Environmentalism: Land, Spirit, and the Idea of Wilderness*. Reprint ed. Winnipeg, M.B.: Bison Books, 2014.

Robertson, Christina, and Jennifer Westerman, eds. *Working on Earth: Class and Environmental Justice*. Reno: University of Nevada Press, 2015.

Shabecoff, Philip. *A Fierce Green Fire: The American Environmental Movement*. Washington, D.C.: Island Press, 2003.

Speth, James Gustave. *Red Sky at Morning: America and the Crisis of the Global Environment*. New Haven, Conn.: Yale University Press, 2004.

Stoll, Mark. *Inherit the Holy Mountain: Religion and the Rise of American Environmentalism*. Oxford: Oxford University Press, 2015.

Switzer, Jacqueline Vaughn. *Environmental Politics: Domestic and Global Dimensions*. 6th ed. Boston, Mass.: Wadsworth, Cengage Learning, 2011.

Thoreau, Henry David. *Walden*. Edinburgh, Scotland: D. Douglas, 1884.

Vig, Norman J., and Michael E. Kraft, eds. *Environmental Policy: New Directions for the Twenty-First Century*. 9th ed. Washington, D.C.: CQ Press, 2016.

Wapner, Paul. *Living through the End of Nature: The Future of American Environmentalism*. Cambridge, Mass.: MIT Press, 2010.

Winfield, Mark S. *Blue-Green Province: The Environment and the Political Economy of Ontario*. Vancouver, B.C.: University of British Columbia Press, 2012.

Oceania

Barnett, Jon, and John Campbell. *Climate Change and Small Island States: Power, Knowledge and the South Pacific*. New York: Routledge, 2010.

Bennett, Judith A. *Pacific Forest: A History of Resource Control and Contest in Solomon Islands, c. 1800–1997*. Leiden, Netherlands: White Horse Press, 2000.

Byrne, Jason, and Neil Sipe. *Australian Environmental Planning: Challenges and Future Prospects*. New York: Routledge, 2014.

Crowley, Kate, and K. J. Walker. *Environmental Policy Failure: The Australian Story*. Prahran, Victoria, Australia: Tilde University Press, 2011.

de Freitas, Chris R., and Martin Perry. *New Environmentalism: Managing New Zealand's Environmental Diversity*. Dordrecht, Netherlands: Springer, 2012.

Doyle, Tim. *Green Power: The Environment Movement in Australia*. Sydney, Australia: University of New South Wales Press, 2000.

Emberson-Bain, 'Atu, ed. *Sustainable Development or Malignant Growth? Perspectives of Pacific Island Women*. Suva, Fiji: Marama Publications, 1994.

Filer, Colin, ed. *The Political Economy of Forest Management in Papua New Guinea*. London: The International Institute for Environment and Development and the National Research Institute, 1997.

Garnaut, Ross, ed. *Resource Management in Asia Pacific Developing Countries*. Canberra, Australia: Asia Pacific Press, 2002.

Hamilton, Clive. *Running from the Storm: The Development of Climate Change Policy in Australia*. Sydney, Australia: University of New South Wales Press, 2001.

Hutton, Drew, and Libby Connors. *A History of the Australian Environment Movement*. Cambridge: Cambridge University Press, 1999.

Jost, Christian, ed. *The French-Speaking Pacific: Population, Environment, and Development Issues*. Mount Nebo, Australia: Boombana Publications, 1998.

Morgan, Ruth A. *Running Out? Water in Western Australia*. Perth, Australia: UWA Publishing, 2015.

Rainbow, Stephen. *Green Politics*. Auckland, New Zealand: Oxford University Press, 1993.

Walker, Ken, and Kate Crowley, eds. *Australian Environmental Policy: Studies in Decline and Devolution*. Sydney, Australia: Tilde University Press, 1999.

ISSUES

Air Pollution

Biermann, Frank. *Saving the Atmosphere: International Law, Developing Countries and Air Pollution*. Frankfurt am Main, Germany: Peter Lang, 1995.

Calhoun, Yael, ed. *Air Quality*. Philadelphia, Pa.: Chelsea House, 2005.

Chandrappa, Ramesha, and Umesh Chandra Kulshrestha. *Sustainable Air Pollution Management: Theory and Practice*. Dordrecht, Netherlands: Springer, 2015.

Everard, Mark. *Breathing Space: The Natural and Unnatural History of Air*. London: Zed Books, 2015.

Gonzalez, George A. *The Politics of Air Pollution: Urban Growth, Ecological Modernization, and Symbolic Inclusion*. Albany: State University of New York Press, 2005.

Jacobs, Chip, and William J. Kelly. *Smogtown: The Lung-Burning History of Pollution in Los Angeles*. New York: Overlook Press, 2015.

Jacobson, Mark Z. *Air Pollution and Global Warming: History, Science, and Solutions*. 2nd ed. Cambridge: Cambridge University Press, 2012.

Kidd, J. S., and Renee A. Kidd. *Air Pollution: Problems and Solutions*. New York: Chelsea House, 2006.

Leonard, H. Jeffrey. *Pollution and the Struggle for the World Product*. Cambridge: Cambridge University Press, 1988.

Markowitz, Gerald, and David Rosner. *Deceit and Denial: The Deadly Politics of Industrial Pollution*. Berkeley: University of California Press, 2002.

McGranahan, Gordon, and Frank Murray. *Air Pollution and Health in Rapidly Developing Countries*. London: Earthscan, 2003.

Miller, Debra A., ed. *Pollution*. Detroit, Mich.: Greenhaven, 2007.

Nadadur, Srikanth S., and John W. Hollingsworth. *Air Pollution and Health Effects*. Dordrecht, Netherlands: Springer, 2015.

Sliggers, Johan, and Willem Kakebeeke, eds. *Clearing the Air: 25 Years of the Convention on Long-Range Transboundary Air Pollution*. New York: United Nations, 2005.

Sokhi, Ranjeet S., ed. *World Atlas of Atmospheric Pollution*. London: Anthem Press, 2007.

Sternberg, Steven P. K. *Air Pollution: Engineering, Science, and Policy*. Glen Allen, Va.: College Publishing, 2015.

Vallero, Daniel A. *Fundamentals of Air Pollution*. 5th ed. Waltham, Mass.: Academic Press, 2014.

Automobiles

Berger, Michael L. *The Automobile Industry in American History and Culture: A Reference Guide*. Westport, Conn.: Greenwood, 2001.

Boehmer-Christiansen, Sonja, and Helmut Weidnet. *The Politics of Reducing Vehicle Emissions in Britain and Germany*. London: Pinter and Associated University Presses, 1995.

Dunn, James A., Jr. *Driving Forces: The Automobile, Its Enemies, and the Politics of Mobility*. Washington, D.C.: Brookings Institution Press, 1998.

Freund, Peter, and George Martin. *The Ecology of the Automobile*. Montreal, Que.: Black Rose Books, 1993.

McShane, Clay. *Down the Asphalt Path: The Automobile and the American City*. New York: Columbia University Press, 1994.

Newman, Peter, and Jeffrey Kenworthy. *Sustainability and Cities: Overcoming Automobile Dependence*. Washington, D.C.: Island Press, 1999.

Nieuwenhuis, Paul, and Peter Wells. *The Global Automotive Industry*. Chichester, England: Wiley, 2015.

Oge, Margo T. *Driving the Future: Combating Climate Change with Cleaner, Smarter Cars*. New York: Arcade Publishing, 2015.

Paterson, Matthew. *Automobile Politics: Ecology and Cultural Political Economy*. Cambridge: Cambridge University Press, 2007.

Porter, Richard C. *Economics at the Wheel: The Costs of Cars and Drivers*. San Diego, Calif.: Academic Press, 1999.

Rajan, Sudhir Chella. *The Enigma of Automobility: Democratic Politics and Pollution Control*. Pittsburgh: University of Pittsburgh Press, 1996.

Ryan, Lisa, and Hal Turton. *Sustainable Automobile Transport: Shaping Climate Change Policy*. Cheltenham, England: Edward Elgar, 2007.

Sinclair, Stuart. *The World Car: The Future of the Automobile Industry*. London: Euromonitor Publications, 1983.

Wall, Derek. *Earth First! and the Anti-Roads Movement*. New York: Routledge, 1999.

Wells, Christopher. *Car Country: An Environmental History*. Seattle: University of Washington, 2012.

Zachariadis, Theodoros I. *Cars and Carbon: Automobiles and European Climate Policy in a Global Context*. Dordrecht, Netherlands: Springer, 2012.

Biodiversity and Biosafety

Bail, Christoph, Robert Falkner, and Helen Marquard. *The Cartagena Protocol on Biosafety: Reconciling Trade in Biotechnology with Environment and Development*. London: Earthscan, 2002.

Barnosky, Anthony D. *Dodging Extinction: Power, Food, Money, and the Future of Life on Earth*. Berkeley: University of California Press, 2014.

Chester, Charles C. *Conservation across Borders: Biodiversity in an Interdependent World*. Washington, D.C.: Island Press, 2006.

Chivian, Eric, and Aaron Bernstein, eds. *Sustaining Life: How Human Health Depends on Biodiversity*. Oxford: Oxford University Press, 2008.

Cooney, Rosie, and Barney Dickson, eds. *Biodiversity and the Precautionary Principle; Risk and Uncertainty in Conservation and Sustainable Use*. London: Earthscan, 2005.

Deke, Oliver. *Environmental Policy Instruments for Conserving Global Biodiversity*. Dordrecht, Netherlands: Springer, 2008.

Huettmann, Falk, ed. *Central American Biodiversity: Conservation, Ecology, and a Sustainable Future*. Dordrecht, Netherlands: Springer, 2015.

Jeffery, Michael I., Jeremy Firestone, and Karen Bubna-Litic, eds. *Biodiversity Conservation, Law and Livelihoods: Bridging the North-South Divide*. New York: Cambridge University Press, 2008.

Jeffries, Michael J. *Biodiversity and Conservation*. 2nd ed. Oxford: Routledge, 2006.

Kolbert, Elizabeth. *The Sixth Extinction: An Unnatural History*. New York: Henry Holt, 2014.

Lindenmayer, David, and Emma Burns. *Biodiversity and Environmental Change: Monitoring, Challenges and Direction*. Clayton, Australia: CSIRO Publishing, 2014.

Mackenzie, Ruth, et al. *An Explanatory Guide to the Cartagena Protocol on Biosafety*. Gland, Switzerland: World Conservation Union, 2003.

McManis, Charles R., ed. *Biodiversity and the Law: Intellectual Property, Biotechnology and Traditional Knowledge*. London: Earthscan, 2007.

O'Riordan, Tim, and Susanne Stoll-Kleemann. *Biodiversity, Sustainability and Human Communities: Protecting Beyond the Protected*. Cambridge: Cambridge University Press, 2002.

Robinson, Daniel F. *Biodiversity, Access and Benefit-Sharing: Global Case Studies*. New York: Routledge, 2014.

Root, Terry Louise, and Kimberly R. Hall. *Biodiversity in a Changing Climate: Linking Science and Management in Conservation*. Berkeley: University of California Press, 2015.

Shiva, Vandana. *Biopiracy: The Plunder of Nature and Knowledge*. Toronto, Ont.: Between the Lines, 1997.

———. *Monocultures of the Mind: Perspectives on Biodiversity and Biotechnology*. London: Zed Books, 1993.

Vernooy, Ronnie, Pitambar Shrestha, and Bhuwon Sthapit, eds. *Community Seed Banks: Origins, Evolution and Prospects*. New York: Routledge, 2015.

Wilson, Edward O. *The Diversity of Life.* New ed. Cambridge, Mass.: Belknap Press, 2010.

Wood, Alexander, Pamela Stedman-Edwards, and Johanna Mang, eds. *The Root Causes of Biodiversity Loss.* London: Earthscan, 2000.

Climate Change

Adger, W. Neil, Jouni Paavola, Saleemul Huq, and M. J. Mace, eds. *Fairness in Adaptation to Climate Change.* Cambridge, Mass.: MIT Press, 2006.

Brown, Lester R. *Plan B: Rescuing a Planet under Stress and a Civilization in Trouble.* New York: Norton, 2003.

Bulkeley, Harriet, Liliana B. Andonova, Michele M. Betsill, Daniel Compagnon, Thomas Hale, Matthew J. Hoffmann, Peter Newell, Matthew Paterson, Charles Roger, and Stacy D. VanDeveer. *Transnational Climate Change Governance.* Cambridge: Cambridge University Press, 2014.

Ciplet, David, J. Timmons Roberts, and Mizan R. Khan. *Power in a Warming World: The New Global Politics of Climate Change and the Remaking of Environmental Inequality.* Cambridge, Mass.: MIT Press, 2015.

DiMento, Joseph F. C., and Pamela M. Doughman, eds. *Climate Change: What It Means for Us, Our Children, and Our Grandchildren.* Cambridge, Mass.: MIT Press, 2007.

Emanuel, Kerry. *What We Know about Climate Change.* Cambridge, Mass.: MIT Press, 2007.

Fisher, Dana R. *National Governance and the Global Climate Change Regime.* Lanham, Md.: Rowman & Littlefield, 2004.

Flannery, Tim. *The Weather Makers: The History and Future Impact of Climate Change.* Melbourne, Australia: Text Publishing, 2006.

Giddens, Anthony. *The Politics of Climate Change.* 2nd ed. Cambridge: Polity, 2011.

Harris, Paul G. *What's Wrong with Climate Politics and How to Fix It.* Cambridge: Polity, 2013.

Held, David, Charles Roger, and Eva-Maria Nag. *Climate Governance in the Developing World.* Cambridge: Polity, 2013.

Hickmann, Thomas. *Rethinking Authority in Global Climate Governance: How Transnational Climate Initiatives Relate to the International Climate Regime.* New York: Routledge, 2016.

Hoffmann, Matthew J. *Climate Governance at the Crossroads: Experimenting with a Global Response after Kyoto.* Oxford: Oxford University Press, 2011.

———. *Ozone Depletion and Climate Change: Constructing a Global Response.* Albany: State University of New York Press, 2005.

Mendelsohn, Robert, and Ariel Dinar. *Climate Change and Agriculture: An Economic Analysis of Global Impacts, Adaptation, and Distributional Effects*. Cheltenham, England: Edward Elgar, 2008.

Newell, Peter. *Climate for Change: Non-State Actors and the Global Politics of the Greenhouse*. Cambridge: Cambridge University Press, 2000.

Newell, Peter, and Matthew Paterson. *Climate Capitalism: Global Warming and the Transformation of the Global Economy*. Cambridge: Cambridge University Press, 2010.

O'Lear, Shannon, and Simon Dalby, eds. *Reframing Climate Change: Constructing Ecological Geopolitics*. New York: Routledge, 2015.

O'Riordan, Jon, Robert William Sandford, and Deborah Harford. *The Climate Nexus: Water, Food, Energy and Biodiversity*. Victoria, B.C.: Rocky Mountain Books, 2015.

Page, Edward A. *Climate Change, Justice and Future Generations*. Cheltenham, England: Edward Elgar, 2006.

Parr, Adrian. *The Wrath of Capital: Neoliberalism and Climate Change Politics*. New York: Columbia University Press, 2013.

Paterson, Matthew. *Global Warming and Global Politics*. New York: Routledge, 1996.

Princen, Thomas, Jack P. Manno, and Pamela L. Martin, eds. *Ending the Fossil Fuel Era*. Cambridge, Mass.: MIT Press, 2015.

Rowlands, Ian. *The Politics of Global Atmospheric Change*. Manchester, England: Manchester University Press, 1995.

Soroos, Marvin S. *The Endangered Atmosphere*. Columbia: University of South Carolina Press, 1997.

Stern, Nicholas. *The Economics of Climate Change: The Stern Review*. Cambridge: Cambridge University Press, 2007.

———. *Why Are We Waiting? The Logic, Urgency, and Promise of Tackling Climate Change*. Cambridge, Mass.: MIT Press, 2015.

Volk, Tyler. *CO2 Rising: The World's Greatest Environmental Challenge*. Cambridge, Mass.: MIT Press, 2008.

White, Wayne A. *Biosequestration and Ecological Diversity: Mitigating and Adapting to Climate Change and Environmental Degradation*. Boca Raton, Fla.: CRC Press, 2012.

Deserts and Forests

Barber, Charles Victor, and James Schweithelm. *Trial by Fire: Forest Fires and Forestry Policy in Indonesia's Era of Crisis and Reform*. Washington, D.C.: World Resources Institute, 2000.

Behnke, Roy H., and Michael Mortimore, eds. *The End of Desertification? Disputing Environmental Change in the Dry Lands*. Dordrecht, Netherlands: Springer, 2016.

Brezina, Corona. *Disappearing Forests: Deforestation, Desertification, and Drought*. New York: Rosen Publishing, 2014.

Cashore, Benjamin, Graeme Auld, and Deanna Newsom. *Governing through Markets: Forest Certification and the Emergence of Non-state Authority*. New Haven, Conn.: Yale University Press, 2004.

Chabay, Ilan, Martin Frick, and Jennifer Helgeson, eds. *Land Restoration: Reclaiming Landscapes for a Sustainable Future*. London: Academic Press, 2015.

Chomitz, Kenneth M., et al. *At Loggerheads? Agricultural Expansion, Poverty Reduction, and Environment in the Tropical Forests*. Washington, D.C.: World Bank, 2007.

Dauvergne, Peter. *Loggers and Degradation in the Asia-Pacific: Corporations and Environmental Management*. Cambridge: Cambridge University Press, 2001.

———. *Shadows in the Forest: Japan and the Politics of Timber in Southeast Asia*. Cambridge, Mass.: MIT Press, 1997.

Dauvergne, Peter, and Jane Lister. *Timber*. Cambridge: Polity, 2011.

Geist, Helmut. *The Causes and Progression of Desertification*. Aldershot, England: Ashgate, 2005.

Grainger, Alan. *The Threatening Desert: Controlling Desertification*. New York: Routledge, 2015.

Gulbrandsen, Lars H. *Transnational Environmental Governance: The Emergence and Effects of the Certification of Forests and Fisheries*. Cheltenham, England: Edward Elgar, 2010.

Humphreys, David. *Forest Politics: The Evolution of International Cooperation*. London: Earthscan, 1996.

———. *Logjam: Deforestation and the Crisis of Global Governance*. London: Earthscan, 2006.

Kolk, Ans. *Forests in International Environmental Politics: International Organisations, NGOs and the Brazilian Amazon*. Utrecht, Netherlands: International Books, 1996.

Lister, Jane. *Corporate Social Responsibility and the State: International Approaches to Forest Co-Regulation*. Vancouver, B.C.: University of British Columbia Press, 2011.

Moran, Emilio F., and Elinor Ostrom, eds. *Seeing the Forest and the Trees: Human-Environment Interactions in Forest Ecosystems*. Cambridge, Mass.: MIT Press, 2005.

Owusu, J. Henry. *Africa, Tropical Timber, Turfs, and Trade: Geographic Perspectives on Ghana's Timber Industry and Development*. Lanham, Md.: Lexington Books, 2012.

Place, Susan E., ed. *Tropical Rainforests: Latin American Nature and Society in Transition*. Rev. ed. Wilmington, Del.: Scholarly Resources, 2001.

Rozario, Paul. *Spreading Deserts*. Chicago, Ill.: Raintree, 2004.

Rudel, Thomas K. *Tropical Forests: Regional Paths of Destruction and Regeneration in the Late Twentieth Century*. New York: Columbia University Press, 2005.

Spray, Sharon L., and Matthew D. Moran, eds. *Tropical Deforestation*. Lanham, Md.: Rowman & Littlefield, 2006.

Straumann, Lukas. *Money Logging: On the Trail of the Asian Timber Mafia*. Basel, Switzerland: Bergli Books, 2014.

Tuck-Po, Lye, Wil de Jong, and Abe Ken-ichi, eds. *The Political Ecology of the Tropical Forests in Southeast Asia: Historical Perspectives*. Kyoto, Japan: Kyoto University Press, 2003.

Vandermeer, John H., and Ivette Perfecto. *Breakfast of Biodiversity: The Political Ecology of Rain Forest Destruction*. 2nd ed. Oakland, Calif.: Food First Books, 2005.

Endangered Species

Baier, Lowell E. *Inside the Equal Access to Justice Act: Environmental Litigation and the Crippling Battle over America's Lands, Endangered Species, and Critical Habitats*. Lanham, Md.: Rowman & Littlefield, 2015.

Baillie, Jonathan E. M., Craig Hilton-Taylor, and Simon M. Stuart, eds. *IUCN Red List of Threatened Species: A Global Species Assessment*. Gland, Switzerland: IUCN—The World Conservation Union, 2004.

Beatley, Timothy. *Habitat Conservation Planning: Endangered Species and Urban Growth*. Austin, Texas: University of Texas Press, 2014.

Broswimmer, Franz J. *Ecocide: A Short History of Mass Extinction of Species*. London: Pluto Press, 2002.

Dickson, Barnabas, and Jon Hutton, eds. *Endangered Species Threatened Convention: The Past, Present and Future of CITES, the Convention on International Trade in Endangered Species of Wild Fauna and Flora*. New York: Routledge, 2013.

Donald, Paul F., Nigel J. Collar, Stuart J. Marsden, and Deborah J. Pain. *Facing Extinction: The World's Rarest Birds and the Race to Save Them*. 2nd ed. London: T & AD Poyser, 2013.

Donlan, Josh C. *Proactive Strategies for Protecting Species: Pre-Listing Conservation and the Endangered Species Act*. Berkeley: University of California Press, 2015.

Gunter, Michael M., Jr. *Building the Next Ark: How NGOs Work to Protect Biodiversity*. New ed. Lebanon, N.H.: Dartmouth College Press, 2006.

Hutton, Jon, and Barnabas Dickson, eds. *Endangered Species, Threatened Convention: The Past, Present and Future of CITES.* London: Earthscan, 2000.

McGavin, George C. *Endangered: Wildlife on the Brink of Extinction.* Buffalo, N.Y.: Firefly Books, 2006.

Meacham, Cory J. *How the Tiger Lost Its Stripes: An Exploration into the Endangerment of a Species.* New York: Harcourt Brace, 1997.

Mills, J. A. *Blood of the Tiger: A Story of Conspiracy, Greed, and the Battle to Save a Magnificent Species.* Boston, Mass.: Beacon Press, 2015.

Myers, Norman. *The Sinking Ark: A New Look at the Problem of Disappearing Species.* New York: Pergamon Press, 1979.

Pearce, Fred. *The New Wild: Why Invasive Species Will Be Nature's Salvation.* Boston, Mass.: Beacon Press, 2015.

Reeve, Rosalind. *Policing International Trade in Endangered Species: The CITES Treaty and Compliance.* London: Royal Institute of International Affairs, 2002.

Saulitis, Eva. *Into Great Silence: A Memoir of Discovery and Loss among Vanishing Orcas.* Boston, Mass.: Beacon Press, 2014.

Westley, Frances, and Philip S. Miller. *Experiments in Consilience: Integrating Social and Scientific Responses to Save Endangered Species.* 2nd ed. Washington, D.C.: Island Press, 2013.

Wignall, Paul B. *The Worst of Times: How Life on Earth Survived Eighty Million Years of Extinctions.* Princeton, N.J.: Princeton University Press, 2015.

Wijnstekers, Willem. *The Evolution of CITES: A Reference to the Convention on International Trade in Endangered Species of Wild Fauna and Flora.* 7th ed. Geneva, Switzerland: CITES, 2003.

Wilcove, David. *No Way Home: The Decline of the World's Great Animal Migrations.* Washington, D.C.: Island Press, 2007.

Energy

Bradford, Travis. *Solar Revolution: The Economic Transformation of the Global Energy Industry.* Cambridge, Mass.: MIT Press, 2006.

Byrne, John, and Young-Doo Wang, eds. *Green Energy Economies: The Search for Clean and Renewable Energy.* New Brunswick, N.J.: Transaction Publishers, 2014.

Ekins, Paul, and Mike Bradshaw. *Global Energy: Issues, Potentials, and Policy Implications.* Oxford: Oxford University Press, 2015.

Gallagher, Kelly Sims. *The Globalization of Clean Energy Technology: Lessons from China.* Cambridge, Mass.: MIT Press, 2014.

Goldblatt, David L. *Sustainable Energy Consumption and Society: Personal, Technological, or Social Change?* Dordrecht, Netherlands: Springer, 2005.

Gunkel, Darrin, ed. *Alternative Energy Sources*. Detroit, Mich.: Greenhaven, 2006.

Knechtel, John, ed. *Fuel*. Cambridge, Mass.: MIT Press, 2008.

Lewis, Joanna I. *Green Innovation in China: China's Wind Power Industry and the Global Transition to a Low-Carbon Economy*. New York: Columbia University Press, 2013.

Nersesian, Roy L. *Energy for the 21st Century: A Comprehensive Guide to Conventional and Alternative Sources*. Armonk, N.Y.: M. E. Sharpe, 2006.

Rifkin, Jeremy. *The Hydrogen Economy: The Creation of the Worldwide Energy Web and the Redistribution of Power on Earth*. New York: TarcherPutnam, 2002.

Ristinen, Robert A., and Jack J. Kraushaar. *Energy and the Environment*. 2nd ed. Hoboken, N.J.: Wiley, 2006.

Skjærseth, Jon Birger, and Tora Skodvin. *Climate Change and the Oil Industry: Common Problem, Varying Strategies*. Manchester, England: Manchester University Press, 2003.

Smil, Vaclav. *Energy at the Crossroads: Global Perspectives and Uncertainties*. Cambridge, Mass.: MIT Press, 2003.

Spellman, Frank R. *Environmental Impacts of Renewable Energy*. Boca Raton, Fla.: CRC Press, 2014.

Wolfson, Richard. *Energy, Environment, and Climate*. New York: Norton, 2008.

Yang, Ming, and Xin Yu. *Energy Efficiency: Benefits for Environment and Society*. Dordrecht, Netherlands: Springer, 2015.

Food

Ali Brac de la Perriere, Robert, and Franck Seuret. *Brave New Seeds: The Threat of GM Crops to Farmers*. London: Zed Books, 2000.

Andrée, Peter. *Genetically Modified Diplomacy: The Global Politics of Agricultural Biotechnology and the Environment*. Vancouver, B.C.: University of British Columbia Press, 2007.

Barrientos, Stephanie, and Catherine Dolan, eds. *Ethical Sourcing in the Global Food System*. London: Earthscan, 2006.

Blatt, Harvey. *America's Food: What You Don't Know about What You Eat*. Cambridge, Mass.: MIT Press, 2000.

Bourne, Joel K., Jr. *The End of Plenty: The Race to Feed a Crowded World*. New York: Norton, 2015.

Campbell, W. Bruce, and Silvia López-Ortíz, eds. *Sustainable Food Production Includes Human and Environmental Health*. Dordrecht, Netherlands: Springer, 2014.

Chase, Lisa. *Food, Farms, and Community: Exploring Food Systems*. Lebanon, N.H.: University of New Hampshire, 2014.

Clapp, Jennifer. *Food*. 2nd ed. Cambridge: Polity, 2016.

Clapp, Jennifer, and Doris Fuchs, eds. *Corporate Power in Global Agrifood Governance*. Cambridge, Mass.: MIT Press, 2009.

Clark, Lisa F. *The Changing Politics of Organic Food in North America*. Cheltenham, England: Edward Elgar, 2015.

Falkner, Robert, ed. *The International Politics of Genetically Modified Food: Diplomacy, Trade and Law*. New York: Palgrave Macmillan, 2007.

Fridell, Gavin. *Coffee*. Cambridge: Polity, 2014.

Gay, Kathlyn. *Superfood or Superthreat: The Issue of Genetically Engineered Food*. Berkeley Heights, N.J.: Enslow, 2008.

Gordon, Susan, ed. *Critical Perspectives on Genetically Modified Crops and Food*. New York: Rosen Publishing, 2006.

Heller, Chaia. *Food, Farms, and Solidarity: French Farmers Challenge Industrial Agriculture and Genetically Modified Crops*. Durham, N.C.: Duke University Press, 2013.

Martineau, Belinda. *First Fruit: The Creation of the Flavr Savr Tomato and the Birth of Genetically Engineered Food*. New York: McGraw-Hill, 2001.

Oliver, Margaret, Thomas Bishop, and Ben Marchant, eds. *Precision Agriculture for Sustainability and Environmental Protection*. New York: Routledge, 2013.

Oppenlander, Richard. *Food Choice and Sustainability: Why Buying Local, Eating Less Meat, and Taking Baby Steps Won't Work*. Minneapolis, Minn.: Publish Green, 2013.

Pimentel, David, and Marcia H. Pimentel. *Food, Energy, and Society*. 3rd ed. Boca Raton, Fla.: CRC Press, 2008.

Richardson, Ben. *Sugar*. Cambridge: Polity, 2015.

Rose, Nick, ed. *Fair Food: Stories from a Movement Changing the World*. Brisbane, Australia: University of Queensland Press, 2015.

Schlosser, Eric. *Fast Food Nation: The Dark Side of the All-American Meal*. Boston, Mass.: Houghton Mifflin, 2001.

Scholz, Roland W., Amit H. Roy, Fridolin S. Brand, Deborah T. Hellums, and Andrea E. Ulrich, eds. *Sustainable Phosphorus Management: A Global Transdisciplinary Roadmap*. Dordrecht, Netherlands: Springer, 2014.

Shiva, Vandana. *Stolen Harvest: The Hijacking of the Global Food Supply*. Cambridge, Mass.: South End Press, 2000.

Thompson, Paul B. *Food Biotechnology in Ethical Perspective*. 2nd ed. Dordrecht, Netherlands: Springer, 2007.

Thomson, Jennifer A. *Seeds for the Future: The Impact of Genetically Modified Crops on the Environment.* Ithaca, N.Y.: Cornell University Press, 2007.

Weirich, Paul, ed. *Labeling Genetically Modified Food: The Philosophical and Legal Debate.* Oxford: Oxford University Press, 2007.

Zeeuw, Henk de, and Pay Drechsel, eds. *Cities and Agriculture: Developing Resilient Food Systems.* London: Earthscan, 2015.

Hazardous Chemicals and Pesticides

Bahadori, Alireza. *Waste Management in the Chemical and Petroleum Industries.* Chichester, England: Wiley, 2013.

Carlile, W. R. *Pesticide Selectivity, Health and the Environment.* Cambridge: Cambridge University Press, 2006.

Carson, Rachel. *Silent Spring.* Boston, Mass.: Houghton Mifflin, 1962.

Freeze, R. Allan. *The Environmental Pendulum: A Quest for the Truth about Toxic Chemicals, Human Health, and Environmental Protection.* Berkeley: University of California Press, 2000.

Geiser, Ken. *Chemicals without Harm: Policies for a Sustainable World.* Cambridge, Mass.: MIT Press, 2015.

Hough, Peter. *The Global Politics of Pesticides: Forging Consensus from Conflicting Interests.* London: Earthscan, 1998.

Lansdown, Richard, and William Yule. *Lead Toxicity: History and Environmental Impact.* Baltimore, Md.: Johns Hopkins University Press, 1986.

Levine, Marvin J. *Pesticides: A Toxic Time Bomb in Our Midst.* Westport, Conn.: Praeger, 2007.

McCormick, John. *Acid Earth: The Politics of Acid Pollution.* 3rd ed. London: Earthscan, 1997.

Pretty, Jules N. *The Pesticide Detox: Towards a More Sustainable Agriculture.* London: Earthscan, 2005.

Rosenfeld, Paul E., and Lydia Feng. *Risks of Hazardous Wastes.* Oxford: William Andrew, 2011.

Rossol, Monona. *Pick Your Poison: How Our Mad Dash to Chemical Utopia Is Making Lab Rats of Us All.* Chichester, England: Wiley, 2011.

Selin, Henrik. *Global Governance of Hazardous Chemicals: Challenges of Multilevel Management.* Cambridge, Mass.: MIT Press, 2010.

Hazardous Waste Trade

Albers, Jan. *Responsibility and Liability in the Context of Transboundary Movements of Hazardous Wastes by Sea: Existing Rules and the 1999 Liability Protocol to the Basel Convention.* Dordrecht, Netherlands: Springer, 2015.

Clapp, Jennifer. *Toxic Exports: The Transfer of Hazardous Wastes from Rich to Poor Countries.* Ithaca, N.Y.: Cornell University Press, 2001.

Fletcher, Thomas H. *From Love Canal to Environmental Justice: The Politics of Hazardous Waste on the Canada-US Border.* Peterborough, Ont.: Broadview Press, 2003.

Iles, Alastair. *Piling Up E-Wastes in Asia: Impacts and Design Solutions.* Berkeley: University of California Press, 2004.

Jacott, Marisa, Cyrus Reed, and Mark Winfield. *The Generation and Management of Hazardous Wastes and Transboundary Hazardous Waste Shipments between Mexico, Canada and the United States, 1990–2000.* Austin: Texas Center for Policy Studies, 2001.

Kojima, Michikazu, and Estuyo Michida, eds. *International Trade in Recyclable and Hazardous Waste in Asia.* Cheltenham, England: Edward Elgar, 2013.

Kuehr, Ruediger, and Eric Williams, eds. *Computers and the Environment: Understanding and Managing Their Impacts.* Tokyo: United Nations University Press, 2003.

McCarthy, James. *Recycling Computers and Electronic Equipment: Legislative and Regulatory Approaches for E-Wastes.* Washington, D.C.: Library of Congress Congressional Research Service, 2002.

Omohundro, Ellen. *Living in a Contaminated World: Community Structures, Environmental Risks, and Decision Frameworks.* Aldershot, England: Ashgate, 2004.

O'Neill, Kate. *Waste Trading among Rich Nations: Building a New Theory of Environmental Regulation.* Cambridge, Mass.: MIT Press, 2000.

Pellow, David Naguib. *Resisting Global Toxics: Transnational Movements for Environmental Justice.* Cambridge, Mass.: MIT Press, 2007.

Rahm, Dianne. *Toxic Waste and Environmental Policy in the 21st Century United States.* Jefferson, N.C.: McFarland, 2002.

Oceans and Fisheries

Bhattacharya, Hrishikes. *Commercial Exploitation of Fisheries: Production, Marketing and Finance Strategies.* New York: Oxford University Press, 2002.

Caveen, Alex, Nick Polunin, Tim Gray, and Selina Marguerite Stead. *The Controversy over Marine Protected Areas: Science Meets Policy*. Dordrecht, Netherlands: Springer, 2015.

Clover, Charles. *The End of the Line: How Overfishing Is Changing the World and What We Eat*. New York: Random House, 2004.

DeSombre, Elizabeth R. *Flagging Standards: Globalization and Environmental, Safety and Labor Regulations at Sea*. Cambridge, Mass.: MIT Press, 2006.

DeSombre, Elizabeth R., and J. Samuel Barkin. *Fish*. Cambridge: Polity, 2011.

Ebbin, Syma A., Alf Håkon Hoel, and Are K. Sydnes, eds. *A Sea Change: Exclusive Economic Zones and Governance Institutions for Living Marine Resources*. Dordrecht, Netherlands: Springer, 2005.

Ellis, Richard. *The Empty Ocean: Plundering the World's Marine Life*. Washington, D.C.: Island Press, 2003.

Gerdes, Louise I., ed. *Endangered Oceans: Opposing Viewpoints*. San Diego, Calif.: Greenhaven, 2004.

Hall, Stephen J. *The Effects of Fishing on Marine Ecosystems and Communities*. Oxford: Blackwell Science, 2000.

Hannigan, John. *The Geopolitics of Deep Oceans*. Cambridge: Polity, 2015.

Jacques, Peter. *Globalization and the World Ocean*. Lanham, Md.: AltaMira Press, 2006.

Johnson, Magnus L., and Jane Sandell, eds. *Marine Managed Areas and Fisheries*. London: Academic Press, 2014.

Jones, Peter J. S. *Governing Marine Protected Areas: Resilience through Diversity*. New York: Routledge, 2014.

M'Gonigle, Michael R., and Mark W. Zacher. *Pollution, Politics and International Law: Tankers at Sea*. Berkeley: University of California Press, 1979.

Mitchell, Ronald. *Intentional Oil Pollution at Sea: Environmental Policy and Treaty Compliance*. Cambridge, Mass.: MIT Press, 1994.

Roberts, Callum. *The Unnatural History of the Sea*. Washington, D.C.: Island Press, 2007.

Seckinelgin, Hakan. *The Environment and International Politics: International Fisheries, Heidegger and Social Method*. New York: Routledge, 2006.

Skjaerseth, Jon B. *North Sea Cooperation: Linking International and Domestic Pollution Control*. Manchester, England: Manchester University Press, 2001.

VanDeveer, Stacy D., and Geoffrey D. Dabelko, eds. *Protecting Regional Seas: Developing Capacity and Fostering Environmental Cooperation in Europe*. Washington, D.C.: Woodrow Wilson International Center for Scholars, 1999.

Webster, D. G. *Adaptive Governance: The Dynamics of Atlantic Fisheries Management*. Cambridge, Mass.: MIT Press, 2008.
———. *Beyond the Tragedy in Global Fisheries*. Cambridge, Mass.: MIT Press, 2015.

Ozone Depletion

Andersen, Stephen O., and K. Madhava Sarma. *Protecting the Ozone Layer: The United Nations History*. London: Earthscan, 2002.
Benedick, Richard Elliot. *Ozone Diplomacy: New Directions in Safeguarding the Planet*. Enlarged ed. Cambridge, Mass.: Harvard University Press, 1998.
Cagin, Seth, and Philip Dray. *Between Earth and Sky: How CFCs Changed Our World and Endangered the Ozone Layer*. New York: Pantheon Books, 1993.
Fabian, Peter, and Martin Dameris. *Ozone in the Atmosphere: Basic Principles, Natural and Human Impacts*. Dordrecht, Netherlands: Springer, 2014.
Lu, Qing-Bin. *New Theories and Predictions on the Ozone Hole and Climate Change*. Singapore: World Scientific Publishing, 2015.
Molina, Mario J., and F. Sherwood Rowland. "Stratospheric Sink for Chlorofluoromethanes: Chlorine Atom-Catalysed Destruction of Ozone." *Nature* 249 (28 June 1974): 810–12.
Parson, Edward A. *Protecting the Ozone Layer: Science, Strategy, and Negotiation in the Shaping of a Global Environmental Regime*. Oxford: Oxford University Press, 2002.
Sethi, Rajat, and Shubham Manchanda, eds. *Ozone and Ozone Depletion: Sources, Environmental Impact and Health*. New York: Nova Science Publishers, 2013.
Ward, Bud, ed. *Reporting on Climate Change: Understanding the Science*. 3rd ed. Washington, D.C.: Environmental Law Institute, 2003.
Ward, Peter Langdon. *What Really Causes Global Warming: Greenhouse Gases or Ozone Depletion?* New York: Morgan James Publishing, 2015.

Persistent Organic Pollutants

Chandra, Ram, ed. *Environmental Waste Management*. Boca Raton, Fla.: CRC Press, 2015.
Downie, David Leonard, and Terry Fenge, eds. *Northern Lights against POPs: Combatting Toxic Threats in the Arctic*. Montreal, Que.: McGill-Queen's University Press, 2003.

Johansen, Bruce E. *The Dirty Dozen: Toxic Chemicals and the Earth's Future*. Westport, Conn.: Praeger, 2003.

Olsen, Marco A. *Analysis of the Stockholm Convention on Persistent Organic Pollutants*. Dobbs Ferry, N.Y.: Oceana Publications, 2003.

O'Sullivan, Gwen, and Court Sandau, eds. *Environmental Forensics for Persistent Organic Pollutants*. Amsterdam, The Netherlands: Elsevier, 2014.

Rose, Martin, and Alwin Fernandes, eds. *Persistent Organic Pollutants and Toxic Metals in Foods*. Sawston, Cambridge: Woodhead Publishing, 2013.

U.S. Environmental Protection Agency. *Persistent Organic Pollutants: A Global Issue, a Global Response*. Washington, D.C.: U.S. Environmental Protection Agency, 2013.

Urbanization

Anguelovski, Isabelle. *Neighborhood as Refuge: Community Reconstruction, Place Remaking, and Environmental Justice in the City*. Cambridge, Mass.: MIT Press, 2014.

Benton-Short, Lisa, and John Rennie Short. *Cities and Nature*. 2nd ed. New York: Routledge, 2013.

Bouteligier, Sofie. *Cities, Networks, and Global Environmental Governance: Spaces of Innovation, Places of Leadership*. New York: Routledge, 2013.

Brand, Peter, with Michael Thomas. *Urban Environmentalism: Global Change and the Mediation of Local Conflict*. New York: Routledge, 2005.

Bulkeley, Harriet. *Cities and Climate Change*. New York: Routledge, 2013.

Bulkeley, Harriet, and Michele M. Betsill. *Cities and Climate Change: Urban Sustainability and Global Environmental Governance*. New York: Routledge, 2003.

Chapple, Karen. *Planning Sustainable Cities and Regions: Towards More Equitable Development*. New York: Routledge, 2015.

Cockrall-King, Jennifer. *Food and the City: Urban Agriculture and the New Food Revolution*. Amherst, New York: Prometheus Books, 2011.

Doucet, Clive. *Urban Meltdown: Cities, Climate Change and Politics as Usual*. Gabriola Island, B.C.: New Society Publishers, 2007.

Heberle, Lauren C., and Susan M. Opp. *Local Sustainable Urban Development in a Globalized World*. Aldershot, England: Ashgate, 2008.

Jabereen, Yosef. *The Risk City: Cities Countering Climate Change; Emerging Planning Theories and Practices around the World*. Dordrecht, Netherlands: Springer, 2015.

Kahn, Matthew E. *Green Cities: Urban Growth and the Environment*. Washington, D.C.: Brookings Institution Press, 2006.

McLaren, Duncan, and Julian Agyeman. *Sharing Cities: A Case for Truly Smart and Sustainable Cities*. Cambridge, Mass.: MIT Press, 2015.

Portney, Kent E. *Taking Sustainable Cities Seriously: Economic Development, the Environment, and Quality of Life in American Cities.* Cambridge, Mass.: MIT Press, 2013.

Sheehan, Molly O'Meara. *City Limits: Putting the Brakes on Sprawl.* Washington, D.C.: Worldwatch Institute, 2001.

Stone, Brian, Jr. *The City and the Coming Climate: Climate Change in the Places We Live.* Cambridge: Cambridge University Press, 2012.

Water

Barlow, Maude. *Blue Future: Protecting Water for People and the Planet Forever.* Toronto, Ont.: House of Anansi Press, 2014.

Colten, Craig E. *Southern Waters: The Limits to Abundance.* Baton Rouge: Louisiana State University, 2014.

Conca, Ken. *Governing Water: Contentious Transnational Politics and Global Institution Building.* Cambridge, Mass.: MIT Press, 2006.

Dombrowski, Ines. *Conflict, Cooperation, and Institutions in International Water Management.* Cheltenham, England: Edward Elgar, 2007.

Feldman, David Lewis. *Water.* Cambridge: Polity, 2012.

Finger, Matthias, Ludivine Tamiotti, and Jeremy Allouche, eds. *The Multi-Governance of Water: Four Case Studies.* Albany: State University of New York, 2006.

Fishman, Charles. *The Big Thirst: The Secret Life and Turbulent Future of Water.* New York: Free Press, 2011.

Gleick, Peter H., et al. *The World's Water 2006–2007: The Biennial Report on Freshwater Resources.* Washington, D.C.: Island Press, 2006.

Goldsmith, Edward, and Nicholas Hildyard. *The Social and Environmental Effects of Large Dams.* Wadebridge, England: Wadebridge Ecological Centre, 1984.

Khagram. Sanjeev. *Dams and Development: Transnational Struggles for Water and Power.* Ithaca, N.Y.: Cornell University Press, 2004.

Lassiter, Allison, ed. *Sustainable Water: Challenges and Solutions from California.* Berkeley: University of California Press, 2015.

Leb, Christina. *Cooperation in the Law of Transboundary Water Resources.* Cambridge: Cambridge University Press, 2013.

Leslie, Jacques. *Deep Water: The Epic Struggle over Dams, Displaced People, and the Environment.* New York: Farrar, Straus & Giroux, 2005.

McCully, Patrick. *Silenced Rivers: The Ecology and Politics of Large Dams.* Enlarged and updated ed. London: Zed Books, 2001.

Pearce, Fred. *When the Rivers Run Dry: Water—The Defining Crisis of the Twenty-First Century.* Boston, Mass.: Beacon Press, 2006.

Piper, Karen. *The Price of Thirst: Global Water Inequality and the Coming Chaos.* Minneapolis: University of Minnesota Press, 2014.

Reisner, Marc. *Cadillac Desert: The American West and Its Disappearing Water.* New York: Viking Penguin, 1986.

Turton, Anthony, and Roland Henwood, eds. *Hydropolitics in the Developing World: A Southern African Perspective.* Pretoria, South Africa: AWIRU, 2002.

Waterbury, John. *The Nile Basin: National Determinants of Collective Action.* New Haven, Conn.: Yale University Press, 2002.

Whaling

Burns, William C. G., and Alexander Gillespie, eds. *The Future of Cetaceans in a Changing World.* Ardsley, N.Y.: Transnational Publishers, 2003.

de Groot, Laurens. *Hunting the Hunters: At War with the Whalers.* Translated by Laura Vroomen. London: Adlard Coles Nautical, 2014.

Dorsey, Kurkpatrick. *Whales and Nations: Environmental Diplomacy on the High Seas.* Seattle: University of Washington Press, 2013.

Epstein, Charlotte. *The Power of Words in International Relations: Birth of an Anti-Whaling Discourse.* Cambridge, Mass.: MIT Press, 2008.

Estes, James A., et al., eds. *Whales, Whaling, and Ocean Ecosystems.* Berkeley: University of California Press, 2006.

Fitzmaurice, Malgosia. *Whaling and International Law.* Cambridge: Cambridge University Press, 2016.

Friedheim, Robert L., ed. *Towards a Sustainable Whaling Regime?* Seattle: University of Washington Press, 2001.

Heazle, Michael. *Scientific Uncertainty and the Politics of Whaling.* Seattle: University of Washington Press, 2006.

Hoyt, Erich. *Marine Protected Areas for Whales, Dolphins and Porpoises: A World Handbook for Cetacean Habitat Conservation.* London: Earthscan, 2004.

Mulvaney, Kieran. *The Whaling Season: An Inside Account of the Struggle to Stop Commercial Whaling.* Washington, D.C.: Island Press, 2013.

Nolt, John. *Environmental Ethics for the Long Term: An Introduction.* New York: Routledge, 2014.

Starkey, David J., Poul Holm, and Michaela Barnard, eds. *Oceans Past: Management Insights from the History of Marine Animal Populations.* New York: Routledge, 2008.

Stoett, Peter J. *The International Politics of Whaling.* Vancouver, B.C.: University of British Columbia Press, 1997.

Vincent, Sam. *Blood and Guts: Dispatches from the Whale Wars.* Collingwood, Victoria, Australia: Black Inc., 2014.

ENVIRONMENTAL ETHICS AND PHILOSOPHIES

Ethics

Arnold, Denis G. *The Ethics of Global Climate Change.* Cambridge: Cambridge University Press, 2014.

Attfield, Robin. *Environmental Ethics: An Overview for the Twenty-First Century.* 2nd ed. Cambridge: Polity, 2014.

Blanchard, Kathryn D., and Kevin J. O'Brien. *An Introduction to Christian Environmentalism: Ecology, Virtue, and Ethics.* Waco, Tex.: Baylor University Press, 2014.

Boylan, Michael. *Environmental Ethics.* Upper Saddle River, N.J.: Prentice Hall, 2001.

Brereton, Pat. *Environmental Ethics and Film.* New York: Routledge, 2015.

de Vrind, Rob, and Rainer Paslack. *Environmental Ethics: An Introduction and Learning Guide.* Sheffield, England: Greenleaf, 2012.

Des Jardins, Joseph R. *Environmental Ethics: An Introduction to Environmental Philosophy.* 5th ed. Belmont, Calif.: Wadsworth/Thomson Learning, 2012.

Hardin, Garrett. *Exploring New Ethics for Survival: The Voyage of the Spaceship Beagle.* Baltimore, Md.: Pelican, 1972.

———. "Living on a Lifeboat." *Bioscience* 24, no. 10 (1974): 561–68.

Hourdequin, Marion. *Environmental Ethics: From Theory to Practice.* London: Bloomsbury Academic, 2015.

Keller, David R., ed. *Environmental Ethics: The Big Questions.* New York: Wiley-Blackwell, 2010.

Light, Andrew, and Avner De-Shalit, eds. *Moral and Political Reasoning in Environmental Practice.* Cambridge, Mass.: MIT Press, 2003.

Light, Andrew, and Holmes Rolston III, eds. *Environmental Ethics: An Anthology.* Oxford: Blackwell Publishing, 2003.

Maltais, Aaron, and Catriona McKinnon, eds. *The Ethics of Climate Governance.* Lanham, Md.: Rowman & Littlefield, 2015.

Newton, Lisa H. *Ethics and Sustainability: Sustainable Development and the Moral Life.* Upper Saddle River, N.J.: Prentice Hall, 2003.

Pojman, Louis P., ed. *Environmental Ethics: Readings in Theory and Application.* 3rd ed. Belmont, Calif.: Wadsworth/Thomson Learning, 2001.

Schmidtz, David, and Elizabeth Willott, eds. *Environmental Ethics: What Really Matters, What Really Works.* Oxford: Oxford University Press, 2002.

Stenmark, Mikael. *Environmental Ethics and Policy-Making.* Aldershot, England: Ashgate, 2002.

VanDeVeer, Donald, and Christine Pierce, eds. *The Environmental Ethics and Policy Book: Philosophy, Ecology, Economics.* 3rd ed. Belmont, Calif.: Wadsworth/Thomson Learning, 2003.

Wenz, Peter S. *Environmental Ethics Today.* Oxford: Oxford University Press, 2001.

Westra, Laura, and Patricia H. Werhane, eds. *The Business of Consumption: Environmental Ethics and the Global Economy.* Lanham, Md.: Rowman & Littlefield, 1998.

Philosophies

Amster, Randall. *Peace Ecology.* New York: Routledge, 2015.

Baber, Walter F., and Robert V. Bartlett. *Deliberative Environmental Politics: Democracy and Ecological Rationality.* Cambridge, Mass.: MIT Press, 2005.

Beder, Sharon. *Environmental Principles and Policies: An Interdisciplinary Introduction.* London: Earthscan, 2007.

Boyd, David R. *The Optimistic Environmentalist: Progressing Toward a Greener Future.* Toronto, Ont.: ECW Press, 2015.

Callicott, J. Baird, and James McRae, eds. *Environmental Philosophy in Asian Traditions of Thought.* Albany: State University of New York Press, 2014.

Cianchi, John. *Radical Environmentalism: Nature, Identity and More-Than-Human Agency.* New York: Palgrave Macmillan, 2015.

Costanza, Robert, John Cumberland, Herman Daly, Robert Goodland, and Richard Norgaard. *An Introduction to Ecological Economics.* Boca Raton, Fla.: St. Lucie Press, 1997.

Dobson, Andrew. *Green Political Thought.* 4th ed. New York: Routledge, 2007.

Dobson, Andrew, and Derek Bell, eds. *Environmental Citizenship.* Cambridge, Mass.: MIT Press, 2006.

Drenthen, Martin, and Jozef Keulartz, eds. *Old World and New World Perspectives in Environmental Philosophy: Transatlantic Conversations.* Dordrecht, Netherlands: Springer, 2014.

Dryzek, John. *The Politics of the Earth: Environmental Discourses.* 3rd ed. Oxford: Oxford University Press, 2013.

Goldsmith, Edward. *The Way: An Ecological World-View.* London: Rider, 1992.

Guha, Ramachandra, and Joan Martínez-Alier. *Varieties of Environmentalism: Essays North and South.* London: Earthscan, 1997.

Hawken, Paul. *Blessed Unrest: How the Largest Movement in the World Came into Being and Why No One Saw It Coming*. New York: Viking Penguin, 2007.

Hay, Peter R. *Main Currents in Western Environmental Thought*. Bloomington: Indiana University Press, 2002.

James, Simon P. *Environmental Philosophy: An Introduction*. Cambridge: Polity, 2015.

Liddick, Donald R. *Eco-Terrorism: Radical Environmental and Animal Liberation Movements*. Westport, Conn.: Praeger, 2006.

Lovelock, James. *The Ages of Gaia: A Biography of Our Living Earth*. Rev. ed. New York: Norton, 1995.

———. *Gaia: A New Look at Life on Earth*. Oxford: Oxford University Press, 1979.

———. *The Vanishing Face of Gaia: The Final Warning*. New York: Basic Books, 2009.

Martínez-Alier, Joan. *The Environmentalism of the Poor: A Study of Ecological Conflicts and Valuation*. Cheltenham, England: Edward Elgar, 2003.

Merchant, Carolyn. *Radical Ecology: The Search for a Livable World*. 2nd ed. New York: Routledge, 2005.

Mies, Maria, and Vandana Shiva, eds. *Ecofeminism*. London: Zed Books, 1993.

Nixon, Rob. *Slow Violence and the Environmentalism of the Poor*. Cambridge, Mass.: Harvard University Press, 2011.

O'Connor, James. *Natural Causes: Essays in Ecological Marxism*. New York: Guilford, 1998.

Sessions, George. *Deep Ecology for the Twenty-First Century*. Boston, Mass.: Shambhala, 1995.

Sutton, Philip W. *Explaining Environmentalism: In Search of a New Social Movement*. Aldershot, England: Ashgate, 2000.

Thiele, Leslie Paul. *Environmentalism for a New Millennium: The Challenge of Coevolution*. Oxford: Oxford University Press, 1999.

Wilson, Edward O. *The Future of Life*. New York: Knopf, 2002.

Zimmerman, Michael E., et al., eds. *Environmental Philosophy: From Animal Rights to Radical Ecology*. 4th ed. Upper Saddle River, N.J.: Prentice Hall, 2005.

EVENTS AND PEOPLE

Environmental Disasters

Bryan, Nichol. *Danube: Cyanide Spill*. Milwaukee, Wis.: World Almanac Library, 2004.

Caldicott, Helen. *Crisis without End: The Medical and Ecological Consequences of the Fukushima Nuclear Catastrophe*. New York: New Press, 2014.

Eckerman, Ingrid. *The Bhopal Saga: Causes and Consequences of the World's Largest Industrial Disaster*. Hyderabad, India: Universities Press, 2005.

Fortun, Kim. *Advocacy after Bhopal: Environmentalism, Disaster, New Global Orders*. Chicago: University of Chicago Press, 2001.

George, Timothy S. *Minamata: Pollution and the Struggle for Democracy in Postwar Japan*. Cambridge, Mass.: Harvard University Asia Center, 2001.

Gibbs, Lois Marie. *Love Canal: My Story*. As told to Murray Levine. Albany: State University of New York Press, 1982.

Gunn, Angus M. *Unnatural Disasters: Case Studies of Human-Induced Environmental Catastrophes*. Westport, Conn.: Greenwood, 2003.

Juhasz, Antonia. *Black Tide: The Devastating Impact of the Gulf Oil Spill*. Hoboken, N.J.: Wiley, 2011.

Lochbaum, David, and Edwin Lyman. *Fukushima: The Story of a Nuclear Disaster*. New York: New Press, 2014.

Lustgarten, Abrahm. *Run to Failure: BP and the Making of the Deepwater Horizon Disaster*. New York: Norton, 2012.

Mahaffey, James. *Atomic Accidents: A History of Nuclear Meltdowns and Disasters: From the Ozark Mountains to Fukushima*. New York: Pegasus Books, 2015.

Mishima, Akio. *Bitter Sea: The Human Cost of Minamata Disease*. Translated by Richard L. Gage and Susan B. Murata. 1st English ed. Tokyo: Kosei, 1992.

Mould, R. F. *Chernobyl Record: The Definitive History of the Chernobyl Catastrophe*. Bristol, England: Institute of Physics Publishing, 2000.

Niedenthal, Jack. *For the Good of Mankind: A History of the People of Bikini and Their Islands*. 2nd ed. Majuro, Marshall Islands: Bravo Publishers, 2001.

Rees, Joseph V. *Hostages of Each Other: The Transformation of Nuclear Safety since Three Mile Island*. Chicago: Chicago University Press, 1994.

Schweithelm, James. *The Fire This Time: An Overview of Indonesia's Forest Fires in 1997/98*. Jakarta, Indonesia: WWF Indonesia, 1999.

Smith, Jim T., and Nicholas A. Beresford. *Chernobyl: Catastrophe and Consequences*. Dordrecht, Netherlands: Springer, 2005.

Walker, J. Samuel. *Three Mile Island: A Nuclear Crisis in Historical Perspective*. Berkeley: University of California Press, 2004.

Biographies and Autobiographies

Axelrod, Alan, and Charles Phillips. *The Environmentalists: A Biographical Dictionary from the 17th Century to the Present*. New York: Facts on File, 1993.

Berman, Tzeporah. *This Crazy Time: Living Our Environmental Challenge*. Toronto, Ont.: Vintage Canada, 2012.

Brown, Michael, and John May. *The Greenpeace Story*. Scarborough, Ont.: Prentice Hall Canada, 1989.

Davidson, Cliff I., ed. *Clean Hands: Clair Patterson's Crusade against Environmental Lead Contamination*. Commack, N.Y.: Nova Science Publishers, 1999.

Essemlali, Lamya (with Paul Watson). *Captain Paul Watson: Interview with a Pirate*. Buffalo, N.Y.: Firefly Books, 2013.

Faber, Doris, and Harold Faber. *Nature and the Environment*. New York: Scribner, 1991.

Foreman, Dave. *Confessions of an Eco-Warrior*. New York: Three Rivers Press, 1993.

Hill, Julia Butterfly. *The Legacy of Luna: The Story of a Tree, a Woman and the Struggle to Save the Redwoods*. New York: HarperCollins, 2000.

Humes, Edward. *Eco Barons: The New Heroes of Environmental Activism*. New York: Ecco/HarperCollins, 2010.

Hunter, Robert. *The Greenpeace to Amchitka: An Environmental Odyssey*. Vancouver, B.C.: Arsenal Pulp Press, 2004.

———. *Warriors of the Rainbow: A Chronicle of the Greenpeace Movement*. New York: Holt, Rinehart & Winston, 1979.

Lear, Linda. *Rachel Carson: The Life of the Author of "Silent Spring."* New York: Henry Holt, 1997.

Maathai, Wangari Muta. *Unbowed: A Memoir*. New York: Knopf, 2006.

McKibben, Bill. *Oil and Honey: The Education of an Unlikely Activist*. New York: Henry Holt, 2013.

Parkin, Sara. *The Life and Death of Petra Kelly*. New York: HarperCollins, 1995.

Pearce, Fred. *Green Warriors: The People and the Politics behind the Environmental Revolution*. London: Bodley Head, 1991.

Peterson, Dale. *Jane Goodall: The Woman Who Redefined Man*. Boston, Mass.: Houghton Mifflin, 2006.

Revkin, Andrew. *The Burning Season: The Murder of Chico Mendes and the Fight for the Amazon Rain Forest*. Washington, D.C.: Island Press, 2004.

Rosebraugh, Craig. *Burning Rage of a Dying Planet: Speaking for the Earth Liberation Front*. Herndon, Va.: Lantern Books, 2004.

Souder, William. *On a Farther Shore: The Life and Legacy of Rachel Carson, Author of Silent Spring*. New York: Broadway Books, 2012.

Tucker, Linda. *Saving the White Lions: One Woman's Battle for Africa's Most Sacred Animal*. Berkeley, Calif.: North Atlantic Books, 2013.

Watson, Paul. *Seal Wars, Twenty-Five Years on the Front Lines with the Harp Seals*. Buffalo, N.Y.: Firefly Books, 2003.

Weyler, Rex. *Greenpeace: How a Group of Journalists, Ecologists, and Visionaries Changed the World*. Vancouver, B.C.: Raincoast Books, 2004.

INTERNET RESOURCES

Environmental Issues

Air Pollution

Convention on Long-Range Transboundary Air Pollution
www.unece.org/env/lrtap/lrtap_h1.html
Environment Canada: Air
www.ec.gc.ca/Air
National Geographic: Air Pollution
http://environment.nationalgeographic.com/environment/global-warming/
    pollution-overview
Natural Resources Defense Council
www.nrdc.org/air
U.S.-Canada Air Quality Agreement
www.ec.gc.ca/Air/default.asp?lang=En&n=83930AC3-1
U.S. Environmental Protection Agency: Air and Radiation
www.epa.gov/air

Bhopal Disaster

Bhopal Medical Appeal
www.bhopal.org
International Campaign for Justice in Bhopal
www.bhopal.net
Union Carbide Corporation

www.bhopal.com

Biodiversity and Biosafety

Action Group on Erosion, Technology and Concentration (ETC)
www.etcgroup.org
Biodiversity Convention
www.cbd.int
Biotechnology Industry Organization (BIO)
www.bio.org
Cartagena Biosafety Protocol
www.cbd.int/biosafety
Genetic Resources Action International (GRAIN)
www.grain.org
International Service for the Acquisition of Agri-Biotech Applications
www.isaaa.org
Navdanya: Earth Democracy Movement (Vandana Shiva)
www.navdanya.org

Climate Change

David Suzuki Foundation
www.davidsuzuki.org/issues/climate-change/science/climate-change-basics/
 climate-change-101-1
Friends of the Earth Climate Page
www.foe.co.uk/campaigns/climate
Greenpeace International Climate Page
www.greenpeace.org/international/campaigns/climate-change
Kyoto Protocol to the UN Framework Convention on Climate Change
unfccc.int/Kyoto_protocol/items/2830.php
NASA: Climate Change
http://climate.nasa.gov
Union of Concerned Scientists
www.ucsusa.org
United Nations Framework Convention on Climate Change
unfccc.int/2860.php
World Resources Institute
www.wri.org/our-work/topics/climate
WWF Climate Page
http://wwf.panda.org/about_our_earth/aboutcc

Desertification

United Nations Convention to Combat Desertification
www.unccd.int
World Day to Combat Desertification
www.un.org/en/events/desertificationday/background.shtml

Endangered Species

Convention on International Trade in Endangered Species (CITES)
www.cites.org
Convention on the Conservation of Migratory Species of Wild Animals
www.cms.int
World Wide Fund for Nature/World Wildlife Fund (WWF)
www.wwf.org

Forests and Deforestation

Center for International Forestry Research
www.cifor.org
Forest Ethics
www.forestethics.org
Forest Stewardship Council
www.fsc.org
Global Forest Watch
www.globalforestwatch.org
International Tropical Timber Association
www.itto.int
Rainforest Action Network
www.ran.org
World Resources Institute: Forests
www.wri.org/our-work/topics/forests

Hazardous Chemicals and Pesticides

Environmental Working Group
www.ewg.org
Minamata Mercury Convention
www.mercuryconvention.org
Pesticide Action Network: North America and International
www.panna.org

Rotterdam Convention on the Prior Informed Consent Procedure for Certain
    Hazardous Chemicals and Pesticides in International Trade
www.pic.int
Stockholm Convention on POPs
www.pops.int

Hazardous Waste Trade

Basel Action Network
www.ban.org
Secretariat of the Basel Convention
www.basel.int

Ozone Depletion

Montreal Protocol on Substances That Deplete the Ozone Layer
http://ozone.unep.org/en/treaties-and-decisions/montreal-protocol-sub-
    stances-deplete-ozone-layer
Vienna Convention for the Protection of the Ozone Layer
http://ozone.unep.org/en/treaties-and-decisions/vienna-convention-protec-
    tion-ozone-layer

Persistent Organic Pollutants

Greenpeace Chemicals Page
www.greenpeace.org/international/campaigns/toxics/chemicals-out-of-con-
    trol
International POPs Elimination Network
www.ipen.org
Pesticides Action Network
www.panna.org
Stockholm Convention on POPs
www.pops.int

Whaling

Greenpeace Whales Campaign
www.greenpeace.org/international/campaigns/oceans/whaling
International Convention for the Regulation of Whaling
https://iwc.int/convention
International Whaling Commission

https://iwc.int/home
Sea Shepherd Conservation Society
www.seashepherd.org

International Environmental Agreements (Opened for Signature/ Entered into Force)

African Convention on the Conservation of Nature and Natural Resources (1968/1969)
https://treaties.un.org/doc/Publication/UNTS/Volume%201001/volume-1001-I-14689-English.pdf
Agreement for the Implementation of the Law of the Sea Convention Relating to the Conservation and Management of Straddling Fish Stocks and Highly Migratory Fish Stocks (1995/2001)
www.un.org/Depts/los/convention_agreements/convention_overview_fish_stocks.htm
Antarctic Treaty (1959/1961)
www.ats.aq
Cartagena Protocol on Biosafety to the Convention on Biological Diversity (2000/2003)
www.cbd.int/biosafety
Comprehensive Nuclear Test Ban Treaty (1996/not in force)
www.ctbto.org
Convention for the International Council for the Exploration of the Sea (1964/1968)
http://www.ices.dk
Convention for the Prohibition of Fishing with Long Driftnets in the South Pacific (Wellington Convention) (1989/1990)
www.unep.ch/regionalseas/legal/dnet.htm
Convention for the Protection of the Ozone Layer (Vienna Convention) (1985/1988)
http://ozone.unep.org/en/treaties-and-decisions/vienna-convention-protection-ozone-layer
Convention on Access to Information, Public Participation in Decision-Making and Access to Justice in Environmental Matters (Aarhus Convention) (1998/2001)
http://www.unece.org/env/pp/treatytext.html
Convention on Biological Diversity (1992/1993)
www.cbd.int
Convention on Fishing and Conservation of the Living Resources of the High Seas (1958/1966)

https://treaties.un.org/Pages/ViewDetails.aspx?src=TREATY&
   mtdsg_no=XXI-3&chapter=21&lang=en
Convention on Long-Range Transboundary Air Pollution (1979/1983)
www.unece.org/env/lrtap
Convention on Nuclear Safety (1994/1996)
www-ns.iaea.org/conventions/nuclear-safety.htm
Convention on Persistent Organic Pollutants (Stockholm Convention) (2001/
   2004)
www.pops.int
Convention on the Ban of the Import into Africa and the Control of Transboundary Movement and Management of Hazardous Wastes within Africa
   (Bamako Convention) (1991/1998)
www.unep.org/delc/BamakoConvention
Convention on the Conservation of Antarctic Marine Living Resources
   (1980/1982)
www.ccamlr.org
Convention on the Conservation of Migratory Species of Wild Animals
   (1979/1983)
www.cms.int
Convention on the Continental Shelf (1958/1964)
https://treaties.un.org
Convention on the Control of Transboundary Movements of Hazardous
   Wastes and Their Disposal (Basel Convention) (1989/1992)
www.basel.int
Convention on the High Seas (1958/1962)
https://treaties.un.org
Convention on the International Commission for the Protection of the Rhine
   against Pollution (Berne Convention) (1963/1965)
www.iksr.org
Convention on the International Trade in Endangered Species of Wild Fauna
   and Flora (CITES) (1973/1975)
www.cites.org
Convention on the Law of the Non-navigational Uses of International Watercourses (1997/2014)
www.internationalwaterlaw.org/documents/intldocs/watercourse_status.html
Convention on the Prevention of Marine Pollution by Dumping of Wastes
   and Other Matter (London Convention) (1972/1975)
www.imo.org
Convention on the Prior Informed Consent Procedure for Certain Hazardous
   Chemicals and Pesticides in International Trade (Rotterdam Convention)
   (1998/2004)
www.pic.int

Convention on the Protection and Use of Transboundary Watercourses and International Lakes (1992/1996)
www.unece.org/env/water
Convention on the Territorial Sea and the Contiguous Zone (1958/1964)
https://treaties.un.org
Convention on Third Party Liability in the Field of Nuclear Energy (Paris Convention) (1960/1968)
www.nea.fr/html/law/nlparis_conv.html
Convention on Wetlands of International Importance Especially as Water-fowl Habitat (Ramsar Convention) (1971/1975)
www.ramsar.org
Convention Relative to the Preservation of Fauna and Flora in their Natural State (1933/1936)
http://sedac.ciesin.org/entri/texts/fauna.flora.natural.state.1933.html
International Convention for the Conservation of Atlantic Tunas (1966/1969)
www.iccat.int
International Convention for the Prevention of Pollution of the Sea by Oil (1954/1958)
www.imo.org
International Convention for the Protection of Birds (1950/1963)
http://sedac.ciesin.org/entri/texts/protection.of.birds.1950.html
International Convention for the Regulation of Whaling (1946/1948)
https://iwc.int/convention
International Plant Protection Convention (1951/1952)
www.ippc.int
International Treaty on Plant Genetic Resources for Food and Agriculture (2001/2004)
www.planttreaty.org
International Tropical Timber Agreement (1983/1985)
www.itto.int
Kyoto Protocol to the United Nations Framework Convention on Climate Change (1998/2005)
www.unfccc.int
Minamata Convention on Mercury (2013/not in force)
www.mercuryconvention.org
Montreal Protocol on Substances That Deplete the Ozone Layer (1987/1989)
http://ozone.unep.org/en/treaties-and-decisions/montreal-protocol-sub-stances-deplete-ozone-layer
Protocol on Environmental Protection to the Antarctic Treaty (1991/1998)
www.unep.ch/regionalseas/legal/antarc.htm
Protocol on Heavy Metals to the Convention on Long-range Transboundary Air Pollution (1998/2003)
www.unece.org (see protocols)

Protocol on Persistent Organic Pollutants to the Convention on Long-Range Transboundary Air Pollution (1998/2003)
www.unece.org (see protocols)
Treaty Banning Nuclear Weapon Tests in the Atmosphere, in Outer Space and Under Water (1963/1963)
www.ctbto.org
United Nations Convention on the Law of the Sea (LOS) (1982/1994)
www.un.org/Depts/los
United Nations Convention to Combat Desertification in Countries Experiencing Serious Drought and/or Desertification, Particularly in Africa (1994/1996)
www.unccd.int
United Nations Framework Convention on Climate Change (1992/1994)
http://unfccc.int

Nongovernmental Organizations and Global Agencies

African Conservation Foundation
www.africanconservation.org
African Wildlife Foundation
www.awf.org
Australian Conservation Foundation
www.acfonline.org.au
Center for International Environmental Law (CIEL)
www.ciel.org
Centre for Science and Environment, India
www.cseindia.org/index.html
Ceres
www.ceres.org
Coalition for Environmentally Responsible Economies
www.ceres.org
Conservation International
www.conservation.org
Ducks Unlimited
www.ducks.org
Earth Charter Initiative
www.earthcharter.org
Earth First!
www.earthfirst.org
Earthjustice
www.earthjustice.org
Earthtrust

www.earthtrust.org
Earthwatch Institute
www.earthwatch.org
Environmental Defense Fund (EDF)
www.edf.org
Environmental Foundation for Africa
www.efasl.org
Environmental Investigation Agency
www.eia-international.org
Environmental Performance Index
http://epi.yale.edu
European Centre for Nature Conservation
www.ecnc.org
Food and Water Watch
www.foodandwaterwatch.org
Forest Stewardship Council
www.fsc.org
Forests and the European Union Resource Network (FERN)
www.fern.org
Friends of the Earth International
www.foei.org
Friends of the Earth, U.S.
www.foe.org
Global Compact
www.unglobalcompact.org
Global Environment Facility (GEF)
www.gefweb.org
Global Witness
www.globalwitness.org
Green Belt Movement
www.greenbeltmovement.org
Green Cross International
www.gcint.org
Greenpeace International
www.greenpeace.org/international
Heifer International
www.heifer.org
ICLEI: Local Governments for Sustainability
www.iclei.org
International Institute for Environment and Development (IIED)
www.iied.org
International Institute for Sustainable Development (IISD)
www.iisd.org

International Rivers Network
http://internationalrivers.org
International Union for Conservation of Nature (IUCN)
http://cms.iucn.org
International Whaling Commission
https://iwc.int
Living Earth
www.livingearth.org.uk
Marine Stewardship Council (MSC)
www.msc.org
National Audubon Society
www.audubon.org
Natural Resources Defense Council
www.nrdc.org
The Nature Conservancy (TNC)
www.nature.org
Ocean Conservancy
www.oceanconservancy.org
OCEANA
www.oceana.org
Oxfam International
www.oxfam.org
Pesticides Action Network
www.panna.org
Rainforest Action Network (RAN)
www.ran.org
Rainforest Alliance
www.rainforest-alliance.org
Resources for the Future
www.rff.org
Sea Shepherd Conservation Society
www.seashepherd.org
Sierra Club
www.sierraclub.org
Socioeconomic Data and Applications Center (SEDAC) (Hosted by the Earth
    Institute at Columbia University)
http://sedac.ciesin.org
Slow Food
www.slowfood.com
SumOfUs
http://sumofus.org
Union of Concerned Scientists
www.ucsusa.org

United Nations Development Programme
www.undp.org
United Nations Environment Programme
www.unep.org
Wetlands International
www.wetlands.org
Wilderness Society (Australia)
www.wilderness.org.au
Wilderness Society (United States)
www.wilderness.org
Women's Global Green Action Network
www.wggan.org
World Bank (Environment)
www.worldbank.org/environment
World Business Council for Sustainable Development
www.wbcsd.org
World Resources Institute
www.wri.org
World Wide Fund for Nature/World Wildlife Fund (WWF)
www.wwf.org
Worldwatch Institute
www.worldwatch.org

About the Author

Peter Dauvergne is professor of international relations at the University of British Columbia, Canada. His research focuses on global environmental politics, multinational corporations, and environmental theory in international relations. He also has subfield interests in the international political economy of sustainable consumption and the politics of environmental management in the Asia-Pacific. Dauvergne is the founding and past editor (2001–2007) of the MIT Press journal *Global Environmental Politics*. Since joining the University of British Columbia in 2002, he has also served as associate dean in the Faculty of Arts (2006–2008), senior advisor to the university president (2008–2009), and director of the Liu Institute for Global Issues (2009–2014).

Professor Dauvergne has previously published 14 books and more than 50 journal articles and book chapters. His books include *Environmentalism of the Rich* (2016); *Protest Inc.: The Corporatization of Activism* (2014, with Genevieve LeBaron); *Eco-Business: A Big-Brand Takeover of Sustainability* (2013, with Jane Lister); *Timber* (2011, with Jane Lister); *Paths to a Green World*, 2nd ed. (2011, with Jennifer Clapp); *The Shadows of Consumption: Consequences for the Global Environment* (2008), winner of the Gerald L. Young Award for the best book written in 2008 in the field of human ecology; *Loggers and Degradation in the Asia-Pacific: Corporations and Environmental Management* (2001); and *Shadows in the Forest: Japan and the Politics of Timber in Southeast Asia* (1997), winner of the 1998 Sprout Award from the International Studies Association for the best book in global environmental affairs. A Japanese translation of the first edition of *Paths to a Green World* (2005) was published in 2008, an Arabic translation of *The Shadows of Consumption* was published in 2013, and a Korean translation of *Protest Inc.* was published in 2015.